INTERESTING TIMES

Other works by
Chas W. Freeman, Jr.

Cooking Western in China 西餐菜单—中国原料烹调
—with P. T. Freeman（芮敏）and Deng Baorong （邓宝荣）
(South China Press, 1987)

Arts of Power: Statecraft and Diplomacy
(U.S. Institute of Peace Press, 1997)

The Diplomat's Dictionary
(U.S. Institute of Peace Press, 2nd ed., 2010)

America's Misadventures in the Middle East
(Just World Books, 2010)

"In *Interesting Times*, Chas Freeman shares with readers four decades of his prolific and intelligent thinking on China and the Sino-American relationship. His aim consistently has been to challenge sloppy and misguided American thinking, whether engaged in by President Nixon in connection with his 1972 trip to China or the U.S. intelligence community that 'missed so many . . . major developments over the years.' Freeman challenges comfortable banalities, using words as a scalpel to reveal the tissue of slanderous euphemisms, delusions, and misunderstandings that constitute much of the corpus of discourse about China. Ambassador Freeman calls for America to develop a realistic, long-term, mutual interest–based conception of Sino-American relations capable of achieving the positive potential of ties between these two great nations."

—**DAVID M. LAMPTON**
Professor and Director of China Studies at Johns Hopkins—SAIS
Former President of the National Committee on U.S.-China Relations

"*Interesting Times: China, America, and the Shifting Balance of Prestige* is a widely perceptive analysis of the history of the Sino-American normalization process and the prospect that China can build on its economic success and growing defense capabilities to assume global political leadership like that which the U.S. exercised in the last century."

—**NICHOLAS LARDY**
Anthony M. Solomon Senior Fellow
Peterson Institute for International Economics

"Bold, incisive, innovative thinking and analysis are as rare in the field of foreign affairs as in other intellectual disciplines. Throughout his distinguished career in the Foreign Service, Ambassador Chas Freeman was renowned, and on occasion chastised, for his fearless determination to identify the consequences of trends and policy options without regard for the strictures of political correctness. Invariably, he assessed the implications of current developments in a longer-term time frame than most of his colleagues. Nowhere is this better illustrated than in this fascinating, enlightening, and provocative compilation of his writings, speeches, and musings on China and its complex relationships with the United States and the world. China's rapid rise is the dominating feature of the international landscape and is likely to confront the United States with its principal national security challenge over the next several decades. Anyone with an interest in foreign relations will benefit from exposure to the wealth of material, both historical and forward-looking, in this stimulating book."

—**J. STAPLETON ROY**
Former U.S. Ambassador to China

ABOUT

JUST WORLD BOOKS
"TIMELY BOOKS FOR CHANGING TIMES"

Just World Books produces excellent books on key international issues—and does so in a very timely fashion. Our titles are all published first as quality paperbacks. Most are later also released as e-books and some in hardcover. Because of the agility of our process, we cannot give detailed advance notice of fixed, seasonal "lists." To learn about our existing and upcoming titles, to download author podcasts and videos, to find our terms for bookstores or other bulk purchasers, or to buy our books, visit our website:

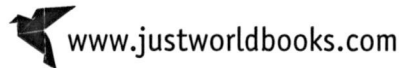 www.justworldbooks.com

Also follow us on Facebook and Twitter!

Our recent titles include:

- *Wrestling in the Daylight: A Rabbi's Path to Palestinian Solidarity*, by Brant Rosen

- *Watches Without Time: An American Soldier in Afghanistan*, by Matt Zeller

- *The General's Son: Journey of an Israeli in Palestine*, by Miko Peled

- *Troubled Triangle: The United States, Turkey, and Israel in the New Middle East*, edited by William B. Quandt

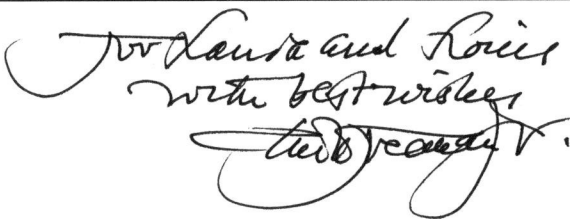

Interesting Times

China, America, and the Shifting Balance of Prestige

Chas W. Freeman, Jr.

JUST WORLD
BOOKS

Charlottesville, Virginia

Just World Books is an imprint of Just World Publishing, LLC.

Cartography and typesetting by Jane T. Sickon for Just World Publishing, LLC. Cover design by Lewis Rector for Just World Publishing, LLC.

Publisher's Cataloging-in-Publication
(Provided by Quality Books, Inc.)

Freeman, Charles W.
    Interesting times : China, America, and the shifting
balance of prestige / Chas W. Freeman, Jr.
    p. cm.
    LCCN 2012950762
    ISBN 978-1-935982-26-5

    1. United States—Foreign relations—China. 2. China
—Foreign relations—United States. 3. Balance of
power.   I. Title.

E183.8.C5F74 2012   327.73051
                    QBI12-600220

Contents

Map 1:
China's Provinces

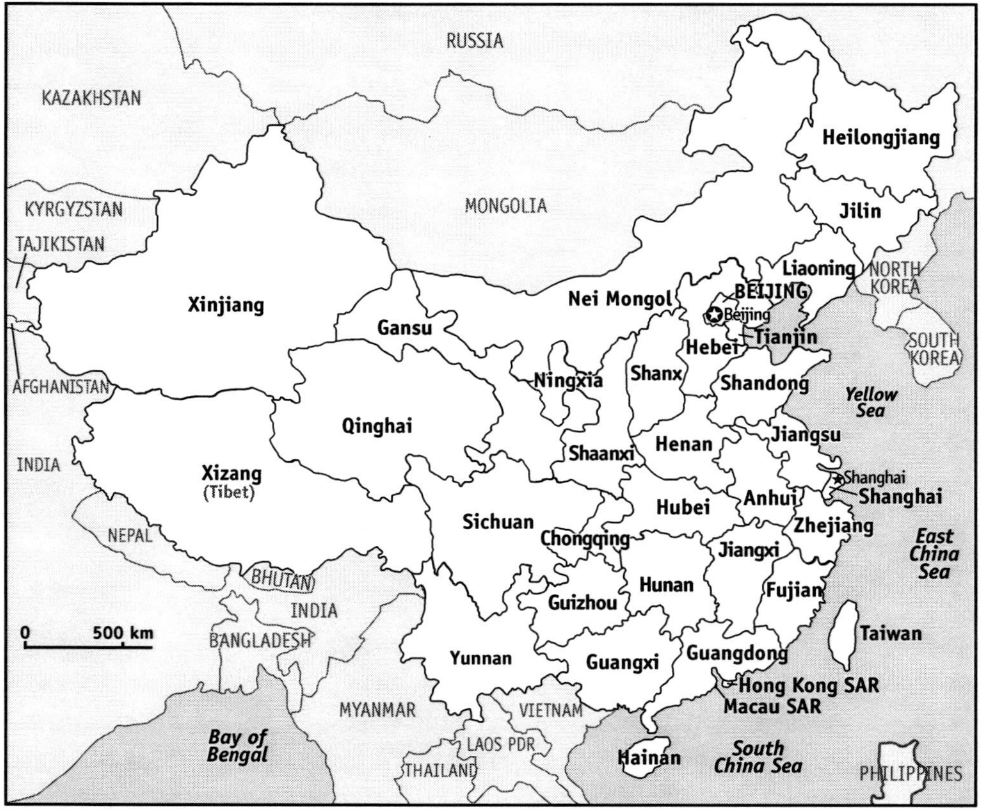

Cartography by Jane T. Sickon
and © 2013 Just World Books

Map 2: Maritime Claims in the South China Sea

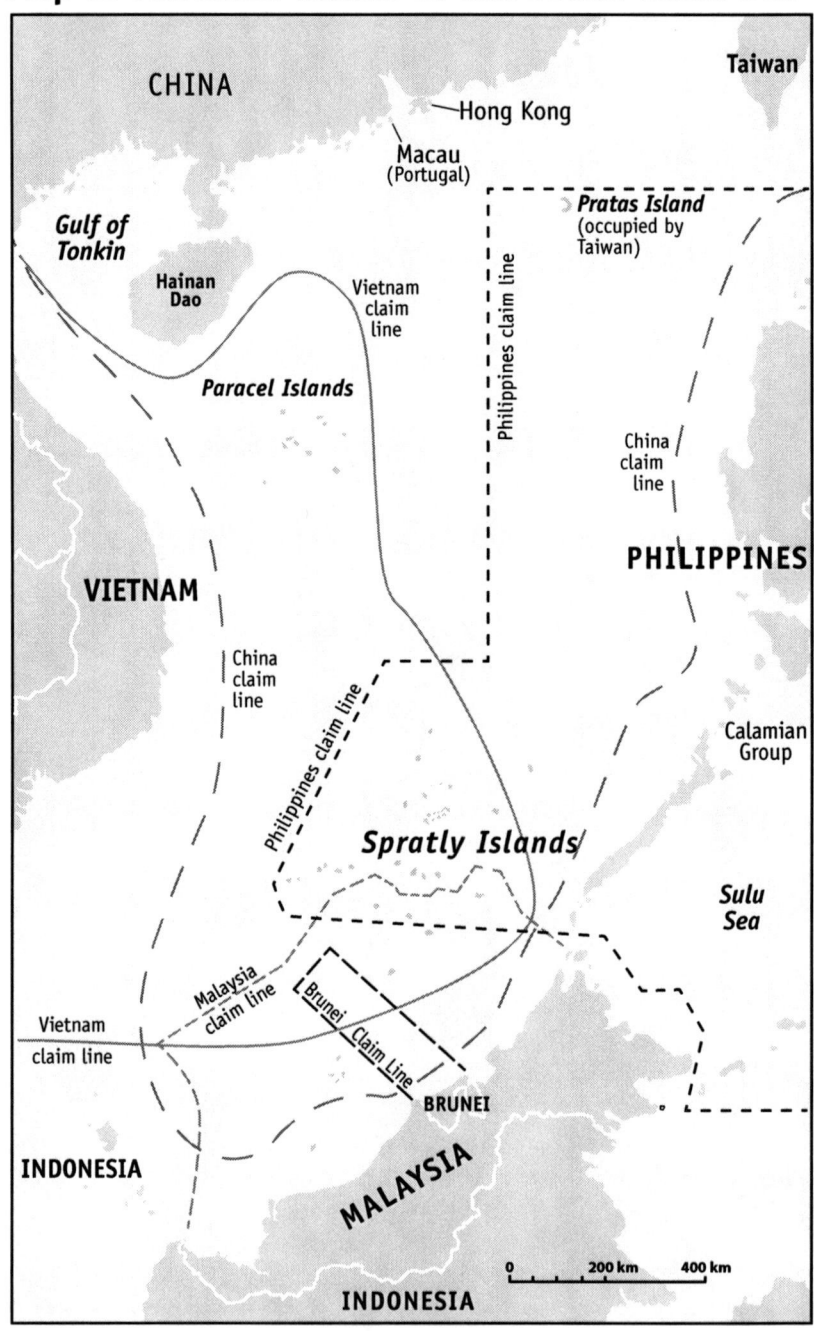

Cartography by Jane T. Sickon and © 2013 Just World Books

Introduction

China and America in "Interesting Times"[1]
October 2012

This is a book about the progress of the first forty years of official inter-action between the United States and the People's Republic of China and the prospects for the next forty. The printed text is supplemented by mate-rial that resides on the Internet. The author participated in many of the events that formed the Sino-American relationship. This is a work born of experience and a life in the public policy arena, not academic theory or scholarship. The analyses in this book were not written to confirm the conventional American wisdom about China, but to challenge it.

Sentiment and fantasy have always played a large role in America's poli-cies toward China. They caused Franklin Delano Roosevelt to overestimate China's strategic utility in the Second World War and to imagine that it was committed to democracy. They led America to embrace China as a founding, permanent member of the United Nations Security Council at a time when that country's poverty, isolation, and powerlessness made it irrelevant to global governance. Nostalgia for the lost cause of Chiang Kai-shek contributed greatly to Washington's thirty-year delay in recognizing Beijing, rather than Taipei, as the actual capital of China.

The United States' belated rediscovery of China four decades ago (under the presidencies of Richard Nixon, Jimmy Carter, and Ronald Reagan) led to popular infatuation with the Chinese, who most Americans imagined were democratizing, consumerizing, and otherwise Americanizing them-selves. Such illusions set the stage for a widespread sense of betrayal when, at Tiananmen Square on June 4, 1989, the Chinese Communist Party vio-lently suppressed peaceful opposition to its rule. Since then, the prevailing American view of China has been tinged with broad ideological antipathy, including disbelief that the People's Republic and its ruling "Communist" party could possibly enjoy legitimacy among the Chinese people.

Yet China's continuing political stability and growing wealth and power continue to confound the dogmatic predictions of American politicians and pundits alike. China's autocracy seems in many respects to be outperforming the world's democracies in coping with the challenges of globalization and the current Great Recession. China's continuing success is therefore very annoying to American ideologues. It calls into question oft-reiterated suppositions they have taken to be axiomatic. Do technological innovation and success in market economies really require full-blown freedom of speech? Do rising productivity and living standards inevitably lead to democratization? Do government-orchestrated industrial policies necessarily smother rather than empower entrepreneurship? Mounting evidence suggests perhaps not.

China's current wealth and power were simply unimaginable forty years ago, when Mr. Nixon ignored the domestic Chinese distemper and abuses of the Great Proletarian Cultural Revolution and invoked the People's Republic to balance the now-disappeared Soviet Union. The many surprises of the past four decades[2] make it clear that no one can be at all sure what China will be like forty years hence. Some consider China's success foreordained. Others imagine reasons that China, like the USSR, might collapse—or at least, like twentieth-century Argentina, fall short of its projected advance to world leadership. Whatever the prognosis, in a period of political paralysis, deindustrialization, falling living standards, social immobility, self-doubt, and business malaise in the United States, American politicians find China's uninterrupted progress more than a little unnerving. American unease has grown apace with China's economy and its centrality to global prosperity.

After World War II, the United States crafted and then, to one degree or another, managed both the world order and the regional order in the Indo-Pacific. Far from posing a threat to these arrangements, China is now fully integrated into them. But the growing weight of China's political economy inevitably challenges American dominance and threatens to displace it.

China's return to wealth and power has made it the decisive factor driving the evolution of the Indo-Pacific region at a moment when that region is once again becoming the center of gravity for the world economy. China's economic mass is drawing West, Central, and South Asia into increasingly active relationships with it, giving rise for the first time in history to something approaching a sense of Asia as a single geopolitical region. In the lands and seas that lie between it and the United States, China is already the most attractive and dynamic economic force. Its political and cultural clout in the Western Pacific is growing apace with its economic centrality. At the same time, however, China's military potential is viewed by its neighbors with disquiet as something to be appeased or resisted. They are realigning and rearming themselves to do both.

In a limited sense, China is already a world power. Its commercial and financial interests cannot be ignored and must be addressed in the management of economic issues in every region of the globe or sector of the world economy. Where economic power leads, political influence usually follows. Everyone, including the Chinese themselves, sees China as ultimately destined to play a preeminent role in global governance. China's political influence is still minimal, but if it is not yet an irresistible military force, China has already become an immovable military object.

Americans alternate between apprehension that the Chinese will displace their leadership of world and Asian affairs and frustration that China does not use its influence actively to intervene in regional conflicts. This has led to a variety of U.S. responses, ranging from renewed military confrontation in the Western Pacific (the "pivot to Asia") to schemes for a Sino-American duumvirate (the "G2"). Despite superficial differences, these responses have in common a tendency to view China as an analogue or mirror image of the United States and to interpret trends relating to it in military, zero-sum terms reminiscent of the bipolar struggle of the Cold War.

The logic of the U.S. "pivot" derives from its attribution to China of ambitions to become a "peer military competitor" of the United States or to impose a "Chinese version of the Monroe Doctrine" on Asia. But there is precious little evidence in Chinese policy and political discourse to support the thesis that China aspires to emulate the United States in either way. The People's Liberation Army (PLA) remains focused on internal security, the defense of the Chinese homeland against neighbors with a history of invading it, and countering the powerful U.S. naval and air forces constantly mapping and probing its coastal defenses.

The notion of China directing world affairs as the United States once did assumes a degree of confidence and assertiveness on the part of China's leaders that is at odds with their sense of vulnerability to foreign intervention and their aversion to risking their own political survival as well as that of the Chinese Communist Party. It is also at odds with China's obsessive deference to the sovereignty of foreign nations and its resolutely noninterventionist approach to their internal affairs. Whatever China's role in global governance may come to be, it is certain to follow a Chinese rather than an American model.

While U.S. understanding of China suffers from a persistent tendency to misinterpret Chinese developments by viewing them in an American mirror, the Chinese are no less guilty of such "mirror-imaging" in their analysis of the United States. Chinese political culture extols the importance of both grand strategy and stratagem. This leads many in China to mistake American policies for expressions of coherent strategy. (In fact, they are the vector of many contradictory special interests—an amalgam of tactical impulses that does not constitute a strategy.) The Chinese establishment thus routinely attributes guile and gamesmanship to American actions and outcomes that are more fortuitous than calculated. And Chinese are, if anything, guiltier than Americans of applying the logical fallacy of *post hoc ergo propter hoc* as they interpret events, imputing baleful motives and devious manipulations where none were in fact in play.

The difficult Sino-American interaction over the question of Taiwan's relationship with the rest of China has illustrated the problems of reciprocal incomprehension as well as or better than any other issue. This unresolved issue has always been the most important single factor inhibiting the smooth development of relations between the United States and China. The ways in which Richard Nixon, Mao Zedong, and Zhou Enlai finessed it and Jimmy Carter, Ronald Reagan, and Deng Xiaoping accommodated each other with respect to it are outstanding examples of statecraft and the diplomatic arts. They deserve more careful study than they have received.

Taiwan long presented the only conceivable *casus belli* in Sino-American relations. From time to time, the issue has engendered exercises in brinkmanship by both sides. It remains difficult but is now slowly being resolved between Chinese on the two sides of the Taiwan Strait. The danger that fighting will resume in the unresolved civil war that divided China is clearly diminishing apace with cross-Strait interdependence and rapprochement. Neither Beijing nor Washington has taken adequate account of this or of the extent to which it is reducing Taipei's deference to the United States and to American influence on Taiwanese attitudes and policies. Today's continuing Sino-American acrimony over the Taiwan issue seems increasingly outdated and inconsequential.

Meanwhile, in an effort to reaffirm its relevance to Asian security, the United States has taken the initiative to interpose itself between China and Brunei, Japan, Malaysia, the Philippines, and Vietnam, entangling itself in ancient territorial quarrels from which it had previously kept its distance. These countries have long had competing claims to islets, rocks, and reefs in the South and East China Seas. (Taipei has claims too, but these are legally indistinguishable from those of Beijing and derive from Taiwan's ancient status as a province of "China.") For China, the claims of others awaken angry memories of Chinese impotence in the age of Western colonialism, when these counterclaims to China's arose. Japan's stand on the Senkaku/Diaoyu islands issue serves as a particularly unfortunate reminder of its belligerent past. China's claims recall to apprehensive neighbors the millennia in which the Middle Kingdom exercised hegemony in Asia. Those with territorial disputes with China quite naturally seek U.S. backing to balance rising Chinese power.

As the naval and other maritime capabilities of all the various claimants (not just China) have improved, both their efforts to enforce their claims and the frictions between them have grown. The United States has defense treaty obligations to Japan and the Philippines and a developing security partnership with Vietnam. Armed clashes between China and any of these countries could pull America into the conflict. The U.S. "pivot" has greatly increased the potential for this. Ironically, therefore, as tensions over Taiwan recede, strategic antagonism between Beijing and Washington is broadening and deepening, not attenuating. For the United States, the possibility that Americans will feel compelled to join Asian allies in fighting over barren islands, rocks, and reefs in China's near seas now eclipses Taiwan as a potential cause of war with China.

The last forty years have illustrated the potential for cooperation between America and China to change not just China but the world for the better. Immediately after "normalizing" its relations with the United States, China began to transform itself through eclectic borrowing of policies and practices from the United States, other Western countries, and overseas Chinese. This process of "opening and reform" deserves close study.[3] It has lifted hundreds of millions of Chinese out of poverty. It is about to make China's the largest economy on the planet, overtaking the United States in that status. (Some economists argue that this has already happened.)

China's integration into the American-crafted world order helped end the Cold War, to globalize capitalism, and to usher in an era of widening prosperity. These developments in turn fostered a dramatic reduction in the dangers of nuclear or other hostilities between the world's great powers. If military rivalry now becomes a dominant feature of Sino-American relations, the effects are likely to be equally far-reaching. The next forty years could see the world—in the words of the apocryphal Chinese curse—compelled to live through "interesting times."

The current Sino-American relationship is a bundle of discontinuities. Bilateral relations are highly developed. Dozens of intergovernmental committees coordinate official interaction bilaterally and facilitate cooperation between enterprises and individuals in the two countries. The two economies are interdependent, with two-way trade set to approach $600 billion in 2012. Human ties are also very strong and getting stronger, with rapidly increasing flows of tourists, businesspeople, and students traveling in both directions. (More than 1.5 million Chinese tourists will visit America in

2012, while well over 2 million Americans will travel to China. There are more than two hundred thousand Chinese students in the United States.)

Political cooperation between the two countries at the international level is more limited and shows contradictory trends. China has taken a leading role in supporting the American-led diplomatic effort to denuclearize the Korean Peninsula. It endorsed the U.S. invasion of Afghanistan. It has cooperated with efforts to cap the Iranian nuclear program. It has been less enthusiastic about U.S. attempts to win international backing for humanitarian and other interventions in former European colonies like Libya and Syria. These issues have made it plain that China does not accept recent Western attempts to alter the Westphalian system by introducing concepts of limited sovereignty like "humanitarian intervention" and the "responsibility to protect." China has accepted the existing Western-crafted order. It will not allow the West to dictate what succeeds this.

Military contacts between China and America have been both discontinuous and substantively unproductive. The United States had much more interaction and insight into the Soviet military at the height of the Cold War than it does with today's Chinese PLA. Crisis management mechanisms to control the possible escalation of conflict between the two countries are almost nonexistent. Indeed, the recently announced U.S. concept of "air-sea battle" envisages strikes deep in China that would almost certainly invite retaliation against the American homeland as well as bases abroad. The U.S. actions this concept envisages could well provoke China to cross the threshold into nuclear warfare. Given the difficulty the two militaries have had in communicating with and understanding each other, this should be a matter for grave concern.

Overall, the uneven development of Sino-American relations raises questions about their stability as well as the international orientation of China's neighbors. Can two such large, proud countries compartmentalize their differences, continuing to enjoy close economic cooperation and expanding political partnership while their military relations turn hostile? Given nationalist passions in China and the martial traditions of the United States, this seems doubtful.

In many ways the effects of an increasingly antagonistic relationship are already manifest in the evolution of the two sides' military force structures and armaments. Mutual hostility is also reflected in Washington's opposition to Chinese investment in U.S. industry and infrastructure that local politicians seek to attract. It is apparent in the deteriorating tone of each side's commentary about the other. Each has become the enemy of choice for the other's war planners and military-industrial complex. China has not yet joined the United States in developing systems to attack across the Pacific, other than through cyberspace. But China's perceived need to deter and counter the hostile U.S. forces at its twelve-mile limit now seems likely to drive it toward doing so.

Both the United States and China are now in poorly understood transitions. America's political economy no longer provides the superior results it once did. The export-oriented Chinese model of economic growth has come to the end of its useful life. Both China's economic system and its politics require reform. As a result, large uncertainties cloud the futures of both the United States and China, and hence the future roles of each in world affairs.

To look back forty years is to be reminded that it is entirely possible that past experience may not reliably predict the future. In 1972, President Nixon and Chairman Mao surprised the world by setting aside irreconcilable differences to cooperate. In late 1978, Deng Xiaoping put China on a very different course than anyone had expected, with implications that very few understood. A decade later, much to the surprise of both Americans and Chinese, the U.S. strategy of "containment" finally worked, producing the collapse of the Soviet Union and fundamentally altering the global strategic geometry. Past American and Chinese leaders got many policies right. There is no guarantee that coming generations of leaders on both sides will prove equally wise or farsighted. It matters greatly whether they are.

Forty years ago, China's economy was about the size of Italy's—one-tenth that of the United States. Today (at nominal exchange rates), China has a GDP nearly four times Italy's and a bit less than half of America's. It is about to overtake the American economy in size. For the first time in more than 130 years, the United States will not possess the world's largest economy. All things remaining equal (as, of course, they won't), the magic of compound growth could give China a GDP that is two to three times bigger than that of the United States in 2052. If China is then still spending 1.5 to 2 percent of its GDP on defense, it could have a defense budget at least twice that of the United States today, with all of the capabilities this implies. Even if China falls well short of current projections, it has the potential to be a much more influential force in Asia and on the world stage.

It is impossible to imagine that, with the largest economy in the world, China will continue to defer to American leadership as it has throughout the first decades of its emergence from poverty and powerlessness. A difficult process of adjustment in bilateral interaction and global roles is clearly in prospect. The Sino-American relationship is bound to become both more equal and more competitive. Neither side is capable of striking a "grand bargain" to manage this transition. It will be defined by the responses of both to events that test both their interests and the quality of their statecraft. Each side needs to recognize what is at stake in these responses. What happens between China and the United States in the coming decade will decide how China deploys its wealth and power. It will set the strategic alignments of China's neighbors. It will dictate China's role on the world stage. And it bids fair to be the greatest single external determinant of America's future.

Chapter 1

What Mr. Nixon Wrought

It is hard to overstate how extraordinary President Richard Nixon's 1972 visit to Beijing was. He traveled to the capital of a regime he had spent his political career badmouthing and which the United States, under policies he had advocated, had spent over two decades successfully excluding from international society.

Mr. Nixon's debut in Beijing was also my debut as an interpreter in anything other than a classroom setting. My first significant act as interpreter in Beijing was to refuse an order from my president to interpret for him.

Richard Nixon's vanity had led him to demand that I interpret a banquet toast he had memorized and that he wished to deliver so it would seem extemporaneous. No problem. But the final text,[1] I had heard, included bits and pieces of Chairman Mao Zedong's poetry in English translation. I asked to see it. Through an intermediary, the president denied to me that there was a text. I knew this was a lie. I decided I could not interpret his remarks under circumstances that would require me to attempt to ad-lib an English rendering of unknown excerpts from Chairman Mao's poetry back into Chinese. This angered Mr. Nixon, but to have done what he demanded would have been to embarrass both him and my country before the ruling elite of China as well as hundreds of millions in American and foreign television audiences. A couple of days after the incident, Mr. Nixon tearfully apologized for his misjudgment and prevarication. He thanked me for having stood up to him on the matter.[2]

The three pieces that follow review the very wide-reaching effects Mr. Nixon's visit had on China, America, and the world. They also note some of the contradictions and dilemmas in current and prospective U.S. relations with China and analyze the principles that have guided the development of Sino-American relations.

Forty years after the president's opening to China, I was asked to deliver a commemorative speech at the Center for the National Interest (formerly the Nixon Center) in Washington, D.C. This was a chance to reminisce, but also an opportunity to consider some of the contradictions inherent in America's current policies toward China, as I did in the piece that opens this first chapter, "The United States and China Forty Years On."

China is now widely seen as the leviathan on the horizon even as American power and influence decline and the hegemony of the United States is ever more widely challenged or ignored. Some react to China's return to wealth and power with denial, others with alarm. For American businesses, China is where the market growth and industrial challenges are. For U.S. diplomats, it is a largely passive actor to be pushed into endorsing U.S. foreign policy objectives against its own (obviously misguided) judgments. For the Pentagon, it is the military rival of choice. All acknowledge that the consequences of American mismanagement of relations with China would be huge.

Before Americans "go abroad in search of monsters to destroy,"[3] we would be prudent to make a serious effort to understand both contemporary China and what its rise might mean for our global leadership, assuming we wish to retain a measure of it amidst the major shifts in the international balances of wealth, status, and power that are now underway. To appraise the Chinese challenge we need also to understand the China model, if there is one. In this chapter's second section, "Will China Rule the World as the United States Once Did?," I take a look at the strengths, weaknesses, and degree of exportability of "socialism with Chinese characteristics" and at China's potential to displace American hegemony on the global and regional levels. Having reviewed the previous forty years, I conclude with some thoughts about the probable course of the next forty.

Find More in the Online Archive

A few years ago, on the thirtieth anniversary of the establishment of diplomatic relations between the United States and the People's Republic of China, I offered some reflections on the factors driving our ties. I think what I said continues to have some predictive value. You can find it in this book's companion online archive under the title "Eight Theses on Sino-American Relations": http://bit.ly/interesting-times.

The United States and China Forty Years On[4]
February 2012

Forty years ago next Tuesday,[5] on a clear, cold afternoon in Beijing, I followed President Nixon onto the tarmac at Beijing's Capital Airport. I have a belated confession to make. When I tried to sleep on Air Force One on the way to Beijing, I was jolted awake by a nightmare. I dreamed that Generalissimo Chiang Kai-shek would be standing there with his old political sparring partner and secret pen pal, Zhou Enlai. In my dream, Chiang stepped forward to greet his former friend and political backer Richard Nixon with a loudly sarcastic "Long time, no see!" As we pulled up to the shabby old structure that was then the only terminal at Beijing's airport, I peered anxiously out the window. Others were elated to see Premier Zhou emerge to greet us. I was merely relieved that he was there pretty much by himself.

It's almost impossible today to recall the weirdness of that moment, when an American president who had made a political career of reviling Chinese Communism strode without apology into the capital of the People's Republic of China—a state and government the United States did not recognize—to meet with leaders that Chiang Kai-shek—whom we officially viewed as the legal president of all China—called "bandits at the head of a bogus regime." I had entered the foreign service of the United States and learned Chinese because I thought we would eventually have to find a way to recruit China geopolitically. I was thrilled to be the principal American interpreter as our president led an effort to do exactly that. My job was to help him and his secretary of state discuss with China's Communists what to do about other even more problematic Communists.

Next Tuesday, on the precise anniversary of that February 21, 1972, personal introduction to Beijing, I expect to be back there—not to try to rearrange the world again but to make Chinese financiers aware of specific investment opportunities in the United States. In 1972, it was necessary for the leader of the capitalist world to save China from Soviet Communism. In 2012, the world looks to China to save capitalism—and the world's capitalists flock to China in search of funds. How very much was changed by the forces Nixon and Mao put in motion that afternoon forty years ago!

There is no more Soviet Union; the bipolar world it helped define is gone, as is the unipolar American moment its collapse created. The famous Shanghai Communiqué of 1972[6] opened with a long recitation of the irreconcilable differences between the United States and China on almost every major international question of the time. Encounters between Chinese and American leaders now produce far less dramatic laundry lists of relatively minor and entirely manageable frictions, as well as grumbles, growls, and whines about highly technical issues that lower-level officials in both countries need to work.

China has risen from poverty, impotence, and isolation to retake its premodern place atop the world economic order. The People's Republic is now a major actor in global governance. It is fully integrated into every aspect of the international system it once sought to overthrow and, in some ways, more devoted to that system than we are. Forty years ago, China's backwardness and vulnerability were the wonder of the world. Now the world envies China and ponders the strategic implications of its rapidly growing wealth and power.

Reality, unlike ghosts in China,[7] seldom travels in straight lines. But if current trends advance along current lines, as early as 2022, China will have an economy that is one-third to two-fifths larger than that of the United States. If China continues to spend roughly 2 percent of its GDP (or 11 percent of its central government budget) on its military as it does now, ten years hence it will have a defense budget on a par with ours today. Even with the exchange rate adjustments that will surely take place by 2022, $600 billion or so is likely to buy a lot more in China than it can here. And all that money will be concentrated on the defense of China and its periphery, whereas our military, under current assumptions, will remain configured to project our power simultaneously to every region of the globe, not just the Asia-Pacific.

What sort of relationship do we want with the emerging giant that is China? The choice is not entirely ours, of course. China will have a lot to say about it. To the extent we pay attention to the views of allies like Japan, so will they. But we do have choices, and their consequences are portentous. This suggests that they should be made after due reflection rather than as the result of strategic inertia.

Right now, the military strategic choice we've made is clear. We are determined to try to sustain the global supremacy handed to us by Russia's involuntary default on its Cold War contest with us. In the Asia-Pacific region, this means "full-spectrum dominance" up to China's twelve-mile limit. In effect, having assumed the mission of defending the global commons against all comers, we have decided to treat the globe beyond the borders of Russia and China as an American sphere of influence in which we hold sway and all others defer to our views of what is and is not permissible.

This is a pretty ambitious posture on our part. China's defense buildup is explicitly designed to counter it. China has made it clear that it will not tolerate the threat to its security represented by a foreign military presence at its gates when these foreign forces are engaged in activities designed to probe Chinese defenses and choreograph a way to penetrate them. There's no reason to assume that China is any less serious about this than we would be if faced with similarly provocative naval and air operations along our frontiers. So, quite aside from our on-again, off-again mutual posturing over the issue of Taiwan's relationship to the rest of China, we and the Chinese are currently headed for some sort of escalating military confrontation.

At the same time, most Americans recognize that our own prosperity is closely linked to continued economic development in China. In recent years, China has been our fastest-growing export market. It is also our largest source of manufactured imports, including many of the high-tech items we take pride in having designed but do not make. And we know we have to work with China to address the common problems of humanity.

So our future prosperity has come to depend on economic interdependence with a nation we are also setting ourselves up to do battle with. And, at the same time, we hope to cooperate with that nation to assure good global governance. Pardon me if I perceive a contradiction or two in this China policy. It looks to me more like the vector of competing political impulses than the outcome of rational decision-making.

Of course, no Washington audience can be the least surprised that Capitol confusion, intellectual inertia, and the prostitution of policy to special interests—rather than strategic reasoning—determine policy. Why should China be an exception? But even those of us long callused by life within the Beltway ought to be able to see that we've got a problem. Our approach to managing our interactions with China does not compute.

Actually, we have a much bigger problem than that presented by the challenge of dealing with a rising China. We cannot hope to sustain our global hegemony even in the short term without levels of expenditure we are unprepared to tax ourselves to support. Worse, the logic of the sort of universal sphere of influence we aspire to administer requires us to treat the growth of others' capabilities relative to our own as direct threats to our hegemony. This means we must match any and all improvements in foreign military power with additions to our own. It is why our military-related expenditures have grown to exceed those of the rest of the world combined. There is simply no way that such a militaristic approach to national security is affordable in the long term, no matter how much it may delight defense contractors.

In this context, I fear that the so-called "pivot" to Asia will turn out to be an unresourced bluff. It's impressive enough to encourage China to spend more on its military, but what it means, in practice, is that we will cut military commitments to Asia less than we cut commitments elsewhere. That is, we will do this if the Middle East comes to need less attention than we have been giving it. At best, the "pivot" promises more or less more of the same in the Indo-Pacific region. This would be a tough maneuver to bring off even if we had our act together both at home and in the Middle East. But we do not have our act together at home. Our position in West Asia and North Africa is not improving. And some Americans are currently actively advocating war with Iran, intervention in Syria, going after Pakistan, and other misguided military adventures in West and South Asia.

So what's the affordable alternative approach to sustaining stability in the Asia-Pacific region as China rises? My guess is that it's to be found in adjustments in our psychology. We need to get over World War II and the Cold War and focus on the realities of the present rather than the past.

Japan initially defeated all other powers in the Asia-Pacific region, including the United States. We then cleaned Japan's clock and filled the resulting strategic vacuum. We found our regional preeminence so gratifying that we didn't notice as the vacuum we had filled proceeded to disappear. Japan restored itself. Southeast Asians came together in the Second Indochina War (popularly known in the United States as "the Vietnam War"). The Association of Southeast Asian Nations (ASEAN) incorporated Indochina and Myanmar. India rose from its postcolonial sick bed and strode forward. Indonesia did the same.

But we have continued to behave as though there is an Asian-Pacific power vacuum only we can fill. And as China's rise has begun to shift the strategic equilibrium in the region, we have stepped forward to restore it. We seem to think that if we Americans don't provide it, there can be no balance or peace in Asia. But quite aside from the fact that there was a balance and peace in the region long before the United States became a Pacific power, this overlooks the formidable capabilities of re-risen and rising powers like Japan, south Korea, India, Indonesia, and Vietnam. It is a self-realizing strategic delusion that powers the self-licking ice cream cone that is the American military-industrial complex.

If Americans step forward to balance China for everyone else in the region, the nations of the Indo-Pacific will hang back and let us take the lead. And if we put ourselves between them and China, they will not just rely on us to back their existing claims against China—they will up the ante. It cannot make sense to empower the Philippines, Vietnam, and others to pick our fights with China for us.

The bottom line is that the return of Japan, south Korea, and China to wealth and power and the impressive development of other countries in the region should challenge us to rethink the entire structure of our defense posture in Asia. Unable to live by our wallets, we must learn to live by our wits. In my view, President Nixon's "Guam Doctrine"[8] pointed the way. We need to find ways to ask Asians to do more in their own interest and their own defense. Our role should be to back them as *our* interests demand, not to pretend that we care more about or understand their national security interests better than they do, still less to push them aside to take on defense tasks on their behalf.

We need to think very differently than we have done over the nearly seven decades since the end of World War II. To be sure, a less forward-leaning American approach to securing our interests in Asia would require painful adjustments in Japan's and south Korea's dependencies on us as well as in our relations with the member states of ASEAN and India and Pakistan. It would almost certainly require an even stronger alliance with Australia. Paradoxically, it would be more than a little unnerving for China, which has come to like most aspects of, even if not everything about, the *status quo*.

It is not in our interest to withdraw from Asia. But more than six decades after we deployed to stabilize Cold War Asia, we should not be afraid to adapt our strategy and deployments to its new post–Cold War realities. Both the strategic circumstances of our times and the more limited resources available to us demand serious reformulation of current policies. These policies cannot effectively meet the evolving challenges of the world the Nixon visit to China—forty years ago next week—helped create.

Will China Rule the World as the United States Once Did?
March 2012

Forty years ago, China was ostracized by the world's great powers, large and small. It was openly admired only by tiny, idiosyncratically Communist Albania. Having rejected Soviet tutelage, China stood angrily outside the bipolar world order of the Cold War. Today China is a central participant in global governance. It has emerged as a formidable competitor of established powers like the United States, Europe, and Japan in many spheres, with expanding prestige and influence not just in Asia but well beyond it.

Many see the multiple effects of China's rise as the primary challenge to American dominance of world affairs—the *Pax Americana* that succeeded the collapse of the Soviet Union—as well as to the liberal international order that America helped create and lead after World War II. If nothing else, the rapid growth of China's economy and defense capabilities is proving to be a lucrative cure for post–Cold War enemy deprivation syndrome. As such, it has become a principal justification for increased funding for the U.S. military-industrial complex. But is China destined to supplant American global military supremacy, displace the worldwide ascendancy of Western values, replace the U.S.-crafted world order with a system "made in China," or project its military power around the globe? Does it even aspire to do any of things? Could it if it wanted to?

China's return to wealth and power is indeed one of several factors hastening the end of the *Pax Americana* by bringing into being a more complex and pluralistic global order. China is about to become both the world's biggest economy and an immovable military object, if not an irresistible military force. But China lacks the ambition, the exportable ideology, the political appeal, and the geopolitical circumstances to assume the global leadership roles that America played in the last century. China will participate in crafting an international order to succeed the crumbling *status quo*, but for a wide variety of reasons, it is unlikely to lead this process or to become the global hegemon, the world's supreme military power, or an economic model for others. It is entirely possible—even likely, if current trends continue—that the United States and China will stumble into various forms of confrontation, including military confrontation. But this is far from inevitable. Let me explain.

From Strategic Cooperation to Ideological Contention
In 1972, President Richard Nixon boldly invoked the People's Republic of China[9] to balance the apparently growing strategic menace of Soviet Communism. The Soviet Union simultaneously challenged both the interests and values of the United States.[10] Soviet-American rivalry had divided the world into two hostile camps from which only a few major powers were then aloof.[11] China remained hostile to American values as it then understood them, but it had been alarmed by Moscow's willingness to invade neighbors (like Czechoslovakia) in the name of enforcing ideological discipline in the "socialist camp." Battles between Soviet and Chinese forces had taken place at several points along the then-undemarcated Sino-Soviet frontier.

Beijing thus shared U.S. concerns about rising Soviet power and assertiveness. Chairman Mao Zedong's government did not share American views on much else, but it was prepared, like the Nixon administration, to set aside the "essential differences" in the "social systems and foreign policies" of the two countries in order to cooperate strategically against the nonideological aspects of the Soviet threat.[12]

Having declared that ideological differences were essentially irrelevant to the development and conduct of their bilateral relations,[13] China and America were able to cooperate militarily and otherwise for the next seventeen years, until the collapse of the Soviet empire in 1989 eliminated the strategic rationale for doing so. In that same year, the Chinese government's violent suppression of student demonstrators in Beijing's Tiananmen Square and elsewhere caused widespread indignation and disillusionment with China in the West, especially in the United States. Within months, ideological contention over democracy and human rights had replaced strategic cooperation as the dominant theme of U.S. China policy.

From Triumphalism to the Eclipse of the Euro-American Model

This policy inversion began amidst American triumphalism, as the U.S.-led international order overwhelmed the collapsing Soviet sphere. At least in its own estimation, the United States became the "indispensable nation,"[14] an invincible superpower and a unilateralist manager of processes of global governance, financial and economic deregulation to spread the American model of capitalism around the world, and political change to replace autocracy with democracy everywhere. But time, the rise of other powers (including but not limited to China), and experience soon challenged this ill-considered ideological certitude and national arrogance.

Campaigns in Afghanistan and Iraq, undertaken in part to show the futility of resistance to American military power, resulted instead in demonstrating the limits of that power. U.S. intervention in Iraq failed to reshape either that country or the greater Middle East to American or Western advantage. None of the several approaches to the pacification of Afghanistan that America and NATO tried yielded convincing progress. Deference to American leadership by U.S. allies visibly subsided as hostility to U.S. policies mounted around the world. The result has been to begin to bring home to the United States the futility of unilateralism and the pragmatic requirement to enlist others, including the so-called "BRIC" countries (Brazil, Russia, India, and China), in crafting solutions to global and regional problems, regardless of the nature of their domestic politics and legal practices.

Meanwhile, the costs of two large, unfunded wars in Iraq and Afghanistan have left the United States heavily in debt, fiscally hollow, and monetarily at risk. A global economic crisis brewed up by ingenious financial chicanery on Wall Street has discredited American financial leadership, institutions, and economic ideology. The air has gone out of the "Washington Consensus" balloon. Economies with industrial policies are outperforming those committed to doctrinaire laissez-faire economics.[15] At the same time, it has become apparent that history has not after all "ended" in an irreversible victory of democracy over autocracy. In the second decade of the twenty-first century, autocracies like China are widely seen to be outdoing democracies at the tasks of governance. The United

States and Europe have joined Japan in economic doldrums, political grid-lock, and self-doubt as China powers ahead and democratic India falters.

Is China a Model? Can It Be One?

In 2012, everyone abroad acknowledges the military prowess of the U.S. armed forces, but almost no one still sees the United States as a political or economic model to be emulated. Almost no one looks to China as a model either. China continues to advance, but its political economy is a work in progress that lacks both a doctrine and an operating manual. China's success serves to power skepticism about American political values and economic doctrines that predict China's failure. China's example doesn't present an adoptable alternative to these values and practices.

Unlike the United States, contemporary China shows no interest in altering, still less overthrowing, the political or economic systems of the nations with which it interacts internationally. It has embraced respect for diversity as a pragmatic tool of statecraft. It doesn't even insist on constitutional or ideological uniformity in its own space, tolerating Hong Kong's unsurpassed economic freedoms and Macau's reliance on gambling while offering Taiwan even greater autonomy than either of these city-states within some sort of yet-to-be-crafted Greater China commonwealth. China's performance calls into question American self-confidence, competitiveness, and self-regard, not American values or ideology. This distinguishes it from all past challenges to the Euro-American model of political economy that has ruled the world for the past two centuries.

Fascism and Communism repudiated and sought to replace Western forms of democracy and capitalism with alternative models of political economy based on authoritarianism and collectivism. The Chinese Communist Party (CCP) has voiced no objection to others practicing democracy, laissez-faire capitalism, or any other system—as long as they refrain from insisting that China follow their example. Like their forebears, today's Chinese seem content to let foreigners be foreigners, while working at modernizing their own country in their own way.

So far the Chinese system appears to be working well for the Chinese, even if they can't explain to non-Chinese how it works. Meanwhile, all sorts of mistaken assumptions about the nature of the Chinese political economy have been attributed to contemporary China.[16] China's evolving socioeconomic order and the domestic and foreign implications of this order cannot be accurately analyzed by applying labels that impute characteristics to China. The role of the "state," in the sense of the central government and its instrumentalities pursuing national as opposed to special interests, is far less in China than most suppose. Contemporary China doesn't fit the mold of past systems in other countries. It has come up with something new and different that must be understood in its own terms.

"Cadre Capitalism"

Confucius once remarked despairingly that for most people "gluttony and lust are what life's all about."[17] Officials in China's many political subdivisions often seem determined to prove him right. Deng's "reform and opening" (especially the opening to Chinese investors and entrepreneurs from Hong Kong and Taiwan) grafted the capitalist notion of the legitimacy of greed onto physical appetites long acknowledged by Chinese culture. This has inspired a uniquely Chinese economic architecture of profit-seeking public-private partnerships at every level of government and enterprise. The result is a formidable alliance between political boosterism and entrepreneurship that is best described as "cadre capitalism."

In this system, CCP members (the "cadres" who staff government and quasi-governmental functions in China from the village level up) play the economic role that "angels," fund managers, and other investors do elsewhere, but with a political twist—they have the power of the layers of the government and party apparatuses they represent behind them. Cadres stimulate the growth of production, employment, and civic pride by embracing enterprises in which the fragments of China they manage have an ownership interest. They provide homegrown and overseas Chinese entrepreneurs with exemptions from government regulations and licensing regimes, cheap loans, free land, political protection, and security from labor unrest, among other benefits. Cadres gain in many ways from this. They create jobs for those for whose welfare they are accountable; elevate their own patronage power; boost their communities' reputations; and improve their prospects for promotion within the party apparatus, while living the good life that revenue from the enterprises in which they have "invested" affords.

Cadre capitalism is something new to the world. It has delivered over three decades of relentlessly rapid economic growth to China. In the process, it has also administered affront after affront to long-standing Western assumptions about the dependency of innovative economic advance on freedom of information and the inevitability of political liberalization in prospering societies. Just as the fact that bees can fly was once thought to be "scientifically impossible," China's perverse success at moving forward appears to refute the canons of economic liberalism and laissez-faire ideology.

A Market Economy with Chinese Characteristics

In cadre capitalism, as in other forms of market economy, the profit motive rules. But in cadre capitalism, government behaves like the private sector, the country's vigorous private sector is exceptionally government-friendly, and many entrepreneurs are inseparable from the CCP, which runs the government entities with which businesses are partnered and which delivers the decisions they need to turn a profit. Economically, each political fragment of China is a cutthroat competitor of every other. Since China has a million villages, a couple of dozen provinces, and more than 120 cities with populations of a million or more people, that's a lot of very fierce competition. As an ironic result, Chinese markets for goods and services are much more fragmented and competitive—much more classically "capitalist"—than those in the contemporary West.[18]

But China combines its nearly "perfect" national markets with a CCP apparatus that is able to enact and implement industrial policies, harnessing market forces to shape cadre capitalist decisions to the long-term advantage of the overall political economy. The party, with more than 80 million members,[19] pervades the private sector as well as every level of government. The CCP requires its members to master policy-relevant disciplines, like economics, and to stay current with the rationales for its policies. It controls personnel selection and promotions in every area of the political economy. In China, the invisible hand is a Communist Party cadre. The cadre is the policy-responsive herdsman of his or her part of a ferociously competitive political economy.

Chinese themselves are neither eager to analyze their own commercial culture nor inclined to provide a theoretical framework for explaining it, analyzing its strengths and weaknesses, or predicting its probable future evolution. There are, however, plenty of Western political scientists and economists who make a good living by putting out predictions of Chinese collapse, which they update annually when China once again annoyingly fails to fail as they think it should. Generally speaking, when something works in practice but not in theory, reality needs a closer look and theory needs a tune-up. That is the case with Western understanding of the Chinese political economy.

The Chinese Ideology

Chinese themselves describe their socioeconomic system as "socialism with Chinese characteristics." Many in the West snicker at this, interpreting it as an ideological evasion by China's ruling Communist Party that will let it endorse capitalism without having to say it's sorry. There's something to this interpretation, but it misses not only the incestuous relationships between government and enterprises that are at the heart of cadre capitalism but two other key points.

The first is that, although China's system is operationally capitalist in its emphasis on competition and reliance on market forces, it is doctrinally socialist in its recognition of the responsibility of government to promote equality and social justice and in its continuing aspirations to do so. Chinese socialism rejects the indifference to inequality of income distribution, private affluence, and public squalor that capitalism, at least in its extreme American form, sometimes exhibits. China regards these as social maladies that must be cured by state policies directed at ameliorating them.

The second point is that the "Chinese characteristics" the system integrates are not an ideology but a comprehensive hierarchy of values. These values are integral to Chinese culture. They impart vigor, agility, and both adaptability and predictability to the Chinese political economy. They dictate that the social disciplines of propriety (礼) be the primary regulators of economic behavior in China, much as law is in the West. These disciplines aim at social harmony and fair outcomes rather than transactional justice. They are not enforced by lawyers and judges but by peers and social networks.[20]

In brief, Chinese rank the emotional bonds (情) that animate *guanxi* (关系), or the reciprocal obligations of carefully cultivated human relationships, above the calculus (理) of selfishness that measures private gain (利) in transactions, which is what classical economic theory supposes drives human behavior. They think that one has an obligation to one's partner and one's peers to do *what is right* rather than *what one has a right* to do. They place both social comity and mutual interest, rather than self-interest, ahead of legal strictures (法). Chinese culture has always emphasized the virtues of harmony (once 大同, now 和谐). This remains an important objective of Chinese culture, including its highly competitive business subculture.

This hierarchy of values demotes the rule of law but operates no less effectively than Western legal systems to enable contracts to be made and enforced—at least among Chinese, if not between Chinese and foreigners. It engages "face" (面子), or self-respect that depends on constant reaffirmation of one's status and perceived reliability by those to whom one is emotionally connected, in the enforcement of terms of cooperation that are mutually fair. The Chinese obsession with preserving face is at least as efficacious in this regard as the compulsion to adhere to legal obligations is in the West, and perhaps more so. (Risking the forfeit of moral standing in one's social circle by generating disharmony, demonstrating impropriety, showing disregard for the interests of friends, and evidencing unreliability is much more emotionally stressful than resorting to the impersonal processes and risks of litigation.) In China, social comity *is* business; the social *is* the economic.

"Chinese Characteristics"

A socioeconomic system with "Chinese characteristics" is thus a market economy in which social bonds are a stronger regulator of economic behavior than other forms of self-interest, and in which the logic of relationships trumps the rule of law in the conclusion and implementation of contracts. In such a system, conviviality—drinking and dining together— is not just a lubricator of business; it is a central affirmation and guarantor of contractual obligation. Gifts are expected to be traded for privileged information, competitive advantages, mentoring, and other favors. Hiring depends mostly on *whom* rather than *what* one knows. Family members, classmates, and members of other important social networks have a duty to yield the keys to bank and corporate treasuries. Direct and indirect kickbacks are part of mutually beneficial transactions. Yesterday's helpful gesture justifies tomorrow's repayment of the favor. Transactions are not ends in themselves but elements of relationships that all concerned wish to sustain into the future.

These "Chinese characteristics" dispense with lawyers; speed deals; emphasize cooperation to mutual benefit; position transactions within social networks that reinforce their underlying logic; assure that each party to a deal attends to the broad and not just the narrow interests of the other; closely relate expectations of future business to current demeanor and performance; and regulate dispute resolution. They are thus a major source of the evident efficiencies of China's cadre capitalist economy. They are also the source of most of its hidden costs as well as frictions with foreign business partners. In an economy in which all levels of government and business are joined at the hip, these elements of business culture engender cronyism, bribery, nepotism, and other forms of corruption.[21] These practices are contagious. They have a corrupting effect on those doing business with China and the Chinese. They also stimulate local disturbances as people object to their interests being injured by corrupt transactions like "land snatching."[22] Above all, however, these practices are built into a culture that operates through social networks from which foreigners are mostly excluded.

China's challenge to the supremacy of Euro-American economic doctrine derives from the relative success of China's unique combination of cadre capitalism with Chinese values. It does not arise from China's espousal of an exportable alternative doctrine. China has made intermittent efforts to come up with a comprehensive statement of guiding principles based on a fusion of Confucian notions of social harmony, Marxist dialectics, and the scientific method. Notwithstanding these efforts, China currently has no ideology it can explain to its own people, still less one to propose as an alternative to that of the United States or other Western countries.

Given the culture-specific characteristics of cadre capitalism, it is improbable that China could formulate a coherent or compelling statement of ideological principles for cadre capitalism. If it were to do so, the likelihood that its formulation would have much resonance in non-Chinese societies is negligible. Meanwhile, China faces problems of corruption and difficulties in cooperating smoothly with foreign businesses that seem to be inherent in the essence of its cadre capitalist system.

Political Legitimacy or the Lack of It
The lack of a clearly thought-through ideology to justify cadre capitalism or CCP rule poses no difficulty for the Chinese government as long as things continue to go well. The CCP has earned—and continues to earn—the confidence and support of the Chinese people by delivering renewed wealth, power, and visible international respect in ever-larger dollops. If life is getting better and the prestige of the nation is rising, why question the right to rule of those delivering such socioeconomic and psychological advances? Polls show that ordinary Chinese have a lot of pride in their country and a great deal of confidence in the system under which they live.[23] Of course, the system is not currently under severe stress, as it would be were China's economic advance to falter.

Unlike ethnic separatist causes, local grievances about property takings, tax levies, wages and working conditions, environmental damage, police activities, and the like are readily reduced to their negotiable particulars. They do not easily morph into broad protest movements. The Chinese learned the hard way in the Cultural Revolution that someone must be in charge. They fear the chaos that results from a lack of authority on the part of the state. The Chinese authorities are now well practiced in the arts of managing public disturbances about such matters. There is no apparent alternative to CCP rule and the CCP is determined to ensure that none emerges. Only a few in China currently question the legitimacy of the CCP's leadership of the nation's affairs.

Foreign Putdowns
The CCP enjoys no such legitimacy abroad. As a matter of principle, liberal democrats do not recognize the legitimacy of governments whose authority derives from anything other than free expression of political preferences at the ballot box. Anticommunists judge that it is impossible for any Communist party to enjoy popular support. Human rights advocates seek to convert the world to the gospel of the eighteenth-century Euro-American Enlightenment and are outraged by the not-infrequent deviations from this standard at every layer of the Chinese establishment. American politicians exemplify all these beliefs, and the less they know

about China, the more firmly they espouse them. They do not conceal their essential disbelief in the legitimacy of China's Communist government. Despite their interest in cultivating profitable ties for themselves and their constituents with a prospering China, they frequently bear witness to their hope that Communist rule there will in time be overthrown, as it was in the USSR and Eastern Europe. For some, this stance is cynically calculated to ingratiate themselves with their constituents and not a matter of conviction, but for most, it is both.

American disdain for China's political system complicates cooperation between the United States and China. On the U.S. side, beneath both the self-interested pursuit of cooperation and disputes with China, there is invariably a tinge of ideological antipathy alloyed with envy, apprehension, and denial of the likely implications of China's rapidly growing wealth and power in relation to the United States. Chinese, in turn, are quick to judge that America is trying to put China down or hold it back. The message they hear from the U.S. commentariat is that Americans are more likely to delight in Chinese difficulties than to sympathize with them.

China's Unattractive Politics and Their Consequences

Meantime, China's Communist-run government has a real, rather than just an imagined, legitimacy problem to solve. The CCP's authority once rested firmly on widespread admiration for its heroic role in creating a new China and its cadres' reputation for moral rectitude and probity. No more. Today, the CCP's hold on power depends on sustaining economic progress and safeguarding China's newly revived international prestige.

China's leaders know how very vulnerable they could be to a withdrawal of popular support were a major economic setback or foreign humiliation to cut confidence in their ability to keep living standards rising and national pride intact. Hence their unwillingness—even in the face of intense pressure from foreign trading partners—to compromise policies (like those affecting exchange rates) that underpin continuing rapid growth in employment at home. Hence, too, their hypersensitivity to any reminder of their still-limited ability to defend China's interests and honor and their disinclination to engage in any risky, large-scale military activity that could result in failure.

Until the CCP can find credible substitutes for past sources of moral support, it will remain fearful of the possibly inflammatory effects of foreign influences and unpredictable events on domestic restlessness and opposition to CCP rule. Managing the domestic politics of foreign relations is difficult when a policy stumble could call into question not just the competence of particular leaders but the reasonableness of the constitutional order they administer. Awareness of the brittleness of their popular mandate has made China's leaders simultaneously edgily cautious, harshly repressive of activities they see as attempts to organize political opposition to their rule, and quick to take offense at anything they perceive as a foreign putdown.

Despite its impressive ability to deliver results, these features of the Chinese system make it singularly unattractive to outsiders. They complicate the cause of national reunification by turning off people in democratic Taiwan. They disqualify China as a political model for other nations and limit Chinese influence abroad. Lack of a mandate to rule that is independent of sustaining an unbroken record of upward mobility for China and the Chinese people is therefore a serious political problem. This is recognized by the CCP, which is realistic about its and China's many weaknesses and deficiencies.

Despite the urgency of the issues this problem presents, it nonetheless remains unresolved. As long as the sustainable authority of the Chinese political system is not put on a firmer footing, there is no prospect that China could assume global political leadership like that which the United States exercised in the last century. There is also no evidence that China aspires to such a role. It remains absorbed in the difficult tasks inherent in maintaining order and progress in a society of nearly 1.4 billion people. Self-doubt adds further to the natural caution of Chinese leaders who come to power in a system in which the scale of governance is unprecedented, the margin for error is narrow, and misjudgments can result in unforgivable catastrophe.

The Imperatives behind China's Conservatism

Chinese officials justly consider it a minor miracle that the country for whose well-being they are responsible has so far managed to feed 20 percent of the world's people on less than 10 percent of its arable land with only 7 percent of its fresh water.[24] Memories of starvation and civil strife disturb their sleep as well as that of China's elderly. To them, China seems ever poised between a famine and a fracas.

Moreover, unlike the United States, which has no great-power or hostile neighbors, China is surrounded by both. Some of them—Japan and Russia, for example—have recent histories of invading it and annexing its territory. Behind an unsettled border on which Chinese and Indian forces confront each other, India dreams of besting China and countering its influence in Asia. U.S. and Indian Cold War covert action programs directed at destabilizing Tibet and Xinjiang have long since ended, but the ethnic resistance to Chinese rule they exploited has not ceased. In both Korea and Vietnam, which have long traditions of combat with China, U.S. and Chinese forces have fought each other both directly and indirectly. The

U.S. Navy and Air Force probe China's defenses along its coasts. Over the past hundred years, China has fought bloody battles with all these forces, most of which it failed to win.

Not surprisingly, as a reflection of these many internal and external challenges, China's leaders are notably risk averse. In their own view, they have much less margin for error than the leaders of any other great power. A misjudgment in economic policy could result in mass unemployment, the starvation of tens of millions, and popular uprisings that could prove fatal to the regime. Mismanagement of relations with the powerful nations on China's periphery could catalyze war and risk military humiliation, culminating in regime overthrow. The mishandling of ethnic minorities could turn a relatively minor annoyance into a real challenge to the territorial integrity of the Chinese state. There are ample precedents in recent Chinese history for all these things.[25] Well-founded concerns about internal and external factors bearing on continuing prosperity and domestic tranquility combine to make China an inherently cautious, conservative power, famed for its defensiveness and patience rather than its aggressive pursuit of short-term advantage.

China's Politico-Military Posture

China expanded over millennia to its present geographically natural mountain, desert, and maritime limits mainly by assimilating rather than annihilating neighboring peoples. It claims no land beyond its historic borders; indeed, it has abandoned claims to much territory it could claim historically (especially in what is now the Russian Far East). In China's uniquely long history, it was several times overwhelmed by neighbors with more militaristic societies. The stalwart independence of Korea, Mongolia, and Vietnam—some of which invaded China, but all of which China repeatedly failed to conquer—underscores the reality of China's basically defensive orientation, with rare exceptions, over the last two millennia.

Early in its uniquely long history as a society, China built a "Great Wall" to exclude foreign invaders. In 1433, it voluntarily abandoned its naval supremacy in the Indo-Pacific region by burning and scuttling its fleet. Those who cite European precedents to predict aggressive behavior from a newly prosperous and powerful China strangely choose to treat this history as irrelevant. China is certainly not a pacifist power. But China's traditionally defensive posture is deeply rooted in the geopolitics, geography, and political traditions of East Asia. It is unclear why academic theories drawn almost entirely from European history should prove more predictive of East Asia's future than realistic extrapolations from its present or past might do.[26]

Despite the multiple internal and external challenges to its national security and territorial integrity, since China's "opening and reform" began in 1979, the CCP has given priority to the modernization of agriculture, industry, and science and technology. It has held defense spending to 2 percent or less of GDP and less than 10 percent of the central government's budget.[27] Its strategic forces remain modest in size and configured to deter and respond to a nuclear attack, not to initiate one.

China's economy has, of course, been growing very fast, and its central government budget has grown even faster. In recent years, this has permitted a very rapid rise in Chinese military spending[28] and much progress in closing the gap between China's military capabilities and those of the United States and other developed countries. (Still, with a few exceptions, China's military disposes of weaponry that is a generation or more behind that of the United States, Japan, and most NATO members.) China is now able to defend itself—and could overwhelm Taiwan, if need be. It could prevail in battle with rival claimants to islands in its near seas like the Philippines or Vietnam, but not Japan. Over the past two centuries, China was repeatedly invaded from the sea. But despite its desire to be able to defend itself from seaborne attack by a major naval power like the United States, China cannot yet project its power much beyond its immediate periphery.

China's Self-Perceived Weakness and Some of Its Consequences

China sees itself as having had a history of weakness and vulnerability to foreign invasion. For over a third of the last millennium, it was under foreign occupation and rule.[29] In the nineteenth and twentieth centuries, China was variously invaded or garrisoned by forces from Russia, British India, Western European countries, the United States, and Japan. China remains the only great power with borders still actively contested by neighbors and territory separated from it by ongoing foreign intervention.[30] Having been bullied itself, it has repeatedly expressed determination not to bully others or to be seen as doing so.[31]

China has fought wars on its borders in modern times.[32] But, despite its rising power, it has not pressed a single territorial dispute to resolution through the use of force.[33] China's maritime borders remain unresolved, but all but one of its land frontiers—that with India—have been demarcated through peaceful negotiations.[34] (The prolonged failure to settle the Sino-Indian border seems to have as much or more to do with India as it does with China.)

In a misguided attempt to avoid irritating other claimants, China early on decided to postpone efforts to settle its more than half-century-old claims to islands and reefs in the South and East China Seas that others dispute.[35] These claims, now imbued with nationalist passion and competition for access to seabed oil and gas resources, pit other claimants against China. Southeast Asians fear that China, for the first time in more than a century, is rapidly acquiring the military strength to impose solutions in their disputes with it. In response, these countries have become much more active in asserting their own claims, as has China.

Sino-American Military Dynamics

The growth in China's economic power and military capabilities is inexorably shifting the balance of power in the Indo-Pacific region. This dynamic naturally concerns China's neighbors, especially those with unsettled borders with China, like India, or maritime boundary disputes with China, like Malaysia, the Philippines, and Vietnam. Perceiving an increasingly formidable potential threat from China, these countries have embarked on major efforts to modernize their naval and other forces. At the same time, they are trying to buttress their claims by populating formerly uninhabited islets and actively exploring for oil and gas in partnership with foreign companies. They don't want to alienate China by taking sides with America against it. They have nonetheless sought to enlist American support for their continuing rejection of China's claims. This effort has met with increasing success as America itself reacts to rising Chinese power.

Much of these nations' interest in U.S. military posturing on their behalf (as opposed to American expressions of interest in their continuing independence and freedom from coercion) would likely disappear if the territorial disputes that now inflame their relations with China were to be resolved. Neither they nor China have seriously pursued resolution of their differences. But increased American backing emboldens nationalists and hardens their positions on territorial disputes. It also riles nationalist sentiment in China. It thus adds to each side's domestic political difficulties in pursuing compromise.

The U.S. sees its intervention as assuring peaceful outcomes without prejudice to the positions of the parties. Ironically, however, it actually reduces the likelihood that negotiations will take place or succeed. It also increases the danger of U.S. military clashes with Chinese forces over issues that are of passionate concern to China and other claimants but not to the United States.

The United States' concerns about China's rising military power have centered on two issues: (1) its effects on U.S. deterrence of the possible use of force by the People's Liberation Army (PLA) to coerce Taiwan's political reunification with the rest of China; and (2) the extent to which China may be establishing a defensive perimeter in which it can inhibit or exclude the ability of U.S. naval and air forces to attack it. The two issues have traditionally been related, as the only contingencies that anyone could imagine for armed conflict between Chinese and American forces were related to Taiwan. As tensions between Taiwan and the Chinese mainland and the danger of war between them have diminished,[36] however, American concern about China's ability to keep U.S. forces at bay has had to find other justifications.

The United States has now attributed to China strategies of "anti-access" and "area denial" directed at U.S. forces. These terms represent an American assessment of the possible effects of greater Chinese military competence on U.S. forces; they are not strategic concepts or terms used by Chinese military planners. American concerns reflect the post–Cold War U.S. determination to sustain the ability to dominate the global commons and to prevail in battle against any and all foreign opponents, including China.[37] China's rising military power threatens to erode this absolute U.S. superiority even if it does not threaten the U.S. homeland.

For its part, China sees itself as acquiring the ability to defend itself against attack from its near seas and the land masses within them, not seeking to impede U.S. non-hostile access to these areas or to deny U.S. forces passage through them. China has a greater stake in freedom of navigation in the South China Sea than any other country. Sixty percent of its imports and exports pass through that sea.

U.S. force structure and forward deployments are configured to interrupt this trade and to exert overwhelming military power on China's borders. Current and planned U.S. capabilities vastly exceed the requirements of deterrence (which does not demand absolute assurance of the ability to crush enemy defenses to be successful). This slights the defensive capabilities of U.S. allies and security partners in the Indo-Pacific region. It also complicates rather than accords with their desire for cordial, if wary, relations with a rising China. U.S. deployments and operations embody a fundamentally confrontational policy. This is inconsistent with the oft-stated U.S. willingness to accommodate China's rise or to deal with its consequences in ways that minimize the risk of conflict.

An ambitiously aggressive U.S. military posture designed to preserve the capability to attack China at will precludes less expensive and risky American strategies aimed at buttressing regional balances and sustaining deterrence without appearing to threaten attacks on the Chinese homeland. The evolving U.S. battle plan presupposes that, from the outset, any war that occurred would involve U.S. strikes on forces and facilities on Chinese territory or immediately adjacent to it. This does not address the obvious difficulties of escalation control in these circumstances. It is simply unrealistic, given China's possession of nuclear weapons.

Sino-American Mistrust

The major source of distrust between the Chinese and American armed forces has long been the possibility of war over Taiwan. Taiwan has now been joined as a cause of mistrust by the contradiction between the stated U.S. ambition to be able to overpower the defenses of any and all potential foreign adversaries, including China, and China's attempts to develop credible defenses against foreign attack, including from the United States. This contradiction is at the root of an emerging arms race between China and the United States. America is striving to sustain its past and present overwhelming military superiority in the Indo-Pacific region. China is attempting to offset America's massive advantages in conventional military strength through innovative, asymmetric, and relatively inexpensive means.[38]

Military rivalry and mistrust imbue American backing of China's neighbors with a polarizing sense of strategic hostility to China that these neighbors do not wish to convey. It tinges other aspects of Sino-American relations with mutual suspicion verging on hostility. It reduces the prospects for bilateral cooperation on key areas of overlapping common interest. The earnest protestations of American diplomats to the effect that the United States "seeks to develop a positive, cooperative, and comprehensive relationship with China," not to counter it, ring hollow in China and the region alike. They detract from, rather than add to, American credibility.

Given the current fiscal and monetary difficulties that the United States faces, it is unclear how long America will be able to afford the pursuit of global military predominance of this extremely expensive kind in East Asia or anywhere else. Sooner or later, the United States will be driven to less resource-intensive and risky approaches to sustaining the regional stability that its interests demand. These will involve enhanced rather than diminished cooperation with American allies and security partners. Such policies will also require more honest and effective communication between the American and Chinese military establishments than at present. In the meantime, thoughtful Chinese strategists seem prepared to wait America out.

Few performances are as self-righteously unpersuasive as those of American political and military leaders who profess to be mystified by the purpose of Chinese defense modernization. With awesome indifference to irony, they have sometimes done so right after having proclaimed their resolve to maintain an inherently threatening military presence on China's borders, sold advanced weaponry to Taiwan, bombed a Chinese embassy abroad,[39] stridently sided with China's neighbors against it, or argued for some form of regime change in China.[40] Chinese officials who mouth euphemistic platitudes to describe the purposes of China's defense build-up or who espouse conspiracy theories about the United States do equal damage to China's credibility. Of such hypocrisy and self-deception are accidental wars concocted. The avoidance of potentially catastrophic conflict between great powers deserves more effective diplomacy than this.

Immediate Prospects

China and the United States are both in the midst of uncertain political, economic, and military transitions. As 2012 merges into 2013, a new generation will come to power in China. At the same time, a new team (either a reelected Obama administration or a new Republican-led administration) will be organizing itself to govern in Washington, D.C. American politics are mired in gridlock, a debilitating condition that is unsustainable and must eventually be overthrown by political change. Chinese politics have experienced more reform than many are prepared to admit, but no one in China or anywhere else believes that the Chinese political system has achieved a mature and stable form. China has yet to find a way to deal with a citizenry that is no longer prepared to let officials do its thinking for it. As the second decade of the twenty-first century unfolds, political upheavals of one sort or another seem more likely than not in both countries, though no one knows when or how they might occur.[41]

Meanwhile, China's generous investments in human and physical infrastructure, intelligent uses of industrial policy, and rising competency in science and technology are beginning to pay off. They contrast with the United States' tolerance of mediocrity and disinvestment in education, abandonment of efforts to maintain—still less upgrade—transportation systems, special-interest-tax-code-directed economic decision-making, and avid interest in high-tech products of all kinds but not the science and mathematics that result in them. China is now in the early stages of building effective social safety nets and public health systems for its aging population. These systems are now under increasing economic and political stress in America. The qualitative gaps between the two economies are closing even as the gross balance between them shifts in favor of China, which will soon displace the United States as the largest economy in the world.

Even as this happens, however, the export-oriented, high-investment, low-consumption, low–public services model on which China has built its success is coming to the end of its useful life. And the high-consumption, low-savings, generous-welfare American system is now in chronic crisis. China and America each confront the need to make painful adjustments in their economic structures and strategies in order to sustain growth and prosperity.[42] Both countries have reached turning points in their political economies. As they respond (or fail to respond) to the challenges before them, their politico-economic interaction will also change in often stressfully trying ways. The short-term prospect is for increased trade friction as the two economies grow into ever-greater interdependence.

Strategic Rivalry

A similar dynamic is at work in the Sino-American military balance. For the foreseeable future, the United States will command formidable armed forces with power projection capabilities that are second to none. But chronic deficits, ballooning debt, and competing socioeconomic priorities foretell deep cuts in U.S. defense budgets and related military spending.[43] (Political denial has so far held back fiscal realities, but the need for the United States to manage its national debt will clearly not permit this to go on much longer.) The U.S. armed forces are about to enter a prolonged period of fiscally dictated downsizing. They will be configured to be able to confront a range of specific and limited contingencies rather than to dominate the global commons.

On the other hand, there is no reason to expect anything but further rapid growth in Chinese defense budgets. Even if China continues to hold its overall military spending at its current, relatively low level (about 1.5 to 2 percent of GDP or 10 to 11 percent of the central government budget), given continued rapid economic expansion in China, sometime in the third decade of the twenty-first century, Chinese military-related spending will exceed that of the United States.[44] Spending is only loosely correlated with capabilities. Nevertheless, these trends strongly suggest that within a decade and a half, China will be able to achieve its stated objective of defending itself against even as capable a military power as the United States.

China will also have gained the economic means to develop significant military power projection capabilities. Whether it decides to do so will depend on the extent to which its global interests and the demands of an evolving world order compel such a decision. The extent to which China enjoys a cooperative rather than a hostile military relationship with the United States and other major powers will be a major determinant in this regard. Should the United States appear to pose an escalating threat to China in alliance with China's neighbors, rather than to participate in an East Asian security balance that makes room for China, China will have the capacity to respond on a global level.

China has so far been very careful to avoid political or military rivalry with America. It has not sought to disrupt American alliances in Asia or anywhere else. On the contrary, while objecting to some specific U.S. policies, China has repeatedly expressed appreciation for the stabilizing effects of the U.S. presence in the Asia-Pacific region. This attitude has reflected China's judgment that its interests are best served by "a peaceful international environment," to which the U.S. presence in Asia is a significant contributor. It also resonates with an assessment that, as things stand, it could not win a military contest with America in any event. China is unlikely to revise its judgment that peace along its borders is in its best interest. In the future, however, it will be increasingly confident about its ability to hold its own against the United States in its "near abroad."

If China comes to feel undue military pressure from America, it is less likely to respond in the Indo-Pacific (where its actions might easily exacerbate rather than relieve apprehensions by its neighbors about its power) than elsewhere. China could, for example, come to see distracting the United States by fostering challenges to U.S. interests in the Western Hemisphere as strategically advantageous. Some countries in the Caribbean and South America have been eager to enlist China as a counterweight to U.S. power. (Were China to decide to accommodate their demands, it would bring considerably greater capabilities to bear than previous adversaries of the United States—Imperial and Nazi Germany, Imperial Japan, and the USSR.)

Yet such a Chinese move toward mounting a global challenge to American power seems unlikely. The common interests of the two countries in global order, peace, and prosperity vastly outweigh their few areas of serious disagreement, and both sides are well aware of this. Only a major American or Chinese misstep could tip U.S.-China relations toward broad strategic antagonism rather than the continuing mixture of cooperation and competition that both sides' political leaders judge to be appropriate, desirable, and mutually advantageous. Still, the possible consequences of strategic antagonism are a pointed reminder of how much is at stake in the prudent management of Sino-American relations.

For better or ill, China has now joined America as a leading influence in global governance, the world economy, and Indo-Pacific politico-military affairs. Over the coming decade and more, China will become a more formidable player on the world stage. There is no more consequential bilateral relationship at present than that between the United States and China. That is likely to be the case for many decades to come. The world must hope for wise statesmanship from the leaders of both countries. To date, China has proven to be a remarkably cautious and conservative international actor. In most respects, it has become the "responsible stakeholder" the United States has desired it to be. Whether China will continue to behave this constructively as its power grows will be decided in large measure by decisions and policies made in America.

A Few Features of the Next Forty Years

One way or another, by the middle of the twenty-first century, most of the current conflicts between the United States and China are almost certain to have been resolved. The most troubling such question, Taiwan's relationship to the rest of China, is a case in point. So are the current controversies over provocative U.S. patrols in China's near seas, claims and counterclaims in the South China Sea between China and its neighbors, north Korea, alleged currency manipulation, the protection of intellectual property, and the terms of trade and investment. Differences on still other issues, like human rights, seem destined to moderate. No doubt other contentious Sino-American differences will emerge to succeed these. Every resolution of a problem creates new problems. And the United States and China will become even more interdependent than they now are and therefore have even more to bicker about than they do now.

Taiwan and Other Territorial Disputes

The cross-Strait relationship seems very likely to be worked out in coming decades—though perhaps not without a war scare or two—by peaceful acts of mutual accommodation by both sides. After a decade of disruption by actions and events that originated in Taiwan,[45] a process of pragmatic reintegration of the two sides of the Taiwan Strait resumed in 2005. The January 2012 Taiwan elections made it clear that a decisive majority of Taiwanese voters have come to see independence as a dead option. The only course now acceptable to large majorities on both sides of the Strait is to continue economic integration and cultural rapprochement. Both sides hope this can culminate in the eventual elimination of military confrontation between them. Both sides know that accomplishing this will ultimately require difficult compromises. Both are culturally Chinese and prepared to be patient.

But Beijing and Taipei (with some involvement by Hong Kong and Macau) now seem poised to resume and perhaps accelerate the establishment of the "suprastatal" frameworks[46] that enable cooperation within an ambiguous concept of "one China." Such frameworks transcend issues of sovereignty by creating negotiated assignments of regulatory power to institutions that can manage cross-Strait engagement and cooperation. These frameworks and the rules they administer are, in a sense, supra-sovereign. They facilitate cross-Strait rapprochement on the basis of a common Chinese identity that they themselves are beginning to define. In time, as such an identity permeates all of greater China, these frameworks promise to constitute the foundations of some sort of Chinese commonwealth. As such a commonwealth emerges and ever more divisive issues are bridged, those within greater China will have the opportunity to determine the name, constitution, provisions for national defense, and lawmaking institutions of their community. Their choices may well surprise the world, as so many developments among Chinese have over the past forty years.

U.S.-China confrontations in China's near seas will also be a thing of the past. Even if it could afford such operations, which is doubtful, the U.S. will not be able to continue them indefinitely in the face of active and ever-more-competent Chinese obstruction of them. America will have found ways to pursue its intelligence-collection objectives by less expensive and provocative means. Or perhaps China, by initiating similar activities off America's coasts, will have driven the United States toward the reciprocal abandonment of aggressive patrolling. One way or another, the United States will discontinue this aspect of its current misguided attempt to preserve the global hegemony bequeathed to it by the collapse of the USSR and the end of the Cold War.

It also seems very likely that sovereignty over disputed islands, islets, rocks, and reefs in the South China Sea will be settled through negotiations. China now seems to recognize that early resolution of these issues, politically difficult as it may be in terms of nationalist sentiment, is in China's interest. Other claimants see time working against them as China's position strengthens relative to theirs, regardless of the level of American backing they may enjoy.

There is an obvious sequence of steps that leads to resolution of these issues. All concerned now appear to comprehend it.[47] This path or something like it will be pursued by China and other claimants with or without the intervention of the United States. South China Sea questions will then no longer be "wedge issues" for U.S. policymakers interested in enhancing American influence in Southeast Asian states. Ironically, both the case and the prospects for effective U.S. political, economic, and military engagement with these states to help them balance their ties with China would be enhanced, not weakened, by the dialing down of alarmism.

Korea

The Korea question may very well also find resolution over this period. The danger of conflict on the peninsula has subsided but not disappeared, as occasional armed clashes between the two Korean states periodically illustrate. The situation on the Korean Peninsula has long since ceased to be a major U.S.-China issue. Still, it remains a strategic irritant. For many reasons, it has been easier for the United States to treat the Democratic People's Republic of Korea (DPRK) as a nuclear problem rather than as a state or country. America has sought to manage tensions on the Korean Peninsula rather than to seek a lasting peace there, as China would have preferred.

A peace would require American as well as south Korean acceptance of the exceptionally unattractive regime in the north and the replacement of the armistice with a treaty. A continuing focus on nuclear disarmament is a distraction in this regard. Despite the DPRK's interest in ensuring its continuing existence through normalization of relations with the United States, it is highly unlikely to be willing to give up the security it has gained from building a modest nuclear deterrent to a foreign or Republic of Korea (ROK) attempt to overthrow it or push it around.

China has a major interest in stability and avoiding war on its borders, especially war that could draw great-power intervention and require a Chinese military response. To this end, China has taken the lead in convening talks about the Korean situation between all interested parties. (It has—it must be admitted—done so less out of hope that the DPRK could be persuaded to abandon its nuclear program than from a desire to pre-empt destabilizing moves by either the DPRK or the United States.) Still, in the end, the state of tensions in Korea and whether north and south are at peace or reunified will not be determined by China and the United States. These questions will be decided in interactions between Pyongyang, Seoul, and Washington, none of which now seems inclined toward bold moves.

Shifting Asian Balances

The disappearance of the China-specific and regional security issues that now agitate Sino-American relations will not, of course, mean the end of strategic balancing and bilateral foreign policy differences between the two countries. To cite an obvious example, consider the question of how China and America should respond to India's growing military power and its aspirations to rival China for leadership in Asia and Africa.[48] The many facets of this issue will play out over decades. Other examples are to be found in the possibly shifting strategic orientations of Japan and Russia.

After its defeat and occupation in 1945, Japan accommodated an unpopular American military presence on its soil to protect it from aggression by the Soviet Union and its allies, which then included a militant but militarily impotent China as well as north Korea. But the Soviet threat is no more. Japan's strategic orientation is now driven by the rising strength of China and the two Korean states, one of which (the DPRK) is Japan's avowed nuclear-armed enemy.

In reaction, Japan first began quietly to augment its independent self-defense capabilities and to draw closer to its American protectors. More recently, it has begun to diversify its defense relationships by exploring collaboration with others, like Australia, India, and Vietnam. As the military capabilities of China, the ROK, and Japan itself have improved, so have their efforts to enforce their sovereignty where it is disputed. The resulting military frictions annoy all three countries but, so far, have proved manageable. There is no reason to doubt that they will continue to be so.

Despite two-thirds of a century of exclusive reliance on the United States for defense of both its homeland and its interests abroad, it is improbable that Japan will entrust itself entirely to American protection very much longer. It could end up downplaying its ties to the United States and peacefully accommodating a more powerful China or rearming and seeking to enlist the United States and other Indo-Pacific nations against China—or somewhere in between. Japan's decisions, which will be heavily influenced by America's, will have a major bearing on China, its policies, and its relations with the United States.

Russia is now rebounding from its post-Soviet nadir. It is doing so in association with its heavyweight Chinese neighbor rather than in opposition to it, as was so often the case in the past. This reflects a patient effort by China to cultivate good relations with Russia in its years of economic relapse, strategic resentment, and need as well as common interests that have found expression in the post–Cold War era. Russia and China are senior partners in the Shanghai Cooperation Organization (SCO), an effort to contain Islamist extremism while neutralizing great-power contention for influence in the newly independent states of Central Asia. For economically booming China, Russia has become a major source of oil, metals, coal, and timber as well as advanced weaponry. For oil-rich, consumer industry–poor, and diplomatically downgraded Russia, China is a key source of capital and manufactured goods as well as political backing against the humiliations of the post-Soviet U.S.-dominated world order.[49]

The past volatility of Sino-Russian relations[50] advises considerable caution about their future course. Sources of strain include the demographics and politico-economic orientation of the Russian Far East. This vast part of the Russian Federation, just to the north of the nearly 110 million inhabitants of China's Northeast,[51] remains both underdeveloped and very lightly populated. Chinese investment in Russian Siberia is currently running at a rate at least three times that of Russia, and Chinese migrants have become the primary means of meeting labor shortages. This causes natural concern in Moscow. China will also continue to calibrate its Russia policy to take account of its relations with the European Union (EU). And as the memory of an American-dominated world order recedes, China and Russia could find themselves more frequently at odds on issues of global governance.

Trade, Investment, Peace, and War

All of the paradoxes of interdependence are also likely to play out in U.S.-China economic relations, which will progress through a series of difficult adjustments over the decades to come. Current differences over currency alignments are likely to disappear as China's Renminbi yuan[52] becomes fully internationalized and available as yet another reserve currency. But new difficulties will doubtless arise as the United States ceases to enjoy the privileges of seignorage and exemption from the rules applied to lesser economies and as China takes a more active and self-interested role in global monetary councils.

Similarly, as China turns toward consumerism and a more labor-friendly workplace, the United States, now chronically in deficit, could well regain the trade surplus it once enjoyed with China, shifting the balance of political whining along with the trade imbalance. America has the resource base and productivity to accomplish this, especially if it begins to address some of the hobbles on its economic competitiveness imposed by special-interest-dictated decisions on taxes, tax subsidies, public sector investment, regulatory regimes, tort litigation, and popular culture. In any event, bilateral trade and investment flows are clearly destined to continue to increase. With more intensive transactions come more trade and investment frictions and disputes. As Chinese politics become more responsive to public opinion, the number of complaints originating on the Chinese side could well come to equal or exceed those in America.[53] As the volume of economic interaction between the United States and China increases, so will the sound level.

If the economic order that is emerging promises to test America's self-discipline and restraint and China's willingness to lead as well as complain, so too does the arena of international law and organizations. Both China and the United States have a stake in preserving as much as possible of the current United Nations system. After all, it gives both countries the status of permanent Security Council members and the power to veto the initiatives of other, less favored great powers. Yet to the extent to which this system is failing to adjust to and represent shifting balances of global power and influence, it is becoming progressively less useful and effective. As proud beneficiaries of the *status quo*, both China and America will be challenged to yield a necessary measure of their status to other rising powers.

International law is now undergoing a fairly rapid evolution to reflect recent Western deviations from past norms as well as the moral outlooks of the various non-Western powers now taking the lead in international affairs. These changes increasingly pit the United States and China in argument, sometimes with each other, sometimes with still others. The large shifts in the global constellation of power, capabilities, and influence now taking place are multiplying the examples of this. Let me cite a few.

The regime applied to the world's oceans is unlikely to remain the same when the single national navy that has dominated it is joined by other navies determined to play a role in defending their homelands while policing the global commons.

Non-state and transnational actors—previously essentially unknown to international law—have now seized global roles. There is no agreement on how properly to deal with them.

Newly asserted doctrines of preventative war cannot be reconciled with either the UN Charter or traditional concepts of the law of war, raising the prospect of a world in which the law offers no protection from assault and there is therefore a premium on highly destructive deterrent capabilities.

As robot and other electromechanical systems like drones replace human-operated instruments of war, both the concept of territorial sovereignty and the law of war demand further updating.

The consequences of global interdependence and real-time planet-wide awareness of events, meanwhile, challenge the international community to rebalance traditional concepts of sovereignty and humanitarian accountability.[54] And so forth.

Then, too, there is an abundance of unsolved issues of global governance, beginning with the crafting of an effective response to climate change, natural resource and energy management, and environmental remediation. All these matters and others must be thrashed out between the United States and China, testing the vision and statesmanship of both sides and the quality of their relations with still other great powers.

Conclusion

The world of the future is one in which the United States will no longer reign supreme, but neither will China nor any other nation. China is not and will not be in a position to inspire and lead the world politically and economically, as the United States did in the twentieth century. Nor, barring ill-considered challenges from the United States that stimulate it to do so, will China aspire to dislodge America as the world's greatest military power.

The challenge before the two countries in coming decades is to manage a transition to a new world order to which each contributes and from which each benefits, like the rest of the world. In such an order, the United States and China must share political and economic power with each other and with others, and Sino-American military cooperation and arrangements for multilateral burden-sharing must first supplement, then incorporate, capabilities now exercised by the United States alone. Such a world will not be perfect, but it is better than the conceivable alternatives. Getting to it will be difficult but not impossible. This is a transition that wise statecraft by the two countries can help the world make.

Chapter 2

How Diplomatic Normalization Happened

The American opening to China (and of China to the world) is properly remembered as a turning point in the geopolitics of the last third of the twentieth century, as a remarkable example of imaginative statesmanship, and as an extraordinary political volte face for the man who engineered it, Richard Nixon. It was all of these things. But it was also a complex set of diplomatic maneuvers. After more than two decades of antagonism and mutual distrust, the normalization of relations with the People's Republic of China did not come easily.

The central obstacle was the status in American law and policy of the Republic of China (on Taiwan), rather than the People's Republic of China, as the sole legal representative of China internationally and in the United States. The resolution of this problem in Sino-American relations could not and did not, however, resolve the Taiwan issue per se. As the Chinese never cease to assert, even today the question of Taiwan's relationship to the rest of China and the American position on this question severely complicate U.S.-China relations, especially in the military sphere, and prevent the realization of their full potential. Still, before the United States and China could begin to deal with Taiwan and other problems between them, they had to find each other and lay the basis for a degree of cooperation.

This wasn't as easy as it might seem in retrospect. Washington and Beijing had begun ambassadorial-level talks at Geneva in 1955 and continued them intermittently at Warsaw from 1958 on, but from 1950 through 1968, the United States otherwise maintained a policy of total non-intercourse and embargo against China. It was illegal for Americans to visit mainland China, to do business with its companies, and to buy its products abroad or import them. No financial transactions in dollars were permitted with the China mainland. Chinese with mainland passports were not allowed to visit the United States or to transit its territory.

America devoted an enormous amount of diplomatic energy and effort to assuring that Taipei, rather than Beijing, continued to be recognized at the United Nations and internationally as the seat of the legal government of China. It intervened actively in support of Taipei's efforts to bar representatives of the Chinese Communist regime or its society from attendance at governmental and nongovernmental gatherings abroad. American officials referred to the Chinese Communist capital, Beijing, only by the name Chiang Kai-shek had given it to commemorate China's unification under his rule: Pei-p'ing.[1] A large American bureaucracy earned a living enforcing these strictures. When I joined the United States Foreign Service (USFS), I became part of this apparatus.

In my first overseas tour, in an India where memories of the 1962 Sino-Indian border war were still fresh, I gained an appreciation for the highly suspicious Indian view of China and for India's aspirations for Tibet, which was by then fully incorporated into China.[2] In the fall of 1968, I helped other U.S. diplomats sustain Taipei's position as the legally recognized representative of China in the United Nations. As a Chinese-language and area studies student in Washington and then in Taiwan from 1969 to 1971, I was tapped to interpret at the ambassadorial-level talks with "Communist China" at Warsaw.

As a junior officer on the State Department's China desk in the spring and early summer of 1971, I helped write background papers in support of the visit of an American envoy to Beijing. I was not supposed to know about the proposal for a high-level American emissary to the Communist regime, but having read the transcripts of the Warsaw talks, I did. I guessed but did not know that the emissary would be Henry Kissinger. (At that time, the degree of his personal involvement in secret diplomatic activities on behalf of the president, e.g., talks with the north Vietnamese in Paris, was not public.)

In late 1971 and early 1972, I also played a supporting role, though I no longer had to pretend anymore that I didn't know what I was doing or why, in the preparations for President Nixon's February 21–28 visit to the China mainland. I accompanied the president as the principal American interpreter on that visit. In the spring of 1973, I was a member of the advance team that set up the United States Liaison Office in Beijing. Though asked to stay on in any one of several capacities, I declined. In terms of either the opportunity to get to know China better or to move the bilateral relationship forward, I judged that diplomatic service in Beijing during the Great Proletarian Cultural Revolution, then morphing into the domination of the "Gang of Four," would be barely distinguishable from house arrest. My first prolonged service in Beijing was as chargé d'affaires ad interim and then as Deputy Chief of Mission (July 1981–November 1984) under the splendidly professional leadership of Ambassador Arthur W. Hummel Jr.

In 1980, when I was serving as Country Director for Chinese and Mongolian Affairs at the Department of State, a Chinese-American lawyer friend named Gene Hsiao asked me to write a detailed account of the diplomatic process of Sino-American rapprochement for a book he was editing. He wanted me to document the many small signals that helped to begin and advance the relationship. He correctly considered it effectively impossible for someone who hadn't actually participated in the execution of these minutiae to produce such an account, even though almost all of the details were in the public record. I had participated in the run-up to President Nixon's 1972 visit to Beijing and accompanied him on it. My friend was also aware of the work I had done on legal issues that would arise from "derecognizing" Taipei and recognizing Beijing as the seat of China's government. After initially resisting his invitation to write for him, I accepted it.[3]

As far as I know, the account of the nitty-gritty diplomacy of the initial Sino-American rapprochement that I wrote for my friend remains unique as a chronicle of what can be required to initiate and establish communication with an estranged foreign power. Quite aside from its value to meticulous diplomatic historians, I would like to think that it may be useful to others who may have occasion to attempt to build relations with other formerly hostile foreign countries in the future.

I am not normally a colorless writer, but what I wrote in this case was deliberately understated. After all, as I wrote, Ronald Reagan was campaigning for the presidency on a pledge to restore official relations with the Republic of China on Taiwan and to institute a policy of unrestrained arms sales to the island. Many associated with his campaign had made it clear that they intended to carry out a purge of anyone associated with U.S.-China normalization, to which they viscerally objected. (To this day, some remain essentially unreconciled to the termination of the U.S. defense treaty with Taiwan.) Members of Senator Jesse Helms's staff made a point of informing me that I was on the list of those to be done in.

Once in office, President Reagan came to appreciate the strategic advantages that his predecessor's opening to China had gained for the United States. Ever a pragmatist beneath his ideology-laden rhetoric, he revised his position on China accordingly. Still, the ugly political tone in 1980 could not help but remind any career diplomat involved with China of what had happened to a previous generation of "China hands" charged with insufficient loyalty to Chiang Kai-shek's Chinese Nationalist cause. (Less than thirty years before, one of my predecessors as Country Director for China had been physically hauled away by security personnel from the very desk at which I then sat, in response to charges from Senator Joe McCarthy.) Even when it does not come naturally, there are circumstances when it is best to be bland.

The possibility of the American political conversation lapsing into a "who sold out Taiwan" debate was all too obvious. The sad fact was that the "normalization" of relations with the People's Republic of China necessitated the "abnormalization" of relations with its politico-military rival across the Taiwan Strait, which the United States had supported so thoroughly for decades. Despite the persuasive strategic rationale for doing this, no one with a personal acquaintance with Taiwan and its people could fail to find this distressing.

Of course, the relaxation of tensions in the Taiwan Strait that the new relationship with China catalyzed eventually led to the end of martial law and the birth of a democratic system of government in Taiwan. But for many, this just compounded the irony: in effect, the United States had to continue officially to turn a cold shoulder to the increasingly attractive, modernized Chinese society that was emerging on the island. Taiwan's diplomacy has skillfully played on this awkward situation and the ambivalence with which Americans inevitably regard it.

It is hard to think of other examples of a great power deliberately sacrificing relations with a basically inoffensive and friendly former protectorate in order to court strategic cooperation with the mortal enemy of that protectorate. As the post-normalization debate over the Taiwan Relations Act[4] revealed, many who had applauded President Nixon's opening to China had remained in a state of denial about its inevitable costs in terms of relations with Taiwan. They saw President Jimmy Carter's implementation of his two (Republican) predecessors' diplomatic undertakings to break with Taipei and switch diplomatic relations to Beijing as probably expedient but certainly dishonorable. It is fair to say that many Americans continue to be troubled by the U.S. shift of embassies from Taipei to Beijing, more than three decades later.

The piece I wrote for my friend Professor Hsiao carries the story of U.S.-China antagonism and rapprochement from the last years of the Lyndon Johnson administration through those of Jimmy Carter's presidency. The Taiwan problem may have been finessed, but it did not go away when formal U.S. relations with Taipei ended. Some of the subsequent iterations of the Taiwan problem are described in the pages that follow this article. This contentious story is not over. There will be more trends and events to ponder in the years to come.

The Process of Rapprochement: Achievements and Problems[5]
August 1980

In the October 1967 issue of *Foreign Affairs*, presidential candidate Richard M. Nixon, repudiating almost two decades of his own rhetoric, urged that American policy "come urgently to grips with the reality of China."[6] Moving with all deliberate speed, the United States and the People's Republic of China finally succeeded—on January 1, 1979, twelve years and three American administrations later—in establishing mutual recognition and diplomatic relations.

The entire process of normalization was a unique experience in the conduct of American diplomacy, involving a complete reassessment of the American position toward bilateral relations with China as well as the objective circumstances in other parts of the world that they affected. The long and difficult process was filled with tensions, frustrations, secret diplomatic maneuvers, hard bargaining, and much spectacle. The end result was a reversal of mutual hostilities dating from the Korean conflict and the beginning of a new relationship with a country whose importance to the United States and the rest of the world seems certain to increase with the passage of time.

From Confrontation to Summit Negotiation
The China policy inherited by the new Republican administration in 1969 was essentially that formulated by the Truman administration in May 1951 in the aftermath of Chinese intervention in the Korean conflict. It rested on the assumption of closely coordinated Soviet and Chinese policies (the Sino-Soviet bloc) jointly devoted to achieving Communist hegemony over the weak new states of postwar Asia and the Pacific. This assumption had seemingly been confirmed by the Korean conflict and made an article of faith for much of the American body politic by the virulent anticommunism of the time.

The goal of American policy from 1951 through 1969 was to isolate and contain "Communist China." The United States refused to recognize the Chinese Communists as the legitimate rulers of China, strongly opposed proposals for their seating in the United Nations or other international fora, firmly supported the international position of the defeated Chinese Nationalist regime on Taiwan, underwrote the control of the "Republic of China" over Taiwan and other areas of China from which it had not been driven, and gave vigorous support to nations on the periphery of China that American policy makers saw as threatened by Chinese "aggression."

By 1968, the assumptions on which this policy rested had begun to come under serious question. Sino-Soviet unity, never so great as it was perceived to be, was demonstrably a thing of the past. The Soviet invasion of Czechoslovakia on August 21 of that year, justified by the Brezhnev doctrine of "limited sovereignty" on September 26, seemed ominously to provide a precedent and rationale for Soviet escalation of the war of words with China into armed conflict. In March 1969, following a series of minor incidents, serious fighting broke out along the Sino-Soviet frontier. The "Cultural Revolution," while heightening Chinese rhetorical aggressiveness, had meanwhile revealed a China so at odds with itself as to present a diminished threat to neighboring countries, which, in any event, achieved considerable viability as independent nations. In the United States, the Vietnam War had created a mood in which, for the first time in two decades, the old anticommunist assumptions were subjected to reexamination.

It was against this background that prominent leaders of the Republican and Democratic parties began to propose changes in our China policy during the 1968 presidential campaign. Stressing the need to replace "bamboo curtains" with "open doors," the Democratic candidate, Hubert H. Humphrey, called for "the building of peaceful bridges to the people of mainland China."[7] Governor Nelson A. Rockefeller of New York followed suit in his bid for the presidency by urging Americans to make more "contact and communication" with China.[8] Meanwhile, Undersecretary of State Nicholas DeBelleville Katzenbach assured a National Press Club audience that the United States would be "happy to respond positively" to any future Chinese wish for better relations. He quoted a letter from President John Tyler to the Chinese Emperor in 1843: "The Governments of two such great countries should be at peace. It is proper and according to the will of Heaven that they should respect each other and act wisely."[9]

By June 21, Vice President Humphrey had told the editors of the *New York Times* that the United States should lift its embargo on trade with China except for strategic materials.[10] For the first time in two decades, the presidential nominees of both parties, Nixon and Humphrey, were both on record as favoring reconciliation with China.

After his election but before his inauguration, Nixon approved a resumption of the Sino-American ambassadorial talks at Warsaw. This would be the 135th meeting since their inception in 1954 at Geneva, and the first since 1967. The meeting, scheduled for February 20, 1969, was abruptly canceled by the Chinese on February 18, ostensibly because of the defection of a Chinese diplomat in the Netherlands to the United States. While expressing disappointment, the new administration pledged "new initiatives to reestablish more normal relations with Communist China."[11]

In early February, the new president initiated a major study of policy options toward China.[12] On May 24, President Nixon had Secretary of State William Rogers, then in Pakistan, ask Pakistani chief of state Yahya Khan to feel out the Chinese about expanded talks with the United States.[13] On July 21, the administration began a series of actions to relax barriers to Sino-American trade and contact, announcing that beginning July 23, U.S. citizens traveling abroad could bring back up to one hundred dollars' worth of Chinese goods and authorizing travel by several categories of U.S. citizens (including members of Congress, journalists, and scholars) to the Chinese mainland.[14] On August 1, President Nixon, visiting Pakistan, reiterated U.S. interest in expanded dialogue with China to Yahya Khan. The next day, in Romania, he made a similar démarche to President Nicolae Ceauşescu.[15]

On September 5, Undersecretary of State Elliott L. Richardson formally enunciated what later evolved into the doctrine of "evenhandedness" that governed relations between Washington, Beijing, and Moscow throughout the 1970s, stating that the United States would not seek to exploit the Sino-Soviet split but would "pursue a course of progressively developing better relations" with both countries.[16] About two months later, on November 7, the United States quietly ended the Seventh Fleet's nineteen-year patrol of the Taiwan Strait. Placed there during the Korean War to protect Taiwan from invasion from the Chinese mainland, the patrol had become a symbol of the United States' commitment to the Chinese Nationalist regime.[17]

On December 3, the United States ambassador at Warsaw proposed a resumption of the Warsaw talks to his Chinese counterpart, whom he met at the Chinese embassy on December 11.[18] Eight days later, the Department of State announced the removal of most restrictions on U.S. business participation in third-country trade in mainland Chinese goods, abolished the hundred-dollar ceiling on tourists' purchases of such goods, and liberalized customs regulations for their noncommercial importation.[19]

In his February 18, 1970, report to Congress on U.S. foreign policy, President Nixon reiterated his desire for "improved practical relations" with Beijing and described the actions his administration had taken over the previous year as "specific steps that did not require Chinese agreement but which underlined our willingness to have a more normal and constructive relationship." He noted that the United States had "avoided dramatic gestures which might invite dramatic rebuffs."[20]

Earlier, in mid-December 1969, the Chinese had in fact responded to the Americans' secret overtures through Pakistan and Romania.[21] On January 8, 1970, the Department of State announced the resumption of the Warsaw talks on January 20.[22] This 135th formal session of the Warsaw talks differed from its predecessors in several important respects. It was held in the Chinese embassy rather than in facilities provided by Poland, which had been vulnerable to electronic eavesdropping by third countries. After posing for the press in a formal setting replicating the sterile atmosphere of previous sessions, the American ambassador and the Chinese chargé adjourned to another room and met less formally.

The Chinese negotiator lost no time in complaining that the U.S. ambassador, in his previous informal discussions, had "failed to mention a single word about Taiwan." He added that "we must point out that there have long existed serious disputes between China and the United States, and that the crux of these lies in the question of Taiwan." The American ambassador assured the Chinese chargé that "the limited United States military presence on Taiwan is not a threat to the security of your government, and it is our hope that as peace and stability in Asia grow, we can reduce those facilities on Taiwan that we now have."[23] He went on to say that the United States "would be prepared to consider sending a representative to Peking [Beijing] for direct discussions . . . of any of the subjects I have mentioned in my remarks today or other matters on which we might agree."[24]

When the 136th session of the Warsaw talks convened on February 20, 1970, the Chinese accepted the proposal that an American emissary visit Beijing.[25] At that same meeting, the American ambassador, stating the U.S. position "as clearly and frankly as possible," said—in language that was to become a major element of the Shanghai Communiqué—that "it is my government's position that the question of Taiwan . . . is one to be resolved by those directly involved. . . . We do not intend to interfere in any peaceful settlement. . . . It is my government's intention to reduce those military facilities which we now have on Taiwan as tensions in the area diminish."[26]

This was to be the last session of the Warsaw talks; the Chinese canceled the next meeting, scheduled for May 20, 1970, as a protest against the U.S. "incursion" into Cambodia. In the months that followed, dialogue between the China and the United States continued through other channels of communication, particularly Pakistan and Romania.

Pakistani president Yahya Khan visited Beijing on November 10, 1970, and informed the Chinese of an American proposal, dated October 25 the same year, that a "high-level" U.S. official travel to the Chinese capital for talks. After conferring with Chairman Mao Zedong, Premier Zhou Enlai told the Pakistani chief of state the following day (November 11) that "in order to discuss the vacation of Chinese territories called Taiwan, a special envoy of President Nixon's will be most welcome in Peking."[27] The United States responded through Pakistan on December 16, accepting the invitation but redefining the scope of the forthcoming talks to embrace "a broad range of issues which lie between the People's Republic of China and the

United States, including the issue of Taiwan."[28] Two days later (December 18), Mao Zedong told the American journalist Edgar Snow that he would be happy to receive President Nixon in China "either as a tourist or as president." (Mr. Snow inexplicably failed to report this directly or indirectly to the U.S. government, which learned of it just prior to its publication in the April 30, 1971, issue of *Life* magazine.)

Meanwhile, the Romanians also informed the United States on January 11, 1971, of a proposal by Premier Zhou Enlai that President Nixon visit China. Zhou's invitation made it clear that although the "one outstanding issue" between the United States and China—Taiwan—would have to be addressed, he was interested above all in the Soviet challenge to the interests of both countries.[29] Subsequent discussions continued through the Pakistani channel, paving the way for the historic secret visit by National Security Adviser Henry A. Kissinger to Beijing in the summer of that year.

While China and the United States were exchanging messages through third parties, each government also took some direct actions to ease tensions. On the U.S. side, all restrictions on the use of American passports to visit China were removed within a year (March 15, 1970, to March 15, 1971);[30] licenses were granted for commercial export of certain selected goods to the People's Republic;[31] and American carriers abroad were permitted to transport certain goods consigned to the China mainland between ports in third countries.[32] Moreover, President Nixon, in his second annual foreign policy report to Congress, stressed that "the United States is prepared to see the People's Republic of China play a constructive role in the family of nations," explicitly abandoning two decades of U.S. efforts to isolate the Chinese, and for the first time using the formal name of the Chinese Communist regime in an official U.S. document.[33] On the Chinese side, the government had begun since 1969 to release American prisoners.[34]

Responding to these gestures in a dramatic manner typical of Premier Zhou's diplomatic style, the Chinese Ping-Pong team, while participating in an international competition in Japan on April 6, 1971, formally invited its American counterpart to visit China.[35] The visit began on April 10. Four days later, the Department of State announced that the twenty-one-year embargo on trade with the Chinese mainland would be relaxed, with trade permitted in commodities nearly equivalent to those traded with the Soviet Union, and that U.S. currency controls affecting China would be ended. In addition, the Department of State declared that visas for any Chinese seeking to visit the United States would be expedited.[36] To a bemused gathering of the American Society of Newspaper Editors, President Nixon on April 16 announced his hope to visit China someday.[37] He reiterated this at an April 29 press conference.[38] On the same day, Secretary of State Rogers told a British television audience that a visit to China by President Nixon "might well be possible" if relations continued to improve.[39] The April 30 issue of *Life* made public Mao's invitation to President Nixon.

Meanwhile, currency controls were abolished[40] and export restrictions formally modified.[41] Finally, on June 11, Zhou Enlai formally accepted an American proposal of a July 9–11 Kissinger visit to Beijing, as presented earlier through the Pakistani channel.[42] The visit took place as planned, with the result that President Nixon was able to announce to a surprised world on July 15 that he had accepted an invitation to visit Beijing.[43]

The principal immediate objective of the Nixon initiatives toward China was to gain room for diplomatic maneuver in U.S.-Soviet relations and with respect to Vietnam, and to induce more responsible Soviet behavior.[44] It was no accident that the first Strategic Arms Limitation Talks agreements (SALT I) with the Soviet Union followed Nixon's successful visit to Beijing by less than two months. But the United States was also pursuing a variety of longer-range objectives remarkably parallel to those implemented by the European great powers toward post-revolutionary France in the early nineteenth century, as described by Henry Kissinger in his doctoral thesis, published as *A World Restored*.[45] These goals were later summarized as follows:

1. To facilitate China's entry into the international community in a way that would contribute to world peace and stability, not threaten it;
2. To acknowledge our national interest in the development of a strong, secure, prosperous, and friendly China that could play a legitimate and constructive role in the Asia-Pacific region and ultimately in the world;
3. To defuse contentious issues dividing the United States from China, such as the Taiwan issue, and eliminate the danger of possibly catastrophic miscalculation by an emerging nuclear and major regional power;
4. To develop constructive patterns of consultation with the Chinese on international issues and build friendly and cooperative economic, commercial, cultural, and other relationships with the Chinese necessary to sustain these ends.[46]

From the very outset, the United States made it clear that it sought an opening to China not as a matter of expediency but as a long-term and strategic move. Drawing in part on a third-party source based on mainland Chinese documents and on Premier Zhou Enlai's speech to the Tenth

National Congress of the Communist Party of China (August 24, 1973),[47] I would summarize Beijing's initial objectives as follows:

1. To balance relations with the United States against those with the Soviet Union, reducing the danger of Soviet attack;
2. To eliminate the danger of an American attack on China, either unilaterally or in collusion with the Soviet Union, Japan, or others;
3. To prevent the feared development of a U.S.-USSR "joint super-power dominance" over the world, from which China would be excluded and to which it would be subject;
4. To achieve U.S. and thereby world recognition of the legitimacy of the People's Republic of China, the validity of China's national interests, and its status as a major regional and world power with something to say about the shape of current and future international policies;
5. To gain access to and enlist the economic and technological resources of the United States in the buildup of Chinese industry and defense capability (simultaneously eroding and eventually eliminating American-sponsored multilateral barriers to importation of sophisticated technologies by China);
6. To obtain U.S. acquiescence in the eventual reincorporation of Taiwan into China under the sovereignty of the People's Republic.

Implementation of the Shanghai Communiqué

American and Chinese objectives were largely congruent internationally, while bilateral relations were complicated by "the crucial question obstructing normalization"—Taiwan. It figured heavily in the Kissinger-Zhou talks, although Kissinger's pathbreaking visits to Beijing in July and October 1971 were largely devoted to exploring each side's views of international issues in their strategic context. "By tacit agreement," neither side pressed "controversial issues to the hilt."[48] This established the pattern of the dialogue through the process of rapprochement, with each side seeking to enlarge areas of agreement and to set aside differences for later resolution.

During Kissinger's October visit, the greater part of a joint communiqué was hammered out by a hastily formed State Department and National Security Council working group. This included the most important portions of what became the Shanghai Communiqué: strategic agreement on a joint commitment to oppose "hegemonism" in the Asia-Pacific region (language proposed by the United States but later adopted as anti-Soviet shorthand by the Chinese); mutual adherence to the "five principles of peaceful coexistence" (at American initiative, resolving a major issue of the Warsaw talks in the 1950s); and joint subscription to the desirability of "normalization." Bilateral questions, including the all-important issue of Taiwan as well as such questions as trade and cultural exchange, were left for later.

Inasmuch as the United States affirmed that it was prepared to endorse, though with qualifications, the principle of one China, including Taiwan, it had now become apparent that the differences between the two sides could be bridged by a mutual resort to creative ambiguity. Between visits, the two sides maintained direct contact through the American and Chinese embassies at Paris in accordance with a suggestion first made by the United States in 1970.[49]

President Nixon's visit to China took place from February 21 to 28. Just before his departure from the United States, he ordered a further relaxation of U.S. export controls. The effect was to carry forward the "evenhanded" policy by placing China on the same basis as the Soviet Union.[50] As in the earlier Kissinger visits, discussion during the Nixon visit was largely devoted to a comprehensive review of international relations and exploration of strategic perspectives that began to seem increasingly parallel.[51] The communiqué was negotiated in English. The contentious matter of American expectations regarding "peaceful settlement" of the Chinese civil war was not finally incorporated in agreed-upon communiqué language until the early morning hours of February 26.[52] An American interpreter reviewed the Chinese and English texts for conformity on the following afternoon, finding and later confirming to the National Security Council staff that the Chinese had been scrupulously fair in their translation of the text into Chinese and that the Chinese version was in fact somewhat more favorable to the United States than the English.[53]

The Taiwan section of the "Shanghai Communiqué" which was issued at Shanghai on February 28 and in Washington on February 27, due to the International Date Line, recorded an "agreement to disagree." The Chinese side gracefully refrained from spelling out their conditions for normalization, which remained as stated earlier by Zhou Enlai to a delegation of the Committee of Concerned Asian Scholars on July 19, 1971: the United States must recognize Beijing as the sole legitimate government of China; break diplomatic relations with Taipei; withdraw its forces from Taiwan; and abrogate the 1954 Mutual Defense Treaty with the Chinese Nationalist regime.[54] Having reached agreement with the Americans temporarily to disagree on the Taiwan issue, the Chinese finally abandoned their twenty-one-year-old restrictions against trade and cultural exchange with the United States.

For the next six and a half years, until agreement on "normalization" was finally reached and announced in the Joint Communiqué of December 15, 1978, the Shanghai Communiqué served as the basic charter of the Sino-American relationship.

In the first year following the issuance of the Shanghai Communiqué, progress in Sino-American relations was rapid. The two sides remained in day-to-day contact through Paris, and there were occasional visits by Dr. Kissinger and members of his staff to New York for meetings with the Chinese mission to the United Nations. Sino-American strategic dialogue was advanced by a third Kissinger visit to Beijing in June 1972. Both sides seemed content to explore the possibilities inherent in the new relationship without pressing for normalization, which both expected would come during Nixon's second term. Visits by congressional delegations and other prominent Americans to China began. (By the end of 1978, most key members of the Senate and the House of Representatives had visited Beijing.) Although no Chinese "officials" per se visited the United States (other than the United Nations headquarters in New York), cultural delegations came in increasing numbers. Trade boomed, exemplified by China's purchase of ten Boeing 707s in the summer of 1972. As the end of 1972 approached, established channels of communication were overtaxed.[55]

In part for this reason, the Department of State persuaded a reluctant Dr. Kissinger to propose a more efficacious (and conventional) method of contact. The idea of some sort of representation for the United States in Beijing had been perfunctorily explored prior to and during the Nixon visit in February 1972 but dropped by both sides as premature under then-existing circumstances. During Kissinger's fourth visit to Beijing (February 15–19, 1973), it was agreed that each side would establish a "liaison office" in the capital of the other.[56] Since the "liaison office" was then unknown to international law and practice, it would not imply a level of formality in the relationship inappropriate before mutual recognition. At the same time, however, the liaison offices could assist the transition to normalized relations that both sides expected shortly to come about, and solidify the relationship against setbacks incident to the succession crisis the United States expected to occur soon in China. To symbolize the importance attached by both sides to the relationship, each named one of its most distinguished senior diplomats—David K. E. Bruce and Huang Zhen, respectively—as chiefs of the liaison offices.[57] Diplomatic privileges and immunities were conferred on the offices and their personnel.[58]

The timing of this agreement on more concrete forms of contact was unexpectedly fortunate. Within a matter of weeks, the Nixon administration was preoccupied with its own "succession crisis" arising from the Watergate affair, and by the latter half of 1973 China had begun to slip under the influence of the xenophobic and ideologically extremist "Gang of Four." Promising negotiations on bilateral matters, such as settlement of reciprocal claims for frozen assets (on which agreement in principle had been reached in Paris in February 1973), were soon stymied by Chinese obstructionism.

Dr. Kissinger returned to Beijing on November 10, 1973, for his fifth visit, his first as secretary of state. The visit produced a communiqué in which growing strategic agreement was recorded through the extension of the anti-hegemony clause of the Shanghai Communiqué to cover the entire globe rather than just the Asia-Pacific region. It also evoked a pointed reminder by the Chinese that normalization could "be recognized only on the basis of confirming the principle of one China."[59] This reflected heightened Chinese sensitivity to the Taiwan issue and fears that the Nixon administration would prove incapable of achieving normalization. The atmosphere was not aided when, on March 3, 1974, the Senate confirmed a new American ambassador to Taipei, Leonard Unger, whose unexpected nomination to that post had been made by President Nixon largely for domestic political reasons.[60]

Neither Secretary Kissinger's visits of November 25, 1974, and October 19, 1975, to Beijing nor the visit of President Gerald Ford to China on December 1, 1975, produced any visible further progress in bilateral relations, which remained stalemated by political factors on both sides of the Pacific. Although each side saw it as in its own politico-military interest to maintain an appearance of steady progress in the relationship and a commitment to "normalization," neither side seriously attempted to achieve a breakthrough during this period, resting content with continuing exploration of each other's increasingly convergent strategic viewpoints. Nevertheless, the process of American military withdrawal from Taiwan, proposed at Warsaw in 1970 and recorded in the Shanghai Communiqué, continued. By the end of 1976, all U.S. combat forces and most U.S. military personnel had been removed from the island.

Normalization Achieved under New Leaders
On October 6, 1976, following the deaths of both Premier Zhou Enlai and Chairman Mao Zedong, a coalition led by Hua Guofeng arrested the Gang of Four in Beijing. Less than a month later, Jimmy Carter was elected the twenty-ninth president of the United States. The political leadership on both sides of the Pacific had changed. While both the United States and China continued, understandably, to stress the importance of their strategic relationship over bilateral issues, it soon became clear that each was now prepared seriously to consider the negotiation of normalization, which would remove the political barriers to closer cooperation.

The Chinese had made their position public years before. They had indicated in the November 1973 communiqué that they required some more explicit American "confirmation" of the "principle of one China" than that in the Shanghai Communiqué, which reads in part: "The United States acknowledges that all Chinese on either side of the Taiwan Strait maintain that there is but one China and that Taiwan is part of China. The United States government does not challenge that position."

The Chinese adhered to their position of July 1971: the United States must recognize Beijing as the sole legitimate government of China, break diplomatic relations with the rival Chinese regime in Taipei, "abrogate" the 1954 Mutual Defense Treaty with that regime, and withdraw all military forces and installations from Taiwan. Thereafter, the United States—they said—could follow the "Japanese model" in unofficial relations with Taiwan, maintaining practical relationships with the people of the island intact but refraining from any official contact.[61] The Chinese consistently rejected any post-normalization arrangement that would derogate from Chinese sovereignty over Taiwan or appear to confer a color of officially recognized status upon the Taiwan authorities.[62]

Even before his inauguration, President-elect Carter, speaking through Secretary of State–designate Cyrus Vance (after a meeting at the State Department with the chief of the Chinese liaison office on January 8, 1977), had endorsed the Nixon and Ford administrations' policy of normalizing relations with Beijing.[63] On February 8, after a similar meeting, President Carter reaffirmed the Shanghai Communiqué.[64] Although the president stated that there was no set schedule or deadline for doing so,[65] the administration made clear its intention to "move toward full normalization of relations" on the basis of the recognition of one China, while reiterating the importance of settlement of the Taiwan question by the Chinese themselves by peaceful means.[66] Exploratory talks with the Chinese on the subject (which tested the limits of Chinese flexibility and found them narrow) began with Secretary Vance's visit to Beijing in August of 1977. This was followed by National Security Adviser Zbigniew Brzezinski's meetings with Chinese leaders in May 1978. It was during those meetings in Beijing that Dr. Brzezinski formally indicated to the Chinese that Leonard Woodcock, chief of the United States Liaison Office in Beijing, would soon be ready to begin discussions with the Chinese foreign minister "to see whether normalization could be reached on mutually acceptable terms."[67]

Based on extensive consultation with members of Congress and others, the Carter administration had determined that the United States could "only establish diplomatic relations with Beijing if such action could be accomplished in a way that did not damage the well-being of the people on Taiwan or reduce the chance for a peaceful settlement of the Taiwan question by the Chinese themselves."[68] This basic consideration found expression in several specific concerns:

1. The Mutual Defense Treaty with the Chinese Nationalists could not be "abrogated," as Beijing had demanded, but should rather be terminated in accordance with its own terms, which would allow it to expire after either side gave one year's notice.[69] Furthermore, the United States wished to establish that all other treaties and agreements in force with Taiwan would not automatically lapse with derecognition of the Taipei regime, as had been the case with other countries at the time of their recognition of the People's Republic of China.
2. The United States attached special importance to the settlement of the Taiwan issue between the Chinese parties by peaceful means; the normalization process "could not move forward if Beijing continued to talk and think about the Taiwan issue in . . . inflammatory terms."
3. It was essential that the United States be able effectively to continue a wide range of relationships with the people on Taiwan after normalization (in accordance, at a minimum, with the Japanese model, modified to meet the more stringent requirements of the U.S. systems of government and domestic law): "In particular, these post-normalization relations would have to include continued sale of defensive weapons to Taiwan."[70]

With these major exceptions, Beijing's conditions posed few problems for the United States. The U.S. executive branch had long been prepared to "confirm" the principle of "one China" and to transfer recognition from Taipei to Beijing. Earlier discussions (during the Nixon and Ford administrations) had established that some variation of the Japanese model was the best arrangement that could be obtained for future relationships with Taiwan. And the United States had already removed all but a few hundred of its military personnel from Taiwan in accordance with its pledge in the Shanghai Communiqué.

In the early summer of 1978, following Dr. Brzezinski's visit to Beijing, President Carter authorized Ambassador Leonard Woodcock to begin a series of presentations on normalization to the Chinese foreign minister, Huang Hua. In five meetings, Ambassador Woodcock laid out the American position. (On September 19, 1978, President Carter met personally with Ambassador Chai Zemin, chief of the Chinese liaison office at Washington, to emphasize American concerns about the well-being of the people on Taiwan.) In completing his presentations on November 4, Woodcock told the Chinese that the United States would be willing to work toward a January 1, 1979, target date for normalization if its concerns were met,[71] and also offered the Chinese a draft of a possible joint communiqué.[72]

The Chinese response was delayed until early December by the illness of Foreign Minister Huang. After further negotiations, Woodcock was invited to meet with Vice Premier Deng Xiaoping on December 13. This was the crucial meeting. It led directly to a second meeting with Deng the following day in which an agreement that met the fundamental concerns of the United States was finally reached.[73] In view of the danger of leaks, the two governments simultaneously announced the agreement in the form of a Joint Communiqué (formally dated January 1, 1979) and two unilateral statements on December 15, 1978, in both Washington and Beijing. According to the communiqué, the two countries agreed to recognize each other and to establish diplomatic relations, to take effect from January 1, 1979.

Reaffirming the principle of one China, the Joint Communiqué states: "The United States of America recognizes the Government of the People's Republic of China as the sole legal Government of China." Significantly, the newly recognized Chinese government lent its approval to the follow-on statement that: "Within this context, the people of the United States will maintain cultural, commercial, and other unofficial relations with the people of Taiwan." To dispel any doubt with respect to the status of Taiwan, the government of the United States further made it clear that it "acknowledges the Chinese position that there is but one China and Taiwan is part of China"—in language that was a strengthened abbreviation of the Shanghai Communiqué formula.

The unilateral U.S. government statement, which the Chinese had seen in advance, committed the United States to maintain such "cultural, commercial, and other unofficial relations" with Taiwan at the people-to-people level "without official government representation and without diplomatic relations." It further stated that appropriate adjustments would be made in U.S. laws and regulations to sustain such relationships with the people of Taiwan. The document also emphasized that "the United States continues to have an interest in the peaceful resolution of the Taiwan issue and expects that the Taiwan issue will be settled peacefully by the Chinese themselves."

The simultaneous unilateral Chinese statement, which also had been seen by the United States government in advance, took issue with the statement of U.S. "interest" in the manner by which the Chinese would settle the Taiwan question, asserting that "the way of . . . reunifying the country is entirely China's internal affairs." Nevertheless, the Chinese government did not contradict the U.S. expectation that "settlement" of the Taiwan issue would be achieved by peaceful means. Subsequent statements and actions by the Chinese government were premised on the possibility of peaceful "reunification" of Taiwan with the Chinese mainland rather than, as always in the past, its armed "liberation."

In addition, the United States also announced its intention to give one year's notice of termination as required under Article 10 of the Mutual Defense Treaty with the Chinese Nationalists. It thus simultaneously rid itself of an instrument incompatible with the transfer of recognition and diplomatic relations to Beijing and made it clear that treaties and agreements previously concluded with Taipei on a government-to-government basis would not automatically lapse due to derecognition, but would remain in effect until terminated in accordance with law. Remaining U.S. military forces in Taiwan were to be withdrawn by April 30, 1979, two months after the exchange of ambassadors on March 1.[74]

On the difficult question of supplying Taiwan with arms, the United States publicized the fact that in the course of negotiations for normalization, it had "made clear its intention to continue the sale of defensive weapons on a restrained basis after termination of the defense treaty."[75] However, in deference to Chinese sensitivities, a moratorium on new sales commitments was imposed while the treaty remained in force during 1979.[76] (This moratorium was duly lifted on January 2, 1980, after the treaty's expiration.)

Speaking through Premier Hua Guofeng on the day normalization was announced (December 16, 1979, Beijing time), the Chinese government insisted that it could "absolutely not agree" to continued U.S. arms sales to Taiwan but, after stating the basis of its opposition, went to note that on this issue "the two sides had differing views, but nevertheless the Joint Communiqué was reached." This disagreement, which falls short of an agreement to disagree, and the subsequent reiteration by the United States Congress of U.S. policy on arms sales to Taiwan in the Taiwan Relations Act, have posed new problems to the otherwise successful development of Sino-American relations since "normalization."

Post-normalization Achievements

In the two years following the exchange of mutual recognition and diplomatic missions between the United States and China, bilateral relations in virtually all spheres progressed with surprising speed. This was exemplified by the establishment of an elaborate framework for agreements for cooperation in the cultural, scientific and technological, economic, consular, and other fields, and by the exchange of visits by leaders of both countries to discuss matters of mutual interest. These visits and other important events are reviewed in the following discussion.

Until the end of 1978, two incumbent presidents of the United States, Nixon and Ford, had journeyed to Beijing, but no top Chinese leader had reciprocated due to the continued presence of the Kuomintang (Chinese Nationalist) embassy in Washington. With the removal of this obstacle on January 1, 1979, Vice Premier Deng Xiaoping paid a week-long visit (January 28 to February 5) to Washington and other parts of the United States.

In both ceremonial and substantive terms, Deng's visit was a milestone in Sino-American relations, setting, in President Carter's words, "a new and irreversible course" in the history of the two countries.[77] During this visit, the two sides concluded several basic agreements for cultural, scientific, and technological cooperation and for the establishment of consular relations. A Joint Press Communiqué issued by Carter and Deng on February 1 further promised to facilitate the accreditation of resident journalists in Beijing and Washington and undertook to conclude trade, aviation, shipping, and related agreements in the near future.

After this historic visit, the interflow of personnel, ideas, goods, and services between the two countries increased by leaps and bounds. At the end of September 1980, the Department of State summarized the state of U.S.-China relations as follows:

Despite ideological, cultural, and social differences between us, our countries share a common concern with global peace and stability. Consultation between our governments on specific issues is now a normal feature of the international landscape. Although our perspectives on global problems are rarely identical, our policies are often parallel and mutually supportive. Our dialogue proceeds from enlightened self-interest and mutual respect, embracing almost every issue on the international agenda—from questions of war and peace, to world economic problems, environmental protection, and the organization and management of our Foreign Services. Regular consultative mechanisms now exist between us with respect to global and regional strategic problems, politico-military questions, UN and other multilateral organization affairs, arms control, regional political and economic problems, international narcotics matters, and all aspects of our bilateral relations.

The Department of State further noted the extraordinary growth in human contact between the two countries, since the establishment of diplomatic relations, citing as examples:

1. Vice President Mondale and five U.S. Cabinet members have visited China; Vice Premiers Deng Xiaoping, Fang Yi, Kang Shi'en, Geng

Biao, and Bo Yibo, as well as many Chinese ministers and department heads, have visited the U.S.;

2. Almost every department and agency of our Federal government, including the Department of Defense, now has a productive relationship with its Chinese counterpart. State and local governments as well as universities and other private institutions have begun to forge similar ties;

3. More than 100 Chinese delegations now visit the U.S. each month (up from about two per month in 1978); perhaps 70,000 Americans will visit China in 1980, compared with 10,000 in 1978.

4. Almost 5,000 Chinese scholars and students are now in the U.S., while hundreds of Americans are working, doing research, or studying in China (virtually no such exchanges took place two years ago).

With respect to trade and economic exchange, the Department of State took note of the fact that:

Sino-American trade . . . has significantly exceeded the most optimistic earlier projections. . . . China now buys about half of all U.S. cotton exports and is a major importer of U.S. wheat, corn, and soybeans; exports of U.S.-manufactured goods are the fastest growing item in our trade. Textiles and oil head the list of Chinese imports to the U.S.[78]

Finally, the Department of State recorded activities and exchanges in other fields:

A large and growing number of cultural exchange activities, undertaken at both the governmental and private levels, are giving the American and Chinese peoples broad exposure to each other's artistic and cultural achievements. Early in 1981, the US–PRC Joint Science and Technology Commission will hold its second annual meeting in Washington to review the hundreds of joint research projects and cooperative programs the U.S. and China have initiated since early 1979 under the Agreement on Cooperation in Science and Technology. These programs currently cover 13 fields, from high energy physics to earthquake studies.[79]

Vice President Mondale's visit to China (from August 25 to September 1, 1979) had provided an impetus for these remarkable developments in the new relationship. It removed any doubt that the United States would seek to temper the pace at which relations with China developed to match developments in U.S.-Soviet relations, or would apply mechanical evenhandedness in its approach to relations with those two very different Communist countries. Speaking at Beijing University and to an unprecedented nationwide television audience in China on August 27, the vice president proclaimed American support for "a strong and secure and modernizing China." He told the Chinese people that "despite the sometimes profound differences between our two systems, we are committed to joining with you to advance our many parallel strategic and bilateral interests. Thus any nation which seeks to weaken or isolate you in world affairs assumes a stance contrary to American interests." He then declared that the objectives of the United States with respect to China were:

1. To build concrete political ties in the context of mutual security;
2. To establish broad cultural relations in a framework of genuine equality;
3. To forge practical economic bonds with the goal of common benefit.

In announcing that U.S. experts would be available to help with several massive Chinese hydroelectric and irrigation projects, the vice president confirmed the designation of China as a "friendly nation" for purposes of the Foreign Assistance Act.[80] And he told the Chinese that the United States was prepared to extend up to $2 billion in credits over the coming five years through the U.S. Export-Import Bank.

Another major fillip had been provided by Secretary of Defense Harold Brown's visit to Beijing. By the time of Vice President Mondale's trip to China, most elements of the Chinese and American governments had established normal contacts and relationships. However, there was one notable omission in this pattern—the Department of Defense. During Mondale's visit it was agreed in principle that Secretary Brown would make a trip to Beijing, and a tentative schedule was subsequently set for early January 1980.

The Soviet invasion and occupation of Afghanistan on Christmas Eve 1979 directly challenged Chinese interests as well as those of the United States and its European and Japanese allies, with the result that the context and outcome of Secretary Brown's discussions with the Chinese were profoundly altered. At this January 6, 1980, welcoming banquet in Beijing, the secretary noted that "under these circumstances, increased cooperation between China and the United States can be an important—and is a needed—element in the maintenance of global tranquility. Improved relations between China and the United States are not directed against any third country, though the actions of others will affect the nature of relationship. . . . [Our] cooperation . . . should remind others that if they threaten the shared interests of the United States and China, we can respond with complementary actions in the field of defense as well as diplomacy."[81]

Accordingly, contacts in the defense field were also established and developed, including the visit to the United States of Chinese Vice Premier Geng Biao and a high-level delegation from the People's Liberation Army (PLA) in late May and early June 1980, and another PLA delegation to study the U.S. Army's logistics management system in September, when Undersecretary of Defense William Perry paid a reciprocal visit to Beijing.

Meanwhile, controls on exports of high-technology items from the United States to China were significantly liberalized. For the first time, the United States government permitted the sale of such items to China specifically for military end-use. Moreover, the United States agreed to consider the commercial sale, on a case-by-case basis, of military support equipment (but not weapons) to the Chinese, subject only to the approval of U.S. allies in the Coordinating Committee (COCOM) at Paris. Specifically, the Department of State published a list of military support equipment that could be considered for sale to China in its *Munition Control Newsletter* No. 81. The Department of Commerce also moved China to a new and distinct category of export control, technically known as "Category P," which stipulated that exports of dual-use equipment and technology to China would not be considered a precedent for exports to other controlled destinations such as the countries of the Warsaw Pact.[82] As a matter of fact, in retaliation for the Soviet invasion of Afghanistan, the United States and its allies were at the same time further restricting sales of such high-technology items to the Soviet Union.

Related to this was the agreement between the United States and China to conduct a series of regular consultations on developments in Southwest Asia and the Indian Ocean area. It was for this purpose that Vice Minister of Foreign Affairs Zhang Wenjin visited the Commander-in-Chief, Pacific Area Command in Honolulu as well as officials in Washington with a small delegation in mid-March 1980. Zhang's discussions with senior American officials marked a new stage in friendly and candid consultation on international issues. These discussions were soon broadened to include European, Northeast and Southeast Asian, Middle Eastern, and African affairs.

Several senior State Department officials visited Beijing separately in the summer of 1980 to continue the dialogue, which—it was agreed—would be institutionalized so that the two sides could meet several times a year in the future.[83] Vice Minister of Foreign Affairs He Ying met with State Department officials in Washington in September to discuss United Nations and other multilateral diplomatic issues. The extent to which the broad consultative relationship that had quickly emerged was taken for granted was illustrated by the total lack of press attention to He's presence in the American capital.

These achievements notwithstanding, Sino-American relations in the first two years of normalization were not entirely trouble-free. China's attack on Vietnam in February 1979 caused some irritation in Washington. Through State Department spokesman Hodding Carter III, the U.S. government called for "immediate withdrawal of Vietnamese troops from Cambodia and Chinese troops from Vietnam."[84] On a visit to Beijing to negotiate for the settlement of frozen assets issues in the same month, Secretary of the Treasury W. Michael Blumenthal publicly criticized the Chinese "incursion" into Vietnam. However, the strain in Sino-American relations caused by the fighting did not affect the otherwise warm atmosphere of his visit. Beyond this, the knottiest problem remained the status of Taiwan.

Back to the Taiwan Problem
In its unilateral statement of December 15, 1978, concerning the establishment of diplomatic relations with China, the United States government had declared that it "will seek adjustments to our laws and regulations to permit the maintenance of commercial, cultural, and other non-governmental relationships in the new circumstances that will exist after normalization." Proceeding from this premise, President Carter issued a memorandum on December 30 directing all departments and agencies of the federal government to continue their current programs and other relations with Taiwan on an unofficial basis, through a designated nongovernmental instrumentality. An American Institute in Taiwan (AIT), consisting of three trustees appointed by the secretary of state, was incorporated on January 16, 1979, as a nonprofit District of Columbia corporation "to maintain commercial, cultural, and other relations" with Taiwan "without official Government representation or diplomatic relations."

And on January 26, the president submitted a bill, H.R. 1614, to Congress for legislative implementation of the Joint Communiqué that had been issued on December 15, 1978. The bill sought to achieve three purposes: to confirm the continued eligibility of the people on Taiwan for participation in U.S. programs and activities that, under U.S. law, would normally be carried out with foreign countries, states or governments; to provide for the execution of such programs and activities on an unofficial basis through AIT and the corresponding instrumentality to be established by Taipei (i.e., the Coordination Council for North American Affairs, or CCNAA); and to permit funding, staffing, and administrative support for the AIT.[85] A series of very contentious congressional hearings followed.

The Senate Committee on Foreign Relations viewed the president's draft bill as deficient in several respects. First, it contended that although the Carter administration had recognized the People's Republic as the sole legal government of China and acknowledged the Chinese position that "Taiwan is a part of China," "the United States has not itself agreed to this position." Conceding to the opinions of "legal scholars" that it would be unwise to try to define Taiwan's international legal status, the Senate Committee believed that "the best approach would be to spell out the specific manner in which relations with Taiwan will be maintained by the United States." Second, the Senate Committee sought clarification with regard to "the legal standing of the people on Taiwan to sue and be sued in the United States courts, and the protection of property rights of entities and persons in both countries." Third, it recommended a provision for congressional oversight of the AIT. Fourth, it requested the president "to provide extensive privileges and immunities" for members of the Taiwan instrumentality, CCNAA, in the United States on a reciprocal basis. Finally, the Senate Committee wanted "to make clear to the PRC that its new relationship with the United States would be seriously endangered if it resorted to force in an attempt to bring about the unification of Taiwan with the mainland."[86] For these reasons, the Senate Committee introduced its own redrafted bill, the Taiwan Enabling Act (S. 245) to implement the new Taiwan policy.[87]

The House Committee on Foreign Affairs took a similar view of the alleged deficiencies of the executive branch bill, H.R. 1614, and introduced its own bill, H.R. 2479, with special emphasis on the security aspects of Taiwan. The Committee stated its view that

> the future of Taiwan must be determined through peaceful means in a way that will not prejudice the well-being of the people on Taiwan. . . .
>
> If, nonetheless, an armed attack or use of force against Taiwan were to occur, the legislation makes it clear that there should be a prompt response by the United States. What would be appropriate action, including possible use of force in Taiwan's defense, would depend on the specific circumstances. The committee does not attempt to specify in advance what the particular circumstances or response might be; and, in any event, U.S. action is to be according to constitutional processes. In the committee's opinion, at the very least, the United States should seriously consider withdrawing recognition of the PRC.
>
> Finally, the committee takes particular note of recent statements by Chinese leaders, most notably by Chinese Vice Premier Teng Hsiaoping [Deng Xiaoping], which indicate that the PRC will accept a Taiwan that will maintain its present economic and social system, that will

continue foreign trade and investment and people-to-people contact, and that will maintain its own armed forces. These policy statements are welcomed and are of some consolation to the many Americans concerned about the future security of Taiwan.[88]

After additional debate and hearings, both houses reached a compromise over some technical differences and language[89] and adopted the Taiwan Relations Act. The Act became law on April 10, 1979. As passed, it achieved the basic purposes sought by the president, and has since been an effective domestic legal underpinning for nongovernmental relations between the people of the United States and the people of Taiwan.

As could be expected, Beijing strongly objected to many of the congressional amendments to the law, particularly to Section 2(b), which embellished the long-stated interest of the United States in a peaceful settlement of the Taiwan issue by the Chinese themselves, enumerating the following six specific policy objectives of the United States:

1. To preserve and promote extensive, close, and friendly commercial, cultural, and other relations between the people of the United States and the people on Taiwan as well as the people on the China mainland and all other peoples of the Western Pacific area;
2. To declare that peace and stability in the area are in the political, security, and economic interests of the United States, and are matters of international concern;
3. To make clear that the United States' decision to establish diplomatic relations with the People's Republic of China rests upon the expectation that the future of Taiwan will be determined by peaceful means;
4. To consider any effort to determine the future of Taiwan by other than peaceful means, including by boycotts or embargoes, a threat to the peace and security of the Western Pacific area and of grave concern to the United States;
5. To provide Taiwan with arms of a defensive character; and
6. To maintain the capacity of the United States to resist any resort to force or other forms of coercion that would jeopardize the security, or the social or economic system, of the people of Taiwan.

Among other provisions of the law which met with Beijing's objection was Section 4(b)(3)(B), which states:

For all purposes under the laws of the United States, including actions in any court in the United States, recognition of the People's Republic of China shall not affect in any way the ownership of or other rights or interests in properties, tangible and intangible, and other things of value, owned or held on or prior to December 31, 1978, or thereafter acquired or earned by the governing authorities on Taiwan.

The basis of Beijing's objections to this provision was that it had over-ridden the normal principles of international law which permit the successor government to assume control of the property of its predecessor. (An immediate consequence was effectively to preclude the United States from successfully prosecuting its own diplomatic and consular property claims, dating from 1949, in China.)

For these and other reasons, the Chinese government lodged a strong protest, stating that the law, as passed, contravened the principles of the Joint Communiqué. Beijing was reassured, however, by the president's statement when he signed the law on April 10:

In a number of sections of this legislation, the Congress has wisely granted discretion to the President. In all instances, *I will exercise that discretion in a manner consistent* with our interest in the well-being of the people on Taiwan, and *with the understandings reached on normalization of relations with the People's Republic of China, as expressed in our Joint Communiqué.* [italics mine]

The Taiwan Relations Act was not an international agreement, but domestic legislation which the United States did not expect Beijing to accept. Nevertheless, Vice Premier Deng Xiaoping bluntly told a visiting Senate Foreign Relations Committee delegation on April 19, 1979, that the congressional rewrite of the bill had come close to "nullifying" the newly normalized Sino-American relationship.[90]

The continuing connections between the United States and Taiwan, though unofficial in nature, seem to have occasioned considerable controversy at the Second Session of the Fifth National People's Congress, held in Beijing in June 1979. The principal issue in the minds of the Chinese was the continuation of American arms sales to Taiwan. As noted earlier, the Carter administration had imposed a moratorium on new sales commitments to Taiwan in 1979. Nevertheless, deliveries of weapons and parts under pre-normalization commitments continued until the expiration of the Mutual Defense Treaty on January 1, 1980. Taiwan was in fact the eighth largest recipient of arms from the United States that year.

On January 2, 1980, the Carter administration announced new sales commitments to Taiwan in the amount of $280 million. This drew immediate protest from Beijing. The Chinese argued that such sales and deliveries were contrary to the Joint Communiqué commitments of the United States and that they diminished the prospects for a peaceful settlement of the Chinese civil war between the mainland and Taiwan. The Chinese government contended that continued American arms sales had the effect of depriving Taipei of any incentive to respond to the series of conciliatory gestures Beijing had initiated immediately after its establishment of diplomatic relations with the United States.

These gestures amounted to an offer that, after "reunification," Taiwan could continue to be ruled by the Kuomintang on the conditions of virtually complete autonomy cited by the congressional reports mentioned earlier. In addition, Beijing had offered open travel between the two parts of China: direct postal, telecommunications, shipping, and air links (including allowing Taiwan's China Airlines to fly to Beijing and Shanghai); trade free of tariff barriers; and a wide range of cultural, scientific, and technological exchange. The People's Liberation Army had ceased shelling the Chinese Nationalist–held islands of Quemoy and Matsu on January 1, 1979, and the Chinese government had invited the Taiwan authorities to join in party-to-party (Chinese Communist Party–Kuomintang) talks on a basis of equality, to reduce and ultimately eliminate military confrontation in the Taiwan Strait as well as to work out the modalities of "reunification."

Taipei formally rejected all of Beijing's overtures, terming them a "Communist united front trick." In practice, however, over the following months, indirect contact between Chinese from Taiwan and the mainland became an ever-more-common occurrence. Such contacts took place primarily in third countries, such as the United States and Japan, but occasionally directly. One highly interesting example was the Taiwan authorities' entertainment of twenty-eight Beijing foreign ministry officials on January 15, 1981, when their plane, a Singapore airliner, was forced to land at Chiang Kai-shek Airport on its way from Hong Kong to San Francisco.[91] Trade between Taiwan and the Chinese mainland, conducted indirectly through such *entrepôts* as Hong Kong, grew rapidly to an estimated level of $400 to $500 million in 1980, up dramatically from the negligible totals of previous years.[92] These developments, plus diminished military activity on both sides of the Fujian front, reduced tension in the Taiwan Strait area to their lowest level in thirty years.

Contrary to fears expressed at the time of American derecognition, Taiwan prospered under the new arrangements stipulated by the Joint Communiqué. Approved major U.S. investment in Taiwan amounted to $70.7 million in 1979 and $200 million in 1980, bringing the total of U.S. investment since 952 to $866.2 million. In the field of trade, Taiwan's total exports amounted to $16.1 billion in 1979 (an increase of 27 percent over 1978) and $19.8 billion in 1980 (an increase of 23 percent over 1979). On the import side, figures were $14.8 billion for 1979 (an increase of 34 percent over 1978) and $19.7 billion for 1980 (an increase of 33 percent over 1979). Bilateral trade with the United States continued to grow rapidly, totaling $11.6 billion in 1980, an increase of 27 percent over 1979. Of this, Taiwan enjoyed an export surplus of $2.06 billion.[93] Taiwan experienced no difficulty in obtaining necessary trade and investment financing from private U.S. banks and the U.S. Export-Import Bank.

Beyond these developments, a private air transport agreement between AIT and CCNAA was concluded on March 5, 1980, to replace the previous intergovernmental air transport agreement. Similarly, a private agreement for scholarly and scientific cooperation was effected through an exchange of letters between those two instrumentalities on September 4. As authorized by Section 10 of the Taiwan Relations Act, the AIT also concluded an agreement with CCNAA on the mutual grant of functional privileges, exemptions, and immunities to the two organizations and their designated employees on October 2. While this private accord is unusual from the standpoint of international law, it facilitates—on the basis of a nongovernmental agreement—the performance of necessary functions by the two organizations.

Conclusion

In the larger view, the lengthy and difficult process by which the United States and China moved from mutual hostility through cautious détente to rapprochement represents more than the mere normalization of political relations. In advancing relations to a new stage beyond détente—to a close consultative relationship based on equality, enlightened self-interest, and mutual respect for the differing ideologies and social systems of the two countries—normalization promises to mark the end of almost two centuries of inequality, discrimination, and occasional violence between the two nations since their first contact in 1784.

Normalization has consolidated a strategic relationship of great importance to both China and the United States. For the first time in a century, the United States is provided with an opportunity simultaneously to develop close and cooperative relationships with both China and Japan, no longer having to choose between them. Normalization has encouraged progress toward a relaxation of tensions in Korea, opened possibilities of Sino-American cooperation in pursuit of common objectives elsewhere in Asia and the Pacific region, and enhanced the prospects for the peaceful settlement of the Chinese civil war.

Most important, assuming continued care by both sides in the handling of the Taiwan issue, the normalization process has paved the way for a close and cooperative relationship of true equality and mutual benefit between the American people and the Chinese: one-quarter of humankind.

Chapter 3

The Origins of the Taiwan Issue

My career in the United States Foreign Service focused on the opening of strategic ties to the People's Republic of China. My anticipation of this was a major reason I became a diplomat; yet my involvement in U.S. interaction with Beijing was in many ways tinged with irony. From 1969 to 1971, I daresay I was the only member of my class at the Foreign Service Institute's Chinese-language and area studies school in Taichung, Taiwan, to see Taiwan as in many ways a more dynamic and interesting new proto-democratic Chinese polity than the mainland. This fascination and my desire to understand the evolution of Taiwan's political economy were the reasons I applied myself to studying Taiwanese (Minnan), a dialect of Chinese so different from Mandarin that anywhere else it would qualify as a separate language.[1] Although I never overcame a slight Mandarin accent in Taiwanese, I became fluent enough to deliver speeches in that dialect and prided myself on the empathy I developed for Taiwan's second-earliest Chinese settlers and their descendants.[2]

I expected to serve in Taipei. Instead, I found myself drafted first to interpret for the Warsaw talks with Communist China and then to accompany President Nixon to Beijing as the principal American interpreter for his delegation. Much of the discussion during and after that visit was devoted to our differing views of Taiwan and its international standing. All three of the joint communiqués that are the fundamental documents governing U.S.-China relations center on the Taiwan problem.

But long before there was a Taiwan problem between the United States and China, there was a Taiwan issue. The issue is what form and substance should govern the relationship between Taiwan and the rest of China. This question reflects the history of Taiwan, which the various participants in that drama see differently.

I tried to bring out these differences—and some of the causes underlying them—in a piece I composed (during a long flight to Taipei in 1995) for

Dr. Gerrit Gong, who then held the Freeman Chair[3] in China Studies at the Center for Strategic and International Studies in Washington, D.C. As my article noted, in the mid-1990s, the Taiwan issue was at an inflection point. The article ("Same Strait, Different Memories") will help readers unfamiliar with Taiwan's complex history to understand its apparent drift toward independence under President Lee Teng-hui (Li Denghui). This drift threatened the framework for peace in the Taiwan Strait and produced a crisis in U.S.-China military interaction (see Chapter 4.)

Taiwan's history includes several attempts by foreign powers to exploit its strategic location against China. These powers include the United States, though the American relationship with Taiwan after World War II and after the defeat of Chiang Kai-shek's Republic of China in its civil war with the Chinese Communist Party was much more a response to events than the product of strategic calculation.

Find More in the Online Archive

As I began my study of Chinese in 1969, I wrote a short paper on historical views of Taiwan's strategic importance. I believe it remains useful background reading on the subject. I caution the reader, however, that in 1969, despite the hints of a thaw in U.S. relations with the China mainland that are discussed in detail in Chapter 2 of this book, no one wanted to admit that this would require adjustments in the U.S. relationship with Taiwan. Memories of the McCarthy witch hunt over "who lost China" and the hammerlock of the "China Lobby" on U.S. policy were powerful inhibitions on anyone who was inclined to discuss this. The logic of a turn to the People's Republic of China (then called "Red China") seemed obvious to me. My perception of it had played a large role in my decision to enter the Foreign Service of the United States. Still, I thought the question of Taiwan's geostrategic status was relevant to possible changes in U.S. China policy and decided to devote my research to it. The result of this effort is available under the title "The Strategic Significance of Taiwan to the United States: An Historical Appreciation" at http://bit.ly/interesting-times.

Same Strait, Different Memories[4]
March 1995

On February 28, 1947, a minor, nonpolitical incident in Taipei led to a bloodbath in Taiwan, in which thousands of the island's inhabitants perished at the hands of Kuomintang (KMT) forces. The KMT had occupied Taiwan and proclaimed the island's reannexation to China less than two years before. The KMT's brutality was born of fear that the rolling victory of its Chinese Communist Party (CCP) rivals on the mainland might extend to the island.

For decades thereafter, public mention of the "2/28 incident" was taboo in Taiwan. The millions of officials, military personnel, and others who had fled the fall of the Republic of China (ROC) on the mainland to seek refuge in Taiwan recalled it as a Communist-inspired internal security problem, justifying rule by martial law. Propagandists in the People's Republic of China (PRC) inaccurately echoed this view by attempting, though without success, to portray 2/28 as a Communist-led popular uprising. Politically active natives of the island remembered it as a symbol of martyrdom and repression by an undemocratic regime imposed on them by transient outsiders from the China mainland. For mainlanders and Taiwanese alike, 2/28 long stood as a symbol of alienation, division and competing nationalisms.

On February 28, 1995, however, mainlanders and Taiwanese joined in commemorating 2/28 at Taipei's Suchow University. They were addressed by Chang Hsiao-yen, a highly regarded mainlander. Chang[5] is minister of Overseas Chinese Affairs, but everyone in Taiwan knows him also as the grandson of Chiang Kai-shek and the son of Chiang Ching-kuo, whose presidency of the ROC on Taiwan laid the basis for democratic rule by the Taiwanese majority. Chang spoke with poetic eloquence in Mandarin, the official language, though, like many of his generation, he is bilingual in the Taiwanese dialect.

Minister Chang began:

We have come here today from different places. We may have been born in different provinces, regions and cities; we may speak different dialects. We have each grown up in different circumstances. We may have different religious faiths. We may also have different political philosophies, belong to different age groups, and be of different sexes. We may have different appreciations of the value of human life and of fate or the explanations for these. But we would not have gathered here today if we did not have a common concern and love for this piece of earth we now stand upon—this piece of earth we depend upon for our survival and our growth.

Chang closed his remarks with an appeal to his audience to transcend their disparate memories of 2/28 and to replace them with a common realization:

> We all belong to this piece of earth. We all belong to this nation. Among us, there are no longer any "transients"; there can no longer be any "outsiders." . . . We must enable our children and our children's children to recall with pride this time in which their parents and their parents' parents committed ourselves to forgive, to atone, and to love so that they might . . . [live] free of alienation, in mutual respect, and in the warmth of companionship.

Minister Chang did not describe Taiwan as his homeland, as a subsequent generation may do. Nevertheless, his appeal to substitute a sense of common identity and destiny for the malice of the past dealt movingly—and skillfully—with the reality that differing memories of the same events can divide a people. Memories inspire the myths by which nations coalesce or cleave asunder. They are the hidden root of political discourse. They shape a people's vision of the future even as they define its view of the past and present. Incompatible memories lead to incompatible perspectives. The story of Taiwan is woven from the different memories of Chinese on Taiwan and the mainland. It is told differently in Tokyo, and in yet another way in Washington. This story is understood one way in Beijing and in quite another in Taipei and Kaohsiung. It seems certain to enter a new chapter, and perhaps an ending, over the coming year. It is uncertain whether the story of Taiwan will have a happy ending and, if so, for whom.

The Taiwanese Experience of China

The Chinese ancestors of the pre-ROC Taiwanese came to Taiwan in trickles and waves over centuries. China was then under foreign (Manchu) rule. Han Chinese had yet to conceive of the idea of the nation-state, still less to be animated by nationalism. The Chinese who came to Taiwan were loyal to family and to clan; larger polities were for them an irksome reality to be avoided as much as possible. They sought land and a life free of famine and political turbulence as well as the taxes and exactions of Chinese officialdom. In Taiwan they found a frontier area nominally governed from Fuzhou but, in practice, beyond the *de facto* jurisdiction of the emperor's officials.

Beijing's casual attitude toward the island was exemplified in its response to the 1871 murder (and subsequent eating) by aborigines of

Japanese sailors shipwrecked on Taiwan's east coast. In July 1873, after two years of Japanese protests and demands that the Chinese government punish the perpetrators, Beijing informed the Japanese foreign minister that China had no jurisdiction over Taiwan's tribal areas and had no intention of asserting it. Only after a Japanese expeditionary force had occupied these areas did China claim sovereignty over all of Taiwan and send its own forces to deal with the situation in Taiwan's eastern marches. Beijing's belated interest led it to discover that Taiwan's Chinese-inhabited areas, which were experiencing a surge of immigration from the mainland, were also in a state of lawlessness. In 1885, Beijing elevated Taiwan to the status of a separate province. Taiwan Province soon led China in economic modernization. Taipei was the first Chinese city to have electricity; Taiwan was the first Chinese province to have a railroad. The island's experience of effective Chinese government was, however, brief. Nine years later, following China's defeat in the Sino-Japanese War of 1894–95, Taiwan and its people were ceded to Japan. This transfer of territory and people aroused less indignation among China's ruling elite than did the simultaneous recognition of Japanese suzerainty in Korea.

For fifty years, until Japan's surrender in August 1945, Taiwan's people were subjects of the Japanese emperor, under the jurisdiction of the Imperial Japanese Navy. The Japanese efficiently suppressed sporadic resistance from both Chinese and—with special brutality—aborigines on Taiwan. Japanese policies favoring assimilation of Taiwan's largely illiterate peasant and tribal population rapidly succeeded. By the 1930s, many Taiwanese were living in Japanese-style houses, eating Japanese food, and reading Japanese newspapers. Some were winning distinction in Japanese universities. Taiwan's economy developed along with that of Japan, giving Taiwanese an economic infrastructure, level of literacy, sophistication in modern ways, and standard of living superior to that of all but a privileged few on the China mainland. Tens of thousands of Taiwanese demonstrated loyalty to the emperor by serving as support troops and camp followers during the Japanese armed forces' invasion of the Chinese mainland. Many young Taiwanese gave their lives as *kamikaze* pilots in the last stages of Japan's defense against advancing American forces.

Given the extent to which Taiwan had been "japanized," the KMT forces sent to regain Chinese sovereignty over the island treated Taiwanese with both hostility and envy. Taiwanese therefore experienced the initial period of their "recovery" by China as a harsh occupation by a brutal and unsophisticated alien military, accompanied by widespread confiscations of property. This atmosphere set the stage for the 2/28 incident and for a decade of severe repression of Taiwanese by the KMT authorities following their ejection from the China mainland. Taiwanese were treated like a conquered population, and regarded with suspicion. Land reform succeeded in KMT-ruled Taiwan in the 1950s, unlike earlier on the KMT-ruled mainland, in no small measure because the lands of a disempowered Taiwanese elite were at issue, rather than those of a landlord class with significant ties to KMT officials.

In the 1950s and '60s, the KMT sought energetically to reassimilate the Taiwanese to Chinese ways. It taught them Mandarin while banning discourse in Japanese. It tutored them in Chinese culture and inculcated them with Chinese nationalism. The KMT indoctrinated Taiwanese in its vaguely socialist ideology of *san min zhuyi*.[6] It instructed them in its version of twentieth-century Chinese history, introducing them to events they had previously seen through Japanese rather than Chinese eyes. The KMT filled them with fear of the Chinese Communist Party (CCP) and wariness of Beijing's perfidy. It conscripted Taiwanese to fight in a renewal of the civil war it had lost to the CCP. It sought to inspire them to be willing to lay down their lives to reunite Taiwan with the China mainland. The KMT tolerated no dissent from its dogma. Despite the ROC on Taiwan's economic and military dependence on the United States, it brushed aside American expressions of concern over its harsh treatment of Taiwanese and dissidents of both Taiwanese and mainland Chinese origin.

By the late 1960s, Taiwanese had been at least superficially re-sinicized. Literacy in Chinese and fluency in Taiwan's peculiarly accented version of Mandarin were virtually universal among those under the age of fifty. A modernized Chinese culture was emerging in which Taiwanese were full participants. Taiwan's dispossessed landlords became a newly prosperous entrepreneurial class, as the American advisers who helped craft land reform on the island had hoped they would. Living standards rose rapidly as Taiwan liberalized and opened its economy and became one of the world's great manufacturing centers. Politics began to relax. The KMT's leadership remained with its mainlander old guard, but its membership began to be heavily Taiwanese. Younger mainlanders increasingly identified their future with Taiwan rather than with the restoration of KMT rule over the mainland. Many left for a more secure future in the United States or Canada. Taiwanese, too, migrated to the United States in increasing numbers. Agitation for rule of Taiwan by Taiwanese rather than mainlanders ("Taiwan independence") thus added a secure American rear area to its original base in Japan.

On Taiwan itself, however, a process of mutual assimilation was manifestly underway between Taiwanese and mainlanders. Taiwanese were slowly advancing into positions of authority. When Chiang Ching-kuo succeeded his father Chiang Kai-shek as president of the ROC in 1975, he clearly recognized that the island's future depended on the participation of its Taiwanese majority in government. He steadily increased the political role of Taiwanese, suspended martial law, and laid the basis for a transition to a locally elected democracy. At his death in 1988, the presidency passed to a Taiwanese, Lee Teng-hui. Taiwan had become a boisterous democracy.

By the 1980s, Taiwan's living standards exceeded those of many European countries. A relaxation of tensions in the Taiwan Strait, brokered by U.S. policy, made it possible for Taiwanese to travel to the China mainland to see for themselves what they had only read about and seen in old films. They marveled at the mainland's size and its ubiquitous evidence of past Chinese greatness. They were dismayed by its squalor and backwardness. They saw the mainland's CCP-directed political system as an extreme version of the KMT rule they had endured in the 1950s. The experience reinforced both their pride in their Chinese heritage and their sense that that heritage had been renovated and improved in Taiwan. It added to their pride in their own achievements and to their determination to see these achievements acknowledged. It also aggravated an identity crisis born of a century in which Taiwanese have been successively nationals of Japan, of a mythical China ruled from Taipei, and now of an internationally unrecognized, democratic polity in which the transition from Chinese mainlander dominance of politics to Taiwanese control is soon to be completed.

The growing familiarity of Taiwanese with the mainland reminded them that for ninety-six of the past hundred years[7] Taiwanese have had no political connection with Chinese across the Strait. This century has culminated in Taiwan's development of a distinctive, but still undefined, identity as a modernized, democratic polity in which Taiwanese, as well as mainlanders on Taiwan, take pride and satisfaction. As Taiwanese prepared for the parliamentary elections of 1995 and presidential elections in 1996, they were sure, whatever the outcome, that they would assume full control of their island's government for the first time. The idea of surrendering some of this hard-won political power to yet another group of mainlanders through reunification with a larger Chinese polity had little appeal to them. Increasingly, Taiwanese politicians from the opposition Democratic Progressive Party (DPP) openly advocated a declaration of Taiwan's independence from China. They argued that, without effective refutation either from the ruling KMT or from Washington, Beijing could not act militarily to prevent Taiwan's independence despite its pledge to do so, because the United States was committed to defending Taiwan against attack from the China mainland. If the PRC did attempt military action, they asserted, American forces were bound to defend Taiwan's right of self-determination.

Mainlanders on Taiwan View China and Taiwan

Most mainlanders arrived in Taiwan in a state of shock. The KMT had just been defeated in savage fighting with its CCP rivals. The arriving mainlanders had lost their homes and been separated from their wives, children, and extended families. The bulk of them were soldiers, many of them peasants with no real commitment to Chiang Kai-shek or his KMT. Not a few had been forced to Taiwan at gunpoint by their officers. They knew little, if anything, about Taiwan or the Taiwanese. Most were unaware of 2/28. Few of those who were aware of the incident and its aftermath had any reason for questioning the KMT's version of events or its actions to deal with Taiwanese unrest.

These mainlanders arrived to live amongst a Taiwanese populace that was sullen, if not actively hostile, after four years of harsh repression. The new arrivals were lodged with Taiwanese, willy-nilly, throughout the island. They saw themselves as transients. Taiwanese hopefully regarded them as such. Everyone expected the CCP soon to extend its victory in the Chinese civil war to Taiwan. The newspapers were full of horror stories about the CCP's advances on Taiwan as the People's Liberation Army (PLA) rolled up KMT resistance across the Strait. Arriving mainlanders found Taiwanese more rural than urban and more Japanese than Chinese in their habits. Mainlanders met Taiwanese resentment of their presence with contempt for their crude and uncultured (un-Chinese) Taiwanese hosts.

Kim Il-sung's July 25, 1950, surprise attack on south Korea brought the KMT and Taiwan an unexpected reprieve. The warships of the U.S. Seventh Fleet took up station in the Taiwan Strait for the alleged purpose of preventing either party to the Chinese civil war from attacking the other. No mainlander on Taiwan, any more than any Communist ruler in Beijing, was fooled by this pretense of U.S. neutrality. They knew that the KMT's armies were barely capable of mounting a defense of the island, let alone taking the offensive against the China mainland. The KMT, which had blamed the absence of U.S. support for the CCP's victory in the Chinese civil war on the mainland, found itself even more dependent on U.S. military and economic backing for its survival on Taiwan. This support was not clearly offered until the PRC's intervention to prevent a UN victory over Kim Il-sung in Korea. That decision in Beijing led to a decision in Washington to provide generous American economic and military aid to the ROC on Taiwan.

The KMT's weak position on Taiwan forced Chiang Kai-shek to heed advice from Americans and economic technocrats he had excluded from decision-making when he ruled the mainland. Sound KMT policies built on earlier Japanese investment in infrastructure and human resources to lay the basis for steadily escalating economic growth in Taiwan. Throughout the 1950s, however, mainlanders in Taiwan lived in fear of conquest by the PLA, in apprehension of the Taiwanese, and in resentment of American tutelage. These fears were reflected in Taiwan's brutal internal security controls.

By the mid-1960s, Taiwan's economic success had ended the need for U.S. aid. Fading fears of attack from the mainland or insurrection by Taiwanese allowed the KMT regime to relax the enforcement of martial law. The passage of time had helped mainlanders and Taiwanese to learn to live with each other. Taiwanese had learned Mandarin and increasing numbers of mainlanders born on the island could speak Minnan, the Taiwanese dialect of Chinese. Intermarriage was increasingly common. In the economy, mainlanders increasingly found themselves working for Taiwanese. Even in the armed forces, Taiwanese officers began to be promoted to positions of command over mainlanders.

Some mainlanders had come to accept Taiwan as their home and to identify their fortunes with it. For many in the older generation, however, Taiwan remained a place of sojourn in which the dream of return to the China mainland provided the principal source of hope. For KMT soldiers separated from their wives and children on the mainland and unable to find brides on Taiwan, this dream had particular force. For these mainlanders, the international community's switch to recognizing Beijing, rather than Taipei, as the government of China over the course of the 1970s was especially traumatic. This trauma culminated in the American announcement, on December 15, 1978, of normalization with the PRC (which meant the corresponding abnormalization of relations with the ROC on Taiwan).

Over the course of the 1980s and '90s, mainlanders were forced to accept the increasing economic and political ascendancy of the ROC's Taiwanese majority and to adjust to minority status in the island's evolving polity. The opening of the PRC to travel that followed Washington's normalization of relations with Beijing allowed Taiwan's mainlanders to rediscover their homeland. Many of them were startled by their encounter with its primitive realities. These realities had the effect of awakening them to the extent to which they had become accustomed to living in Taiwan's modernized Chinese society. Many had pined for the wives and children they had abandoned during the KMT's panicked flight to Taiwan and had dreamed of returning to their homes. After viewing the PRC's realities first hand, few chose to return permanently to their mainland points of origin.

Mainlanders on Taiwan had prided themselves on the idea that the PRC had repudiated Chinese tradition while the ROC on Taiwan had preserved it. Their visits to the mainland showed them that Taiwan's adjustments of Chinese tradition to fit the requirements of a universally educated, industrial society had, surprisingly, been much more successful and, to some extent, gone farther than the mainland's. The appeal of reunification, however loosely contrived, with the China mainland was tempered by the desire of Taiwan's mainlanders to preserve the advantages hard work and great achievement had gained for them in Taiwan. Many returned from visits to the mainland recommitted to the continued development of Taiwan as a separate Chinese society from which modern ideas and practices might be disseminated to modernize the rest of China. Reunification should be realized, they believed, only when China's transformation into a society more closely resembling that of Taiwan was well advanced. As the 1995 legislative and 1996 presidential elections loomed in Taiwan, most mainlanders continued to support the principle of reunification on such vague and indefinite terms, while rejecting any declaration of independence from China by Taiwan as both inappropriate and unnecessarily risky.

Chinese on the Mainland Remember the KMT

The CCP's victory in the Chinese civil war and its proclamation of the founding of the PRC on October 1, 1949, ended the KMT's presence on the China mainland. Many suffered as the CCP consolidated its rule over the mainland, but for most Chinese the establishment of the PRC marked a welcome end to a century of disorder, foreign domination, civil strife, and foreign invasion that had taken the lives of perhaps 90 million Chinese. If favorable images of the KMT had survived its defeat and flight to Taiwan, these were rapidly erased. The CCP's relentless propaganda against Chiang Kai-shek and his KMT apparatus successfully identified the KMT with the enormous suffering of the past. For the new Chinese elite, the KMT was the relic of a nasty bygone era, propped up on Taiwan by a hostile United States and incapable of surviving without American support. If American backing for the KMT's sanctuary on Taiwan could be removed, they believed, the Chinese civil war would be brought to its logical conclusion, as KMT rule on Taiwan succumbed to stratagem or was pushed aside by insurrection or military conquest.

The CCP's memories of the KMT during the civil war on the mainland blinded it to the changes the KMT was undergoing in Taiwan. Chinese in Beijing neither perceived nor understood the implications of the KMT's rapid "taiwanization" in the 1960s. (Taiwanese constituted a majority of KMT members by the early 1970s.) As Taiwan progressed toward democracy, the KMT was forced to transform itself from the conspiratorial Leninist organization it had been on the mainland into something much more closely resembling a Western political party. The KMT became more concerned about representing its constituency and retaining power on Taiwan than about regaining its lost position on the mainland. By the 1990s, as full democracy came to Taiwan, the KMT was engaged in a difficult balancing act between the "one China" principle dictated by its heritage of Chinese nationalism and the "Taiwan first" imperative imposed by its competition for the loyalty and support of Taiwan's electorate.

The old men who occupied senior leadership positions in the CCP and PLA, however, remembered the KMT as the arrogant and oppressive foe it had been in its last days on the mainland. They burned with righteous nationalist resentment of the KMT's achievement of sanctuary behind the U.S. Seventh Fleet in Taiwan. They saw the KMT as leading a tiny fragment of China's more than one billion people in defiance of the Chinese nationalist ideal of a unified China that could stand up to challenges from foreign powers like the United States. Chinese nationalists in Beijing saw the KMT as traitors who were collaborating with American efforts to weaken and divide China.

The CCP's appeals to the KMT to join it in reunifying China therefore continued for a long time to be couched in terms calculated to divide Taipei from Washington and to appeal to the KMT's own sense of Chinese nationalism. Nationalist ideals were, however, steadily eroding on Taiwan. The PRC's appeals resonated, if at all, only with older mainlander members of the KMT. Beijing's policy seemed stuck on the premise of reunification through some sort of deal with the KMT, based on what the KMT had come to see as the disastrous model of CCP-KMT collaboration in the 1940s. It was not until January 30, 1995, that the CCP put forward a proposal (PRC president Jiang Zemin's eight points) directed more to Taiwan's electorate than to the KMT and its leaders.

Chinese on the Mainland Remember Taiwan
The pain of Beijing's cession of Taiwan to Japan in 1895 quickly faded from the memory of Chinese on the mainland. Taiwan had, after all, been a frontier region only recently incorporated politically and economically into China. Chinese had plenty of other things on their minds as Manchu rule collapsed, revolution was succeeded by warlordism, Japan invaded, and the Chinese civil war unfolded. In the 1930s, Mao Zedong offhandedly suggested to Edgar Snow that Taiwan could be independent once Japan was defeated. It was, however, Chiang Kai-shek's KMT, not Mao's CCP, which then ruled China. Chiang insisted to his wartime American allies that Taiwan should be returned to China at the end of the war. As the KMT recovered Taiwan for China, events on the island were overshadowed for mainland Chinese by the drama of the KMT's mainland collapse under CCP military assault.

Taiwan became of interest to the PRC only when Chiang and his army took refuge there in 1949 and 1950. The PLA then began the difficult task of marshaling an invasion fleet to subdue Chiang's remaining KMT forces in Taiwan. This invasion was frustrated by the American reaction to the sudden north Korean attempt to reunify Korea by force.

Beijing's subsequent decision to intervene to prevent the defeat and disappearance of the north Korean Communist regime led to an American reaffirmation of ties with the ROC on Taiwan. American actions to deny Taiwan to the PRC and to bolster the capabilities of the ROC on Taiwan were seen by most Chinese as a continuation of the pattern of foreign intervention and division of China into spheres of influence that had characterized the "century of humiliation" from which China had just emerged. What had been envisaged as a relatively minor operation on Taiwan to mop up KMT forces defeated in the civil war on the mainland came to be seen as a major challenge to Chinese sovereignty.

This feeling became all the stronger as the ROC in Taipei, with resolute American backing, continued successfully to present itself in the United Nations and internationally as the sole legitimate government of all of China, including Taiwan. Annual battles over Chinese representation in the UN transformed the Taiwan issue from a territorial issue into a major test of international legitimacy for the PRC. The CCP had won its civil war with the KMT. The PRC was denied the international political fruits of its victory by the ROC on Taiwan and its American sponsors. Battles over the right to represent China in international councils spanned a quarter-century. Not until twenty-two years after its founding, in 1971, was the PRC at last able to take a seat in the United Nations as the legitimate government of China, an acknowledged great power and a permanent member of the UN Security Council. Not until the late 1980s, nearly a decade after the 1979 U.S. switch of recognition from Taipei to Beijing as the government of China, was the PRC able to dislodge the ROC on Taiwan's diplomats from the capitals of all internationally significant states. (Among major states, only South Africa now[8] maintains formal diplomatic relations with Taipei.)

The deaths of Chiang Kai-shek in 1975 and of Mao Zedong in 1976 ended their personal duel for China's destiny. Other leaders, with less experience of each other and, presumably, less personal animus, succeeded Chiang and Mao. By the time Deng Xiaoping had come to power in Beijing and the United States had transferred recognition from Taipei to Beijing, the ROC had ceased to pose a serious diplomatic challenge to the PRC's international standing. Under Chiang Ching-kuo, however, the ROC on Taiwan was rapidly emerging both as a more Taiwan-centered polity and as a major manufacturing economy whose financial prowess could be ignored neither by the international community nor by the PRC itself.

With the U.S.-PRC normalization agreement of December 15, 1978, Deng Xiaoping's diplomacy succeeded in removing the American military and formal diplomatic presence from the ROC on Taiwan. This reduced the most visible and obnoxious element of foreign intervention in Taiwan but did not entirely eliminate such "interference in China's internal affairs." Deng's government acquiesced to President Carter's declared intention to "continue to sell carefully selected defensive weapons, on a restrained basis," to the ROC on Taiwan. The PRC protested, but did not retaliate, when Washington renewed the American security guarantee for Taiwan through the Taiwan Relations Act (TRA) in the spring of 1979. Beijing had begun to turn its attention from crafting a solution of the Taiwan problem in Washington to crafting one with Taipei through a series of public and private approaches to the KMT regime there.

This focus was, however, upset by the 1980 American presidential campaign, in which Ronald Reagan noisily insisted on the reestablishment of some form of official American relationship and unrestrained arms sales to the ROC on Taiwan. The newly elected Reagan administration then made a point of proclaiming its intention to sell new fighter aircraft to Taiwan. Beijing responded by demanding that Washington reach an explicit understanding with it on arms sales to Taiwan. The negotiations that followed made the Taiwan issue once again the center of U.S.-PRC relations and completely overshadowed Beijing's approaches to Taipei. Their result was a return to arrangements broadly similar to the 1978 normalization *modus vivendi* on arms sales, but at a price to both sides. Beijing had to acquiesce in continuing U.S. sales of weapons to Taiwan. Washington had to agree to restrict and gradually reduce the level of such sales.

This agreement was controversial in both Beijing and Washington. The Chinese objected that it acquiesced to continued American intervention in the Chinese civil war. The open debate that accompanies congressional approval of U.S. military transfers was a constant reminder of the continuing American role in defending Taiwan against possible attack from the China mainland, and a constant irritant in U.S.-PRC relations. Many Americans found the August 17 communiqué demeaning. American interpretations of the communiqué gradually eroded it. In 1992, President Bush authorized a huge sale of advanced aircraft to Taiwan. The PRC responded by suspending implementation of understandings with Washington that restricted its missile exports, and reportedly sold missiles it had previously agreed not to transfer to Pakistan. It took no action against Taiwan. Meanwhile, the combination of Beijing's continued military modernization, including purchases of major new weapons systems and technology from cash-desperate Russia, with Washington's massive arms transfers to Taiwan intensified the arms race in the Taiwan Strait.

Notwithstanding this arms race, however, dialogue between Beijing and Taipei continued to expand to cover an increasing number of topics. The two sides began to reach agreements on technical matters, facilitating steady growth in the scale and scope of contact between people and institutions on the two sides of the Taiwan Strait. In the late 1980s, Taiwan had emerged as an increasingly crucial source of trade, technology, and investment for the modernizing economy of the China mainland. In some areas, such as those on the mainland just across the Taiwan Strait, Taiwanese investors became a dominant force in the local economy. The influence of Taiwan was, however, not restricted to these areas. By the mid-1990s, there were virtually no areas of mainland China where Taiwanese entrepreneurs were not engaged in applying the lessons (and the labor-management model) of Taiwan's industrial modernization.

As Chinese became familiar with the magnitude of Taiwan's social and economic achievements, they sought to emulate them. With the 1997 recovery of Hong Kong before them, few Chinese had any sense of urgency about Taiwan's reunification with the rest of China. None wished to tackle the politically unsettling process of working out concrete political and military arrangements for relations across the Strait after Taiwan's reunification with the rest of China. (Beijing's reunification proposals foreswore the sending of mainland officials or soldiers to Taiwan, but allowed Taiwan to retain its armed forces and invited officials from Taiwan to participate in government on the Chinese mainland.) Most Chinese seemed content with Taiwan's continued *de facto* separation from them, as long as interaction across the Strait continued to advance and Taipei continued to deal pragmatically with Beijing in ways that held open the possibility of loose reunification at some later, perhaps much later, date.

Most Chinese remained ignorant of the historical and policy factors that had produced Taiwanese success and of the changes in the KMT that had facilitated it. Some, however, began to look to the political, as well as the economic, precedent of the modernization of the Chinese society on Taiwan as a model for future evolution toward free market–based democratic rule on the mainland. A few saw the KMT's transformation from a Leninist to a democratic political party as a model for the future evolution of the CCP.

Almost no one on the mainland, however, understood, still less sympathized, with the identity crisis history had imposed on the Taiwanese. The nationalism and worldview of Chinese on the mainland had been formed in the tumultuous events of twentieth-century Chinese history—the fall of the Manchu (Qing) Dynasty; the establishment of the Republic of China; the May 4th movement; the rise and fall of warlords; the Northern Expedition; the struggle between the CCP and KMT; the Japanese occupation of northeast China (Manchuria); the Long March; the Japanese invasion of north and central China; the anti-Japanese war; the Chinese civil war; the founding of the PRC; the Korean war; Soviet tutelage; the anti-rightist campaign and the Great Leap Forward; the Sino-Soviet split; the Cultural Revolution; the rise and fall of the Gang of Four; and the rolling process of Deng Xiaoping's subsequent reforms. The inability of Taiwanese to identify with a China formed by these events and inspired by memories of them, was incomprehensible to Chinese on the mainland. Few stopped to ponder the implications of the fact that Taiwanese had not participated in these formative events (except, to some extent, as members of the Japanese armed forces in World War II).

The increasing insistence of Taiwanese that Taiwan's unique character and its economic and political achievements merited international acknowledgment in the form of recognition of Taiwan's independence was therefore greeted with angry disbelief in Beijing. Most Chinese saw a foreign hand—a clumsy American hand or perhaps a more subtle Japanese one—behind the Taiwanese drive for recognition of a separate political identity for their island. As Taiwan's 1995–96 election season approached, however, growing appreciation of the fundamental political forces at work on the island led to apprehension in Beijing that the PRC might be forced to intervene militarily to halt moves by Taiwan toward independence. This was a course of action that virtually all Chinese understood would be disastrous for themselves as well as for their relations with Americans and Japanese. It was also one that they saw no way of avoiding if they were to remain true to the spirit of Chinese nationalism.

Japanese Memories Repressed

When Japan came out from its self-imposed isolation in the Meiji period, it did not take it long to recognize the strategic importance of Taiwan both to the defense of the home islands and to the southward advance of the Japanese empire. The Japanese seizure of Taiwan during the Sino-Japanese war of 1894–95 reflected both considerations. Unlike Korea, which was administered by the Imperial Army, Taiwan was under the jurisdiction of the Japanese navy, which pursued considerably more enlightened policies of assimilation once initial resistance by Taiwanese had been suppressed. Japanese attributed the ease with which Taiwanese assumed Japanese ways to the largely peasant character of society in Taiwan and to the shallowness with which higher Chinese culture had taken root there before 1895. Japanese were flattered by Taiwanese acceptance of their culture. Assimilated Taiwanese were second-class subjects of the Japanese emperor, rather like Okinawans, to be sure, but much more accepted than Koreans. Taiwan was indeed, in a memorable Japanese phrase later adopted by

Americans, an "unsinkable aircraft carrier," but it was also a southern island extension of the Japanese homeland. The loss of Taiwan in 1945 was seen by most Japanese not only in symbolic terms as the end of empire but also as the poignant loss of a quasi-Japanese population.

Fond Japanese feelings for Taiwanese persisted, even as they were repressed by the policy exigencies of post–World War II and Cold War politics. The ability of Taiwanese to speak Japanese and the resumption of Japanese contact with Taiwan through tourism and trade in the 1950s reinforced these feelings. Japanese had no affection for their wartime KMT enemies (though conservative Japanese appreciated Chiang Kai-shek's anticommunism), but sympathy for Taiwanese aspirations continued to be an unspoken factor in Japanese policy toward Taiwan.

Japan's China policy was long subordinated to the policies of Japan's American defenders. After the shock of President Nixon's sudden announcement in July 1971 of the U.S. shift toward a strategic opening to Beijing, Japanese policy gradually took a more independent course. That course was dictated by strategic realities that required Japan to court and conciliate Beijing. Chinese attitudes toward Japan were pragmatic, but tinged with bitter memories of the tens of millions of deaths the Japanese invasion of the China mainland had caused from 1931 to 1945. The Japanese government's policies toward Taiwan were crafted with a view toward appeasing Chinese on the mainland, but were carried out in such a way as to preserve Japanese economic and other human ties to Taiwan. Japan was free to carry out such policies because management of its strategic interests with regard to Taiwan was the responsibility of its American protectors.

As Taiwanese assumed control of Taiwan's politics, latent sympathy for them found increasingly open expression in Japan. Japanese found the ROC on Taiwan's current president, Lee Teng-hui, a culturally appealing figure. Lee, a former Japanese national, was said to speak Japanese (as some mainlanders on Taiwan sarcastically pointed out) better than Chinese Mandarin. Japanese policy with regard to Taiwan, however, continued prudently to defer to the strategic imperative of avoiding the hostility of the PRC. Japan sought to avoid the open renewal of competition with China for political or military influence in Asia. The history of Japanese involvement in Taiwan made it a point of particular neuralgia in interaction between Tokyo and Beijing. To the extent possible, therefore, Japanese policy continued to strive to hide behind American policy toward Taiwan.

American Memory and Forgetfulness
American attitudes and policies toward Taiwan had, as noted above, been the main determinant in Taiwan's post–World War II relationships

both with the China mainland and internationally. Before World War II, the U.S. military—correctly, as it turned out—had perceived the Japanese presence in Taiwan as a threat to the Philippines and the rest of Southeast Asia. For other Americans, Taiwan was *terra incognita*. The U.S. bombed Taiwan during the war and briefly contemplated invading it. A few Americans assigned to plan a U.S. occupation of Taiwan studied the island's history. (Some of these Americans, like Senator Claiborne Pell, later emerged as prominent sympathizers with Taiwanese aspirations for self-determination and independence.) In the end, however, U.S. forces massing to invade the Japanese home islands bypassed Taiwan. The U.S. assisted KMT forces from the China mainland in occupying the island and raised no objection to Taiwan's reincorporation into KMT China. When the KMT was forced to flee to Taiwan, Washington made it clear that it would not act to prevent a PRC conquest of Taiwan.

These policies of indifference toward Taiwan's fate had been unsuccessfully resisted by General MacArthur's Tokyo headquarters. Having assumed responsibility for the defense of Japan, MacArthur had come to share traditional Japanese views about the strategic importance of Taiwan. The north Korean invasion of south Korea catalyzed Washington's acceptance of policies toward Taiwan favored by the Tokyo-based U.S. military.

Most Americans, however, saw Taiwan purely in terms of anticommunism and the strategic and emotional imperatives of the Korean War. The nasty U.S. debate about who had "lost China" and the rising influence of Senator McCarthy soon made it politically incorrect to withhold "positive loyalty" to the cause of Chiang Kai-shek and his KMT. Escalating American involvement in Taiwan throughout the 1950s and early 1960s ensured that many Americans became aware of the tensions between Taiwan's mainlander and native Chinese populations. The American focus on support for the ROC's position in the "free world" beyond the realm of Communism, however, led all but a few Americans involved with the island to identify themselves strongly with its KMT rulers.

The absurd KMT insistence that it represented all of China, despite its exile to Taiwan and irrelevance to developments on the China mainland, made the Chinese representation issue and the related question of Chinese recognition a zero-sum game. (In 1957, Chiang Kai-shek brushed aside an effort by U.S. Secretary of State Dulles to persuade him to renounce the use of force against the mainland. His reasoning, which paralleled that of the PRC then and in later decades, was that no government of China could ever give an undertaking to a foreign government not to use force against other Chinese challenging its sovereignty over Chinese territory.) The Vietnam War led to much questioning by Americans of the basic assumptions of long-standing U.S. policy in the East Asian and Pacific region. Increasing numbers of Americans came to favor a switch in recognition and diplomatic relations from Taipei to Beijing. In their debate over China policy, some Americans expressed concern about the plight of mainlanders on Taiwan, but few considered the impact of the decisions they advocated on Taiwanese. By the 1968 American presidential elections, all candidates had pledged themselves, in the words of Richard Nixon, "to come urgently to grips with the reality of China."

The American officials who negotiated the February 28, 1972, Shanghai Communiqué with Premier Zhou Enlai were aware that a small group of Taiwanese dissidents in Japan and the United States advocated "Taiwan independence." This awareness came, however, from vociferous CCP and KMT objections to the notion of a status for Taiwan distinct from "China," rather than from sympathy with the Taiwan independence movement. No American official accepted the assertion of these dissidents (which in fact may have reflected substantial opinion among Taiwanese) that "Taiwanese" were something other than "Chinese."

The issue for American policy was not how to deal with self-determination by the island's inhabitants, but how to reconcile a continuing American relationship with the ROC on Taiwan with an opening to the PRC dictated by Cold War strategic considerations. American policy dealt with this problem by endorsing the legal fiction, asserted by both Taipei and Beijing, that there was only "one China" and that Taiwan was "part of China." The phrasing of the American statement in the Shanghai Communiqué, that the United States acknowledged that "all Chinese on either side of the Taiwan Strait" stood for a single China of which Taiwan was part, was intended to mollify the PRC without destroying the ROC on Taiwan's bargaining position in future negotiations between the CCP and KMT. It may, as subsequent legal hairsplitting by Taiwan independence advocates sought to suggest, have theoretically left open the possibility of a distinction between "Taiwanese" and "Chinese," but that was clearly not its intention. On the contrary, if anything, it was intended to clarify that the United States saw no basis for questioning Taipei's and Beijing's common position that no such distinction was admissible.

In the English version of the normalization communiqué of December 15, 1978, the same language "acknowledging" the Chinese position that Taiwan was part of China was repeated in abbreviated form. The Chinese language version of the communiqué changed "acknowledge" (*renshidao*) to "recognize" (*chengren*). No public notice of this change, which was seen in Beijing as an important shift in the U.S. position, was taken in Washington, which learned of it only slightly before the communiqué was released. The normalization communiqué's formula was repeated in the August 17, 1982, communiqué, which recorded the revived U.S.-PRC *modus vivendi* on Taiwan arms sales.

The Tiananmen incident of June 4, 1989, dramatically changed American views of China, and placed human rights concerns at the center of U.S. China policy. Later in 1989, with the fall of the Berlin Wall, the Soviet empire in East and Central Europe collapsed. The subsequent disintegration of the Soviet Union itself removed the strategic rationale for U.S.-PRC relations. Americans welcomed Taiwan's transformation into a democratic polity in the early 1990s, seeing this as part of a worldwide trend toward democracy and respect for human rights that had, tragically, bypassed the PRC. The issue of Taiwan's relationship to the China mainland came to be seen primarily as a human rights issue, pitting Taiwan's prosperous democracy against a repressive regime in Beijing determined to deny Taiwan the place in international affairs to which its economic and political achievements entitled it. Support for Taiwanese aspirations for self-determination received a further boost from significant campaign contributions from the increasingly numerous, well-organized, and well-heeled Taiwanese-American community in the United States.

The ROC on Taiwan's policies were, meanwhile, shifting under the pressure of electoral politics in Taiwan. Taipei no longer claimed to be the capital of anything other than Taiwan. The KMT had replaced its long-standing dedication to the principal of one China with lip service to the notion of Chinese reunification sometime, somehow or other, in the future. The KMT had joined with its Democratic Progressive Party (DPP) opponents in seeking to establish an international personality for Taiwan as a democratic polity separate from the China mainland. For Taiwanese, the issue was the achievement of dignity commensurate with the economic strength and political virtue of the new democracy on Taiwan, including membership in the United Nations. This position attracted overwhelming sympathy and support in the U.S. Congress.

Members of Congress from both parties found an easy political target in the blatant contrast between the Clinton administration's diplomatically correct relations with the undemocratic regime in Beijing and its unwillingness to accord the democratic regime in Taipei comparable honors. Most Americans had forgotten that the basis of the PRC's tolerance of the flourishing U.S.-Taiwan relationship was a U.S.-PRC understanding that the United States would endorse the legal fiction that China was undivided (when manifestly it was divided into two competing polities) and would trade changes in the form of U.S.-Taiwan relations for the continuation, without disruption, of their substance. Many Americans who remembered this U.S.-PRC understanding asserted that the emergence of democracy on Taiwan and the nearly simultaneous unmasking of the repressive nature of the PRC had made Beijing's views no longer worthy of consideration. Others who had strongly endorsed the legal fiction of "one China" when this worked to the advantage of anticommunists in Taipei had always rejected it when it appeared to serve the interests of Communists in Beijing. Liberal members of Congress concerned with human rights or Taiwanese self-determination therefore joined traditional, conservative supporters of the KMT in pressing for an end to the ambiguity and contortions of Washington's relationship with Taipei.

By the fall of 1994, the Clinton administration had been forced by congressional pressure to announce a modest upgrading of American relationships with Taipei, including a restoration of open ministerial-level contact. In May 1995, the Congress sought virtually unanimously to overrule the administration's previous refusal to allow President Lee Teng-hui to visit the United States on the pretext of accepting an award from Cornell University, where he had earned his doctorate. By the end of May, the Clinton administration had capitulated to congressional pressure and agreed to allow Lee's visit to go forward.

Virtually all Americans saw the issue of Lee's visit as a simple case of according due courtesy to the respected leader of a friendly democratic society, and felt that no third party, such as Beijing, had the right to speak against this. There was virtually no public discussion among Americans of the cost of such moves in terms of their potential to buttress the growing view among Chinese on the mainland, including China's highly nationalist younger generation, that the United States was a hostile rather than a friendly power. Nor was there any discussion at all of the implications of American policy changes for perceptions on both Taiwan and the China mainland. Those perceptions increasingly were that the United States was moving toward a Taiwan policy disconnected from China policy, a Taiwan policy that would ignore or defy both Beijing and the legacy of Chinese nationalism.

In this atmosphere, PRC president Jiang Zemin's conciliatory gesture to the ROC on Taiwan of January 30, 1995, went virtually unnoticed in the U.S. Jiang's initiative was, however, taken very seriously in Taipei, which responded with its own conciliatory statement on April 8. Even as Beijing's relations with Washington deteriorated over the Taiwan issue, its dialogue with Taipei proceeded.

1995: A Year of Living Dangerously?

As 1995 unfolded, Chinese leaders in Beijing, while once again extending an olive branch to Taipei, took a series of actions, such as expanded exercises in the Taiwan Strait and military redeployments opposite Taiwan, to signal their resolve to prevent overt secession by Taiwan from the legal fiction of one China. The U.S. Congress continued to press to deepen U.S. relations with—and, implicitly, the U.S. commitment to—Taipei. Some DPP politicians on Taiwan continued to assert on the campaign stump that the TRA provided Taiwan, in effect, with a blank check that it could cash to protect Taiwan against the consequences of a declaration of independence. These politicians claimed that Americans could be invoked to defend Taiwan against the PRC, regardless of the source of the conflict. As of mid-May 1995, these assertions that the bill for a change of Taiwan's name and flag could be paid in American blood had met no rebuttal from either the KMT on Taiwan or the administration in Washington.

Japanese, true to their traditional low profile on the Taiwan issue, studiously avoided discussing it. Neither Americans nor Japanese appeared to be concerned that decisions by Taiwan's electorate, and Beijing's reaction to them, might provoke an armed conflict in the Taiwan Strait sought by no one. The dedication of the United States to the ideal of self-determination would be tested by such conflict, as would the credibility of the American defense commitment embodied in the TRA. The strategic interests of Japan, as well as its affection for the Taiwanese, would be challenged.

An American decision to come to Taiwan's aid would require Japanese acquiescence in the use of U.S. bases and facilities in Japan. A war in the Taiwan Strait would thus force Japan to choose between its alliance with the United States and its strategic interest in a non-hostile relationship with China. So unpalatable a choice would inevitably stimulate many Japanese to seek to regain the right to pursue an independent defense of Japanese strategic interests. Japan would distance itself from the United States while strengthening its own military capabilities. On the other hand, a U.S. failure to respond to a PRC attack on Taiwan would so devalue the U.S.-Japan security relationship that Japanese would feel even more impelled to develop a military capable of independent action to defend their strategic interests. Either way, conflict in the Taiwan Strait clearly had the potential to produce major strategic realignments in Asia, including attenuation of U.S. ties with Japan and the reemergence of a Sino-Japanese military rivalry. As of mid-1995, however, neither Washington nor Tokyo seemed alert to the extent to which their relations with China and with each other, like the prospects for peace in the Taiwan Strait, had been taken hostage by the Taiwan electorate.

Decisions by the Taiwan electorate from November 1995 through March 1996 will determine the extent to which Taiwan defies or continues to tolerate the ambiguities of life within the legal fiction of one China. These decisions about Taiwan's identity, and reactions to them by Beijing, Washington, and Tokyo, have the potential to determine much more than whether there is peace or war in the Taiwan Strait. The Taiwan electorate may also determine whether China enjoys peaceful and cooperative relations with the United States and Japan and whether the Japanese security partnership with the United States will survive as a substitute for an independent Japanese military role in Asia. As all sides approach decisions on matters of great moment to them, they do so as prisoners of their disparate and incompatible memories of each other and of Taiwan and its history.

Chapter 4

The Reemergence of the Taiwan Problem

Relations with China under Ronald Reagan's presidency began inauspiciously. Members of the committee that planned his inauguration invited Cabinet officers from Taipei as official guests. Only strenuous efforts by Secretary of State–designate Alexander M. Haig Jr. and National Security Advisor–designate Robert C. "Bud" McFarlane avoided the crisis that would have followed so serious a lapse in the American undertaking not to have any official relationship with Taiwan. As the president came to understand the importance to American diplomacy vis-à-vis the Soviet Union of sustaining the new relationship with Beijing, he dropped his effort to restore official ties to Taipei.

But President Reagan simultaneously made it clear that he intended to ignore the formula for continuing arms sales to Taiwan that his predecessor had outlined as part of the agreement with Deng Xiaoping to disagree on this issue.[1] The immediate issue was the proposed sale of an advanced fighter aircraft, designated the "FX," to Taiwan. (It was not then clear what specific aircraft this might refer to, though it was clear that the decision would make or break at least one of the two aerospace contractors competing to supply a plane.) China demanded clarification of U.S. policy.

The outcome was almost a year of difficult negotiations, culminating in a U.S.-China agreement commonly known as the 8/17 Communiqué.[2] In that communiqué, the Chinese made a unilateral commitment to make best efforts to resolve the Taiwan issue peacefully, without resort to force, and this was paralleled by a linked unilateral American statement that "the United States . . . does not seek to carry out a long-term policy of arms sales to Taiwan; that its arms sales to Taiwan will not exceed, either in qualitative or quantitative terms, the level of those supplied in recent years since the establishment of diplomatic relations between China and the United States, and that it intends gradually to reduce its sale of arms to Taiwan, leading, over a period of time, to a final resolution."

The 8/17 Communiqué served as a guideline for American arms-sales policy throughout the 1980s. In late 1992, however, during a hard-fought presidential campaign in which job creation was seen as critical, the George H. W. Bush administration authorized what was then the largest single arms sale in history to Taiwan—the sale of 150 F-16 fighters. This resulted in a sharp increase in Sino-American tensions and the progressive remilitarization of cross-Strait relations, which had seen a steady trend away from military confrontation over the preceding decade. U.S.-China relations in President Bill Clinton's first term in office were dominated by the linked issues of American insistence on improvements in Chinese human rights practices and the extension of permanent most-favored-nation (i.e., normal trading) status to China.

It was in this context that Congress insisted on permitting Taiwan's democratically elected president to visit the United States, igniting a nine-month-long crisis that ultimately produced a U.S.-China naval confrontation in March 1996.

Up till 1995, when Lee's visit to Cornell unveiled his vision of self-determination for Taiwan's inhabitants, the aim of Chinese policy was to wait for Taiwan to fall back into a renewed organic relationship with the mainland that was considered both natural and inevitable. Time, in the Chinese consensus view then, could produce only a prolongation of the "one China" status quo or reunification, with no possible third outcome. So Chinese nationalists in Beijing, aware of how unlikely it was that Taiwan would soon agree to terms, favored prolonging the status quo indefinitely. This would certainly, eventually, lead to an end to China's suffering from "national dismemberment," they thought. Patience would thus yield its own reward.

Over the course of 1995 and 1996, Lee made it clearer and clearer that he had an alternative view both of the status quo and of how it might evolve. The status quo could be defined, in Lee's view, as the indefinite separation of Taiwan from the rest of China and its rule by Chinese born on the island— "new Taiwanese," as he eventually phrased this notion. (Lee was perhaps better able than others to come up with an inclusive phrase like "new Taiwanese" because he was a member of a minority within a minority, a Taiwanese Hakka.) This status quo, Lee posited, need not result in reattaching Taiwan to the rest of China. Reassociation between Taiwan and the mainland could come about, in any event, he added, only on the basis of cross-Strait ideological convergence, i.e., the embrace by the mainland of "democracy." This was, of course, a euphemism for the overthrow of the Chinese Communist regime.

The alternative to reunification that Lee gradually unfolded for public inspection was recognition of Taiwan by the international community as an *independent state under the name "Republic of China." As Lee made his case ever clearer for the continued separation of Taiwan from the rest of China and for international recognition of Taiwan as a state distinct from that on the China mainland, Chinese nationalists in Beijing increasingly came to doubt that time was indeed on the side of reunification. The consensus shifted toward alarm that Taiwan was bent on turning the delay to the advantage of separatism.*

If Taiwan was indeed committed to a separatist course, it could not be expected to negotiate any terms for reunification and would not come to the negotiating table unless forced to do so. Without coercion, in other words, reunification could not occur. This logic is why, when Taipei resumed separatist activities soon after Lee's second inauguration, in 1996, most Beijing policy-makers concerned with the Taiwan question came to the conclusion that, more likely than not, force would eventually have to be used to deal with Taiwan. In mid-1995, although this was not widely perceived at the time, the direction of PRC military modernization began to shift toward a single-minded focus on Taiwan contingencies. I reviewed the factors that led to this conclusion in a piece written in the early fall of 1995 which appears as the first section of this chapter under the title "The Renewed Fuss over Taiwan."

In the fall of 1995, when I first understood that China had come to feel compelled to take military actions that would certainly produce a confrontation with the United States, very few Americans were prepared to accept this possibility. In the fall of 1995, I told the Secretary of Defense, the Vice Chairman of the Joint Chiefs of Staff, the Director for Intelligence of the Joint Staff (J-2), and senior officers and analysts of the Department of State, the Central Intelligence Agency, and the National Security Council Staff (including, eventually, the National Security Advisor himself) that the Chinese intended to fire missiles at targets near the Taiwan ports of Keelung [Jilong] and Kaohsiung [Gaoxiong]. My warnings were met with nearly universal disbelief.

As Taiwan's 1996 elections approached, Washington continued to ignore signs of a more muscular Chinese military approach to influencing decisions in Taipei. When the People's Liberation Army did precisely what I had warned it would do, the United States was taken off guard. Some mistook what was clearly intended as a Chinese show of force as a move to launch a broad attack on Taiwan. It seemed to me that, in the context of other uncertainties that had begun to affect post–Cold War Asia, what was about to happen would have very broad strategic implications. I explored these potential effects in the second of the three pieces that follow: "Toward U.S.-China Military Confrontation, 1995–1996."

Amended U.S.-Japan Defense Guidelines revealed over the course of 1996 and 1997 had drawn Chinese attention to the crucial role in any U.S. intervention in the Taiwan area of US Air Force assets based in Japan. The announced arrival of U.S. carriers in the Philippine Sea[3] during the crisis of March 1996 forced the PLA to broaden the focus of its planning to include countering U.S. Navy interference with operations against Taiwan. Overall, however, the results of the 1996 Sino-American naval confrontation over Taiwan were ambiguous, with each side drawing different and, in my view, equally erroneous conclusions about what had happened and why. I analyzed the different lessons that China and the United States drew from the experience and some of its possible consequences in a 1998 article for Foreign Affairs, which appears as the last section of this chapter: "The Aftermath of the 1995–1996 Taiwan Crisis."

Find More in the Online Archive

Some notes on the military dimension of the Taiwan problem as of December 1998 can be found in the online archive in "The People's Liberation Army and Taiwan" at http://bit.ly/ interesting-times. Key documents related to U.S. policies on Taiwan can also be found there, including the Shanghai Communiqué (1972), the Normalization Communiqué and the Unilateral U.S. Government Statement that accompanied it (1979), excerpts from a press conference given by Chairman Hua Guofeng following issuance of the Normalization Communiqué (1979), the Taiwan Relations Act (1979), and the Arms Sales Communiqué (1982): http://bit.ly/interesting-times.

The Renewed Fuss over Taiwan[4]
October 1995

The Taiwan question, which most Americans thought (or hoped) was behind us, is back as a major problem in U.S.-China relations. So is military tension in the Taiwan Strait, at a level not seen since U.S.-China normalization set the stage for trade, investment, and peaceful contacts between Taipei and Beijing. The immediate cause of these unwelcome developments was the private, but very political, visit of Taiwan's leader, Lee Teng-hui to the United States in June. Lee's visit brought Beijing's mounting concerns about the direction of U.S. China policy to a head. The Chinese leadership now believes that the United States government is straying from the basic understandings that made it possible for the two sides to build a normal relationship. They are convinced that the United States is complicitous in efforts by Taiwan to stake out an identity for itself separate from "China."

The return of tension in the Taiwan Strait and of major strain in U.S.-China relations carries obvious dangers. Both Lee Teng-hui, whose efforts to achieve a higher international profile for Taiwan provoked the crisis, and the Clinton administration and U.S. Congress, whose desire to accommodate Taipei ignited the crisis, seriously misjudged the strength of nationalist reaction in Beijing to alterations in long-standing U.S. policy toward Taiwan. Neither Taipei nor Washington sought or foresaw confrontation with Beijing. Nor did Beijing desire confrontation with Taipei or Washington. Beijing is instead reacting to what it sees as a challenge to the *status quo* in the Taiwan Strait. It sees itself as attempting to restore that *status quo* and the framework that made it possible. It remains an open question, however, whether that framework—and the benefits it undergirded—can be put back into place.

The Cold War context in which these agreements were reached, like China's favorable, pre-Tiananmen image in the United States, has manifestly disappeared. Now, China fears, the agreements themselves, and the *modus vivendi* on the Taiwan issue they created, may do likewise.

The basic framework for Sino-American relations and peace in the Taiwan Strait took more than a decade of delicate diplomacy to construct. The three agreements that built this framework have worked so well that few Americans, including few officials in the Clinton administration, bother to read them or remember their negotiating history.

The 1972 Shanghai Communiqué ended more than two decades of U.S. containment policies and began a mutually beneficial strategic dialogue between Washington and Beijing. It marked the end of American backing for Taipei against Beijing in the unresolved Chinese civil war. In this communiqué, the United States noted that "all Chinese on either side of the Taiwan Strait maintain there is but one China and that Taiwan is a part of China" and made it clear that Americans stood for "a peaceful resolution of the Taiwan problem by the Chinese themselves."

In 1979, the United States shifted recognition from Taipei to Beijing as "the sole legal government of China." A key element in the normalization agreement was Washington's acknowledgment of China's position that "there is but one China and Taiwan is part of China." The communiqué committed Americans to maintaining "economic, cultural, and other unofficial relations" with Taiwan "within this context." This tradeoff of form for substance allowed Americans to retain *de facto* ties with Taiwan while exchanging ambassadors with Beijing. Washington continued selling carefully selected defensive weapons to Taiwan to sustain the island's ability to defend itself. This policy, authorized by the Taiwan Relations Act, was intended (in the words of the Act) to assure that "the future of Taiwan [would] be determined by peaceful means." Beijing objected both to U.S. arms sales and the TRA but nevertheless normalized its relations with the United States.

Sino-American differences over the level of U.S. arms sales to Taiwan soon necessitated the conclusion of a third agreement. In the arms sales communiqué of 1982, Beijing accepted the continuation of U.S. arms sales to Taiwan. The Reagan administration agreed to cap the arms' quality and reduce their quantity, with a view to eventually ending the sales. The two sides pledged to "adopt measures and create conditions conducive to the thorough settlement of this issue."

Beijing saw President Bush's campaign-driven sale of 150 advanced F-16 aircraft to Taiwan in 1992 (the largest arms sale in American history) as a blatant violation of the Sino-American understandings on arms sales recorded in the 1982 communiqué. It viewed the Clinton administration's 1994 decision to open cabinet-level dialogue with Taipei as contrary to the 1979 communiqué's stipulation that the United States would maintain only "unofficial" relations with Taiwan. It saw Lee Teng-hui's visit as adding an unacceptable political element to the American economic and cultural relations with Taiwan it had agreed to tolerate at the time of normalization.

Beijing does not now hide its concern that Washington may be returning to the hostile policies the United States abandoned twenty-three years ago in the Shanghai Communiqué. Many Chinese see the U.S.'s tough stand on their membership in the World Trade Organization, along with U.S. restrictions on technology transfer, as part of an effort to retard their country's modernization and block its rise to wealth and power. Chinese leaders view the continuing American focus on human rights as an effort to stir up opposition to them and to divide and weaken China politically. Virtually all Chinese are offended by congressional efforts to promote independence for Tibet. Most see this, like congressional initiatives toward Taiwan, as evidence that the United States hopes that China will collapse and break apart like the former Soviet Union.

Lee Teng-hui's visit to the United States took place in this unpropitious context. Lee himself portrayed his visit as a major step toward Taiwan's determination of its identity and international status by unilateral action rather than in consultation with Beijing. On his return to Taipei, he offered the United Nations a billion dollars for a seat for Taiwan. Rightly or wrongly, Beijing has concluded that Lee's actions are aimed at breaking the delicate understandings that had made confrontation unnecessary in the Taiwan Strait, and at achieving Taiwan independence. Beijing now demands that Taipei, as well as Washington, show that it still sees Taiwan's *de facto* separation from the rest of China as a temporary and unnatural state of affairs—one that negotiators from both sides of the Taiwan Strait should seek to correct through agreement on a process of reunification, even if it takes decades to implement.

This summer,[5] the People's Liberation Army began a series of unprecedentedly large military exercises near Taiwan. Beijing describes these exercises as routine, but clearly intends them to send a message to Taipei. The message is that Beijing will not tolerate secession by Taiwan from the idea of "one China." Chinese can live with Taiwan's *de facto* independence for as long as it takes the two sides to agree on the island's ultimate relationship with the rest of China. Chinese nationalism would, however, compel Beijing to take military action to block a Taiwanese effort at *de jure* secession. Such military action by Beijing, even if provoked by a declaration of independence from Taipei, would compel Washington to decide whether the policies set out in the Taiwan Relations Act required the United States' armed forces to come to Taiwan's defense.

Beijing has put its relations with Washington on hold, and taken steps to improve its dialogue with Tokyo and Southeast Asian capitals, while it concentrates on sending its message to Taipei. The chill in relations with official Washington has not, so far, extended to business relationships with American companies. Beijing seems to have concluded that China's interests are best served by a strategy of strengthening people-to-people and commercial ties with Americans. The Chinese leadership hopes that, in time, broadened support in the United States might help produce less hostile American government policies.

This approach is not, however, cast in stone. Business relations could be seriously affected by a further ratcheting up of the confrontation between Washington and Beijing. This could happen because of actions the Chinese take (or fail to take), for example with regard to missile exports to Pakistan. (U.S. law mandates sanctions for violations of the Missile Technology Control Regime, whether or not the violator is a member of the MTCR. Beijing is not.) It could take place as a Chinese response to further congressional jabs at China over Tibet, human rights, or some other issue of concern to the United States. Unfortunately, however, it could also come about because of an accidental outbreak of conflict in the Taiwan Strait or as a result of decisions of the Taiwan electorate that neither Beijing nor Washington can reliably forecast or control. At their worst, such events could provoke a military confrontation in the Taiwan Strait from which the United States would find it difficult to remain aloof.

Taiwan faces two crucial elections over the coming half-year. Its voters will elect a new Legislative Yuan (parliament) this December 2. In March

1996, they will—for the first time—directly elect a president. On one level, these elections are about who will represent the voters in the island's government. On another, however, they are about Taiwan's domestic self-perception and the island's view of its international identity and status.

Some Taiwan politicians, including many Democratic Progressive Party candidates for the Legislative Yuan and the presidency, espouse a "Taiwanese nationalist" cause at odds with the Chinese nationalist idea of "one China, but not now." They assert that Beijing lacks both the will and the power to forestall a move toward formal separation by the island from "China." (Recent polls show that a third or more of Taiwan's voters interpret the Taiwan Relations Act as committing the United States to go to war with the PRC to protect them, if Beijing sought to use force to prevent or reverse such a declaration of independence.) Others, including some rivals of Lee Teng-hui for nomination by the ruling KMT, favor a policy of negotiation and careful rapprochement with Chinese on the mainland. (A third or more of Taiwan's voters believe the United States would *not* come to their aid if they sought to separate themselves from China.)

Beijing's current military and other actions are clearly intended to influence the decisions of the electorate in Taiwan. That is, presumably, one reason that the mainland has continued to welcome investors and traders from Taiwan, despite the political pressure Beijing is putting on Taipei. No one can now say, however, how Taiwanese will vote in December and March. Still less can anyone be sure that Beijing's efforts to influence the elections will not backfire.

These uncertainties have already had a negative impact on the investment climate in Taiwan, reflected in plummeting prices on Taipei's stock exchange. Escalating tensions with Beijing have also damaged the confidence of Taiwan investors in the mainland. Most are now holding back, pending clarification of future cross-Strait relations. Similarly, American and other foreign companies that once looked to Taiwan as a launching platform and source of key managerial and technical talent for activities on the mainland are—for the time being—looking elsewhere for such support of their China mainland operations. Taiwan's plans to become a regional operations center for international business are now, in effect, on hold.

Meanwhile, most business men and women in the United States, Hong Kong, Taiwan, and the China mainland are justly apprehensive about the mess their political leaderships may produce. Businesspersons with a stake in good U.S.-China and cross-Strait relations seem universally to hope that those concerned will take Henry Kissinger's advice. The former secretary of state has urged that Taipei stop pushing the envelope with Beijing; Beijing stop threatening Taiwan; the U.S. Congress stand down from further pro-Taiwan, pro-Tibet, or anti-China gestures; Beijing resume dialogue with

Washington; and the Clinton administration explain what it means when it says it plans to stand by the three Sino-American communiqués. That is probably what it will take to prevent a further deterioration in an already bad situation.

⟨∅⟩

Toward U.S.-China Military Confrontation, 1995–1996[6]
December 1995

Since the end of the Cold War, only the Asia-Pacific region has seemed at peace and relatively free of change. The collapse of multiethnic states and empires has rocked Europe, Eurasia, and Africa. Anarchy and ethnic or religious strife have broken out in the former Yugoslavia, Afghanistan, Tajikistan, the trans-Caucasus, Liberia, Zaire [now the Democratic Republic of the Congo], Somalia, and Rwanda. The Middle East has seen a brutal Iraqi attempt to annex Kuwait, and the end of civic consensus in Algeria. Major changes have taken place in the relationships between Israelis, Palestinians, and other Arabs, and civil society has gradually reemerged in Lebanon. Confrontation with military regimes in Panama and Haiti and a border war between Peru and Ecuador have marked the advent of the new era in Latin America. Many of these situations have occasioned U.S. military intervention or serious consideration of it—either in the name of the United States itself or under the banner of the United Nations.

At the same time, major adjustments in U.S. military spending and personnel levels have been carried out. As a percentage of GNP, U.S. military spending is now at the levels of the mid- to late 1930s. The size of the U.S. armed forces has shrunk to numbers last seen in 1939. Outside the Asia-Pacific region, the United States has radically adjusted the pattern of American military deployments and has built up its forces in the Persian Gulf. The Atlantic Alliance, which France has now rejoined, is expanding eastward through the Partnership for Peace. The United States had withdrawn two-thirds of its forces from Europe by the time it joined—in the Balkans—in the first military operation in NATO history.

Meanwhile, with American forces out of the Philippines, the United States seeks no further adjustments in the pattern of Asian-Pacific alliances it developed during the Cold War. On the contrary, Washington affirms that the United States will keep the same number of American soldiers, sailors, marines, and airmen—about 100,000—in the Asia-Pacific region that it has stationed there for the past decade or more.

Few in Asia are confident that such an American presence will in fact be sustained. Southeast Asians and Koreans hope that it will be. Increasingly, however, Chinese, and even some Japanese, question whether it should be. They are joined in their skepticism by some Americans who espouse America-first policies. Other Americans doubt the relevance of military alliances. Despite the mounting evidence from other regions, these Americans continue to expect the coming decades to be dominated by economic, rather than political or military, contention. We must all hope they are right.

Beneath the surface calm, however, the Asia-Pacific region is undergoing changes no less profound than those that transformed other regions. These changes go well beyond the well-publicized economic miracle in China and adjacent areas that is making the region the center of gravity of global trade and investment. They include politico-military trends that challenge both the existing strategic balance in the region and the American role in it.

A February 1995 paper from the Pentagon's directorate for International Security Affairs defined the role preferred by the United States for its forces in the region: The "United States Security Strategy for the East Asia-Pacific Region" envisages maintenance of the existing American alliance structure and military presence "as a foundation of regional stability and a means of promoting American influence on key Asian issues."[7] It posits continued cooperation with Asian allies and friends in support of U.S. global strategy and "to deter potential threats, counter regional aggression, ensure regional peace, monitor attempts at proliferation of weapons of mass destruction, and help protect sea lines of communication both within the region and from the region to the Indian Ocean and the Persian Gulf." In short, the United States sees its alliances and cooperative engagement with non-allies as enabling it to underwrite Asian-Pacific balance and peaceful evolution of the *status quo*, while facilitating the nonviolent resolution of disputes within the region.

For this strategy to work, the following conditions must prevail:

- Americans must be prepared to support an indefinite military presence in the Western Pacific similar to that at present;
- Japanese must be prepared to support a continued, substantial American ground, air, and naval presence in Japan and to sustain the division of labor by which Japan's Self-Defense forces defend their home islands while American forces manage the strategic defense of Japan and its more distant interests;
- the United States must have a non-hostile relationship, including dialogue and elements of military cooperation, with China;

- major changes in subregions like the Korean Peninsula and the Taiwan Strait, which have the potential to overthrow the existing military balance, must take place—if at all—by peaceful means rather than as a result of war;
- Southeast Asian nations must continue to exercise with and afford access to American forces based in Japan and the United States;
- the U.S.-Australia alliance must remain close and strong; and
- East Asians must perceive the United States as a wise, reliable, and sympathetic partner in the management of the region's security problems.

Many of these conditions are now under challenge, with the outcome far from clear. The major challenges, however, emanate from domestic factors in the United States, the uncertain evolution of U.S.-Japan relations, and the deteriorating American relationship with China. The United States cannot hope to manage either Korean or Southeast Asian security issues (such as disputes in the South China Sea) if the American people do not support an active U.S. military diplomacy in the region, if U.S.-Japan security ties weaken, or if Sino-American suspicion blossoms into hostility.

The Home Front

The support of the American people for a continued U.S. military role in the Western Pacific cannot be taken for granted. Strong leadership will be needed to sustain it. The collapse of the Soviet Union ended any apparent threat to the survival and independence of the United States. Now that these supreme national interests are no longer at stake, the mood in the United States has turned selfish and inward-looking. This is reflected in the collapse of budgets for the traditional instruments of American statecraft—a global diplomatic and consular presence, direct and indirect economic aid to nations of strategic or commercial significance, cultural exchange and other forms of public diplomacy, contributions to international organizations, and subsidized transfers of weapons to allies to raise the threshold at which they must call for American intervention.

American embassies around the world are closing. The U.S. Agency for International Development's (AID's) foreign assistance programs are rapidly contracting. The agency may be abolished outright. The U.S. Information Agency and its programs face a similar threat. American contributions to the World Bank and other international financial institutions are being cut or eliminated. The United States is now notoriously in arrears in its contributions to the United Nations Organization and its subordinate agencies, from several of which it has begun to withdraw. U.S. military assistance to allies and friends ended some years ago for all but Israel and its Camp David peace process partner, Egypt. Americans seem increasingly to define the appropriate international role for the United States solely in terms of trade and investment. They expect the United States to continue as the world's preeminent political and military power, but no longer seem prepared to pay the bills or sacrifice the lives that this role has traditionally entailed. Even popular issues, like nonproliferation and the environment, can no longer find much support for funding in Congress. More and more of what the United States attempts to do internationally must be done with other people's money.

This trend toward American withdrawal from a leading position in world affairs has yet to have much effect on the U.S. presence in the Asia-Pacific region, though AID missions are being closed and the diplomatic presence drawn down there as elsewhere. So far, with the exception of an unsuccessful challenge to the home porting of U.S. Navy ships in Japan by West Coast shipyard interests, no real debate about the American military presence in the region has emerged. Nevertheless, with the exception of the long-standing U.S. commitment to the defense of the Republic of Korea, the justification for a continuing American military presence in the Western Pacific is poorly understood and thinly supported by Americans. It remains to be seen whether that presence could withstand serious questioning. A compelling case can be made for continuing U.S. military engagement in the region, but no American leader has yet been stimulated to make it.

The U.S.-Japan Alliance

The cornerstone of the U.S. presence in the Western Pacific, as well as of American power and reach in Asia and adjacent areas, is the U.S.-Japan alliance. Without Japanese bases and financial support, the U.S. would be hard pressed to project power into the region, let alone beyond it into the Indian Ocean/Arabian Peninsula theater. Japan's alliance with the United States has precluded any Japanese requirement to develop substantial military forces, power projection capability, or a nuclear deterrent of its own. By furnishing these capabilities to Japan, the United States has made the reemergence of Japan as a potential military rival in Asia unthinkable. It has prevented the possible outbreak of military rivalry and arms races between Japan and China and has managed the emotionally charged Japan-Korea security relationship to the benefit of both sides. By maintaining bases in Japan, the United States has gained a relatively secure forward position from which to guarantee peace in Korea and the Taiwan Strait, project an ongoing presence in Southeast Asia, and secure sea lines of communication to the Indian Ocean. The United States has shared the financial burden of doing all this with Japanese taxpayers. The U.S.-Japan alliance has been, and remains, the basis for the status of the United States as the dominant military power in the Western Pacific.

Smaller U.S. forces, a more constrained defense budget, and reduced basing overseas have, if anything, emphasized the importance of Japan to the United States. For Japanese, however, the elimination—at least for the next decade or two—of Russia as an active strategic rival raised questions about the value of the U.S.-Japan alliance and the American military presence that it authorizes. A quiet debate soon began in Japan.

With the Soviet Union no more, Japanese asked what enemy they now needed Americans to help them deter. Neither Americans nor Japanese wished to posit China as such an enemy. (No one in the region believes that containment is a necessary or appropriate response to rising Chinese power or wishes to foster hostility and confrontation between Japan, China, and the United States.) Before Japan's debate could gather steam, however, north Korea's nuclear and missile threat emerged to provide an apparent answer to the question of who might threaten Japan. The threat of attack or intimidation from north Korea has now been adopted officially by Japan as the organizing principle for its defense. (Since north Korea, unlike the Soviet Union, cannot invade Japan, Tokyo is reducing the size of the Japanese land forces to reflect the lessened risk of ground combat in the home islands.)

The new Japanese focus on the north Korean threat has set aside the debate in Japan. North Korea alone, however, does not provide a long-term basis for U.S.-Japan defense cooperation. Under some circumstances, north Korea might pose a direct threat to Japan. (In the event of conflict in the Korean peninsula, Pyongyang would wish to deter active Japanese cooperation with Seoul's American allies. It would also wish to deny the United States a secure rear area in Japan from which U.S. forces could act against north Korean forces and targets. That is, presumably, a major motivation for Pyongyang's nuclear and missile programs.) By no measure, however, is north Korea as compelling a threat to Japan as the former Soviet Union was. Were Korea to be reunified or north Korea to renounce its nuclear weapons and missile programs, the United States would still wish to maintain forces in Japan. Washington would see this as serving common American and Japanese regional and global interests. Would Tokyo? The rationale for U.S.-Japan securities ties needs broadening, redefinition, and renewal. That is why the Pentagon, through Assistant Secretary Joseph Nye, has sought a security dialogue with Tokyo. Nye's sudden departure from office, however, has raised doubts in Tokyo about how vigorously his successors will pursue this dialogue.

The diminished Japanese sense of external threat has, meanwhile, made Japanese less willing than they once were to tolerate the inevitable frictions from foreign bases and forces on their territory. The replacement of Liberal Democratic Party dominance in Japanese politics has weakened Tokyo vis-à-vis Japanese local authorities. The trend toward less centralized Japanese politics is likely to accelerate as a new election law replacing proportional representation with geographic constituencies takes hold. As local issues assume greater salience in Japanese politics, it will be harder for Tokyo to constrain local resentment and objections to the U.S. military presence and for Washington to finesse complaints from local Japanese communities. The Okinawa child-rape case has served to warn Tokyo and Washington of this. The incident has galvanized a long-overdue dialogue about how to redeploy U.S. forces to minimize friction between them and their Japanese hosts. This process, timely and necessary as it is, is likely to be protracted and contentious. Repeated eruptions in troubled U.S.-Japan trade and investment relations will not ease its management.

The U.S. Presence in Korea

U.S. forces in the Republic of Korea have been, and remain, an essential deterrent to efforts by the failing north Korean regime to solve its problems by conquering the South. The danger of such an attack is now cresting, as Pyongyang's military capabilities reach their apogee amidst economic bankruptcy and political uncertainty. North Korea cannot long sustain the extraordinary burden of war preparations it has assumed. As its capabilities recede, attention will naturally turn to how to arrange a soft landing for the north Korean regime. Having seen the strain reunification placed on Germany, Koreans hope for an evolutionary rather than sudden disappearance of the border between north and south.

As long as U.S. forces must deter north Korean attack, they are strategically immobilized. Their departure from the Korean peninsula would risk north Korean adventurism. (Such adventurism could also be stimulated by an outbreak of major conflict elsewhere that could delay reinforcement of U.S. forces in Korea.) Should the threat from the north disappear, however, Washington and Seoul would have to consider whether to withdraw U.S. forces from Korea.

Some in Seoul argue strongly that U.S. forces should remain even after reunification. They see a continuing U.S. presence as enabling Korea to play a pivotal role in Northeast Asia between China and Japan. They also see utility in a continuing U.S. force presence in Japan to serve as a bridge between the Korean and Japanese militaries. Many Japanese wish U.S. forces to remain in both countries for the same reason. Others see a continuing U.S. presence in Korea as facilitating a U.S. drawdown in Japan. Popular attitudes in Korea are, however, increasingly hostile to the U.S. military presence. Koreans might well prove responsive to a Chinese campaign arguing for U.S. withdrawal, if Chinese came to see a continuing U.S. presence in Asia as threatening or adverse to China's interests.

The U.S.-China Relationship

Cooperative interaction by the United States, including the U.S. armed forces, with China is essential to any American role as balancer and facilitator in Asia-Pacific security matters. How Beijing pursues adjustment of its multiple differences with other Asian capitals (territorial disputes with Japan, the Philippines, Vietnam, Brunei, Malaysia, and India; seabed disputes with both Koreas and Indonesia; rivalry with Taiwan) will determine whether Asia remains at peace or drifts toward confrontation. Without an active dialogue with China, the United States cannot play a moderating role in these disputes. Nor can peace and stability in Korea and South Asia or proliferation issues in these subregions be easily managed. Asian-Pacific transnational issues such as drug trafficking and illegal migration also are intractable without Beijing's help. Regional considerations alone furnish ample reason for the U.S. and China to cooperate. The U.S.-China relationship is, however, increasingly troubled.

The collapse of a common enemy—the Soviet Union—at the end of the 1980s destroyed the strategic rationale for U.S.-China relations. As the Washington–Moscow–Beijing strategic triangle vanished into history, so did the mutual tolerance of ideological differences and patient problem-solving approach that the United States and China had made guiding principles of their relations. The catalytic event was the uprising in Tiananmen Square and the sharp American reaction to its brutal suppression. Since June 4, 1989, the Sino-American relationship has been dominated by American criticism of Chinese human-rights practices and Chinese defiance of U.S. efforts to coerce internal change in China through ostracism and economic pressure.

Mutual understanding between the United States and China, including on matters normally as remote from politics as—for example—the environment, has atrophied along with strategic dialogue. For American politicians, China is no longer "politically correct." For Chinese politicians, the United States is now a bully to be resisted. This atmosphere is not conducive to problem-solving. Under its influence, differences between Washington and Beijing on issues as varied as the rules for global trade, technology transfer, investment, and nonproliferation, Tibet, Hong Kong, territorial disputes in the South China Sea, and the regional balances in South Asia and the Persian Gulf have widened and deepened.

The most dangerous differences between the U.S. and China are, however, those that have arisen over Taiwan. These have their roots in events in Taiwan itself. On the one hand, Taiwan's emergence as a prosperous, modernized, democratic Chinese society has attracted the admiration of many Chinese across the Strait as well as most Americans. Many on the mainland hope that Taiwan's evolution, in which economic liberalization preceded political liberalization, will be recapitulated in the rest of China. They see the gradual reunification of the two sides of the Taiwan Strait as central to the realization of this hope. On the other hand, Taiwan's politics have come to center on the island's identity crisis. The dream of reunification has steadily lost ground to the vision of a distinct Taiwanese national identity, expressed through Taiwan's achievement of internationally recognized independence.

For decades, Taipei enlisted the support of the United States in insisting at the United Nations and elsewhere that there was only one China and that there could be only one legitimate Chinese government, that Taiwan was part of China, and that the capital of China was Taipei, not Beijing. Now that Beijing is almost universally acknowledged as the capital of China, Taipei is seeking to enlist the United States in support of the contrary thesis that, whatever China may be, it consists of "two equal political entities"—two states—that should be recognized as such by the international community and enjoy separate seats in the United Nations. Taipei's efforts to separate itself from the "one China" principle through "pragmatic diplomacy" have already generated serious frictions between Beijing and Washington. Taiwanese separatist impulses now risk military action by Beijing against Taiwan itself.

On one level, the American position is clear. In 1979, the United States switched its diplomatic recognition from Taipei to Beijing as the sole legal government of China. It acknowledged the Chinese position that Taiwan is part of China. (The Chinese version of the joint communiqué accomplishing this states that the United States "recognizes the position of China" that this is so.) Within this context, the United States traded the form of its relations with Taipei for their substance, undertaking to maintain only "economic, cultural and other unofficial relations with the people of Taiwan." On this "one China" basis, Washington's relations with Beijing were normalized while unofficial American ties with Taiwan flourished.

The end of the American military presence in Taiwan and the U.S. defense treaty with Taipei permitted Beijing to set aside threats to "liberate" Taiwan in favor of "a fundamental policy of striving for peaceful reunification." Continuing U.S. arms sales to Taiwan, authorized by domestic U.S. legislation (the Taiwan Relations Act), underscored the abiding American interest in a "peaceful settlement" of the Taiwan issue by the two sides. It assured that Taiwan could maintain a formidable military deterrent against attack from the mainland and gave Taiwan's people the sense of security they needed to risk rapprochement with Chinese across the Strait. Taipei's and Beijing's common view that there was only "one China" removed any sense of urgency about reunification. This consensus was the basis for a tacit *modus vivendi* in the Taiwan Strait. It produced a remarkable relaxation of tensions and facilitated surprisingly rapid expansion of relationships and dialogue between the two sides. It made possible the end of martial law in Taiwan and the island's transformation into a democratic society. Americans, as well as Chinese on the mainland and in Taiwan, reaped major benefits from the emergence and apparent consolidation of the tacit *modus vivendi* in the Taiwan Strait.

It is this *modus vivendi* that has now broken down. Taipei's drive for international recognition as the capital of a state distinct from the rest of China found dramatic expression this spring. Taiwan's president, Lee Teng-hui, made a private but highly political visit to the United States while its premier, Lien Chan, was received officially in central Europe. On their return to Taipei, they offered the United Nations $1 billion for a separate seat for Taiwan in the General Assembly. Beijing saw these actions as a frontal assault by Taipei on the "one China" principle that had undergirded the *modus vivendi* in the Taiwan Strait. It saw the series of policy decisions in Washington that culminated in Lee Teng-hui's visit as signaling an American intention to abandon a "one China" policy. It saw the United States as complicit in Taiwanese separatism.

The Chinese leadership concluded that the United States was attempting to divide China (by permanently slicing off Taiwan, detaching Tibet, and subverting Chinese control of post-1997 Hong Kong), to weaken China politically (by supporting dissidents and fostering opposition to Communist Party rule), and to retard China's modernization (by restricting technology transfer and excluding China from the World Trade Organization). The subsequent U.S. normalization of relations with Vietnam only strengthened perceptions in Beijing that Americans were moving to "contain" China in order to generate a Soviet-style collapse.

Beijing's first priority was to obtain renewed assurances of American fidelity to a "one China" policy. It withdrew its ambassador from Washington, withheld agrément for a new American ambassador, canceled high-level defense and military exchanges, and broke off dialogue on issues of special concern to the United States until it obtained such assurances. With these in hand, Beijing has turned its attention to Taipei.

The People's Republic of China (PRC) has not abandoned its policy of a negotiated settlement with Taipei. Rather than waiting patiently for negotiations to evolve from the past few years informal "Ku-Wang talks," however, Beijing now seeks to compel Taipei either to desist from further efforts to achieve an identity separate from China or to agree to "reunification" on the very loose terms Beijing has proposed. (According to Chinese officials, under reunification, Taiwan would retain its armed forces and continue to buy arms from abroad. No mainland officials would be stationed on Taiwan, which would maintain its own distinct political system and administration. Taiwan officials would, however, be invited to participate in governing the mainland. Recently, Beijing has unofficially suggested that it might be prepared to negotiate a change in the PRC's name, flag, and anthem; that arrangements could be negotiated for Taiwan to take a seat at the United Nations; and that a division of diplomatic labor could be worked out by which Taipei's embassies could represent China in some foreign capitals.)

Beijing has given military backing to its drive to replace the shattered tacit *modus vivendi* in the Taiwan Strait with an explicit one. For the first time in decades, it is mounting military operations against Taiwan. (Initially, these were called exercises, directed by the headquarters of a "military region." They are now called "operations" in a "war zone.") The escalating military pressure is likely to peak as Taiwanese go to the polls for the first direct election of a president on March 23, 1996. If the new president (very likely a convincingly reelected Lee Teng-hui) shows no convincing sign of willingness to turn from "separatism" and open negotiations with Beijing, the People's Liberation Army avows that it is prepared for further escalation, including low-intensity conflict and, possibly, direct strikes by missiles at targets in Taiwan.

In addition to the breakdown of peace and stability in the Taiwan Strait, such an outcome would also mark the discrediting of long-standing American efforts to deter conflict in the Taiwan Strait. At some point, the United States would have to choose between combat support of Taiwan against the PRC and neutrality in their conflict. It is no exaggeration to say that the consequences of either choice for strategic stability in the Asia-Pacific region would be dire, even catastrophic.

Given the strategic importance of Taiwan to Japan, an American decision to stand aside from conflict in the Taiwan Strait would be seen by Japanese as a default on the U.S. responsibility to manage Japan's strategic defense. The Japanese reaction would be all the stronger because of the emotional links between Japanese and many Taiwanese. (Taiwanese are the only former subjects of the Japanese emperor who remain close to their ex–colonial masters.) No longer confident that the United States could be depended upon to do the job for it, Japan would have to reassume responsibility for its own strategic defense.

If the United States decided to intervene in support of Taiwan, it would have to use Japanese bases to do so. Tokyo would then have to decide between its policy of good relations with Beijing, on the one hand, and its alliance with Washington and interests in Taiwan, on the other. It would almost certainly opt for Washington and Taipei. No future Japanese government, however, would be willing ever again to be put in a position where foreigners made such fundamental choices for Japanese. The result would be a slower reassumption by Japan of responsibility for its own defense.

The strategic consequences of conflict in the Taiwan Strait therefore include not just the poisoning of U.S.-China relations for decades and a setback for China's modernization, but fundamental realignment of the Asian strategic balance. Japanese rearmament, in the context of hostility between Japan and China, would polarize the Asia-Pacific region and marginalize the role of the United States. Japan might even, in time, turn to Russia, India, and Southeast Asia as partners in a strategy to balance the rising power of China.

These effects of the outbreak of war in the Taiwan Strait would unfold regardless of whether the United States intervened or not and regardless of whether Beijing succeeded or failed in regaining Taiwan for China. Beijing's arguments that the Taiwan issue is legally a matter of China's internal affairs may be right, but these arguments miss the most important point. Politically and strategically, Taiwan is anything but a local affair. How this issue unfolds in the coming months will decide whether harmony or confrontation prevails in the Asia-Pacific region. It may also decide whether the United States can retain the highly influential role Americans have come to take for granted there.

It is clearly in the interest of the United States to avoid an outbreak of conflict in the Taiwan Strait. Americans do not want to have to make a choice between intervention and nonintervention in the Taiwan Strait, i.e., between war and peace with China. It is therefore in the American interest for Beijing and Taipei to negotiate a renewed *modus vivendi*. The United States should vigorously promote such negotiations as the only viable alternative to confrontation and conflict. Doing so would not be easy. Neither Taipei nor Beijing wants war, but neither is in the mood to compromise. Each needs to be brought to face unpalatable realities. In their own interests, each needs to reach difficult accommodations with the other.

Taipei must confront the reality that it cannot determine its status in defiance of Beijing's views. Taiwan's past and present are linked to the past and present of Chinese across the Strait. Taiwan's future is also linked to them. Whoever rules Taiwan, and whatever the island calls itself, Taipei must have a working relationship with Beijing. The quality of that relationship—not whether Taipei sits in international councils—will determine the level of security and prosperity Taiwan and its people enjoy. Taiwan can win a battle with the Chinese mainland; it cannot win a war.

Beijing must confront the reality that confrontation and combat with Taiwan, rather than accommodation and peaceful interaction, are likely to create a fundamentally adverse and hostile international environment for China. China's modernization, its links to the outside world, and its relationships with other great powers in the Asia-Pacific region and beyond would be the victims of such an environment.

Conclusion

The vision of the United States as the manager of an evolving cooperative security system in the Asia-Pacific region is an appealing one. Without greater efforts by Washington, however, this vision seems likely to be stillborn. Trends and events in the region may already be overtaking it as U.S. attention focuses on Bosnia, Haiti, and other events far from Asia.

Leadership is like muscle tissue. Unless it is exercised, it atrophies. Many in Asia see the last minute decision by President Clinton, in the face of domestic political distractions, not to attend the Asia-Pacific Economic Cooperation (APEC) meeting in Osaka as emblematic of a lack of U.S. interest in and commitment to participating actively in the affairs of the region. Others fear that the drift in U.S.-Japan security relations, which efforts by both sides had begun to reverse, may now resume. Asians are especially disturbed by the erratic course of U.S. relations with China.

American aspirations to help Asians resolve disputes by measures short of war, rather than in combat, now face a major test in the Taiwan Strait. So far, the United States has seemed reluctant to recognize that there is a problem, let alone to bring American diplomacy to bear on the Chinese parties to it. An American default on this urgent challenge will not augur well for the prolongation of the "American century" in the Asia-Pacific region.

The Aftermath of the 1995–1996 Taiwan Crisis[8]
May 1998

A little over two years ago, China and the United States stumbled into a military confrontation in the Taiwan Strait that neither had sought or anticipated. The March 1996 face-off between U.S. aircraft carriers and Chinese warships and rocket forces seems in retrospect, however, to have had some salutary effects. The crisis reminded both countries of the huge stake each has in successful management of relations with the other, and of the continuing centrality of the Taiwan issue to this task. Both have taken that reminder to heart.

Since March 1996, the two governments have worked hard to establish a mutually respectful dialogue about a widening range of bilateral and international issues. Summits and other high level meetings are once again a regular feature of the Sino-American relationship. There have been no further episodes of military confrontation in the Taiwan area. Last fall, when he met with his Chinese counterpart, Jiang Zemin, in the United States, President Bill Clinton urged the earliest possible resumption of dialogue between Beijing and Taipei. In early 1998, after three years of posturing to place the blame for the rupture in dialogue on each other, Beijing and Taipei finally began to exchange proposals about where and how to meet. In late April 1998 (just two months before President Clinton's scheduled return visit to China), Taipei agreed to send a delegation to Beijing to talk about what issues the two sides might take up if they met.

Many observers have concluded from these developments that Washington, Beijing, and Taipei each learned the appropriate lessons from the military confrontation of March 1996. The miscalculations in all three capitals that led to escalating military tensions between them have, they believe, been corrected, making another crisis in the Taiwan Strait unlikely.

But Washington, Taipei, and Beijing see the causes and consequences of what happened—the U.S. carrier deployment, the Chinese missile firings that evoked the U.S. deployment, the Taiwanese drive to alter the international context of the Taiwan question that provoked the Chinese shows of force—very differently. The lessons each has drawn from its experience of three-way brinkmanship are in direct and dangerous conflict. Beijing's and Taipei's conclusions, in particular, are so diametrically opposed as to justify serious concern. The March 1996 crisis may yet turn out to have been the dress rehearsal for a bloody resumption of the long-dormant Chinese civil war that could trigger armed conflict between the People's Republic of China and the United States. To prevent this will require some adjustments in U.S. policy.

Lessons Learned: American Views

President Clinton's skillfully executed decision to deploy two aircraft carriers to the Taiwan area was aimed at reassuring Asian allies and friends that the United States remains committed to the maintenance of peace and stability in the Asia-Pacific region. It was carried out, in particular, to underscore the abiding U.S. interest in assuring that resolution of the Taiwan question occur by peaceful rather than violent means. The deployment achieved both of these objectives.

The major lesson drawn from the crisis by Americans, including most members of Congress, was that the prospect of U.S. military intervention could deter a Chinese attack on Taiwan. When the administration made its deployment decision, however, it did not believe that it was putting U.S. forces in harm's way. It judged, correctly, that the Chinese had no intention of attacking Taiwan. There is also no evidence that the arrival of U.S. forces caused the People's Liberation Army to alter or curtail its March 1996 exercise, the last of six escalating shows of force it had planned and begun in July 1995. Still, the carrier deployment set a benchmark for an American response to any apparent threat to Taiwan that future presidents cannot ignore.

Many Americans believe that the United States is obliged to come to Taiwan's aid regardless of whether Taiwan's own actions have provoked conflict. Nevertheless, the March 1996 war scare in the Taiwan Strait brought home the potential costs of acquiescing in Taiwanese attempts at political one-upmanship, like Lee Teng-hui's ill-advised visit to Cornell University in June 1995. (Lee's private, but congressionally mandated and highly political, visit to the United States—to launch a professorship he had endowed, at an event he had paid for—was the proximate cause of escalating military tensions in the Strait.) Members of Congress are somewhat more cautious than before in voting to support initiatives from Taipei that might have unintended consequences for U.S. relations with China. The Clinton administration—if not yet Congress—has begun to grapple with the need to convince Taipei to refrain from further actions likely to provoke rising military tensions and the danger of war in the Taiwan Strait.

Taiwan's Reactions
In Taiwan, the six PLA shows of force that followed Lee Teng-hui's visit to the United States in July 1995 stimulated fear and dislike of the PRC in Taiwan and accelerated the demise of popular support for the idea of reunification. As military tensions rose, however, many on the island began to consider how to accommodate Chinese on the mainland. The sudden arrival of U.S. aircraft carriers during the sixth and final round of PLA maneuvers in March 1996 halted further consideration of conciliatory moves toward Beijing. It convinced the leaders of Taiwan's ruling and opposition parties that they could count on U.S. intervention to shield them from PRC military challenges to any policy shifts they may undertake. The Clinton administration has attempted to shake this conviction through quiet dialogue with Taipei, but Taiwanese leaders put much more credence in the unqualified public statements of support they hear from sympathetic members of Congress. They make no secret of their belief that, whatever the cause of a future crisis in the Taiwan Strait, any executive branch reluctance to come to their aid would quickly succumb to congressional pressure.

Taiwanese politicians have concluded that they have wide latitude to reject the idea of reunification and to maneuver the island toward international status as a sovereign, independent nation. Some, including President Lee and the leader of the opposition Democratic Progressive Party, Hsu Hsin-liang, define such status as international acceptance of the "Republic of China," now reduced in territory to Taiwan and a few offshore islands, as a sovereign state distinct from the PRC. Lee's Kuomintang still pays lip service to reunification, saying that it can be considered when and if the Chinese mainland democratizes; Hsu's DPP flatly opposes reunification under any circumstances. Other DPP leaders, including the popular mayor of Taipei, Chen Shui-bian (who many see as Taiwan's next president), favor a plebiscite to approve creation of a "Republic of Taiwan."

Beijing's Conclusions

The Lee visit to the United States and subsequent events led the leadership in Beijing to three quite different conclusions.

The first is that, given the evolution of Taiwan's politics, a policy based on the pursuit of peaceful reunification faces diminishing prospects of success. Taipei's agreement to reunification, even under the most generous terms, seems increasingly implausible. Beijing is convinced that Taiwanese leaders are no longer interested in exploring how to reunify China. Rather, their objective is to find a way to internationalize the Taiwan issue so as to keep the island separate from the PRC. Taiwanese nationalism is pushing the island toward ever more overt attempts to achieve international recognition—under one formula or another—as a sovereign state, distinct from China proper, with no organic relationship to Beijing. China's leaders have reluctantly concluded that, more likely than not, they will eventually have to use force to prevent Taiwanese politicians from carrying out actions intended to preclude reunification or to alienate the island irrevocably from Chinese sovereignty.

The March 1996 crisis also forced Beijing to come to grips with the fact that the PLA is still far from ready to take Taiwan by force, if that becomes necessary to prevent its secession. It will take nearly a decade of concentrated effort for China's armed forces to acquire the capabilities, do the planning, and make the other preparations required to have a serious chance of overwhelming Taiwan's formidable defenses. (It may in fact take longer, given the exceptionally rapid force modernization underway in Taiwan.) Building a credible capability to conquer Taiwan has become the highest priority for PLA force planners. China's civilian and military leaders are well aware of the disastrous political, economic, and military costs an effort to conquer Taiwan would entail, even if it succeeded. They hope that demonstrating the capability to invade will be enough to dissuade

Taiwanese from separatism and to persuade them to open serious negotiations about their long-term relationship with the rest of China.

Finally, Beijing concluded that, if it becomes necessary actually to use force against Taiwan, the PLA would almost certainly confront military opposition from U.S. Navy aircraft carriers, possibly backstopped by U.S. Air Force units in Japan. Chinese forces must therefore be prepared either to take Taiwan so rapidly that the United States and Japan are presented with a *fait accompli* or to defeat any U.S. forces that might intervene.

In short, the crisis left Washington confident that war in the Taiwan Strait was deterred and could be deterred indefinitely by bloodless shows of force. It raised hopes among Taiwanese that they would have American military backing for future attempts to end their island's association with China. And it convinced Beijing that, much as it would prefer not to, it must be prepared to invade Taiwan and fight the United States to keep the island at least nominally part of China.

"One China" and "Peaceful Settlement"
Despite recent efforts by Taiwanese nationalists to raise doubts about whether Taiwan ought to be part of China, there is no international dispute that it is. No nation contested China's legal capacity either to cede its island province to Japan in 1895 or to take it back—with American help—after Japan's defeat in 1945. Nor did anyone regard the withdrawal of Chiang Kai-shek's Kuomintang government and armed forces to Taiwan, after the Chinese Communist Party defeated the KMT on the Chinese mainland, as a flight abroad. As the PLA gathered on the other side of the Taiwan Strait in late 1949 and early 1950, the United States made it clear that it had no intention of intervening to prevent the complete victory in the Chinese civil war that CCP conquest of Taiwan would have signified.

North Korea's sudden invasion of south Korea on June 25, 1950, left the United States with little choice but to intervene. Two days later, the U.S. Seventh Fleet deployed to preclude the spread of the Korean conflict to the Taiwan Strait by preventing either party to the Chinese civil war from attacking the other. This decision to enforce a U.S.-declared cease-fire in the Taiwan Strait did not, however, alter Washington's view of Taiwan's status. For more than two decades, the United States championed the right of the Republic of China (ROC) government in Taipei to represent all of China, including areas of the China mainland never under its effective control (like Tibet), in international capitals and the United Nations. The U.S. government did so, in part, on the grounds that the ROC government had not been driven from China and was therefore not a government in exile. It was still on Chinese soil, inasmuch as Taiwan was part of China, American diplomats asserted.

For his part, Chiang Kai-shek was just as insistent on the principle that there was and could be only "one China" as Mao Zedong. His government's claim to be the government of China was central to its legitimacy as ruler in Taiwan. Forty years ago, John Foster Dulles attempted to persuade Chiang to renounce the use of force against Chinese on the other side of the Taiwan Strait. Chiang's answer was the same as that given by Chinese leaders in Beijing today. His was the sole legal government of China, including both Taiwan and the mainland, he asserted. No government wants to have to use force against its own citizens, Chiang said, but no government can give up the right to take military action against armed opposition groups on its own soil.

Until recently, this cross-Strait consensus that Taiwan was a province of China, destined ultimately to be reunited with the rest of the country under a single Chinese government (either the PRC or ROC), defined every element of the contest between Beijing and Taipei. It enabled President Richard Nixon and Premier Zhou Enlai to agree to disagree about Taiwan ("the crucial question obstructing the normalization of relations" between Washington and Beijing) in order to pursue broader strategic interests. In the Shanghai Communiqué of February 28, 1972, the U.S. side declared: "The United States acknowledges that all Chinese on either side of the Taiwan Strait maintain there is but one China and that Taiwan is a part of China. The United States Government does not challenge that position. It reaffirms its interest its interest in a peaceful settlement of the Taiwan question by the Chinese themselves."

The idea of "one China" has deep roots in Chinese nationalism. The related concept of a negotiated resolution of the Chinese civil war through "peaceful settlement of the Taiwan question by the Chinese themselves" was, however, an American innovation. Neither the KMT nor the CCP initially believed that a negotiated settlement was possible. Neither has ever wanted Americans or other foreigners involved in trying to broker one.

The CCP's attitude toward Taiwan, in particular, was driven by its perception that the U.S. military presence and defense commitment to Taiwan were an effort to deny the CCP victory in the Chinese civil war and to perpetuate the colonial-era division of China into foreign-dominated spheres of influence. It was not until the United States began the process of terminating its defense treaty and cutting official ties with Taipei (January 1, 1979) that the PRC officially embraced the idea of negotiations with Taipei. China's new leader, Deng Xiaoping, then abandoned three decades of Maoist rhetoric about the "liberation" of Taiwan and promulgated "a fundamental policy of striving for peaceful reunification." Deng proposed a version of his "one China, two systems" approach (successfully applied in Hong Kong since July 1, 1997), to be agreed upon in negotiations between

Beijing and Taipei. To underscore its interest in peaceful reunification, the PLA halted artillery barrages against the KMT-held islands of Quemoy and Matsu. Taipei's armed forces reciprocated.

"Peaceful Settlement" and U.S. Arms Sales to Taiwan

Taiwan's prosperity and democratic society are mainly the proud creation of the labors and sacrifices of its own people. But they are also an achievement of U.S. diplomacy. The increased sense of security that made it possible for Taiwan to become a prosperous democracy was the direct result of U.S. China policy. For decades, the United States interposed its forces to protect Taiwan from forcible incorporation into the PRC. The United States was able to end this military confrontation with the PRC when it persuaded Beijing that, given the cross-Strait consensus on the principle of "one China," there was a credible prospect that it could peacefully negotiate an end to the division of China. Beijing's belief that this was so was a key factor in its decision to negotiate terms for the return of Hong Kong and Macao to Chinese sovereignty that tolerate more than one politico-economic and social system within "one China." (As many used to remark, Beijing could have "taken Hong Kong [or Macao] with a phone call.") The United States continued arms sales to Taiwan to ensure that Taipei would have a self-defense capability sufficient to prevent Beijing from unilaterally imposing a solution and to bolster Taipei's confidence in its ability to negotiate a mutually acceptable relationship with Chinese across the strait.

The domestic legal authority for the president to continue arms sales to Taiwan is the Taiwan Relations Act (TRA) of April 10, 1979. The TRA is premised on the fact that, on January 1, 1979, the president "terminated governmental relations between the United States and the governing authorities on Taiwan" and transferred diplomatic recognition and relations to Beijing. Washington secured Beijing's agreement to the continuation of American "commercial, cultural, and other [unofficial] relations" with the people of Taiwan before doing so.

The TRA stresses "the expectation [of the United States in switching relations from Taipei to Beijing] that the future of Taiwan will be determined by peaceful means." It declares that "any effort to determine the future of Taiwan by other than peaceful means . . . [would be considered] a threat to the peace and security of the Western Pacific area and of grave concern to the United States." It pledges that U.S. forces will "maintain the capacity . . . to resist any resort to force or other forms of coercion that would jeopardize the security, or the social or economic system, of the people on Taiwan." The overall purpose of the TRA is stated as "to help maintain peace, security, and stability in the Western Pacific." To this end, the TRA authorizes the sale to Taiwan of "arms of a defensive character" to enable it "to maintain a sufficient self-defense capability."

Differences over American arms sales to Taiwan led to a crisis in Sino-American relations in 1981 and '82. On August 17, 1982, President Ronald Reagan announced that he had reached an understanding with the Chinese government on "a mutually satisfactory means of dealing with the historical question of U.S. arms sales to Taiwan." In the U.S.-China Joint Communiqué issued that day, the United States announced a cap on the quality and quantity of arms and a gradual reduction in arms sales to Taiwan, premised on China's efforts to achieve "a peaceful solution to the Taiwan question." President Reagan stressed that future U.S. actions would "be conducted with this peaceful policy fully in mind. The position of the United States Government has always been clear and consistent in this regard. The Taiwan question is a matter for the Chinese people, on both sides of the Taiwan Strait, to resolve."

Progress toward "Peaceful Resolution"
The cause of such a peaceful resolution was well served by subsequent developments. During the 1980s, the PLA withdrew most of its forces and installations from areas across the Strait from Taiwan. Beijing and Taipei turned from military confrontation to the cautious promotion of economic interdependence and human contacts across the Strait. Taipei consistently rejected Beijing's proposals for the formal relaxation of barriers to direct trade, communications, and travel (the so-called "three links"). But the absence of military confrontation and the confidence imparted by continuing U.S. arms sales allowed the Taiwan authorities to acquiesce in a broad de facto expansion of trade and investment ties across the Strait. (There were no economic links at all between Taiwan and the mainland in 1982.) By 1997, cross-Strait trade had reached an annual rate of about $26.5 billion, and some thirty-five thousand Taiwan companies had invested an estimated $30 billion or more in the PRC. Nearly 1.5 million visits—the vast majority of them visits from Taiwan to the Chinese mainland—were taking place each year.

The steady relaxation of tensions between the contending Chinese parties culminated in a 1993 meeting in Singapore between senior, authorized (but nominally "unofficial") emissaries from Beijing and Taipei. The meeting produced agreement on four minor steps to facilitate the exchange of mail and trade across the strait. It also established a regular channel of continuing communication between the non-governmental organizations each side had established to handle discussions with the other.

Beijing went to Singapore to explore ways of giving expression to the "principle of one China" consistent with its concept of "one country, two systems." Taipei entered the Singapore talks under its Guidelines for National Unification. These guidelines envisaged a phased approach to reunification under which talks on private sector exchanges would gradually be succeeded by high-level visits and eventually by formal negotiations between the two sides. The two sides agreed to disagree on what the "principle of one China" might mean in practice. On that basis, they agreed to further talks. A round of such talks was finally scheduled for June 1995, but was cancelled after Lee Teng-hui's speech at Cornell University stressed his government's sovereign, independent status without addressing the question of national reunification.

The End of Rapprochement

Lee's statements, Beijing's subsequent military riposte, and the U.S. reaction to it accelerated the evolution in Taiwan's increasingly lively democratic politics. In December 1996, a four-party "national development conference" produced a consensus between Lee's KMT and the opposition Democratic Progressive Party that set aside the Guidelines on National Unification. The conference formalized Taipei's rejection of Beijing's (and the late Chiang Kai-shek's) insistence on "one China" as well as its "one country, two systems" proposal for negotiations to realize reunification. (A pro-reunification KMT splinter party declined to join this consensus, while agreeing that any talks with Beijing should take as their first priority the interests of the 21 million people of Taiwan rather than those of China as a whole. A pro-independence DPP splinter party walked out on the conference on the grounds that it did not call for outright independence from China.) By late 1997, in case anyone had missed the point, Lee Teng-hui convened reporters from the *Times* of London and the *Washington Post* to assert that his government ruled a "sovereign, independent state" entitled to separate recognition as such by the international community "just like the United Kingdom."

Lee's logic was straightforward and unmuddied by nuance. The ROC, he asserted, has been since 1912 and remains a sovereign, independent state; the jurisdiction of the ROC is now limited to Taiwan, the Pescadores, and the offshore islands of Quemoy and Matsu—the Taiwan area. The ROC is therefore coterminous with and identical to Taiwan. Taiwan is thus a sovereign, independent state under the name "Republic of China." Since Taiwan is already independent from the PRC under that name, it has no need to declare independence under another name, such as "Republic of Taiwan," Lee concluded.

Lee's position neatly combines the thesis that there are now two Chinese states with the cause of Taiwan independence. It has enabled his KMT to reach a consensus on cross-Strait relations with the mainstream of the DPP, represented by Hsu Hsin-liang. At the same time, however, it is a repudiation of the cross-Strait consensus on "one China" that was the basis of both the U.S. position on peaceful settlement and the dialogue between Beijing and Taipei begun at Singapore in 1993. In seeking to defend their claim that their new position is somehow consistent with "one China," KMT spokespeople now argue that the "China" of which Taiwan is a part is a historical or cultural expression rather than a nation-state. (The DPP does not accept Taiwan's status as part of China, so it sees no need to address the issue.)

Taiwan's efforts to redefine itself as a sovereign, independent, even if perhaps "Chinese," nation-state distinct from the PRC have been accompanied by well-financed "pragmatic diplomacy" aimed at changing the international context of the Taiwan question. Lee Teng-hui's fateful visit to the United States in June 1995 is merely the best-known example of this diplomacy. Senior Taiwanese officials have made visits to many other countries to raise the island's international profile. Taipei's efforts to create an international identity as a separate state include the use of economic grants and aid programs to persuade developing countries (primarily in Africa) to establish diplomatic relations with it as well as with Beijing. Taiwan has also mounted a campaign to gain a separate seat for itself among the member states of the United Nations and other international organizations. Taipei justifies these efforts to gain "international space" as essential to its security as a political entity distinct from the PRC.

The skill of Taiwan's diplomacy (which ranks among the world's very best) and the attractiveness of its wealthy and sophisticated democratic Chinese society in comparison with the poor and backward autocracy of the PRC give it natural advantages in this search for international favor. Nevertheless, the principal result of Taipei's campaign to date—as seen most clearly in the events that followed Lee's visit to Cornell—has been to provoke Beijing into counteractions that have resurrected a serious long-term threat to Taiwan's security. Taipei's efforts to purchase favor in foreign capitals have set off a diplomatic bidding war with Beijing in Africa, with some countries shifting relations back and forth between the rival Chinese capitals.

Ironically, Taipei's approach to membership in international organizations as a zero-sum point-scoring contest with Beijing has halted the progress Taipei had been making toward gaining representation in them. (In practice, given Beijing's veto and ability to muster blocking majorities, Taiwan cannot join international organizations unless Beijing agrees. Beijing has been willing to do so when the island has refrained from seeking to establish status as a "state" separate from China. For example, an earlier Taiwan government won Beijing's acquiescence in its membership in the Asian Development Bank as "Chinese Taipei.")

Taipei's search for "international space" is entirely understandable in terms of its people's desire for recognition of their political and economic achievements ("honor" or "face"). Judging by results, however, the pursuit of "international space" is not a strategy that can enhance Taiwan's prosperity and security, or even promote its substantive participation in international society. Taiwan's prosperity and security depend on the character of its relationship with the nearly 1.3 billion Chinese across the Taiwan Strait. Taipei's experience is proving how counterproductive it is to deny or defy this ineluctable reality.

Taipei's recent statements and actions assert a unilateral right to determine Taiwan's future, regardless of the previous cross-Strait consensus on "one China" or the views of non-Taiwanese Chinese on either the island or the mainland. Taiwan's politicians propose to establish Taiwan as a sovereign independent state with its own seat in the United Nations (either under the name "Republic of China" or "Republic of Taiwan"). Taipei is well aware that the solution it proposes implies permanent national dismemberment for China. Given the force of Chinese nationalism, this is an absolutely unacceptable outcome to mainland Chinese. It would be a *casus belli* for any mainland Chinese government; it is such a *casus belli* for the PRC. Taiwan's new focus on separation rather than reunification has thus greatly increased the prospects that the peace, stability, and security of the Western Pacific will be shattered by renewed conflict in the Taiwan Strait.

Much Ado about Little?

Even if Taiwan were somehow to gain international recognition for its status as a sovereign state, independent of China, it is difficult to see what benefits Taiwan would accrue from this other than a flag and other symbols of nationhood. Taiwan is currently a valued *de facto* participant in international and regional affairs, especially in economic affairs. Few foreigners, including Americans, would agree with Taiwanese nationalists that their right to enter foreign ministries by the front rather than the back door is worth a war with China.

Despite the public sympathy Taiwan's aspirations for self-determination evoke in the United States and Japan, independence is, in fact, a less credible option for Taiwan than for the Turkish Republic of Northern Cyprus. Taiwan is as unlikely to achieve broad support by foreign governments for its independence as Chechnya, Kurdistan, Biafra, the Basques, or the Confederate States of America. Recognition of Taiwan's independence by remote mini-states will not help it secure a place in the international community. Quite aside from China's threats to use force to ruin or conquer Taiwan should it attempt to establish a separate sovereignty, there is no nation (including the United States) or bloc of nations with a compelling reason to defy China by recognizing Taiwan's secession from it.

Nor, if the truth were told, would Beijing gain much from reunification, other than an end to the annoyance and expense involved in combating Taiwanese separatism. Mainland China is already benefiting from Taiwan's economic know-how and financial resources and Taipei no longer poses a credible threat to the legitimacy of the government in Beijing. The PRC is now almost universally recognized as the government of China, including Taiwan.

"Reunification"

Beijing's opening offer for negotiations with Taipei (Jiang Zemin's January 30, 1995, "eight-point proposal") appears to acknowledge this. It posits an essentially symbolic reunification rather than the incorporation of Taiwan into the PRC's political and economic system. Jiang's 1995 proposal abjures any intention to alter Taiwan's political, economic, or social system. It renounces Beijing's right to participate in governing Taiwan or to station troops on the island and envisages Taiwan's retention of its own armed forces for purposes of self-defense. Jiang's proposal acknowledges the desirability of Taiwan's continued participation, on an agreed-upon basis, in international organizations as a Chinese economy and society distinct from those in Hong Kong, Macao, or the Chinese mainland.

If Taipei accepted Beijing's reunification offer as made, there would be even fewer changes in Taiwan than there have been in Hong Kong since July 1, 1997. Reunification of Hong Kong with the rest of China involved painful political adjustments in the former British colony. Beijing demands no such changes in Taiwan. There have been no significant alterations to Hong Kong's way of life since its reversion to Chinese sovereignty. Taiwan is much less closely linked to the mainland than Hong Kong. There is even less reason to anticipate that nominal reunification along the lines proposed by Beijing would have much impact in Taiwan. Moreover, given Taipei's formidable negotiating skills, it is hard to imagine that it could not improve upon Beijing's offer while building credible guaranties into an actual deal.

Since what is at stake is mostly symbolism, with little practical consequence, it is tempting to conclude that there is nothing that could justify a fight between the two sides. Yet symbolism ("honor") is often at the root of the most ferocious wars, as events in the former Yugoslavia remind us. From 1979 through 1994, the trend in the Taiwan Strait was toward reconciliation. Since 1995, it has turned toward renewed military confrontation, with a real prospect that, a decade or so hence, it could erupt in war.

Why Not Negotiate?

As a practical matter, Taipei cannot hope either to gain independence from China or to secure guaranties against control from Beijing without Beijing's agreement. (To illustrate: British agreement, reluctantly granted by the Treaty of Versailles after seven years of savage warfare, was necessary to secure American independence. Puerto Rico's status as a self-governing commonwealth associated with the United States derives from Washington's having accorded it such status.) For its part, Beijing cannot hope to persuade Taipei to abandon its separatist impulses by military pressure alone. It needs to conduct a dialogue with Taipei. Nor can Beijing achieve reunification, given its present lack of military capacity to impose it, except with Taipei's agreement. Such agreement can only be obtained through negotiations. Given these realities, why are the two sides finding it so difficult to begin the negotiations they envisaged at Singapore?

Taipei is reluctant to bargain with Beijing about the long-term relationship between Taiwan and the China mainland for many reasons. Taiwan's democratic politics have produced a consensus on its desire to remain a separate society. There is no consensus, however, about what sort of long-term relationship, if any, Taiwan should have with the rest of China.

Reunification is a long-term goal now supported by very few in Taiwan. Almost no one favors reunification in the short term. Taiwan has reached a political consensus against acceptance of any version of Beijing's "one China, two systems" concept. In short, Taiwan's internal political divisions now make it impossible for its leaders to address Beijing's reunification agenda, even if they wanted to. There is no indication that they do. It is likely to remain far easier for Taiwanese politicians to pursue honor abroad than in politically risky talks with Beijing.

Taiwanese public opinion will allow Taipei to enter actual negotiations with Beijing only if the talks are about how to preserve Taiwan's separation from China. Taipei knows that Beijing will not (indeed, cannot) talk with it about that. On the other hand, Taiwan's political establishment does not want to appear to be against dialogue with Chinese across the Strait. Taipei's recent acceptance of talks about talks with Beijing reflects its desire to preempt further urging of cross-Strait negotiations by President Clinton when he visits Beijing in late June 1998. It does not foreshadow Taipei's agreement that negotiations can actually take place.

Taiwan is also divided on the question of whether it should facilitate greater economic interdependence or attempt confidence-building measures between the two sides of the Strait. Taipei's actions have been contradictory, reflecting its inability to reconcile its concerns about the security implications of reliance on the mainland economy with its awareness that its long-term economic prospects are linked to cross-Strait trade and investment. Lee Teng-hui's recent attempts to curb investment in the mainland economy have been very unpopular with Taiwan's business community. Lee continues to ban direct trade across the Strait. On the other hand, he has begun to allow transshipment of mainland imports and exports through Taiwan ports.

Meanwhile, suggestions by some mainland politicians that the two sides begin a military dialogue have gone unanswered by Taipei. The Taiwan armed forces know that many Taiwanese are suspicious of their political orientation and would suspect them of trying to cut a deal with the PRC if they met with counterparts from the PLA. The question of possible military dialogue has been further complicated by Taipei's recent insistence that Beijing agree to a dividing line, much like an international boundary, in the Taiwan Strait beyond which the PLA could not legally venture. Even the technical issues Taipei has proposed for discussion are about how to manage the division of China into separate sovereignties or jurisdictions, rather than about how to bring the two sides of the Taiwan Strait together.

Under these circumstances, Beijing harbors grave doubts about the utility of talking with Taipei. It suspects that Lee Teng-hui would seek to use any talks to seek symbolic validation of his combined "two Chinas, one China—one Taiwan" thesis. Taipei's abandonment of the previous consensus on "one China" and its increasingly vehement rejection of the concept of "one China, two systems" make it difficult for Beijing to imagine a common agenda for talks with Taipei. From Beijing's point of view, the only legitimate purpose of talks is to prevent separatism and to promote some form of reunification consistent with "one China, two [i.e., more than one] systems."

On the other hand, Beijing does not wish, any more than Taipei, to appear to be against cross-Strait dialogue. China's leaders may be skeptical about the prospects for peaceful reunification, but they continue to recognize that it would be less problematic and vastly more advantageous to China than reunification by force. Chinese leaders admit that their major concern is to prevent the separation of Taiwan from the rest of China and to preserve a vision of "one China, even if not now." As long as both sides see reunification as the only alternative to the *status quo*, Beijing would feel no urgency about changing things, they say.

Given the force of Chinese nationalism, it is politically impossible for any politician on the Chinese mainland to admit that anything less than reunification is acceptable. Privately, however, China's leaders are realistic. If Taipei agreed not to pursue alteration of the *status quo*, they suggest, Beijing could defer any effort at changing it for decades to come. Over time, they calculate, Taiwanese nationalism could lose its edge. Equally, the Chinese mainland might become a much more attractive society to Taiwanese than it is at present.

In short, despite the fact that both sides need to talk, each now feels politically constrained from entering serious negotiations. Neither side wishes, however, to be blamed for blocking cross-Strait dialogue. Beijing could accept indefinite extension of the *status quo*, but Taipei cannot. In these circumstances, the two sides will likely meet to talk about talks but be unable to get down to serious discussions about their long-term relationship. In the meantime, Taipei will continue to attempt to create international facts that bolster its claim to independent sovereignty. Beijing will continue to plan to use force to prevent Taipei from succeeding in establishing such status. Taipei will continue to count on its ability to embroil the United States in any conflict it may provoke with the PRC.

U.S. Interests

The fundamental American interest in this contest has been consistent since June 27, 1950, when the U.S. Seventh Fleet first deployed to prevent the outbreak of war in the Taiwan Strait. Under a variety of formulas, the United States has sought to stabilize the military situation in the Taiwan Strait and to ensure that any changes in Taiwan's relationship with the rest of China occur peacefully, through negotiations between the parties, rather than through armed conflict between them. In doing so, the United States has consistently avoided attempting to prescribe solutions to the Taiwan question, leaving these to be worked out between the parties. The focus of U.S. policy statements in the three Sino-American Joint Communiqués and the TRA is at root the same. U.S. policy has always stressed the need to prevent the outbreak of war in the Taiwan Strait by insisting that the parties to the Taiwan dispute settle their differences peacefully, i.e., by reaching a mutually acceptable basis for dealing with each other.

For most of the past fifty years, since Chiang Kai-shek was first "leashed," the threat to the peace and stability of the strait has come from the PRC. For much of that period, Beijing fulminated about its right to "liberate" Taiwan, regardless of the views of the island's inhabitants or the concerns of China's neighbors about the regional and strategic implications of conflict between Taiwan and the China mainland. Now, however, Beijing is on the defensive. It is Taipei, not Beijing, that seeks to change the long-standing "one China but not quite yet" *status quo*. Beijing is prepared to live with this *status quo*. Taipei is not.

This creates a clear dilemma for U.S. policy. U.S. interests dictate an effort to caution Taiwan and to restrain it from actions that might provoke conflict with the PRC, even as the United States continues to constrain the PRC from coercive actions against Taiwan. A century of U.S. rhetoric about self-determination, though it has not led to American willingness to risk war elsewhere (e.g., on behalf of Chechens, Kurds, Kosovo's Albanians, or East Timorese), pulls in the opposite direction.

U.S. Policy

The Clinton administration has responded to this dilemma by reaffirming U.S. adherence to the "one China" policy and interest in "peaceful settlement" that have been the basis of the American approach for a half-century. More recently, it has affirmed that the United States does not and will not support Taiwan's independence or aspirations for a seat as a state separate from China in the United Nations. Separately, Japan (which has more direct historical and strategic ties with Taiwanese than the United States) has said much the same thing. Both in direct dialogue with Taiwan officials and through unofficial emissaries, the administration has sought to caution Taipei that, as it charts its future relationship with Chinese across the Strait, it does not have a blank check it can fill out in American blood. It has urged Taipei to talk seriously to Beijing about a mutually agreeable *modus vivendi* between the two sides. These are sound steps, as far as they go. They have not, however, found much resonance in Congress.

In part for this reason, the administration's efforts to reposition the United States on these issues have not had much cautionary impact on the evolution of political opinion in Taiwan. Taiwanese have instead continued to consolidate and perfect the separatist consensus that has stimulated Beijing, for the first time in years, to think seriously about the possibility that it will have to use force to forestall Taiwan independence or to impose reunification on the island. Taiwanese politicians appear confident that the U.S. Congress will compel the United States to back it militarily, even if Taipei disregards President Clinton's advice and overturns the previous cross-Strait consensus on "one China, even if not now." This calculation is at the heart of Taipei's willingness to take major risks, including the risk of war, to achieve international recognition for Taiwan, under one name or another, as a sovereign, independent state in its own right.

For the first time since the 1950s there is a real danger that decisions in Taipei, not just Beijing, could ignite a conflict in the Taiwan Strait. The United States, as well as both Chinese parties, would be the loser in any such conflict, whether American forces joined it or not. U.S. policy can no longer hope to deter war in the Taiwan Strait by focusing exclusively on preventing actions by Beijing that might destabilize the *status quo*. The United States must now ensure that its policy also effectively precludes decisions and actions by Taipei that could leave Beijing with little or no choice but to react militarily. Such a policy cannot be implemented if the U.S. executive and legislative branches remain at odds.

The administration has yet to do much to obtain congressional backing for its China policy. Nor has it sought to educate Congress on the dangers that recent developments in Taiwan and reactions to them on the China mainland pose to peace in the Taiwan Strait. A serious effort to forge a national consensus on policy toward China, including Taiwan, is overdue. Such an effort must take as its starting point the recognition that attempts by *either* Chinese party to the Taiwan dispute to impose its preferred solution on the other are incompatible with the U.S. interest in peaceful settlement.

That is why the United States should now state unequivocally that it will not support, and will not endorse, any change in Taiwan's status that may be unilaterally contrived or imposed by either Beijing or Taipei. The United States should make it clear that it favors expanded contact, trade, investment, and other ties across the Taiwan Strait as well as the earliest possible opening of high-level negotiations between the two sides. The United States can accept any change in cross-Strait relations that may be mutually agreed upon between the contending parties. Given the importance of Japan in this context, Washington should encourage Tokyo to join it in saying so.

Under current circumstances of increasing disagreement between competing nationalisms on both sides of the strait, it may well be that the best short-term solution to the Taiwan question for all concerned is no solution at all. No change in the "one China, but not now" *status quo*. No reunification. No assertions of independent sovereignty by Taipei.

The United States should encourage Beijing and Taipei to talk about whether they might not agree to defer negotiations about Taiwan's long-term relationship with the rest of China for a specific period—say fifty years. In the interim before such negotiations, neither side would attempt unilaterally to alter the *status quo*. Neither side would threaten the use of force or use force against the other.

Officials in Beijing have consistently stated that their government's primary objective is to prevent Taiwan's secession from "China." If there were no danger of such secession, they say, they could be very patient about the achievement of "peaceful reunification." Taipei needs to be encouraged to test the sincerity of such statements. With the passage of time, much could change to reduce tensions and ease the possibility of cross-strait agreement on Taiwan's role vis-à-vis China and the international community.

The rising military tensions in the Taiwan Strait also dictate a reevaluation of the role of arms sales to Taiwan in preserving peace and promoting prospects for a negotiated settlement between Beijing and Taipei. In the August 17, 1982, Sino-American Joint Communiqué, President Reagan and China's leader, Deng Xiaoping, reached an understanding about how to manage this contentious issue. China declared its determination "to strive for a peaceful solution to the Taiwan question." In acknowledgment of this, the United States declared that

> it does not seek to carry out a long-term policy of arms sales to Taiwan, that its arms sales to Taiwan will not exceed, either in qualitative or quantitative terms, the level of those supplied in recent years . . . and that it intends gradually to reduce its sale of arms to Taiwan, leading, over a period of time, to a final resolution.

It is in the interest of the United States to hold Beijing to its side of the Reagan-Deng bargain. Doing so, however, will require that the United States also keep its word. It is hard to argue that either side is now in full compliance with the August 17, 1982, communiqué.

Ten years after the Reagan-Deng understanding, in August 1992, the United States sold 150 advanced fighter aircraft (F-16s) to Taiwan. This sale—then the largest single arms sale in U.S. history—was an effort by the politically beleaguered [George H. W.] Bush administration to appeal to the voters of Texas, where the F-16 is manufactured, on the eve of the 1992 election. The F-16 sale and many that have followed it cannot be squared with the Reagan-Deng understanding. Since 1992, Taiwan has embarked on a massive program of military modernization. Taiwan's armed forces have not been able to buy everything they want from the United States. (For example, they have so far been denied the submarines with which they would like to be able to attack shipping in Shanghai and other mainland ports in the event of hostilities in the Taiwan Strait.) But they have bought a lot.

The United States should be concerned that Beijing's determination to stick with a policy of peaceful resolution of its differences with Taipei is wavering. How much of this wavering is due to U.S. noncompliance with the Reagan-Deng understanding and how much to the hardening of Taipei's attitudes on reunification is unclear. What is clear is that U.S. arms sales to Taiwan are no longer effective in boosting Taipei's confidence that it can work out its differences with Beijing. They now serve instead to bolster Taipei's view that it can go its own way, regardless of history, geography, and the views of Chinese across the Strait, and that it can count on military backing from the United States as it does so. This is not the message the United States should be sending to Taiwan.

It does not make sense to attempt to sustain Taiwan's current military superiority in the Taiwan Strait or even a long-term military balance between Taipei and Beijing. To do so would be to encourage an arms race between the two sides that Taiwan cannot hope, in the long run, to win against the vastly larger and equally dynamic Chinese society across the Strait. It is not in Taiwan's interest, nor in that of the United States, to cast the Taiwan dispute in mainly military terms. The greatest strength of Taiwan's 22 million people is their superior political and economic system, not their capacity to out-spend, out-arm, or out-fight the nearly 1.3 billion Chinese across the strait. Taiwan's security depends, in the end, on its ability to work out a mutually satisfactory relationship with the rest of China.

That is why, at a minimum, the United States should return to strict compliance with the Reagan-Deng understanding and insist that Beijing do likewise. And as the United States considers future arms sales to Taiwan, it should weigh their impact on Taipei's intentions and behavior as well as Beijing's. Doing so will not threaten Taiwan's self-defense capability. There is already more in the pipeline than Taiwan's military can easily absorb for years to come.

The basic dynamic of cross-Strait relations is now between Taipei and Beijing. Washington is, however, more than a vitally interested observer. Even if the United States is no longer central to cross-Strait relations, its words and actions continue to shape their context. American errors of omission, as well as commission, could lead to the United States being dragged into war with China. It is vitally important that Washington speak and act in such a way as to encourage the contending Chinese parties to the Taiwan dispute to settle their differences through negotiations rather than in battle. The relatively minor adjustments in U.S. policy proposed above would help do this.

Finally, if, despite all the difficulties in their way, negotiations begin between Beijing and Taipei, the United States must be patient and continue to resist the impulse to become directly involved between the parties or on behalf of either of them. Americans should not attempt to dictate the outcome of discussions among Chinese. General George C. Marshall's skillful attempts to compose differences between the KMT and CCP in the mid- to late 1940s failed to satisfy or enlist either party in a viable settlement. The Marshall Mission also helped polarize American politics for more than a decade over the "who lost China" issue. The Taiwan issue is the outgrowth of the resumed Chinese civil war that followed the failure of Marshall's well-intentioned mediation. It holds equal perils for modern-day foreign mediators.

The United States should encourage and support the efforts of the authorities on both sides of the Taiwan Strait to reach a peaceful resolution of their differences. Accomplishing this in the century to come will require nuanced but significant adjustments in American policy. The Clinton-Jiang summit of June 1998 is the time to begin such adjustments.

Chapter 5

War, Peace, and Taiwan

In 1999, the elected president of the Republic of China on Taiwan completed his five-year transition from guardedly advocating independence for the island to openly embracing it. President Lee Teng-hui unequivocally announced in July 1999 that Taiwan is a state distinct from either the PRC or China, ought to be regarded as such internationally, and must be treated as such in terms of cross-Strait relations—a move that, to use a metaphor that once landed the Taiwan intellectual Bo Yang in jail—"broke the political hymen" once and for all. It was now clear to everyone in Beijing concerned with Taiwan policy that, if the PRC did nothing, Taiwan would gradually establish itself internationally as a "state," i.e., Taiwan would eventually achieve the status of independence it had begun openly to declare its due. Lee's moves toward secession catalyzed corresponding transitions in Beijing, which moved from a policy devoted to peaceful settlement on an indefinite timescale toward a policy of coerced settlement within a foreseeable future.

The initial reaction in Beijing to Lee's July 9 pronouncement of his "two-state doctrine" was frenzied examination of military ways to chastise Taiwan, including considering the merits of striking various specific targets of politico-military significance to Taiwan. (If nothing else, this process of target-vetting gave hotheads something to do until cooler heads could regain control.) But the more the Chinese Communist Party looked at actual targets, the more apparent it became that, however potent strikes on them might prove in terms of domestic Chinese politics, the effects on Taiwan and internationally—particularly with regard to the US and Japan —would be highly disadvantageous.

China's politicians were thus finally forced to confront the reality of their impotence (long understood, though spoken of only sotto voce, by the PLA) to impose their will on Taiwan with the forces then under their command. Their response, made more emotional by the humiliating US bombing of China's embassy in Belgrade in May 1999, was to accelerate defense modernization directed at preparing for military action against Taiwan at a time and in a way that Beijing would decide, as opposed to simply reacting to provocations from Taipei. Beijing embarked on this military buildup in full realization of the horrifying possibility that politicians in Taipei might do something so unequivocally challenging that the PLA would have to go after Taiwan, ready or not. At about the same time, the United States' declarations of its intent to field theater missile defense systems in the region led the PLA to conclude that, to deal with Taiwan contingencies, China would need a much larger short- and medium-range missile force than it had traditionally fielded. (The U.S. announcement in early 2000 that it intended to proceed with a national missile defense system added to the PLA's long-range planning a further requirement for a larger nuclear deterrent counterstrike capability.)

But China's response to the threat of Taiwan secession was no means purely military. Conferring at the beachside resort of Beidaihe in early August 1999, China's leaders adopted what traditional Chinese statecraft calls a "two-handed" policy. In addition to launching an unprecedented ten-year military buildup directed at achieving the capability to overwhelm Taiwan militarily by 2008, they greatly expanded their "united front" outreach to the island's interest groups and politically active individuals. They vigorously pursued both the military buildup and the political outreach. Together, these significantly narrowed Taiwan's options and freedom to maneuver and caused some on the island to consider how Taiwan might reverse course to restore the ambiguous cross-Strait consensus on "one China" that Lee Teng-hui, as well as proponents of independence in the official opposition Democratic Progressive Party, had overthrown.

In 2000, Chen Shui-bian, a leader openly committed to independence, was elected to succeed Lee Teng-hui. This underscored to Beijing the necessity of developing coercive measures to prevent Taiwan from successfully establishing an international identity separate from greater China. Coming as it did in the wake of the successful reintegration of Hong Kong and Macau into greater China, Chen's inauguration led to mounting pressure to set a deadline for bringing Taiwan into the fold. Not until 2005, when the Chinese Nationalist (Kuomintang) and Chinese Communist parties established a relationship and began a cross-Strait dialogue behind the backs of the DPP authorities in Taipei, was the domestic pressure for China to set a specific timetable for reunification beaten back by Jiang Zemin's successor, Hu Jintao. This was the background as I described the state of play over Taiwan in early 2004 in a talk that appears as the first of two sections in this chapter: "Sino-American Relations and the Taiwan Issue."

By 2005, China was still three years away from its self-imposed target date for building a credible capacity to devastate Taiwan, but it had substantially reconfigured its armed forces to focus on the island. It was steadily introducing new classes and generations of weaponry, with further "surprises" promised to follow. (This apparently referred primarily to missiles that could sink aircraft carriers and cripple space-based surveillance, communications, and command and control systems as well as to enhanced cyber-warfare capabilities directed at crippling foreign enemies' command and control and logistics systems as well as their homeland economies. It may, however, have embraced other so-far-undisclosed military innovations.) China's force modernization program was calculated to inculcate in Taiwan a sense that the military balance was shifting inexorably to the mainland and that the island was becoming essentially indefensible by military means.

In March 2005, in an ironic echo of the U.S. Taiwan Relations Act, China passed an "Anti-Secession Law." (Among other benefits, this set the stage for setting aside the effort by hardliners to force the setting of a deadline for reunification.) The law emphasized and authorized the use of peaceful means to promote reunification, which it defined in terms generous to Taiwan's continued autonomy, but it also obliged Chinese leaders to use force against Taiwan under specified circumstances. These included: 1) the actual accomplishment by "Taiwan independence" forces, under whatever name and method, of Taiwan's separation from China; (2) the occurrence of a major event that would lead to Taiwan's separation from China; or (3) the loss of all possibility of peaceful unification. Although described as a contingent measure aimed at deterring moves by Taiwan toward independence, this legislation represented a significant escalation of psychological warfare against the island.

The passage of the Anti-Secession Law overshadowed what was in many ways a far more momentous development in cross-Strait relations that was then in preparation. This was the establishment of party-to-party ties between the Chinese Communist Party and the Chinese Nationalist Party (Kuomintang) as well as two parties that had splintered from it. The parties agreed to a detailed agenda of steps to accelerate the economic and social integration of the two sides of the Taiwan Strait and carried it out on a party-to-party basis, sidelining the pro-independence government of Chen Shui-bian. This process changed the dynamic of cross-Strait relations and pulled the rug out from under those on the mainland pressing for a deadline for reunification and flanked the pro-independence DPP administration in Taipei. Eventually, KMT-CCP cooperation facilitated the implementation of the entire menu of cross-Strait links first proposed by the mainland on January 1, 1979. Direct air and shipping for passengers and freight began. Mail flowed back and forth across the Strait. Financial transactions began to be facilitated. After the election of a Kuomintang president, Ma Ying-jeou, in Taiwan in 2008, the two sides made further rapid progress. On June 29, 2010, in Chongqing, they concluded an economic cooperation framework agreement that was widely seen as the most significant advance in political cooperation in over six decades.

However, negotiations on a political cooperation framework agreement that would end the state of war between the two sides remain off the table. And China continues to pursue policies that include a large buildup of military forces opposite Taiwan.

In the fall of 2011, I assessed what all this might mean in a talk that appears as the final section of this chapter: "The Taiwan Problem and China's Strategy for Resolving It."

Sino-American Relations and the Taiwan Issue[1]
April 2004

I have been asked to speak about cross-Strait relations. I do not think this subject can be addressed apart from the prospects for American friendship or enmity with China over the course of this century. Allow me to begin, then, with a few remarks about Sino-American relations in their global context. I will be as direct and brief as I can be.

As the century began, we Americans were still suffering from enemy deprivation syndrome—the sick feeling of disorientation one feels when one has lost a powerful enemy and isn't quite sure how to justify continued high levels of defense spending. For a time, China seemed to be in line to fill in behind the late, unlamented USSR. But on September 11, 2001, America was cruelly assaulted by real, not imaginary, enemies. Only the lunatic fringe and a few of its fellow travelers inside the Beltway now seek to appoint China as enemy-in-chief of the United States. The two countries have found an increasing range of issues on which to work together, and the atmosphere of our relations has steadily improved.

Nevertheless, there is something approaching an American consensus that the rise of China presents the most important long-term challenge to America's currently preeminent wealth and power. In this view, the kind of relationship the United States and China work out is likely to be the decisive factor affecting prospects for the century. I agree.

China is already emerging as the center of economic gravity in the Asia-Pacific region. China's East Asian neighbors, including Japan, are reorienting their economic policies to take advantage of this new reality. Increasingly, all supply chains tie the global economy to China. According to the WTO, the growth in China's foreign trade—imports up 40 percent, exports up 35 percent—accounted for *most* of the growth in world trade in 2003. Nevertheless, China's growth is mainly driven by the size and dynamism of its domestic market. It has proven relatively immune to global economic cycles. Astonishing changes are occurring in China's place in the world. A few examples:

Last year, the United States produced about 90 million tons of steel; Japan about 100 million. In that same year, China produced 220 million tons of steel and imported another 37.5 million, overtaking the United States as the world's largest importer. By 2010, some projections suggest that China may be producing 500 million tons of steel, more than the entire world did in the year 2000.[2] We may, in fact, now be entering an age of rising commodity costs, reversing the trends of the past hundred years, as Chinese demand for energy and raw materials pulls prices up.

China is also likely to become a major center of global technological innovation as it joins Japan as a scientific and technological power. The United States graduates about sixty thousand engineers each year; Japan seventy thousand. China is now graduating about 325,000 engineers annually. The marriage of Chinese genius to science and technology that is now occurring will enable China once again to become a net contributor to global culture. The flow of technology between China and the world, including the United States, will increasingly be in both directions.

There will be many other ways in which China's return to wealth affects the world and the United States. Already Chinese tourists are a key clientele for Southeast Asia's tourist industry. Increasingly, one sees them in Europe. They would be here as well if we had sensible visa policies (but, of course, we don't). In the future, hundreds of millions of Chinese will have the money and the passports to venture abroad.

To deal with Japanese businessmen and tourists, Americans learned to prepare sushi and sashimi. Then we learned to eat seaweed-wrapped sticky rice and raw fish ourselves. What cultural transformations will our future interactions with Chinese bring about? Not, I trust, a passion for CantoPop, sea slugs, or dog meat *baozi*. But you never know. Who would have predicted an American infatuation with Pokémon, manga, or instant ramen?

I cite these things simply to suggest the extent to which China is becoming a force in the world. It is on its way to overtaking Japan as the preeminent economy in East Asia. Within a generation or a generation and a half, in fifteen, twenty, or twenty-five years (pick your economist), China's economy will be larger than ours. East Asia will again be, as it was for most of recorded history, the dominant region in the global economy. Business activity by business activity, one can chart these trends. In economic terms, China is becoming a world power. There are now very few, if any, global economic problems that can be solved without the participation or acquiescence of China. Before long, there will essentially be none.

This is why the failure to include China in the G-7 (or G-8, as it is sometimes called) reduces the relevance of that gathering without addressing the problem of China's increasing connectedness to the issues it is discussing. Asia's prosperity is now inextricably linked to that of China. Without many remarking on it, China's and America's economies are also becoming more interdependent. As our reliance on Japan and China to finance our mounting national debt illustrates, our prosperity increasingly depends on that of others. And China is playing an ever-larger role in this regard.

Americans are already concerned about the value of the Renminbi yuan in relation to the dollar. Given the extent to which the economies of the three parts of so-called "greater China—the China mainland, Hong Kong, and Taiwan—are now interconnected, linking their currencies in some form of monetary union would even now make economic sense. In time, political circumstances may permit this. But whether or not this happens, the size of the Chinese economy and its role in foreign trade means that, as the yuan becomes a hard currency, it is likely to join the euro and the yen as an alternative reserve currency to the dollar. We are destined to become far more interested in Chinese fiscal and monetary policies than we have been.

Of course, as the example of Japan in the last half of the past century reminds us, economic power does not necessarily equate to political influence. Without political reform, China cannot hope to match the international influence of the West, including its most prominent exemplar: the United States. No one now seeks to emulate the Chinese way of governance or to learn the political arts from China. Without political as well as economic modernization, China will continue to have severely limited attractive power, even in its own region, for a very long time to come. The prospects for such political reform are closely linked to the Taiwan issue and are thus at best uncertain. The odds at present are that China's political influence will remain distinctly inferior to that of many other countries much smaller than it.

China's capacity to overawe and coerce its neighbors militarily could, of course, be a different matter. As China's economy grows, Beijing will be able without strain to support an ever-larger defense budget. In the first third of this century, China could emerge as the preeminent military power in Asia. As the century proceeds, if it chooses or is stimulated by others to do so, it could develop military capabilities that begin to rival those of the United States. There is a real risk that the United States and China could be drawn into a series of arms races as military balances shift to reflect China's growing military prowess.

But there is nothing inevitable about the choices China will make, just as there is nothing inevitable about conflict or rivalry with China as a rising power. The analogies that are sometimes drawn to the rise of Russia,

Germany, Japan, and the United States do not ring true. China has articulated no ideologies of imperialism, colonialism, mercantilism, militarism, manifest destiny, territorial aggrandizement, or *mission civilisatrice*. It has instead, to the surprise of many, stressed the equality of nations, the inviolability of national sovereignty, and the supremacy of the United Nations Charter.

There has been no hint of a Chinese "Monroe Doctrine" for Asia; China has not sought to displace the United States or our forces from the region or to fill the vacuums our inattention has sometimes created. The Chinese did not take Hong Kong or Macao by force, though they could have. When they recovered these territories they were respectful of the *status quo* in them; they did not seek to impose their own system there, though they have been less hospitable to postcolonial democratic reforms than they should have been. Similarly, China has now settled all of its land borders with Russia, the newly independent Central Asian states, and Vietnam through negotiations in which it gave as much or more than it got. It says it is prepared to do the same for its maritime boundaries.

All the evidence to date suggests that China is not a new power seeking to stake out an unprecedented status for itself at the expense of the existing regional or international order. The Chinese are a nation returning to a historically preeminent role in Asia. They aspire to resume their traditional status as proud leaders of global civilization after a century and a half of eclipse. As the Chinese do this, they are finally putting the trauma of their earlier weakness, impoverishment, and victimization by foreign powers behind them.

China is thus regaining a welcome measure of poise and self-confidence. Beijing's response to the Asian financial crisis of a few years ago, its recent skillful diplomacy in Korea, its proposals for a northeast Asian security dialogue, its embrace of nonproliferation policies paralleling our own, and its increasingly active role in UN peacekeeping operations all illustrate the return of China as an increasingly mature and responsible international actor. China is, like Japan, becoming a more normal country. It wants to be accepted as such.

All things being equal, China looks to be a force for global and regional stability, not a challenger of the current world order. With a bit of work by both sides, Sino-American relations should therefore be marked by much more cooperation than contention; China should be our friend, not our enemy. If that is so, the prospects for a century of expanded peace, prosperity, and democracy are good.

Unfortunately, all things do not now seem likely to be equal. There is a real possibility that, before the end of the decade, the United States may find ourselves at war with China over Taiwan.

Two Chinese revolutions in the last century, one in 1911 and one in 1949, were fired by the nation's will to erase the imprint of foreign imperialism on China's body and soul, eliminate foreign spheres of influence on Chinese territory, end the capacity of foreign powers to intervene in China's internal affairs, and restore China's national unity along with its wealth and power. As other ideologies have fallen away, the explosive underpinning of Chinese nationalism is all that is left. Taiwan's separation from the rest of China is a monument to all the humiliations both the Kuomintang and Communist revolutions were conceived to overcome. Reunification is a central imperative of the Chinese state.

Remarkably, given the centrality of the Taiwan issue to Chinese nationalism, skillful American diplomacy in the 1970s and '80s persuaded Beijing that Taiwan's status could, like the Hong Kong and Macao issues, be resolved by peaceful means; that is, by negotiation. But, as our friends in Taiwan never tire of pointing out, there are fundamental differences between the circumstances of those colonies and those of Taiwan, which is self-administering and under no foreign sovereignty. No foreign power can cut a deal with Beijing about Taiwan; that can only be done by the Taiwan authorities.

Those authorities were longtime Chinese nationalists, as committed as their Communist rivals to the unity of China. The cross-Strait consensus that there was only one China enabled both sides to finesse sensitive issues like sovereignty while seeking practical means of mutual accommodation. This consensus enabled Beijing to accept the notion of two systems coexisting within one country. It led to proposals for talks about reunification that would guarantee rather than change Taiwan's political, economic, cultural, and military autonomy. These proposals implicitly addressed Japanese and American strategic interests by affirming that there would be no People's Liberation Army forces stationed in Taiwan, thus leaving the military balance in Northeast Asia unaltered. China's position has not changed.

But, over the past few years, Taiwan's position has. The Taiwan authorities have repudiated the idea of one China. The current president, Chen Shui-bian, asserts that the two sides of the Taiwan Strait are separate countries. He says that, since—in his view—Taiwan is already independent, independence is the *status quo* and there is no need to declare it. He has proposed an island-wide referendum on a new constitution that would, among other things, legally consolidate such independence.

The constitution now in force in Taiwan vests sovereignty in the people of China, who approved it in a nationwide vote in 1947. The new constitution would be created in 2006 by a sovereign act of the people of Taiwan without regard to the views of other Chinese. It would go into effect in 2008. By any legal standard, this would constitute an act of self-determination. Mr. Chen has offered to talk with Beijing in the meantime, but only on terms that explicitly or implicitly reaffirm his view of Taiwan as an independent state.

The George W. Bush administration has cautioned Mr. Chen against any effort to change the one-China *status quo* in the Taiwan Strait by such unilateral acts. Mr. Chen has rejected this advice. Instead he denies that the *status quo* is one China and affirms that the United States, as a democracy, is bound to support the democratically expressed will of the people of Taiwan to enjoy their own separate state, regardless of the views of Chinese across the Strait.

But no nation achieves independence without the agreement of the country from which it is separating. Very often, as in our own case and many others, independence is granted only after years of bloodshed. More often still, as the examples of American Southerners, Basques, Biafrans, Kurds, Palestinians, Sri Lankan Tamils, Chechens, southern Sudanese, Kashmiris, and others attest, despite great carnage and human suffering, attempts at separation fail. Rarely, as in the case of the Czech Republic and Slovakia, is separation peacefully agreed upon between the parties.

The positions of both sides on the Taiwan question are now non-negotiable. Mr. Chen insists on independence and has declared a firm, unilateral timetable for making it final. Beijing is prepared to tolerate the current situation of *de facto* separation only if it will lead to negotiations that can produce cross-Strait agreement on some form of reunification. Neither is prepared to address the aspirations of the other, still less to accept them.

In response to the Taiwan authorities' statements and actions, China has raised defense spending and greatly stepped up military preparations to prevent secession by Taiwan. The Chinese say that Mr. Chen's actions are leaving them no choice but to use force against the island. Coincidentally, their preparations to do so will be complete on more or less the same schedule that Mr. Chen has proposed for his referenda consolidating the island's self-proclaimed independence.

Mr. Chen says that Beijing is a paper tiger. As if to underscore this judgment, he has reduced rather than increased Taiwan's defense spending while delaying decisions on American recommendations for upgrading Taiwan's self-defense capabilities. Asked how he would defend Taiwan if, as many outside Taiwan fear, Beijing attacks the island in response to his unilateral actions, Mr. Chen expresses confidence that U.S. forces would feel obliged by the Taiwan Relations Act and pro-Taiwan sentiment in Congress to come to Taiwan's defense. He and his followers seem certain that the result of a war between the United States and China would be an independent Taiwan.

Maybe so. But at what cost to the United States, China, and Taiwan itself? And why should Americans feel obliged to go to war with China to save Taiwan from the consequences of actions it is taking over our objections? With Taiwan's leaders apparently determined to risk a bloody rendezvous with Chinese nationalism, it is time to think and speak clearly about what a Sino-American war over Taiwan would mean.

In the 1950s, the United States several times threatened nuclear attack on China over crises related to the defense of Taiwan. We can no longer do so without risking nuclear counterattack by China. The good news, therefore, is that neither side is likely to risk a nuclear exchange over Taiwan.

But a U.S.-China war over Taiwan would not be fought in a third country or by proxy, as was the case in Korea and Vietnam. In those wars, the United States scrupulously avoided attacking the Chinese homeland. But the defense of Taiwan would require counterattacking the bases and facilities on the Chinese mainland from which Taiwan was being attacked. China has long indicated that it would reply to attacks on its homeland with counterattacks in kind on the United States, including our homeland and our bases overseas. The danger that the conflict could rapidly escalate to the global level is real—all the more so because neither side has done anything to develop a strategy for escalation control, and as a result of reckless decisions in our Defense Department, there is far less communication with the People's Liberation Army than there was with Soviet forces when war with them was a possibility.

China regards Taiwan as part of China, and the world, including the United States, acknowledges this Chinese position. In a fight with China over Taiwan, we would have few, if any, allies, though—given our bases on its territory—Japan would probably find it impossible not to support us.

Such a war would divide Asia and usher in a century dominated by global contention and mutual hostility between China and the United States. This could be even more dangerous and require vastly larger sacrifices of Americans than the Cold War did. China, unlike the Soviet Union, is unhampered by a dysfunctional ideology and economic system. It is unlikely to oblige us by collapsing. The issue between us is not Chinese behavior on the world scene or toward U.S. allies. It is how the Chinese civil war should end.

China would, of course, be severely damaged by war with the United States. I believe that our armed forces could and would rapidly destroy most of China's navy and air force as well as its missile bases. Areas along the coast, where economic development is most advanced, might suffer especially heavy war damage. (I will not speculate about which parts of the United States are most likely to suffer Chinese retaliatory strikes.) An enormous effort would be required to rebuild China's industrial infra-structure and armed forces after the fighting ended.

If China had not succeeded in taking Taiwan, Chinese nationalism would compel it to prepare to try again. The war would thus continue on an intermittent basis until one side or the other gave up. Every aspect of China's modernization would be seriously set back. The country's open-ing to the outside world would be blighted and the political loosening of recent years replaced with the stringencies of martial law. The position of Chinese minorities abroad, especially in the United States, could become very uncomfortable.

But Taiwan would be the main battleground in any such war. Even if there were only one round of warfare, the island would, in all likelihood, emerge with its infrastructure devastated, its prosperity destroyed, and its democracy traumatized, if not suspended. If the result of the fighting was to incorporate Taiwan into China, the PLA would find itself pacifying a sullenly hostile populace. Neither domestic nor foreign investors would want to help the Chinese occupation. China would not gain much of an economic prize if it took Taiwan by force.

If the result was Taiwan's continued *de facto* separation from China, the Taiwan authorities would face the constant threat of renewed Chinese attack. Few investors would wish to risk their money on an island under the Chinese gun. As China reconstituted its armed forces for another try at subduing the island, Taiwan's lamed economy might be unable to afford the weaponry necessary to defend itself. Taiwan might once again, as it did in the 1950s, have to rely on U.S. subsidies to survive. Meanwhile, U.S. and Chinese forces would continue to face off over the island.

The fact is that no one can "win" a war over Taiwan. All will lose. Therefore we must make sure that we avoid such a war. Chinese national-ists will, of course, respond that the obvious way to avoid war is for Taiwan to abandon its dreams of independence. Taiwanese separatists will argue that Chinese across the Strait simply need to respect Taiwan's right of self-determination. Each will find many supporters for its view in the United States but few on the other side of the Taiwan Strait.

In the short term such contradictions are irreconcilable. But so long as neither side actually does anything to challenge the other, there need be no war. And, with the passage of time and the growth of mutual under-standing and goodwill, mutually acceptable compromises may emerge. That is especially the case given the speed of change in China, much of it catalyzed by cross-Strait interaction and the attractiveness of Taiwan's politico-economic model. Given time, differences between the two sides that are problems now may well blur and fade away. Gaining time for such convergence is a worthy objective in itself.

It has long been in the American interest—as well as that of the parties and the world—for this issue to be resolved peacefully, by mutual agreement, through negotiations, not unilaterally and not through war. Beijing knows that we are serious about this and has so far acted with appropriate caution. Taipei, however, now clearly needs to be convinced that if it acts on its own, it may well end up on its own. In short, Beijing needs to continue to avoid acting rashly but Taipei needs to stop doing so. As for Americans, we should explicitly reserve the right not to go to war with China to save Taiwanese from the consequences of their acting against U.S. interests and advice. We should not entrust decisions about war and peace with China to the Taiwan authorities. Such decisions are rightly for us alone to make.

Beijing is currently under mounting domestic pressure to show Taipei that it can bite as well as growl. Mr. Chen's dismissal of the risks he has been taking and his disregard of the consequences for Americans of his provocative behavior vis-à-vis China have alarmed the Bush administration. Neither China nor the United States wants to be forced into another confrontation, still less a war over Taiwan. The obvious answer is for the United States and China to sit down together and figure out how to deter Taipei from provoking such confrontation and how to avoid creating it on our own. Perhaps Vice President Cheney's visit to Beijing will help kick off such a process.

It is in our interest to convince Taipei that it is both playing with fire and becoming dangerously distant from its sole protector, the United States. It is *not* in our interest for Beijing to accomplish this for us by upping the military threat to Taiwan or taking a bite out of the island. The Bush administration, as recently as yesterday,[3] has spoken out ever more bluntly in an effort to instill realism into Taipei and to deter it from taking steps that will provoke such unilateral action by Beijing. Mr. Chen not only brushes these warnings aside, he ensures that his partisans in the press ignore and distort the administration's message in the best totalitarian tradition. It is becoming clear that words may not be enough to convince the Taiwan authorities not to jeopardize its future and our own; punitive actions may be required.

Deterring Beijing from its own unilateral actions is also very much in our interest. Here we confront a subtle problem. China's leaders understand very clearly what the consequences of war with the United States would be. They absolutely do not want such a war. But they have come to believe that Washington is opposed to any form of reassociation of Taiwan with the Chinese mainland, even a negotiated one. Like many people in Taiwan, they judge that the secret purpose of U.S. policy is to help Taiwan become independent and that we will, if necessary, fight

China to accomplish this. But China's national honor requires some form of end to the division of the Chinese nation, even if only symbolically. If accomplishing this will inevitably entail war with the United States, even if China uses peaceful means, then the only choice before China's leaders is when, not whether, to risk such war; China has little, if any, incentive to act responsibly.

For all these reasons, it is time for us to state clearly:

- that we regard the juridical *status quo* in the Taiwan Strait as "one China" and do not accept that the *status quo* is independence;
- that we favor negotiations between the two sides within the context of "one China";
- that we will accept any change in the *status quo* that both sides accept but, conversely, will not accept any change that is not agreed upon by both sides;
- that we will not recognize an independent Taiwan that has not been recognized by Beijing, nor will we recognize any form of reunification that has not been endorsed by the people of Taiwan; and
- that we will implement our obligations under the Taiwan Relations Act and the three U.S.-China joint communiqués and carry out our relations with both sides of the Strait in a manner consistent with these principles.

This is not that far from what the administration stated yesterday[4] in testimony before Congress. If the Taiwan authorities do not get the message or allow it to get through to ordinary people on the island, the administration will—in my opinion—be left with no alternative but to consider appropriate downgrading of selected aspects of American relationships with Taiwan, including our defense and arms sales relationships, as a way of convincing both Taipei and Beijing of our seriousness about managing this issue to avoid war.

Perhaps, given the strength of pro-Taiwan and anti-China sentiment in the United States and the power of the Taiwan lobby in the U.S. Congress, such a return to a balanced policy focused on the maintenance of peace in the Taiwan Strait rather than other agendas is politically impossible. If that is the case, then we must accept that the management of the Taiwan problem to avoid war with China may also be impossible. I, for one, cannot accept that conclusion. The consequences for us and for the world are much too great.

Conversely, successful management of the Taiwan problem is the key to a sound U.S.-China relationship. And the door that key can open is one that leads to a better century than the last one for all concerned, including

Taiwan. That is the key we should be looking for and the door we should strive to open.

Among other things, a People's Republic of China that found a way to reassociate itself peacefully with the democratic Chinese society on Taiwan would be a China that is likely to be much more congenial to both our values and our interests. That kind of China would be one we could work with in the century to come to promote the common prosperity and peaceful international environment for which both Americans and Chinese long. That kind of China is one that would be a friend, not an enemy, of the United States.

The Taiwan Problem and China's Strategy for Resolving It[5]
September 2011

China has always said that Taiwan is the central problem obstructing the development of its relations with the United States.

From this vantage point, the Taiwan problem began on a hot Monday night in Washington, D.C. It was a surprise gift to the Chinese and American peoples from the late north Korean dictator, Kim Il-sung. At four o'clock on the morning of June 25, 1950, local time, he launched a surprise attack to unify Korea by force. Instead of accomplishing this, Kim's violent adventurism ultimately had the effect of perpetuating the division of Korea, cleaving Asia apparently irreversibly into competing American and Chinese spheres of influence, splitting China in two, and making the previously obscure Chinese province of Taiwan into the focus of an ongoing Sino-American military rivalry.

On June 26, 1950, at nine p.m. Washington time, President Truman met at Blair House with key members of his cabinet and the Joint Chiefs. The question before them was what to do about the crisis in Korea and related areas. On the advice of those present, the president directed that "orders be issued to the Seventh Fleet to prevent an attack on Formosa [Taiwan], the National Government of China [i.e., Chiang Kai-shek] be told to desist from operations against the mainland, and the Seventh Fleet be ordered to effect this."[6]

Up to that point, Chinese and Americans alike had confidently expected Mao Zedong's People's Liberation Army (PLA) to pursue Chiang Kai-shek to Taiwan, to which Chiang had fled on December 10, 1949, and to complete the Communist victory in China's civil war. In anticipation of this, on January 5, 1950, President Truman took public note of the fact that "for the past four years the United States and other Allied Powers have accepted the exercise of Chinese authority over" Taiwan. He declared that the United States would not involve itself "in the civil conflict in China . . . [and would] not provide military aid or advice to Chinese forces" on Taiwan.[7]

The reversals of American policy that Kim Il-sung provoked imposed a formidable set of unanticipated strategic challenges on the newborn Communist government of China. As time went on, from Beijing's perspective, the transformation of Taiwan into an American protectorate meant that:

- The objective of unifying China under a single, central authority— a fundamental aim of both the 1911 and 1949 Chinese revolutions— could not soon be accomplished.
- Part of China—Taiwan—would remain subject indefinitely to a foreign—American—sphere of influence, defeating yet another fundamental objective of both Chinese revolutions: the end of foreign domination of any part of Chinese territory.
- The civil war could not be concluded.
- Chiang Kai-shek's Republic of China would continue to function as a rival regime, contesting the right to rule all of China, not just Taiwan, and to represent China internationally. The legitimacy of the People's Republic of China (PRC) would thus be subjected to constant challenge both at home and abroad.
- To rectify these conditions, China would either have to drive the United States from Taiwan by force of arms or persuade it to vacate the island voluntarily.
- In the almost certainly lengthy interim, the United States and China would be locked into a relationship of mutual antagonism and military hostility.

To one degree or another, from Beijing's perspective, these frustrations continue to define what's at stake for China in the Taiwan issue today. The normalization of China's relations with the United States in 1979 altered them less than Washington had appeared to promise or Beijing had hoped. Taiwan's democratization and the emergence of the Taiwan independence movement in the last decade of the twentieth century added another dimension to the complicated issue of Taiwan's political identity, but did not change China's strategic objectives or the domestic imperatives from which they derive. The Chinese Communist Party (CCP) is unalterably committed to unifying China in a way that removes foreign and domestic challenges to the sovereignty and territorial integrity of the Chinese state, while vindicating the Party and its leaders' historic role in the restoration of China's national dignity and self-regard.

Since 1979, China has—with great strategic resolve and even greater tactical flexibility—pursued the goal of reunification by measures short of war. The Chinese have done so in accordance with a concept of the strategic requirements imposed by the perceived imperative of "a peaceful international environment." They judge that only within such an environment can they restore their country to wealth and power. Their concept of what must be done to secure their state in the long run differs in two fundamental respects from American suppositions about what is necessary and appropriate. The unstated presuppositions on both sides contribute to intermittent mutual frustration and misunderstanding. They require clarification.

First, Americans have regarded the situations in Korea and the Taiwan Strait as embodying a more or less stable and peaceful international *status quo* that requires continuing military effort for its sustainment but that is preferable to any feasible alternative. Chinese, by contrast, have seen the *status quo* in both places as reflecting the inherent instabilities of temporary armistices or *de facto* ceasefires in ongoing conflicts. They also consider the underlying political conflicts that drive these situations to be national rather than international in character. These differences of perspective account for many of the differences in the two sides' approaches to these issues.

The basic American objective has been to manage and limit international conflicts along China's borders, deferring them indefinitely rather than resolving them. The fundamental Chinese objective has been to shape these issues so that temporary arrangements can eventually be replaced with long-term agreements that resolve the underlying issues between the parties, eliminate or reduce the possibility of armed conflict or foreign intervention on China's frontiers, and enable peace to be sustained mainly by nonmilitary means. The two sides have shared an interest in deferring conflict that has masked essentially different strategic objectives with respect to it.

In the American view, conflict management avoids politically painful choices. Americans equate a stable *status quo* with peace. As Chinese see it, the *status quo* is one of political struggle and latent military conflict; hence it is inconsistent with peace. They think that replacing strategic dispensations that suspend war with accords to resolve the issues that risk it is ultimately essential to securing China's periphery over the long term. The Chinese also consider that resolution of confrontation-fraught situations on their borders would reduce (or even eliminate) the presence of foreign expeditionary forces—meaning American forces—there. In Beijing's view, this would lower the probability of conflict with the United States or its Asian allies and reduce pressure for increased investment in external defense capabilities at the expense of domestic development.

Thus, the American focus on peace*keeping* contradicts and undercuts the Chinese emphasis on peace*making*. In the case of Taiwan, the United States, though officially ambivalent, acts consistently in practice to support the indefinite extension of the island's peaceful coexistence with the mainland on terms that preserve its *de facto* politico-military separation from the rest of China. China, by contrast, sees reunification of some sort—if only symbolic in nature—as indispensable to creating a lasting peace in the Taiwan area, much as the return of Hong Kong and Macau to Chinese sovereignty ended controversy over their status without altering the character or significantly affecting the operation of their politico-economic systems.

Second, the characteristic American overemphasis on military factors in foreign relations and tendency to confuse campaign plans with strategy have caused many in the United States to slight other elements of China's grand strategy with respect to Taiwan. Americans have tended to view the Taiwan problem as a military problem with political dimensions. The Chinese have seen it as a political problem with military dimensions. Chinese policies toward the island are neither primarily nor exclusively military. They combine political, economic, informational, and cultural instruments of influence with diplomatic and military measures calculated to advance the cause of a negotiated resolution of the nature of Taiwan's relationships with the rest of China in all these aspects of human interaction. The Chinese see weapons as tools with which to change minds, not as instruments whose value is to be measured in how much physical damage they inflict.

In this and other respects, China's strategic culture remains profoundly influenced by its traditions, including Sunzi's notion that measures short of war, politico-military maneuver, and stratagem are the most important elements of campaign plans. As Master Sun put it: 不战而屈人之兵善之善者也 ("to subdue the enemy without actual battle is the acme of skill"). Foreign statements positing a contradiction between China's peaceful engagement with Taiwanese interest groups and elites and the PLA's military buildup against the island strike most Chinese as nonsensical. In China's strategic doctrine, these are two flanks of the same maneuver.

The Chinese are notoriously patient. They also understand that *economic* power, like gravity, is an attractive force that can be attenuated by distance but that cannot repel. Like Europeans, they see economic measures as usually best employed to link peoples rather than to punish them. Beijing is using the allure of mainland markets skillfully to vest a widening range of

Taiwanese economic and social groups with interests in cross-Strait inter-dependence.[8] Unlike Americans, Chinese are not enamored of economic sanctions or blockades. On the other hand, they don't mind a bit of anxiety-driven reflection about the pain a crisis could inflict on the large chunks of Taiwanese society that are now dependent on cross-Strait trade and investment.

To signal political flexibility in future negotiations, Beijing has sus-pended its efforts to dislodge Taipei's diplomatic and quasi-official rela-tionships with foreign capitals. To foster a sense of common identity, it has opened mainland universities to students from Taiwan, licensed Taiwanese professionals to practice there, and facilitated migration as well as tourism.[9] These steps may not generate Taiwanese support for reunifica-tion, but they build a sense of a common Chinese space and erode anxiety about the consequences of formalizing a Chinese commonwealth in which Taiwan is at least symbolically united with the mainland. They thereby diminish potential resistance to negotiated reunification. Under the impact of Beijing's policies, Taiwanese combine a growing stake in avoiding the disruption of cross-Strait relations with a declining stake in remaining politically dissociated from the mainland.

Taiwanese have become accustomed to democracy. China's political system, unlike its economy and culture, remains unattractive to them, but Beijing's international prestige is rising. So is the pride of ordinary Chinese in their country and its achievements. China can be expected to ensure that Taiwanese appreciate, as Chinese, that they too can gain stature from China's enhanced standing and self-confidence. The lure of identification with China seems very likely to rise, not fall, over time. And when Beijing judges that the moment is ripe, it will know how to use inducements as well as implied threats to help Taiwanese rationalize agreement to a long-term cross-Strait accommodation that meets the requirements of Chinese nationalism.

In this context, China's achievement of a credible capacity to devastate Taiwan regardless of U.S. intervention in a cross-Strait conflict answers a key operational question: why should Taiwan negotiate an agreed relation-ship between itself and the rest of China? No one is ever prepared to nego-tiate unless doing so is a path to potential benefits or a credible alternative to substantial setbacks or losses. What Beijing is offering Taipei is essen-tially a symbolically repackaged *status quo*. The offer—definitively outlined in the "eight-point proposal" of 1995—confirms that, under reunification, Taiwan would keep what it already has—self-government on terms it itself has decided, an unchanged political democracy, a globally connected capi-talist economy, its own armed forces, responsibility for its own defense of its part of China, and so forth.

Keeping what you have is not much of an inducement unless you are afraid you could lose it. When the moment is ripe, therefore, Beijing must act to convince Taiwanese that they will be able to retain the benefits of the *status quo* only if they negotiate some form of agreed status consistent with "reunification." The means to do this are increasingly at hand. Beijing will also want to drive home to Americans and Japanese that the only way to guarantee the absence of a PLA presence on Taiwan is for Taipei to accept Beijing's offer to rule this out. China's endgame with Taiwan envisages its eventual preemptive capitulation to the inexorable in response to an offer Taiwan cannot refuse.

China may be prepared to go to war over Taiwan but it is well aware of what a disaster for all concerned actual combat would be. Its strategy is directed at winning without fighting. China now enjoys decisive military superiority over Taiwan. It is acquiring a credible capacity to deflect or counter U.S. intervention in any cross-Strait conflict. In this context, without firing a shot, China has accomplished the deterrence of moves by Taiwan toward independence. It is now beginning to focus on compulsion. With this in mind, China is likely to treat Taiwanese to escalating demonstrations of the PLA's ability to overwhelm Taiwan, notwithstanding whatever military backing it may have from the United States. China's objective will be to couple political measures with demonstrations of irresistible military capabilities. Its objective is to create a sense of inevitability about the need for Taiwan to reach an accommodation with the mainland.

It is in this context that we are seeing a change in the Chinese approach to "transparency." Transparency advertises strength, which is why we have liked it and, up to now, the Chinese have not. Increasingly, however, they do. If cross-Strait military exchanges begin, I would expect the PLA to make every effort to allow Taiwanese officers to observe its exercises so as to impress them with its increasingly formidable capabilities.

The grand strategy China is following is fundamentally directed at manipulating the psychological parameters of decision-making in Taiwan, which China understands are ultimately conditioned by mass opinion as expressed through democratic political structures. This, not U.S. military power, is the "center of gravity" on which Chinese strategy is focused. The convincing perception by Taiwan's elites of overwhelming Chinese military power, not the actual application of that power, is the operative objective of China's continuing military buildup as it relates to Taiwan. In the Chinese context of cross-Strait relations, this approach may well work. It has already led Taipei to deemphasize military means of defense and pay greater attention to political accommodation as a means of reducing the danger of war with the mainland.

Part of the logical force of China's strategy is that, from both Taipei's and Washington's points of view, it is becoming increasingly difficult to argue that agreement to some sort of formal association between Taiwan and the mainland would not be preferable to a Sino-American war to determine the island's relationship to the rest of China. Such a war would devastate both sides of the Strait as well as U.S. bases in the Asia-Pacific region and quite possibly parts of the U.S. homeland. When it ended, if Taiwan remained separate from China, there is no reason to believe that China would accept this as a final outcome. It would be more likely to try again.[10]

If China had succeeded in seizing Taiwan, it would have done so at the cost of long-term Sino-American enmity. In either case, Taiwan as we know it would almost certainly have been destroyed. So whoever "won" a war in the Taiwan Strait, China, Taiwan, and the United States would all have lost.

China's Anti-Secession Law[11] specifies three circumstances in which China's leaders must use force against Taiwan: (1) if "Taiwan independence" forces, under whatever name and method, accomplish the fact of Taiwan's separation from China; (2) if a major event occurs that would lead to Taiwan's separation from the rest of China; or (3) if all possibility of peaceful unification is lost. It is in no one's interest for either these provisions or the ambiguous language of the United States Taiwan Relations Act to be put to the test. Perhaps the United States should try to create circumstances that promote the settlement of the Taiwan problem rather than its perpetuation. But the likelihood of such strategic reasoning and statesmanship in today's policy-gridlocked Washington is as close to zero as you can get.

On several occasions, the Chinese have brought themselves to hope that American diplomacy might help advance rather than obstruct a negotiated resolution between the parties on either side of the Strait. On each such occasion, they have been disillusioned. They now see the United States not as a potential part of the solution but as an incorrigible element of the Taiwan problem—to be flanked, if not removed. The fact that they see the Taiwan issue as ripening to the point where a negotiated resolution may be coming into view adds immediacy to the task of reducing or eliminating U.S. backing for Taiwanese recalcitrance.

Ironically, therefore, as progress is made toward lessened tensions and greater cross-Strait cooperation, U.S. arms sales and other elements of the U.S. defense posture not only become less politically relevant in Taipei but also less tolerable by Beijing, which blames the United States for enabling, if not endorsing, Taiwanese separatism. The prospects are that a good deal of Chinese diplomatic energy and effort is about to be dedicated to raising the costs to the United States of following policies that, in China's view, inhibit rather than encourage cross-Strait accommodation.

The final implications of Kim Il-sung's adventurism and the American response to it are far from having played themselves out in Sino-American relations.

Chapter 6

Where Is China Going?

In December 1978, during the Third Plenum of the Eleventh Central Committee Congress of the Communist Party of China, Deng Xiaoping took the helm in China. He quickly demonstrated his determination to take the country on a new course. At the plenum, he engineered approval of policies of reform and openness to the outside world that promised to set aside Maoist dogma and experiment pragmatically with eclectic borrowing of economic ideas, systems, and practices from the capitalist West. That same month, in a related decision, he agreed to normalize relations with the United States. The years that followed saw Deng use his opening to America to foster an increasingly radical transformation of the Chinese socioeconomic system. But that this was either what he intended or what would happen was far from apparent at the outset.

By 1978–79, when the United States finally accepted Mao's People's Republic as the legal government of China, the world had become accustomed to a poor, weak, unstable, isolated, angry, and internationally uncooperative China. It was hard to see past this familiar image of a country doomed to fall short of its potential. Then, too, Deng's reforms took time to manifest. Few in China or outside it either understood or credited the seriousness of purpose he brought to the task of modernizing his country or the extent to which the policy changes he was enacting could midwife the birth of a post-Maoist China. Deng's reforms broke the cycle of domestic instability and xenophobia that had characterized China for most of the preceding 140 years and throughout the three decades of the People's Republic's history.

For me, the realization that real change might in fact be in progress in China dawned during what seemed like a trivial encounter. I visited Beijing in the early fall of 1979, about nine months after Deng first launched his drive for modernization. I was then Country Director for China, in charge of directing and coordinating U.S. relations with China for the United States Department of State—a much more powerful role in the formulation and implementation of interagency policy than it is now). I was lodged at the Beijing Hotel, then the only hotel in the Chinese capital that came close to internationally acceptable standards. As the first home of the United States Liaison Office at "Peking," in whose establishment I had participated in 1973, it was familiar territory. On the weekend, I walked the two blocks to the northeastern corner of Tiananmen. There I encountered a noodle vendor with a pushcart.

For anyone familiar with 1970s China, this was startling, something like running into a party of pole-sitters and goldfish swallowers doing the Charleston on the Washington Mall. China's service sector, especially its culinary element (which had been one of the great adornments of Chinese civilization), had been swamped in a tidal wave of collectivization and left to drown in a sea of state-socialist commercial torpor. In the China mainland I had come to know since my first visit there in 1972, one ate at home, in dreary canteens in work units, in lackluster public cafeterias, in one's hotel, or in one of a handful of showplace restaurants that had been preserved to impress visiting overseas Chinese and foreigners. There were no xiaochi, small restaurants serving street food, snacks, and light meals.

I like noodles, so I bought a bowl. I was the pushcart's only customer. As I enjoyed my snack, I asked the vendor what "work unit" or commune he belonged to. He replied, "I am my own work unit." Puzzled, I asked him what that meant. He said he was a geti hu, an individually registered enterprise. It struck me at once that, if individuals could now start and operate their own businesses in China, something momentous might be in progress. I began to watch for signs that the Third Plenum really had kicked off a revolution in China—and found more and more such indications.

On a dreary winter evening in Washington a few months later, the small part of the U.S. intelligence community dedicated to long-term forecasting convened a who's who of America's China watchers. The meeting took place at the Smithsonian Castle on the Mall. As an insatiable "end user" of analysis with a professional interest in China and adjacent areas, I attended. The subject was what China might be like in a decade or two. Most who spoke were clearly working off the unstated presupposition that, over the decades to come, China would continue to be poor, weak, unstable, xenophobic, and politically radical.

I was so taken aback by the contrast between the conventional wisdom in the United States and what I had seen, heard, and tasted in China that I went back to my office at the Department of States and spent the night writing a memorandum setting out my own guesstimates of what China might look like twenty years later. (See below for its online location.) A few days later, I circulated the memorandum for discussion to various components of the analytical community. I hoped to stimulate them to make a serious and comprehensive assessment of the implications of the course Deng Xiaoping had charted at the Third Plenum.

My ideas were not well received; my suggestion of a serious relook at what was happening in China was pretty much ignored. At the CIA, I was welcomed with the politely cynical condescension that the analytical cognoscenti reserve for amateur dabblers in their arts. While the discussion was civil, the assembled analysts made it clear that they thought my estimates of possible Chinese industrial and agricultural growth were wildly inflated, that urbanization would not proceed at the pace I thought it would, and that the Chinese military would remain primitive and unable to project significant power beyond China's borders. They insisted that I had vastly overestimated both Deng Xiaoping's ideological innovations and their probable impact. (Among other things, they pooh-poohed my oral suggestion that Hong Kong and Macau might be among the territorial disputes the Chinese would seek to solve by the end of the century. I had omitted mention of this in writing out of concern that I might be mau-mau'd by the residual forces of British colonialism and their American auxiliaries.)

The only predictions I made that the Washington analysts—and the staff of the American Consulate General at Hong Kong, then the U.S. government's premier China-watching establishment—did not question were several that turned out to be fundamentally wrong, especially my assumption that there would be a Soviet Union for China to be concerned about in the year 2000 and that China and the United States would remain obsessed with strategic challenges from it. (Everyone had by then forgotten the premise and purpose of the containment policy proposed by George Kennan in 1946. He saw it as a means to give the USSR time to collapse of its own infirmities, as it eventually did.) No one, certainly not I, could imagine the Cold War ending except in a nuclear exchange that would leave neither side standing. I also predicted that interest groups would arise alongside the Party. Instead, the Party recognized them for what they were and promptly incorporated them into itself. The competition over policies and resources in China therefore did not weaken Party dominance of the process as I had speculated it might.

Battered as I was by criticism, I was left to wonder whether I had not fundamentally misjudged what was happening in China. I was the only one who thought China might be changing fundamentally. The drab and lackluster realities of China in early 1980 and my speculations about what it might become were just too jarringly opposed for those focused on contemporary realities to absorb. In time, however, I proved to be more right than wrong. Ironically, my estimates of how far China could and would travel over the decades to come turned out to be gross underestimates, not exaggerations, of China's potential progress. I got the direction and nature of change largely right—but neither the pace nor the details.

In my experience, estimates by individuals often turn out to be so much more on point than those of large analytical collectives. It may be that correct estimates are just lucky accidents. In my own case, I find that a plausible thesis. But—to shift the topic a bit—it is worth pondering why the U.S. intelligence community not only collectively failed to forecast China's rise and its implications in a timely fashion, but has missed so many other major developments over the years.

With some notable exceptions, our analysts misunderstood and mischaracterized Sino-Soviet relations at the outset of the Cold War; failed to foresee most aspects of the Korean conflict; pandered to the military-industrial complex and its partisans by grossly overestimating Soviet military spending and competence; were surprised by the Soviet strategy that produced the Cuban missile crisis; long denied the reality of the Sino-Soviet split; misestimated the balance of forces and fervor in the Vietnam War; foresaw neither the 1973 Egyptian-Israeli war nor the 1977 Sadat opening to Israel for which it paved the way; were astonished by the Soviet invasion of Afghanistan and its international and domestic consequences for the USSR; did not anticipate the collapse of the Soviet empire or the Soviet Union itself; misread Saddam Hussein's preparations for his lunge at Kuwait; were caught off guard by the Israeli-Palestinian accords at Oslo and did not evaluate the probable consequences of Israel subverting them and setting them aside; were blindsided by the Asian financial crisis of 1997; failed to anticipate the 9/11 terrorist assault on America; mistook the situation in Iraq prior to the U.S. invasion of it; misestimated the strategic consequences of Iraq's invasion and occupation; and did not predict the financial crisis of 2008 and subsequent Great Recession.

This is far from a complete list of lapses. Collectively, the intelligence community has gotten not a few trends and events right but, as this list of failures suggests, its consequential successes are greatly outnumbered by its consequential failures.

This is not the place to attempt a serious examination of why this has been the case. Part of the answer, I think, lies in bureaucratic bloat. Too many analysts, too specialized, too narrowly focused, too inclined to miss the larger contexts that cause straight-line projections of an often-misunderstood present to miss the mark, too much groupthink, too little room for dissent, too little tolerance for outliers, too little challenge from those without access to classified information, too great a propensity to serve the interests of policymakers by providing analysis that corroborates rather than challenges the wisdom of their policies. No doubt there are other factors as well. It would be in the national interest to find and fix them.

Only fifteen years after I wrote my predictions of what China might be like in the year 2000, the Cold War had ended and China had emerged as the greatest change agent in the new era. In early 1996, just over a year after leaving the public service (to which I had by then devoted three decades of my life), I was asked by a private consulting group to provide an appreciation of trends in China and its foreign relations. The result was the first section of this chapter: "China and the Century of the Pacific." It describes how China's self-induced transformation looked to me just before the Taiwan Strait crisis of March 1996. (Many new thoughts then have become commonplaces today.) Most of the issues I identified as important in defining China's future and the shape of the Asia-Pacific region are still important, but the balances of factors within them have shifted, in some cases dramatically, in China's favor over the past decade and a half.

As I wrote that article, a largely overlooked crisis in Taiwan-mainland China relations was well under way.[1] I had warned the most senior levels of the U.S. government in October 1995, in response to Taiwan's moves toward independence, that the People's Liberation Army was planning missile firings and other menacing maneuvers against Taiwan by its forces. These warnings were not taken seriously. Some thought I was delusional. Others dismissed me as a messenger for Beijing, which I most decidedly was not. (Most intelligence failures result from the unwillingness of policy makers to absorb information that contradicts the conventional wisdom. In this case, the conventional wisdom was that China was overawed by American power to the extent that it would not react militarily to provocations from Taiwan.)

In the context of a hurriedly arranged January 4, 1996, discussion of future developments in U.S.-China relations that then–National Security Adviser Anthony Lake convened in the White House Situation Room, I was stunned when the discussion proceeded entirely without reference to the military confrontation in the Taiwan Strait I was confident was about to unfold. About an hour into the meeting, I interrupted the discussion to reiterate my concern that the PLA was embarked on a very threatening course. Tony Lake responded that the Chinese would not dare to risk a military challenge to U.S. policy toward Taiwan, given the overwhelming superiority of the U.S. nuclear arsenal to that of China. In reply, I recounted part of what I had heard from Chinese officials on the issue of nuclear deterrence.

I had warned these officials that their proposed adventurism in the Taiwan Strait would lead to a military confrontation with the United States as well as alienating Japan. Having confused American inattention and complacency about developments in cross-Strait relations with indifference and lack of resolve, these Chinese officials dismissed my prediction as unrealistic. In the ensuing arguments between us they stressed that the United States was no longer in a position to threaten nuclear attack on China, as it had done repeatedly during bilateral confrontations in the fifties and sixties, because China could now strike back at the United States. Inasmuch as "the United States cares more about Los Angeles than it does about Taipei," America could, in their view, be counted upon to avoid risking a nuclear exchange with China over the Taiwan issue.

This was a classic statement of a doctrine of deterrence. Yet two individuals who attended the meeting leaked it to the press as evidence of a Chinese threat to attack the United States with nuclear weapons.[2] This alarmed everyone about the wrong issues. When the military crisis I had predicted actually erupted in the Taiwan Strait, the U.S. government was taken by surprise.[3]

In the spring of 1996, I was asked to put China's growth and its prospects for continuing development into global perspective for members of the Atlantic community meeting in Toronto. A lot had changed by then. Where China was and where it seemed to be going are reflected in the second and final section of this chapter: "Where is China Going?"

Find More in the Online Archive

The prescient memorandum inspired by a bowl of noodles is available as "Forecasting Change in China: Where China Seemed to be Going in 1980" at http://bit.ly/interesting-times.

China and the Century of the Pacific
February 1996

The twentieth century was dominated by events in Europe. The twenty-first century is widely expected to be the century of the Asia-Pacific region, now the location of the world's most dynamic economies. The World Bank forecasts that by 2000 fully half the growth in the world economy will come from East Asia alone. Other economists estimate that, perhaps as early as 2007 to 2015, China will overtake the United States as the world's largest economy.

Few anticipate fundamental political or military change in a region that has—by marked contrast with Europe, Eurasia, and the Middle East—been remarkably tranquil since the end of the Cold War. But the region's politics and military alignments may prove to be no less dynamic than its economics. The last surviving lines of confrontation between "communism" and the "free world" are those in Northeast Asia. The division of Korea and China, like that of Germany, was created and sustained by superpower rivalry. With the disappearance of this rivalry, these divisions too may be subject to erasure. Other aspects of the existing territorial and political order in East Asia are similarly in doubt. It is by no means certain that the region will continue to enjoy the peaceful international environment that underpins predictions of its smooth rise to global preeminence.

What happens in China and between China and its neighbors is key. China's economy is the engine accelerating East Asia toward wealth and power. But rapid growth in China is placing that vast nation's internal stability under increasing stress. A breakdown in China would destabilize the region. China's external power and influence are rising. China is the only great power to have had parts of its territory (Macau, Hong Kong, and Taiwan) detached from it by the intervention of other great powers. The century and a half of Chinese weakness has left behind it the longest list of unsettled territorial issues affecting any country in the world. China has at least as good a legal claim as any other country to most of these territories and borders. Each needs only a relatively minor adjustment in the *status quo* to be settled. In the aggregate, however, these disputes raise the question of how a revitalized China will fit into Asia. China's neighbors are understandably apprehensive that it may do so by combat rather than compromise.

China's Drive for Wealth

Deng Xiaoping was purged in the Cultural Revolution (1964–74) for bluntly asserting that he did not care whether a cat was ideologically black or white as long as it caught mice. In 1978, when he assumed authority over China's destiny, he strangled the ideological cat once and for all. His pragmatic policies, based on the conviction that "getting rich is glorious," kicked off China's longest period of sustained domestic tranquility and economic growth in 140 years. In the countryside, and then in the cities, Deng's policy innovations scraped off decades of accumulated socialist sloth to liberate the entrepreneurial instincts of the Chinese people. As the productivity of labor increased, originally unproductive capital investments proved their worth. The result was sustained growth of about 10 percent annually for over a decade, with recent growth rates as high as 12 to 13 percent. Most economists judge that China's economy can continue to expand at 8 to 10 percent for another fifteen years, during which it would quadruple in size, before growth rates begin to decline. That would be good news for China. The Chinese economy must grow at about 7 percent just to absorb new entrants into the job market.

The East Asian Model of Growth

China is often said to be recapitulating the pattern of growth pioneered by other East Asian societies, like Taiwan and south Korea. This is true up to a point. Trade with the United States is an important factor in Chinese growth, but the American market is less important than it was to the growth of other East Asian economies at comparable stages of development. Intra-Asian trade, including Chinese trade with its East Asian neighbors, is growing faster than trans-Pacific trade. China's domestic market is huge, and growing apace with its economy. China has less need for foreign markets to achieve economies of scale. About 90 percent of China's capital needs can be met from domestic savings.

China is also vastly larger and more diverse than the Asian tigers. Growth rates vary widely between provinces. While economic growth is accelerating in inland provinces, the coastal regions from the Bohai Sea to the Gulf of Tonkin are far ahead and the gap is widening. Shanghai, for example, is now growing at about 20 percent per year. The result is a wave of internal migration from poor places to richer places. As many as 100 million people may have relocated over the past five years, the largest such population movement in history. China is compressing into a few years a process of urbanization that took centuries in Europe, nearly a century in North America, and decades elsewhere in Asia.

Sociopolitical Problems

Such rapid change is generating a growing range of social and other problems. By comparison with most other countries, China is undergoverned and underpoliced. Traditionally, order in China was maintained by social controls backed by the Chinese Communist Party (CCP), rather than by government, the legal system, or police. Social services were provided by the family and local communities or enterprises rather than the state. Whereas the percentage of GNP recycled through all levels of government in the West ranges from about one-third to half, in China, government per se accounts for only about one-eighth of GNP, excluding state-owned enterprises. Such enterprises are now being commercialized, if not privatized. (Restructuring and bankruptcies in state enterprises are likely to cost about 40 million workers their jobs over the coming decade.)

As China develops a more modern state structure and institutions to regulate a market economy, the role of government will grow, but it will be a long time before the Chinese government is able to perform all of the tasks government performs in the West. As family and community break down, and as state enterprise contracts, however, the Chinese government must take an increasingly direct role in the maintenance of law and order and the provision of social services.

China's Margin for Error

China's margin for error as it makes these adjustments is very narrow. The country's population is expected to peak at about 1.6 billion people before falling in the second half of the coming century. No one in human history has ever attempted to govern a society of such size. Moreover, China's ratio of arable land to population is exceptionally low. (China is slightly larger than the United States, including Alaska and Hawaii, but has only one-third of the arable land. If America had the same ratio of arable land to population as China does at present, the U.S. population would be around 3.6 billion!) But as industrial and commercial development continue their dizzy course, more and more farmland is being taken out of cultivation.

These realities account for some aspects of Chinese behavior that perplex foreign observers and complicate Beijing's relations with foreign capitals. China's obsession with order at the expense of individual rights reflects its sense of vulnerability to destabilization as well as lingering horror at the intermittent anarchy and mass starvation the country experienced over the 140 years prior to Deng Xiaoping's reforms. (More than 100 million Chinese lost their lives to foreign invasions and civil strife over that period.) China's draconian policies on birth control reveal fear that population growth could outrun farm productivity. The slow pace with which state enterprise is being dismantled reflects concern about the political effects of sudden unemployment for tens of millions of workers, who remain the last bastion of committed support for the CCP.

China had seemed exempt from the ills of rapid urbanization experienced by Europe in the eighteenth and nineteenth centuries and other Asian countries in the twentieth. It is now feeling the impact of explosive and unplanned change. Chinese cities are the most polluted in the world. The squatter population is growing rapidly—and with it an urban crime wave. Concern about personal security is fueling demands for tougher law enforcement. All of this is creating a backlash against some aspects of reform.

The Challenge of the Market Economy

The political strain is all the greater because of the dominant role of bureaucracy in Chinese entrepreneurial activity. There is no standard for separating public from personal interest. Chinese bureaucrats and soldiers (and their children or other family members) have taken to heart Deng Xiaoping's idea that "getting rich is glorious." They are buying and selling commodities and services and making investments, both on behalf of their "work units" and for themselves. Popular resentment of bureaucratic privilege and corruption is intensifying.

Economic growth is meanwhile altering the relationship between the central and provincial authorities. When the CCP was strong, it, rather than the government, directed provincial decisions. Now that acquisitive individualism has succeeded austere communitarianism as the national ethos, the CCP has lost much of its discipline, along with its ideology. In the absence of government institutions to replace it, the provinces have, to a great extent, gone their own way. New challenges to government posed by the requirement to manage a market economy have been met, if at all, largely at the provincial, rather than the national, level.

Beijing is now intent on creating the central institutions necessary to manage an increasingly dynamic and integrated national economy. To do so, it finds it must bargain with the provincial authorities in order to take away regulatory and other powers they have developed to fill the previous policy vacuum. (A good example is reform in tax policy to suit the new market economy; that took two years of hard central-provincial bargaining to fix.) Provincial apprehensions about the recentralization of authority are balanced by apprehensions about excessive decentralization and devolution of authority to the provinces.

Confusion about which level of government is responsible for what accounts for much of the unpredictability of policy application and other decisions in China. The situation cries out for a "federal" bargain—an agreed-upon division of authority between center and province within the context of a still-centralized state, consistent with Chinese tradition. The post-Deng government is still too weak to drive such a bargain. Sooner or later, however, it must and will do so. The reincorporation of Hong Kong under federal-style guarantees of local autonomy is already emboldening Shanghai and other provincial-level governments to demand comparable privileges.

Analogies to the Soviet Union

The challenges of change in China have led many in the West to speculate that the country will break up or that the CCP will be overthrown. A good deal of this speculation comes from sovietologists who lost their livelihoods when the Soviet Union collapsed and who have retooled themselves to study China. Having failed to predict the disintegration of the Soviet Union, they seem determined to anticipate China's collapse. But analogies between China and the former Soviet Union will not withstand scrutiny.

The Soviet Union was a multiethnic empire in which Great Russians constituted barely half the population. It was imposed by conquest and resettlement over the past 150 years. Moscow sought to impose or export its ideology wherever it could abroad. The failing Soviet economy carried an increasingly insupportable public welfare and defense burden, including subsidies to satellite states and the expenses of a huge troop presence beyond its borders.

China is a country with a strong sense of national unity established over centuries (if not millennia) of gradually digesting minorities at its frontiers.

Ninety-four percent of Chinese now consider themselves to be Han. In western areas of the country, such as Xinjiang and Tibet, minority peoples are a (declining) majority. Much as they may chafe under Han dominance, there is no prospect that they can successfully challenge it.

Beijing does not have an ideology it can explain to its own citizens, still less export to other countries. Finally, unlike the former Soviet Union, China has one of the world's most successful economies, with a relatively small government and low levels of spending on defense and public welfare. China has no satellites to subsidize and stations no troops beyond its borders.

The Taiwan Model

As for the CCP, it remains in power because it is in power; because there is no obvious alternative to it; and because the Chinese people fear national disunity and anarchy. (They take events in the former Soviet Union and Russia as an object lesson in this regard.) Most important, the CCP rules because the Chinese people have had no incentive to dislodge it, given the speed with which their living standards have been improving. Increasingly, the CCP must persuade; it does not command. This weakness does not, however, necessarily point to its collapse.

The CCP would not be the first Leninist party on Chinese soil to lead an economic revolution from the top, inadvertently transforming both the nature of politics and itself in the process. Chiang Kai-shek's Kuomintang, originally a Leninist party with a socialist ideology, did this in Taiwan. The changes the KMT fostered in island China ultimately forced the party to abandon both Leninism and socialism and to seek legitimacy through free elections.

Many Chinese believe the mainland is recapitulating the course of events in Taiwan, though with a lag of twenty-five or thirty years. In doing so, they argue, China is following an East Asian model of modernization, apparent from Korea to Singapore, in which economic liberalization under politically authoritarian rule precedes and establishes the conditions for later political liberalization. Despite all the difficulties in the way of their country's economic growth with continued stability, most Chinese remain optimistic—even cocky—about China's prospects for continued progress toward wealth, power, and a more predictable domestic order. Economic or social collapse in China would blight Asia's economic growth, destabilize the region, and overwhelm it with tens of millions of refugees. Such an outcome is so unthinkable to China's neighbors that they too prefer to be optimistic about China's prospects. (Only the Japanese are somewhat pessimistic. But then many Japanese would prefer a weak and divided China to a strong, united one.)

China's Drive for Power

For most of recorded history, China was arguably the largest, most populous, best-governed, most prosperous, and most technologically advanced of all human societies. Chinese regard their eclipse by the West in what they call "the recent past" (the last few centuries) as an anomaly that time and hard work will inevitably correct. By the end of the twenty-first century, they hope, China will once again be the preeminent society on the planet —a continent-sized Singapore with more than a billion industrious inhabitants.

Military prowess does not have pride of place in this vision. (Military modernization ranks last among the "four modernizations.") Nevertheless, it is China's growing military strength—and its potential to become a world military power by the middle third of the coming century—that most concerns China's neighbors. When China was vulnerable to attack by the United States or the Soviet Union, it sought to deter such attack by concealing as many details of its military force structure and budget as possible in the hope that Washington and Moscow would overestimate its capabilities.

Old habits die hard. In the post–Cold War era, Chinese secrecy continues to generate inflated estimates of Beijing's military capabilities and intentions—less, now, in Moscow and Washington than in Tokyo, New Delhi, Taipei, and Southeast Asian capitals. The result is a growing East Asian arms race aimed at matching what China is presumed to be doing, even though China may not actually be doing it.

Territorial Issues

China lacks secure and recognized frontiers. It disputes seabed boundaries with both Koreas and Indonesia; sovereignty over small islands, rocks, and reefs in the north with Japan (the Senkakus) and in the south with Vietnam, Malaysia, Brunei, and the Philippines; and land borders in the southwest and west with India, Tajikistan, Kyrgyzstan, and Kazakhstan. The civil war that separated Taiwan from the rest of the country remains unresolved. Beijing professes a desire to settle every one of these disputes by negotiation (as it has recently settled its borders with Russia) but does not rule out the use of force, if provoked. The list of places where the Chinese People's Liberation Army might be called upon to defend Beijing's views of China's sovereignty and territorial integrity is therefore very long.

The People's Liberation Army

The PLA is the world's largest armed force, with 3.5 million soldiers in uniform and a huge arsenal based mainly on 1950s technology.

On almost every border —Russia, Korea, Japan, Taiwan, India, and Southeast Asia —Chinese forces are badly outmatched in both training and equipment. The Chinese strike force, with its four ICBMs and handful of nuclear submarines that seldom leave port, is dwarfed by Russian and American strategic forces. On no border, even that with Taiwan, does the PLA concentrate a force superior in numbers to that which confronts it. PLA doctrines and deployments remain defensive rather than offensive.

China's defense budget is organized on different principles from Western budgets and denominated in a currency whose military purchasing power is impossible to estimate. The best guess is that as of 1996, translated into Western terms, China spends the equivalent of about US$50 billion per year on defense. This budget has been rising rapidly to match inflation. It has been stagnant in real terms. PLA leaders have long grumbled about receiving funding well below what they consider necessary to train and equip a credible national defense force, still less one commensurate with China's view of its place in the world. They have compensated for this, to some extent, by going into business and plowing profits back into defense spending.

Four factors are now giving the PLA a basis for demanding a bigger share of the budget. These are: (1) the government's desire to curb military corruption by forcing the PLA to divest itself of the numerous businesses it has created to fund itself; (2) the rapid military modernization going on elsewhere in the region, especially in Taiwan; (3) the opportunities presented by the Russian armaments industry, which is having a sort of going-out-of-business sale; and most persuasively (4) the prospect that military action may be necessary to preclude efforts by Taiwan to separate itself irrevocably from China. The PLA voice in policy-making is more insistent than in the past.

The Taiwan Issue

The Taiwan issue is emerging as the most compelling of these arguments and the focus of PLA political influence. The tacit agreement that kept the peace in the Taiwan Strait collapsed last year. This *modus vivendi* rested on two points of consensus between Beijing and Taipei, both of which Taipei now challenges. Both Beijing and Taipei had accepted that there was only one China, of which Taiwan was part, although they disputed which capital was the legitimate government of China. Both saw only two possible futures for Taiwan—continuation of the *status quo* or eventual reunification with the rest of China. The United States appeared to guarantee this situation. In this context, Beijing could be (and was) relaxed and patient about the Taiwan issue, saying that it could wait "a hundred years" to resolve it.

Taiwan, however, is now a democracy in which local (Taiwanese) voices speak louder than those of post-1949 refugees from mainland China. (Eighty-five percent of Chinese on Taiwan are "Taiwanese.") Taiwan's president is Taiwanese.[4] Taipei has ceased to challenge Beijing's sovereignty over the areas of mainland China the CCP controls. Taiwanese demand that Beijing reciprocate by recognizing Taipei as the capital of an "equal political entity" with sovereignty over Taiwan and a few small islands of mainland Fujian Province (e.g., Quemoy and Matsu). Many in Taiwan now espouse a Taiwanese nationalism at odds with traditional Chinese nationalism.

Taipei's attempt to develop a third possible future for Taiwan—one of statehood separate from China—is deeply rooted in Taiwanese politics. So is Taipei's drive for a separate seat in the United Nations. Taipei's recent words and actions have given Beijing the sense of urgency about the issue that it previously lacked. Ironically, neither Taipei nor Beijing wanted a crisis. Taipei's miscalculations and Beijing's reactions have nonetheless produced one. Mounting military tensions in the previously tranquil Taiwan Strait are the result.

Military Realities in the Taiwan Strait

The crisis has brought Beijing face to face with current military realities in the Taiwan Strait. For the foreseeable future, in the PLA's own judgment, any effort it might make to invade and conquer Taiwan would be decisively defeated by Taipei's armed forces. Military operations normally favor defense, all the more so when there are natural barriers to offensive operations. A hundred miles of water (four times the width of the English Channel) separate Taiwan's heavily fortified beaches from the mainland. Taipei's army is better trained and equipped, and enjoys interior lines of communication. Its air force could maintain air superiority against even the most concentrated and sustained assault by the PLA Air Force. (The F-16s and Mirage 2000s Taiwan will begin to receive this year will give it even greater superiority.) Taipei's navy could be overwhelmed, but only at heavy cost. Even if the PLA could concentrate nearly its entire force against Taiwan (and it can't), it could not hope to overwhelm the island's defenders.

The Current Taiwan Crisis

The PLA is not so stupid as to wish to play its weaknesses against Taiwan's strengths. Nor does it wish to pose a frontal challenge to the United States. Faced with an apparent secessionist challenge from Taipei, Beijing is using the threat, and possible application, of military force as a classic instrument of coercive diplomacy. It is attempting to force Taipei to the negotiating table. Beijing's object in negotiations would be to persuade Taipei to refashion the *modus vivendi* it rashly threw aside last year, i.e., to return to a situation in which reunification is seen as the only alternative to the *status quo*.

The PLA is therefore engaged in very large shows of force. Taiwan is a society of small investors heavily dependent on international trade. Beijing has prepared options for missile strikes and other actions that would drive up shipping and insurance rates, depress the real estate and stock markets, and otherwise force Taipei to take the views of Chinese across the Strait into account. It has communicated its options to Taipei. Some have made it into the press.

The Strategic Consequences of Conflict

This approach may well work, but it is a dangerous game. Conflict in the Taiwan Strait would challenge long-standing American guarantees of peace and stability there, while encroaching on Japan's strategic defense perimeter. The price of Japanese disarmament has been (and remains) reliable U.S. management of Japan's strategic interests. A U.S. failure to come to Taiwan's aid would be seen by Japanese as a default on this American responsibility. It would generate heavy pressure for Japanese rearmament to assure an independent Japanese capacity to defend Japanese interests.

U.S. intervention would require the use of Japanese bases, forcing Japan to choose between a non-hostile relationship with China and its alliance with the United States. Japan would almost certainly choose the United States, but no future Japanese government would ever again wish to be in a position where foreign decisions could impose such choices on it. In either case, the result would be military rivalry between Tokyo and Beijing, hostility between Washington and Beijing, and estrangement between Tokyo and Washington. The Taiwan issue thus has the potential to alter the Asian balance to the detriment of all three of the great powers—America, China, and Japan—most concerned with it.

Asian-Pacific nations have long looked to the United States to keep the unfinished Chinese civil war within bounds by dissuading either Taipei or Beijing from mounting a unilateral challenge to the *status quo* in the Taiwan Strait. Washington's recent inattention and ineptitude are widely blamed for allowing the situation to deteriorate as it has. Asians look for the United States to take diplomatic action to head off conflict in the Strait and to avoid having to decide between military intervention and non-intervention there. So far, the Clinton administration has not effectively engaged either Taipei or Beijing to this end.

Taipei's Options

Even if Washington declines to engage, however, it is far from certain that conflict is inevitable. The current crisis has already sobered Taipei and muffled calls for independence among Taiwanese voters. Beijing has made it clear that it will watch the president Taiwan elects on March 23, 1996 (almost certainly a reelected Lee Teng-hui), and come to a quick conclusion about which way he plans to lead Taiwan. If he shows willingness to abandon the drive for separate status and to accommodate Beijing, tensions will diminish. The issue of reunification will once again be deferred, perhaps to be revisited a decade hence, when Hong Kong and Macau have been fully integrated into China. If, conversely, Mr. Lee seems bent on separation or independence, the military pressure will escalate, perhaps into actual strikes against Taiwan or its interests. The PLA will then have a case for a long-term military buildup to acquire the capability to conquer the island. Fortunately, it currently appears that Mr. Lee has taken this message to heart and plans to launch a series of conciliatory initiatives toward Beijing shortly after he is elected.

China and the Great Powers of the Pacific

As the twentieth century comes to an end, China enjoys the best relations with Russia it has had in three centuries, the most cordial relations with Europe it has had for 150 years, the least troubled relations with Japan in a century, and the best relations with India it has had since the 1962 Sino-Indian border war. Sino-American relations are, however, deeply troubled. Even assuming that the current crisis over Taiwan is finessed, they seem unlikely to improve much for the foreseeable future.

Sino-American Relations

The collapse of the Soviet Union left Sino-American relations without a clear strategic rationale. Neither side has made much effort to develop one. The sharp American reaction to Beijing's brutal suppression of unrest in Tiananmen Square in 1989 ended most aspects of dialogue between the American and Chinese governments. Before 1989, the two governments focused on common interests and how to advance them, deferring differences for later resolution. Since 1989, they have focused on ideological differences, deferring common interests for later exploration. Neither side seems to know how to break this unpromising pattern of interaction.

The reversion of Hong Kong to China in 1997, the impasse between the Dalai Lama and the Chinese authorities in Lhasa, China's obsession with domestic stability under conditions of rapid economic change, tensions between Taipei and Beijing, and intermittent clashes between China and rival claimants in the South China Sea will continue to provide plenty of grist for the mills of congressional China-bashers in the United States. Economic and cultural relations between China and America are flourishing even as political and military relations deteriorate. It is hard to believe, however, that trade relations can remain forever immune to negative political influences, especially given the U.S. propensity for politically motivated sanctions. Already a rising chorus of American armchair strategists posits China as a menace to be confronted and contained. Similar pundits in Beijing claim that the United States desires to dismember China, overthrow its Communist government, and retard its modernization so as to keep China in its place. Sino-American relations are drifting toward hostility.

The Future

China's relations with the United States write the biggest question mark on any effort to assess prospects for peace, prosperity, and stability in both China and the Asia-Pacific region over the next decade. None of America's Asian allies and friends—not even Japan, despite its increasing wariness of China—wishes to pick fights with China or to be drawn into the fights that Washington seems to want to pick. All, even those least sympathetic to China, hope that Washington will deal firmly with Beijing on territorial issues while avoiding ideological confrontation with it. Such an approach is essential to underwriting the American role as balancer and facilitator that most Asians see as desirable. Many in Asia consider that the United States has been doing the opposite. They are worried that, in the absence of American leadership, they will be left to manage their relations with China on their own.

China's drive for wealth and power presents a challenge to the American role in the Asia-Pacific region as well as to China itself and other Asian nations. The conventional wisdom seems to be that American leadership will continue to be welcomed in Asia, that China will modernize successfully without destabilizing itself or its neighbors, and that the Asia-Pacific region can continue its smooth upward progress. Maybe so.

Where Is China Going?[5]
May 1996

The Chinese believe that, for most of recorded history, China was not just the most populous but also the most prosperous, most technologically advanced, most powerful, and—arguably—the best governed of all human societies. Chinese regard their eclipse by the West in what they call "the recent past" (the last few centuries) as an anomaly that time and hard work will correct. Most Chinese now believe that, in the century to come, their nation is destined to resume its natural place as the preeminent society on the planet. They may be right. Even if they are wrong, their cocky confidence that time is on their side has major international implications.

China's rise to wealth and power is the leading factor in the Asia-Pacific region's progressive displacement of the Atlantic community at the center of world economic affairs. The challenge of fitting China into the existing world order does not, however, stop with economics. China's rise also has enormous political and military implications. Its effects will be felt not just in Asia but throughout the world.

The Economic Challenge of China

Between 1980 and 1995, the Chinese economy more than quadrupled in size. From 1991 to 1995, its average annual real growth rate was 11.8 percent. Measured in terms of purchasing power parity, China now accounts for about 8 percent of global GNP. Most economists expect that the Chinese economy will continue to grow at 8 to 10 percent for the next fifteen years. It will again quadruple in size before growth rates begin to decline. Before 2020, they believe, China is likely to overtake the United States as the world's largest economy, thus resuming the rank it had until 1850. By 2030, China's economy may be larger than those of the United States and Japan combined.

The People's Republic of China (PRC) is achieving this growth, in part, by integrating its now largely marketized economy with the more advanced Chinese economies in Hong Kong, Macao, and Taiwan. It is also opening itself to the non-Chinese world. In the past five years, China has absorbed $114.4 billion in direct foreign investment and another $46.9 billion in foreign loans. (About 70 percent of "foreign" investment came from Chinese entrepreneurs in Hong Kong, Macao, and Taiwan.) Over this period, China's trade rose 19.5 percent annually, its imports and exports totaled $1.015 trillion, and the country was visited by more than 200 million foreign tourists. The PRC's foreign exchange reserves rose from $11.1 billion in 1990 to $73.6 billion in 1995 (and will reach $90 billion by the end of 1996). Foreign exchange reserves of the "greater Chinese" economy (comprised of the mainland, Hong Kong, Macao, and Taiwan) now stand at about $225 billion.

The PRC's integration into this "greater Chinese" economy and the East Asian economic region is being accomplished informally, by traders and investors rather than by governments or regional institutions. Now that colonialism, World War II, the civil war, Communism, and Cold

War containment have receded into history, clan and family ties between Chinese overseas and on the mainland are being rapidly reknit. The Taiwan Strait has presented the most dramatic example of these trends. Despite the political estrangement between the authorities in Taipei and Beijing, Taiwan entrepreneurs have invested more than $25 billion on the Chinese mainland. Cross-Strait trade now approaches $28 billion annually. One and a half million people travel to the mainland from Taiwan each year.

The PRC's rates of growth resemble those of other, smaller East Asian societies in recent decades. As in Singapore, Hong Kong, Taiwan, and south Korea, such growth over three or four decades will eventually lift Chinese living standards to levels equivalent to those in middle-income European countries. There are, however, important differences between China and the newly industrialized countries (NICs) of Asia. About 90 percent of China's future capital needs can be met from domestic savings. China's economy has, like other East Asian economies, benefited enormously from access to North American and European markets. Thirty percent of China's exports now go to the United States alone. However, China has a huge internal market, making it less dependent on exports than Taiwan or Korea at comparable stages of development. Moreover, intra-Asian trade, including China's trade with Asia, is now growing much faster than trade with other regions. In the years to come, China's dependence on both external and non-Asian markets, like the United States, will gradually decline.

The Chinese economy is nevertheless the engine that is accelerating the global shift of wealth and power to East Asia. Events in the region or between China and its trading partners may alter the rate of growth but are unlikely to reverse it. As early as the year 2000, the World Bank estimates, East Asia will contribute more than 50 percent of the world economy's growth. If the present is any guide to the future, however, East Asia may do so without having become fully part of the institutions that undergird the current international economic order. This order was crafted over the past half-century of Euro-American global dominance. It is now increasingly unsettled by the rise of China and other East Asian economies.

China's growing economic weight and central position in what is rapidly emerging as the leading economic region of the world economy have yet to be reflected in its inclusion in global institutions and regulatory regimes. China is excluded from the G-7, the World Trade Organization, the New Forum (successor to COCOM), the Missile Technology Control Regime (MTCR), the Nuclear Suppliers Group, and most other institutions devoted to setting global policies on trade, investment, and technology transfer. No one has even thought about how to work toward the ultimate admission of China to the Organization for Economic Cooperation and Development (OECD).

The effort (inaugurated by the United States and others in the early 1970s) to incorporate China into the world order shaped by the Atlantic community over the past half-century has faltered. Yet it is hard to imagine that the institutions that constitute this order can retain their leading position if an economy that is soon to become the world's largest is not fully integrated with them. Meanwhile, a rapidly expanding list of global and regional economic and politico-economic issues cannot be successfully managed without Chinese cooperation.

For example, China will soon overtake the United States as the world's largest emitter of greenhouse gases. Clearly, no effort to moderate the damage to the global environment can hope to succeed unless China is fully a part of it. Despite intense interest in environmental issues in Europe and North America, however, no concerted international effort to engage China in environmental dialogue and cooperation has yet been mounted.

China's rapidly growing export and internal markets continue to develop, to a considerable extent, outside the norms of the global trading system. This is creating vested interests in patterns of Chinese economic behavior that disrupt and damage trade and investment with the industrial democracies. The fact that China is not a member of most multilateral regulatory regimes leaves Beijing free to ignore complaints from its trading partners until they escalate into bilateral confrontation. In such raw tests of power, only a major trading partner like the United States has much chance of prevailing. As China's economic prowess grows, Beijing's bargaining power will also grow, making bilateral solutions to problems with China that are of wider international concern even more problematic. Yet the West has no apparent strategy for achieving China's integration into the multilateral institutions it hopes will regulate the post–Cold War international economic order. Almost without exception, institutions formed since the end of the Cold War have excluded China.

China is already an exporter of high-technology goods, many of them with military applications. As the Chinese economy becomes more sophisticated, such exports will greatly increase. Clearly, no effort to regulate trade with "rogue states" or in technologies relevant to weapons of mass destruction and their delivery systems can hope to succeed if China remains outside it. The limits of what can be accomplished by bilateralism are already apparent. Consider, for example, the decidedly mixed record of unilateral American attempts to regulate exports of Chinese nuclear and missile technology to Pakistan. As China grows, the bilateral leverage of the United States and other countries over it can only diminish. Yet there is no effort being made to bring China into membership in (and hence into compliance with) the multilateral regimes that attempt to regulate the international transfer of sensitive technologies.

Finally, China's opening to the outside world and the concomitant collapse of Chinese totalitarianism have allowed transnational Chinese criminal gangs to emerge. Such gangs are now involved in the drug trade and in smuggling Chinese emigrants under conditions approximating those of the eighteenth-century African slave trade. They are developing linkages to organized crime in Russia, Europe, and the Americas. The full cooperation of the authorities in Beijing with multilateral institutions like Interpol is essential to dealing with these problems. The Asia-Europe Meeting has created a multilateral forum joining European and Asian customs officials to discuss them. Yet the principal markets for drugs and destinations for such migrants are the United States and Canada, which are not part of this forum.

A persistent problem in dealing with China is the inability of the central government in Beijing to obtain the compliance of provincial and local authorities with the agreements it concludes with foreign governments. The current difficulties over intellectual property rights are a case in point. China lacks the legal system, including the courts, trained judges, and legal enforcement mechanisms upon which more developed countries can rely, to implement effective controls over commercial behavior. Everyone knows this to be the case. Even the Chinese will admit it when embarrassed into doing so. Yet there is no concerted international effort under way to aid China in law and administrative reform or in public administration and judicial training.

The absence of an international strategy by which to promote China's adherence to the norms fostered by global institutions is especially striking given the success of efforts to integrate China into the world order in the 1970s and 1980s. China can, of course, be counted upon to bargain for privileged status and exemption from the rules applied to other countries. Nevertheless, once admitted to a club, the record shows, China works hard to learn, adopt, and apply its rules. China's socioeconomic transformation over the past two decades owes much to its admission to institutions like the International Monetary Fund (IMF), International Bank for Reconstruction and Development (IBRD), Asian Development Bank (ADB), and specialized agencies of the UN, and to its subsequent adoption of the modes of analysis and policies they favor.

The lack of a Euro-American (and Japanese) strategy to speed China's integration into global institutions and its effective application of global norms is potentially very serious, given the high stakes involved. It cannot be in the world's interest to wait to begin managing the consequences for the international state system of China's rise to wealth and power.

Problems are accumulating, not diminishing. China's bargaining position is strengthening, not weakening.

The Politico-Military Challenge of China

As China's wealth grows, so do both its military power and political influence. The implications of this for the Asia-Pacific region are well understood by China's neighbors. Without exception, they seek economic benefits from closer ties with China, while keeping a wary eye on Beijing as they move to accommodate it politically. China now enjoys its most cooperative relations with Southeast Asia in five hundred years. China's relations with Russia are the most mutually respectful in more than three hundred years. Its relations with Europe, including Europe's great powers, are the most satisfactory to it in nearly two centuries. Beijing's relations with New Delhi are the least strained since the 1962 Sino-Indian border war. Its relations with Islamabad and Dhaka are as sound as ever. Despite an audible undercurrent of Japanese concern about China, Sino-Japanese relations are as good as they have been in a hundred years. Yet two centuries of weakness have left China with many points of dissatisfaction.

China is now the only great power to have had major portions of its historical territory and population detached from it by the military intervention of other great powers[6]—European powers in the cases of Macao and Hong Kong, Japan and the United States in the case of Taiwan. Beijing is determined to reunite these disparate Chinese societies under a single sovereignty, if not a single politico-economic system. China will accomplish such reunification through negotiations, if possible (as it has proven to be for Hong Kong and Macao), or by force, if necessary (as India did with Goa and Indonesia with Irian Jaya and East Timor). The peaceful reversion of Hong Kong and Macao to China will occur in 1997 and 1999, respectively. The question of Taiwan's relationship to the rest of China remains unsettled.

China is also the only great power to lack secure and recognized borders with most of its neighbors. China has now settled all of its inner Asian frontiers through negotiations with Russia and the newly independent Central Asian states. The list of Chinese border disputes remains, however, the longest such list in the world. China has unsettled economic zone (seabed) boundaries with both north and south Korea. It disputes the Senkaku (or Diaoyu) archipelago with Japan. China contests sovereignty over islets and reefs throughout the South China Sea with Vietnam, the Philippines, Brunei, and Malaysia. Its claims to economic zones in the South China Sea have generated a seabed dispute with Indonesia. The Sino-Indian border has been established *de facto* but not *de jure*. China is determined to define secure and recognized borders with all these neighbors by negotiated territorial adjustments as in the case of its inner Asian frontiers, if possible, or by military action to defend its sovereignty, if necessary.

Unlike reunification with Taiwan, none of these border issues requires major territorial or politico-military adjustments for their resolution. Sino-Korean differences must, in practice, await Korean reunification for their resolution. Neither China nor Japan has so far seen any pressing reason to address the question of sovereignty over the Senkakus.[7] A Sino-Indian border settlement is implicit in the *status quo* and could be formalized whenever the two sides are politically inclined to formalize it. China's full acceptance of the Law of the Sea Treaty (expected to be ratified by the National People's Congress later this year) will provide a legal framework for negotiation of claims in the South China Sea. China's neighbors have few concerns about its actions in the short term. They are all concerned, however, that China's military power relative to them is steadily growing. This has given them an incentive that China has heretofore seemed to lack to explore solutions to territorial issues.[8]

The reemergence of military tensions, including Sino-American naval confrontation, in the Taiwan Strait has changed this situation. Until 1994–95, Chinese leaders (like most politicians in Taiwan) believed that Taiwan had only two conceivable futures: the *status quo* (as it might be amended by cross-Strait interaction) or reunification. In these circumstances, Beijing felt no sense of urgency about the Taiwan issue. China's leaders could live with the *status quo* because the only way they could envisage it changing was by Taiwan's drawing closer to them and eventually accepting their leadership of a loosely reunited China. They sought to promote interdependence and dialogue across the Strait to advance their long-term objective of negotiated reunification.

By 1995, however, Beijing had become deeply concerned that Taiwan's democratic politics were centering on the quest for an identity separate from China. Responding to popular opinion on the island, the leadership in Taiwan began to provide inducements to Third-World capitals to allow the establishment of Taipei embassies alongside Beijing's diplomatic representation. Taipei redoubled its efforts to upgrade its representation in the capitals of great powers. It vociferously sought a separate seat in the United Nations General Assembly. The Taiwan leadership launched a campaign of nominally private but very political travel abroad to raise Taiwan's international profile. Beijing concluded that Taipei was bent on acquiring the attributes of independent statehood on the diplomatic installment plan. Notwithstanding Taipei's protestations of fidelity to the principle of "one China," Beijing saw Taipei's efforts as crafting a basis for long-term separation from China. This conclusion was buttressed by the main opposition party in Taiwan's open espousal of independence. From

Beijing's perspective, Taipei's actions threatened to alter the *status quo* in such a way as to preclude peaceful reunification.

Taipei's efforts to expand its options gave Beijing a sense of urgency about the Taiwan question it had previously lacked. When political warnings failed to deter Taipei, Beijing resorted to intimidation through military measures short of war, such as exercises and missile tests that underscored Beijing's ability to strangle Taiwan's economy. These measures were intended to force Taipei to reverse course or to come to the negotiating table. Chinese posturing, however, belatedly evoked countervailing shows of force by the United States, neutralizing Beijing's pressure on Taipei to negotiate.

American naval deployments were undertaken to underscore the long-standing interest of the United States in a peaceful, rather than violent, settlement of the Taiwan question by the Chinese themselves. They were not intended to signal support for Taiwan independence. Ironically, however, by making it clear that the United States would counter and offset Beijing's use of measures short of war to force Taipei to the negotiating table, U.S. actions have greatly diminished the prospects for peaceful reunification. If Beijing cannot force Taipei to the table, and the United States will not, it is highly unlikely that Taipei will ever negotiate. From Beijing's point of view, China now has only two options: doing nothing while Taipei works toward a "two Chinas" or "one China, one Taiwan" outcome, or going to war for reunification, despite the danger that the United States might be dragged into the conflict. Revising this calculus is now an urgent task for American diplomacy.

Even political dissidents in China see the Taiwan issue as a quarrel among Chinese, to be settled by Chinese without foreign interference. Resentment of American intervention in "China's internal affairs" is high. Beijing is on the verge of embarking on the long-term military buildup necessary to acquire the ability to overrun Taiwan even against U.S. opposition. China's recent embrace of Russian positions on various international issues, including NATO expansion, provides a basis for expanded military cooperation with Russia while calming China's northern flank.

As Beijing increases its military capabilities against Taiwan, it will not abandon its efforts to achieve reunification by peaceful means. It will continue to attempt to intimidate Taiwan into negotiations while seeking to minimize the resulting strain in its relations with the United States. At the same time, it will wish to limit collateral damage to its relationships with its Asian neighbors from tension and possible conflict in the Taiwan Strait. As a result, China is likely to pursue compromise on South China Sea territorial issues (and perhaps even the Senkaku dispute), as it did with Russia and the newly independent Central Asian states. By eliminating potential sources of conflict with the members of ASEAN and Japan, China can hope to provide reassurance that its aggressive stance on the Taiwan issue is *sui generis* and without wider implications for the region. Beijing's most recent military procurement decisions, as well as its diplomatic overtures to Southeast Asia, are consistent with such a strategy.[9]

These ominous trends might, of course, be reversed were Taiwan to be persuaded that it should enter into active negotiations on reunification with Beijing or otherwise provide convincing reassurance that it does not seek a future distinct from association with China. Taipei is, however, unlikely to seek to accommodate Beijing in this manner. Nor are foreign governments likely to be willing or able effectively to press it to do so. Taiwan will continue to attract Western and Japanese sympathy as a democratic underdog menaced by the Communist dictatorship on the Chinese mainland. This will stimulate widening concern about the implications of rising Chinese military power—no matter what Beijing does to allay such concerns.

In terms of deployed forces and raw combat power, if not in terms of technological prowess or power projection capabilities, China is already the preeminent military power in Asia. (The recently reaffirmed U.S. forward presence in Japan and the surge capabilities it facilitates are a potent qualifier to this Chinese military ascendancy.) Chinese defense expenditures have heretofore been relatively low in relation to GNP. Most of China's neighbors (e.g., Russia, Japan, Korea, Taiwan, and even India—let alone the U.S. armed forces in the Western Pacific) have far more advanced capabilities than the PLA. China is determined to match the forces on its borders eventually, but has deferred military modernization while building the economic base for it. In constant dollars, Chinese defense spending grew hardly at all over the past decade. (Nominal budget increases to keep pace with high rates of inflation led the press to perceive increases where none had yet occurred. China's secrecy about its defense budget and force structure aggravates its neighbors' tendency to exaggerate the growth of Chinese military power.)

The relatively low priority assigned to military modernization over the past decade reflected Beijing's judgment that the short-term risk of a major conflict on China's borders was slight and that a resolution of the Taiwan issue could, like the Hong Kong and Macao questions, be peacefully achieved. Recent events in the Taiwan Strait have clearly altered these judgments. The Chinese defense budget is likely to rise accordingly, though the focus of PLA modernization will shift largely to building the eventual capability to conquer Taiwan. Strategic nuclear forces and other weapons systems with the capacity to deter U.S. intervention in any battle for Taiwan are similarly likely to receive much greater emphasis in PLA modernization. Notwithstanding China's single-minded focus on Taiwan, its greater emphasis on military modernization will accelerate its acquisition of significant force projection and strategic weapons capabilities, speeding its emergence as a world, rather than just a regional, military power.

Is China Analogous to the Soviet Union?

The prospect of a more powerfully assertive China inevitably awakens memories of the recent Euro-American struggle with the former Soviet Union. It leads to speculation that China, like the Soviet Union, may disintegrate. It is, however, a mistake to draw many analogies between the USSR and the PRC.

The Soviet Union was a multinational empire, established by tsarist and Communist conquest from Moscow. Its dominant Russian nationality was a bare majority within its imperial structure. The Soviet Union was driven by the impulse to spread its ideology wherever opportunities presented themselves. To that end, it maintained a huge military presence in satellite states along its borders. Moscow's strategic ambitions led it to provide expensive military and economic assistance to like-minded states as far away as Cuba and southern Africa. Rigid central planning ultimately produced a declining economy unable to bear the very high level of military spending the Soviet state demanded. Until its final days, Moscow sought to overthrow the international *status quo* and impose its own rather than to join the existing international order and its institutions.

By contrast, China grew to its present borders over the course of millennia of gradual expansion and assimilation of minority peoples. The 94 percent of the Chinese population who consider themselves Han share a nationalist passion for unity, order, and international respect for their country's historical borders. They have no sympathy and even less tolerance for efforts by Tibetans or other minority peoples within these borders to exercise self-determination. They do not seek to bring additional non-Han peoples into their polity. Contemporary China does not seek to export its ideology (whatever that may be). It has no satellites and maintains no forces beyond its borders. China's increasingly decentralized economy is the fastest growing in the world. Its defense budget could be greatly increased without putting much if any strain on its economy. China seeks to join the existing international order, not to overthrow it.

Nor is China likely to disintegrate as the Soviet Union did. Economic growth has indeed altered the relationship between the central and provincial authorities. As acquisitive individualism succeeded austere communitarianism as the national ethos, the Chinese Communist Party lost much of its discipline, along with its ideology. In the absence of government institutions to replace it, the provinces, to some extent, went their own way. In the early stages of economic reform, new challenges to government posed by the requirement to manage a market economy were met, if at all, largely at the provincial, rather than the national level. Beijing is, however, now well along in its efforts to create the central institutions necessary to manage an increasingly dynamic and integrated national economy. Resistance to this recentralization by the provinces has not led to separatist sentiment. On the contrary, the spirit of nationalism is on the rise throughout China. This makes it less likely than ever that Beijing will tolerate separatism in regions with substantial ethnic minority populations, like Tibetans or Uyghurs.

Finally, the Soviet Union was a horrifying violator of the human rights of all whom it controlled. For all the Western pressure on Moscow on human rights issues, it took the collapse of the regime to bring about significant improvement. Unlike the former Soviet Union, however, China is carrying out far-reaching economic and social reforms. These may or may not lead in time to political reforms, as happened, for example, in the formerly Leninist Chinese society on Taiwan. Nevertheless, it is arguable that the course of events elsewhere in East Asia will prove to be a better predictor of China's future than that in the Soviet Union. (If so, a policy based on protest of egregious incidents while assisting the process of institutional reform in China, similar to the approach followed in Taiwan and south Korea, could work better than a policy based on pressure and protest alone.)

In short, Beijing does not think or behave like Moscow did when it was the capital of the USSR. China is not an implacable foe of the West or the world order the West has created. The PRC is unlikely to follow the USSR into disintegration and collapse. The challenge to the world posed by the rise of China is different. In some ways, it may prove more daunting.

Conclusion

Nearly two centuries ago, Napoleon advised his fellow Europeans, "Let China sleep. When it wakens, it will shake the world." There is now no prospect that China will return to the slumber of past centuries. The twenty-first century will see China resume its traditional pride of place among the world's societies. The question before Europeans and North Americans is not how to prevent what cannot be prevented. It is how to ensure that the rise of China in the new millennium buttresses rather than erodes the international system we have constructed with such difficulty in this century. To that end, we must urgently consider how to speed China's integration into existing institutions on acceptable terms. Equally important, we must decide how best to ensure that China's determination to rectify the borders imposed upon it by the ages of imperialism, fascism, and the Cold War does not lead to long-term confrontation and strategic realignments adverse to Western interests.

Chapter 7

Deng's Revolution in Retrospect

Deng Xiaoping's decision to cast aside ideology in favor of eclectic borrowing from the successful modernization experiences of others ranks as one of the most important events of the twentieth century. Its consequences are a dominant element in the forces shaping the course of this century. The period of Mao Zedong's rule in China should now be called "the pre-Dengist period" of modern Chinese history. Deng wrought a far greater and more lasting revolution in China and the world than his charismatic predecessor did.

In 2006, I had occasion to reflect—in a talk at Johns Hopkins University—on what China might have been like if Deng Xiaoping had not launched the process of revolutionary change he did in December 1978. The result appears as the first section of two: "From Mao to Now" notes that while Deng's revolution has so far worked out very well for China, the country's continued success is far from assured. The chapter ends with a consideration of "What Could Go Wrong for China."

Find More in the Online Archive
More detailed observations on the transformation of China between 1997 and 2001 are available in the online archive at http://bit.ly/interesting-times.

From Mao to Now[1]
October 2006

When Mike Lampton[2] asked me to speak on the thirtieth anniversary of Chairman Mao's demise, I was a bit nonplussed. What, I asked myself, could I say about the famous peasant under glass in Tiananmen? Others, including some who are now ferocious critics of China, were quite taken with him once. I never was. But Mao is worth remembering. I am glad to see so many members of his cult present here tonight. Let me give you my thoughts on the man and his legacy.

Mao Zedong had a force and energy that none but men of equally great spiritual conviction could withstand. His animal appetites, we now know, matched his intellectual vigor. He was an object of adulation to his subjects and of mingled admiration and dread to his subordinates and intimates. While Mao lived, the brilliance of his personality illuminated the farthest corners of his country and inspired many would-be revolutionaries and romantics beyond it.

Few indeed loved Chairman Mao's style of governance, but all but a few of those who despised it most loved the People's Republic he had founded more—and hated him less than they feared him. Had he been less insistent on grand and impractical visions, his ideas would not have convulsed his country as desperately as they did, nor would they have been as thoroughly discredited. Had he not driven his country mad with attempts at sudden, violent change, China would not, however, now be as devoted to domestic tranquility as it is, nor would it have so easily accepted the international order it once rejected but in which it now prospers. Had Mao died earlier, his ideas might have lived on in the new China. He would certainly be seen by history as a greater man.

As it is, Mao is likely to be remembered, unfondly, as a great military strategist and a good poet who was a colossal failure at crafting a sustainable order in the country he sought to liberate from its past as well as from its foreign and domestic oppressors. Had he succeeded in his multiple attempts to eliminate Deng Xiaoping's political influence, the world might still worry about the consequences of China's backwardness and disgruntlement about the international *status quo*, not its rapid advance as a leading participant in the quintessentially capitalist process of globalization. But Mao did not succeed in doing in Deng, and China and the world are greatly the better for that.

Mao was very Chinese, but he aspired to a role in human, not just Chinese, history and philosophy. Generations of soldiers yet unborn will read his thoughts on asymmetric warfare. Only academics—no disparagement of this audience intended—and Communist Party ideologues will ponder his political philosophy or the values it espouses. Today, there are some in northeastern India and Nepal who invoke his name as they struggle for political power and economic leveling in their societies. But they mainly read his military manuals, not his philosophical tracts. There are also those in China for whom Mao remains a god, if now a blessedly undemanding, middle-class god, whose effigy can be mounted on a dashboard or hung above an altar table to be venerated along with one's ancestors. Mao's charisma has transcended the man himself.

In the end, however, Mao Zedong is no more a universal figure than the emperor he most resembles. Qin Shihuang is remembered without reverence by Chinese as the ruthless unifier of China whose violence and oppressions paved the way for the peaceful and tolerant order and the wealth and power of the Han Dynasty. The First Emperor thus created the vessel in which a Chinese culture vastly different than the one he had conceived could take China to greatness. He was the precursor, not the creator, of that China. Still, some of his vision for China was realized in its continued unity of culture and institutions and in the awe that the state he created inspired among its neighbors. Like Qin, Mao was a philosopher king whose philosophy died as his kingdom endured and found its own very different way forward.

That "kingdom"—the People's Republic of China—is Mao Zedong's true monument. And it is one whose achievements are congruent with the goals of the broad pantheon of twentieth-century Chinese revolutionary and nationalist figures, not just Mao himself. Despite the erratic and brutal nature of his reign, both his revolution and the preceding nationalist revolution had in common four inextricably connected objectives:

- unifying China by eliminating warlords and erasing foreign spheres of influence;
- regaining China's independence and deterring foreign invasion and bullying;
- establishing respect for China as a sovereign participant in international affairs; and
- restoring China to prosperity.

When Chairman Mao first proclaimed that China had "stood up," this was what he had in mind. It galled him then, when he wished to stand tall, to have to "lean to one side" to do so. In the end he could not sustain the posture. Thus, China's dependence on the Soviet Union was soon set aside and, after a delay in which he experimented unsuccessfully with means of accelerating China's economic development and used the Cultural

Revolution to affirm the idiosyncratic nativism of his revolution, Mao sought to lean on a suddenly respectful United States to regain China's international balance.

From Mao's perspective, Chiang Kai-shek's defeat and flight to Taiwan reduced him and his "Republic of China" to the status of a warlord whose rump regime could not survive without foreign backing. Mao was determined to bring this vestige of China's turbulent past to heel and to eliminate Taiwan as an American protectorate on Chinese soil. He did not believe in the possibility of peaceful reunification. He was prepared to be patient about reincorporating Taiwan, but expected this to take place through the use of force. Mao lived to see his new Chinese state attain the international recognition as a sovereign great power that the United States had spent so much effort to deny it and to see Chiang's regime reduced to commensurate diplomatic irrelevance. He did not live long enough to see the Taiwan issue begin down the path to peaceful reunification it is now treading.

Chairman Mao insisted on keeping China's distance from the United States as he had not from the Soviet Union. He guarded China's status as an equal and independent actor, standing apart from the sphere of influence that we Americans then, with shameless inaccuracy, called the "free world." And while he was pragmatic in his actual approach, he insisted on a framework for relations with the United States that would realize the objective of a unified China.

Deng Xiaoping embraced this objective, like the other nationalist visions that had animated Mao. But his pragmatism led him both to reject Mao's preferred methods and to risk a degree of intimacy with the United States that Mao would never have contemplated. Deng adopted peaceful reunification as a national objective. He used the cover of improved relations with the United States to force Vietnam to abandon its efforts to build a Soviet-style empire in Indochina. He extended vital assistance to the American-led effort to contain the Soviet Union, for example, enlisting China as a full partner in the Saudi-financed, American- and Pakistani-managed struggle to expel the Soviets from Afghanistan. But most differently of all, Deng boldly initiated an across-the-board exposure of Chinese to American ways. His motive was precisely to overthrow the legacy of Maoism and to replace it with a fundamentally changed socioeconomic order in China.

In the late summer of 1981, Deng Xiaoping remarked in my presence that when the history of the twentieth century was written, Mao's revolution would be described as the prelude to the real Chinese revolution—that which Deng himself had initiated in December 1978. But Deng made it clear that his was a revolution in methodology, not a change in national objectives. His opening of China, of course, was a defining event in the final quarter of the last century, not just for China but for a world in which China now plays an increasingly decisive role. It has greatly accelerated progress toward the objectives of Chinese nationalism—unification, credible deterrence of foreign meddling, international respect, and prosperity.

The establishment in 2005 of party-to-party ties between Taiwan's major opposition parties and the Chinese Communist Party and their inauguration of a partial cross-Strait political entente have reversed the trend toward war in the Taiwan Strait. Their interaction is replacing Taiwan separatism with a process of cross-Strait political integration that parallels the economic integration and cultural rapprochement that have been under way for more than a decade. Meanwhile, Taiwan's political establishment, by repeatedly rejecting massive purchases of American weapons in favor of avoiding an arms race with Chinese across the Strait, has made it clear that the island's elite do not believe their differences with the mainland can or should be addressed by military means.

The leadership in Beijing, for its part, now sees peaceful reunification as the likely result of trends that are increasingly well established. Renewed confidence that time is on their side has restored these leaders' willingness to be patient and forbearing. The last chapter in Taiwan's excursion into an identity separate from the rest of China has, of course, yet to be written—and Chinese leaders do not rule out the possibility that they might have to use force to deter efforts by the Taiwan authorities to alter the legal *status quo*. But they see this as a diminishing possibility, and almost no one in Beijing now expects reunification itself to involve the use of force. In this context, frankly, American and Japanese concerns about Chinese aggressiveness in the Taiwan Strait seem increasingly delusional.

China does seem determined to invest in modernizing its still relatively backward armed forces to be able to deter others from attacking it, as we and many of its neighbors have in the past. Speculation that China should and will aspire to be a "peer competitor" of the U.S. military is, however, made in the USA, not made in China. Threat analysis is, of course, the mother of all defense spending, and Americans are really good at both. Having a potentially formidable high-tech enemy is a great fundraiser for the hyperexpensive advanced weaponry our military-industrial complex prefers to make and our armed forces love to employ. And, in all fairness to purveyors of the China threat, China may yet emulate us by developing the means to invade faraway countries and use gunboat diplomacy against them, or actually do both. But back in the real world, so far, it hasn't; there is no hard evidence that it plans to.

The Lebanese militia's recent frustration of Israel's effort to bomb their country into peaceful coexistence has, meanwhile, provided a splendid example of how Mao's concept of "people's war" remains relevant. Remember "dig tunnels deep, store grain everywhere, and never seek hegemony"?[3] Hezbollah demonstrated how this kind of preparation for defense could support people's war combined with information warfare, including first-class signals intelligence and command and control, to defeat a high-tech invader. Israel, which had no desire or intention to mount a land invasion of Lebanon, was maneuvered by Hezbollah's strategy into engaging it on the ground Hezbollah had chosen for battle, where it could frustrate the invaders of Lebanon militarily and defeat them politically. This evolution should be a caution to anyone contemplating military coercion against a determinedly sovereign people like the Chinese—or, for that matter, the Persians. "People's war," updated to address the challenges posed by technological advances, remains the core of China's defense strategy. It is inherently defensive, rather than offensive, but, as the example of Lebanon shows, it can be very punishing for those who take it on.

This brings me to China's drive for a dignified position of leadership in the world order. In the global contest for political standing, the Chinese are—at present—clear winners. Outside of Germany and our own country, China is by far the most admired great power. This admiration derives from the weight China's own experience has caused it to give to respect for sovereignty. China is popular in no small measure because it now stands against us in its opposition to coercive diplomacy directed at changing the domestic policies of other nations, its rejection of the notion of humanitarian intervention, and its insistence on adherence to the norms of international law.

There is, of course, a great irony in this. China, an Asian nation that long headed an explicitly hierarchical state system, is now the staunchest international defender of once purely European stipulations about the sovereign equality of states. The People's Republic of China, a state created in explicit opposition to the norms on which we and other Western nations built the world order we dominated, has emerged as a stalwart defender of that order against American and other Western second thoughts about it. We have new ideas; China has taken up our old ones. As Beijing's global influence continues to grow, I wouldn't bet on Washington's current radicalism prevailing over China's conservatism. The east wind may indeed prevail over the west, though with results opposite to those Chairman Mao imagined.

China still, however, presents a political model that is not in the least attractive internationally, even to those countries that have become dependent on the Chinese. This will be the case as long as China does not develop a system that gives its citizens a more direct, more visible, and more credible role in selecting their leaders and in formulating and overseeing the implementation of policy. The economic advances of recent years have laid the basis for a gradual political opening that is now overdue. In its absence, China will continue to experience levels of corruption and disrespect for human rights that constantly irk its people and intermittently bring disrepute upon it abroad. Aside from limiting China's international and regional influence, such political backwardness poses a threat to the process of opening and reform that have been the keys to its stunning advances in recent decades. All things being equal, these advances should continue. But nowhere is it written that this must be so.

The greatest threat to China's future global leadership is, I think, neither the deficiencies of its political system nor the risk of American resistance to its rise. It is the danger Mao cautioned against—domineering self-righteousness and overconfidence born of success, translated into hegemonism. China's neighbors share Mao's apprehensions that its return to wealth and power might inspire hegemonic behavior and are watching closely for signs of this. As recent American interaction with the outside world has convincingly demonstrated, a little bit of such behavior can alienate a lot of people very fast. Meanwhile, only the unobservant can fail to notice a rising measure of cocky self-assertiveness in today's China. The American example attests that a country that is "自以为是"—"so full of itself that it has all the answers"—is one that many will wish ill and few will wish to follow.

If China's current, remarkably deft policy of deferential politeness to foreigners is succeeded by arrogance, it will be because of its extraordinary success in advancing the objectives of Chinese nationalism—including, finally, the achievement of levels of wealth that restore China to its historic status as the global economic center of gravity. Mao's misguided efforts to find shortcuts to such economic success derived in large measure from the romantic delusions of Friedrich Engels's ruminations in the *German Ideology*. They failed so badly that the Russians were able, with some justification, to charge him with pursuing "pantsless Communism," a philosophy only the north Koreans now practice. Deng's inspired decision to launch China on a different course has put the pants back on China, along with a fine jacket and tie. The "socialism with Chinese characteristics" that his policies sponsored is derided by some as "bandit capitalism." There may be something to this. But whatever you call its system, China is now a huge success at business, lauded—and feared—here and elsewhere abroad as both the workshop and the potential leader of the capitalist world.

In my view, the challenges from China's economic success lie less in its role as a producer of goods sold throughout the world than in the consequences of its eventual emergence as the world's largest consumer market. These include the likelihood that the Renminbi yuan will join the euro as an alternative to the dollar, as a reserve currency, and ultimately, as a unit of account for trade in energy and other commodities currently traded solely in dollars. And they include the possibility that—if China sustains its remarkable openness to the outside world as well as its commitment to market economics and does not backslide into bureaucratic control of its economy—its current drive to become an innovative society may work, displacing the United States from our long-accustomed role as the global scientific and technological leader. But these are other topics, best left for discussion at another time and place.

China has long strived to restore its unity, sovereign dignity, domestic tranquility, and wealth. These efforts, conducted unsuccessfully under Chairman Mao's erratic baton, are attaining success under the steadier direction of his more pragmatic but equally nationalist successors. China is now not just transforming itself; it is transforming the world. Chairman Mao would have liked that, though he would have hated how it came about and despised how it is proceeding.

China's continued success is far from inevitable, but the challenges we face from a successful China—as well as those that China itself faces—may be quite different than those of concern to us yesterday or today.

What Could Go Wrong for China?[4]
June 2007

Lord Lamont asked me to consider what could go wrong for China. I have concluded, first, that China is a nice place to carp at but you wouldn't want to have to run the place. Second, that a great deal could go wrong with it—and some of it will, but most of it won't. And, third, that we better hope both that things go right for China and that we don't push it into a posture of hostility toward us. That's the summary. Let me speak to it.

Lord Lamont's question is a vitally important one. By now it's a commonplace that what happens in this century will be determined in large measure by developments in China and India. They are recovering their ancient wealth and power, this time in a globalized environment with few economic or cultural barriers.

Many factors suggest caution about the prospects for India, with its unbridled population growth, communal tensions, and fissiparous tendencies; widening gap between highly educated plutocrats and illiterate peasants and proletarians; bureaucratism; nuclear confrontation with Pakistan; and vulnerability to climate change, for example.

In contrast, it's easy to be optimistic about China. Perhaps too easy.

After all, in the nearly thirty years since Deng Xiaoping replaced Mao's utopian dogmatism with eclectic pragmatism, China has enjoyed almost uninterrupted domestic tranquility amidst truly remarkable economic and social transformation. It has emerged as one of the world's greatest economic powers. The Chinese are at long last building the legal and institutional underpinnings of a modern state. The People's Republic has come to expect orderly successions in its leadership. It is creating a meritocratic technocracy and acquiring a vast property-owning middle class. Chinese citizens have expanding freedom to make decisions about how to order their own lives, to travel abroad, and to experiment with unconventional ideas and opinions. The People's Liberation Army, once famously "low-tech," is building an increasingly modern capacity to defend Chinese sovereignty, territorial integrity, and national interests. China is becoming a power in space and in the seas along its coast. The eyes of the world are upon it.

The world used to worry that misgovernance in China would cause its collapse. Now people worry that China's growing strength may lead it to throw its weight around. But the fact that things have mostly gone spectacularly right for China over the past thirty years does not guarantee they will do so in the decades to come. And if things do go wrong for China, the consequences for all of us could be very great indeed. In fact, that could also be the case even if things continue to go right.

For one thing, the world cannot afford the emergence of another self-indulgent, credit-card-financed consumer society along the lines of the one we have built here. Given the size of its population, a China that emulated the United States would, among other things, have 1.1 billion cars on its roads, import more oil than the entire world now consumes, emit ten times the greenhouse gases the Chinese economy currently does, and generate 7.5 billion pounds of garbage every day. Consider, too, the implications of a Chinese decision to seek national security, as we have, through military primacy or preemptive intervention abroad! In these and other respects, the notion of a future China with current American characteristics is unnerving.

Many Americans are frustrated and annoyed by China's obstinate insistence on doing things its way rather than ours. But it may well be that the very worst thing that could happen would be for us to succeed in persuading China to become like us. Arguably, Americans should instead be working with our allies across the Atlantic and Pacific and with progressive-minded people in China to help them avoid our most injurious practices even as we correct them ourselves. In this regard, the prospect that a powerful China might follow us in seeking to exempt itself from the constraints of international law and comity is a reminder of the stake we all have in insisting that every country, including our own, accept and abide by the same standards of conduct in its relations with others.

A truly powerful China is, of course, not an inevitability. Despite much progress over the past decade, China's government revenues are still too small and its civil service too feeble and freewheeling to carry out all the responsibilities of a modern state. Total spending by all levels of government in China this year—though it has almost sextupled over the past decade—will come to only 20.8 percent of GDP. (By way of comparison, in the United States, government spending amounts to 36.4 percent of GDP. In the UK, the figure is 44 percent, more than twice as high as in China.) And China doesn't have much margin for error. It's skating pretty close to the edge in many areas. With only one-fourteenth of the world's arable land, it must feed one-fifth of humanity. (Not for nothing does Chinese cuisine extol the use of ingredients that are elsewhere considered inedible.)

Huge and politically disturbing imbalances in economic development have emerged in China. Some regions of the country now enjoy European levels of affluence, while others remain among the most primitive and poor in the world. Hundreds of millions of people in rural areas are trying to move to cities in which they will live in Dickensian conditions that stimulate crime and invite social unrest. There are more than one hundred Chinese cities with populations of one million or more. Each now has expanding slums overflowing with migrants from the countryside.

In addition to having the world's largest human population, China is home to over half the world's hogs and more than one-fourth of its domestic fowl. Their interactions with exceptionally dense concentrations of people subject Chinese—and, ultimately, everyone else—to the constant risk of crossover by new and often fatal diseases.

Meanwhile, China's largely unregulated economic development is placing an immense burden on its environment. In some respects, China's environment may already have reached the stage of self-sustaining ecological degradation, placing it beyond the possibility of future remediation. Almost 90 percent of the Chinese water supply is polluted, and even that is drying up under the combined impact of deforestation, overuse, and climate-change-induced reductions in snowfall on the Tibetan Plateau. Environmental issues are now the cause of most instances of public disorder in China.

China has a rapidly aging population but no assured funding for the pensions, health insurance, and other elements of the social safety net its elders and their children need. Each Chinese child from a one-child family—as most still are—must prepare to support two parents and as many as four grandparents over their lifetimes. The result is the world's highest rates of individual savings, the suppression of domestic economic demand, an unhealthy dependence on exports for growth, and a resultant vulnerability to the consequences of economic missteps in major foreign economies like our own.

The fact that the government that must deal with these and other issues won a civil war nearly sixty years ago no longer confers legitimacy on it. Nor can the Chinese government claim the legitimation of democratic elections. The mandate of the Chinese Communist Party now depends on its performance—its ability to meet rising expectations and to do something about the widening gap between urban and rural incomes. Failure at either of these tasks could cost the Communist Party its power. Yet the political order in China provides no alternative to the Communist Party other than anarchy, of which the Chinese people have long since had their fill.

Then there's the challenge of assuring national security. Chinese recall their country's subjugation by Western and Japanese imperialism in the nineteenth and twentieth centuries. Within living memory, more than thirty million Chinese perished at the hands of seaborne invaders from Japan. China has land borders with fourteen countries. Since the People's Republic arose in 1949, it has faced limited wars with American-led international forces in Korea, the Indian Army in the Himalayas, the Soviet Red Army in inner Asia, and both Vietnamese Communist and American forces in Indochina. China itself remains divided by an unfinished civil war in which overwhelmingly powerful foreign forces assert a residual right to intervene.

All this is to say that, if you're among those trying to govern China, you have a great many things on your mind and not much inclination to pick fights with foreigners. Not surprisingly, China's leaders have made the maintenance of a peaceful international environment the organizing principle of their foreign policy. They want to get on with domestic development without becoming embroiled in foreign affairs.

China is still the homeland of the great strategist, Sunzi, and it takes seriously his insight that the best wars are those that are never fought. China has been prepared to use limited force for political effect, as with India in 1962 and Vietnam in 1979, but Beijing's strong preference has been to settle borders and other disputes through negotiation, not military coercion. Over the past decade, this approach has achieved the peaceful reassertion of sovereignty over Hong Kong and Macau, the demarcation of both the Russian and Vietnamese land borders, the settlement of borders with the newly independent Central Asian states, and significant progress toward establishing an agreed frontier with India, the only border dispute still unresolved. China is quietly pursuing the same approach to the settlement of its maritime boundaries with its Southeast Asian, Korean, and Japanese neighbors.

The recent sharp increases in Chinese defense budgets do not contradict this focus on managing national security by measures short of war. Spending on the military is, of course, an important indication of the extent to which a nation expects to have to rely on the use of force to secure its defense and foreign policy objectives. Coming after a long period of stagnation in funding for the People's Liberation Army, recent defense budget increases are truly striking. While a good deal of the money has gone into long-overdue pay raises, the net effect is—as intended—the rapid modernization of a previously very backward military establishment. But, to put this in proper perspective, one must realize that other elements of China's political economy are being modernized even more rapidly than the PLA. Increases in the Chinese defense budget, impressive as they are, lag behind even more rapid and larger budget increases for nonmilitary programs and activities in China. The military has yet to seize pride of place in the Chinese budgetary process, as it has here.

It is, of course, true, as is often stated, that the official Chinese defense budget does not include all military and military-related spending. This sounds alarming—until one recalls that this is not at all unusual in other nations. The United States, for example, has an official defense budget of $499.4 billion. The press routinely uses this figure to report that we are spending 3.6 percent of our GDP on our military. But defense-related spending in other parts of the federal budget adds at least another $435.5 billion or so, bringing projected military or military-related outlays this fiscal year to at least $935 billion. Adding in the amount we spend on intelligence, which remains a secret, would push the figure even higher. As it is, $935 billion comes to 6.8 percent—not 3.6 percent—of our GDP.

The proportion of military-related spending that is outside the Chinese defense budget seems in fact to be somewhat less than in the United States, though no one—not even the PLA—has been able to come up with a reliable figure in this regard. For the sake of argument, if the proportion of extrabudgetary military-related expenditures were as high in China as in the United States, Chinese spending on defense could be as much as $84 billion[5]—some $39 billion more than the $45 billion in China's official defense budget—or about 3 percent of GDP, versus the 1.7 percent implied by the defense budget alone. Mirror-imaging is not, of course, a recommended method of extrapolating foreign realities. But it suffices to make two points: first, that Beijing continues to assign a lower budgetary priority to its military than to its domestic development, and second, that defense budget increases in China provide somewhat less cause for concern than alarmists and advocates of defense spending in other countries like to claim.

Despite the rapid improvement in PLA capabilities, Chinese defense spending remains modest. In relative terms, it is a good deal less than half of the proportion of GDP we spend on our military. Of course, our GDP is also much larger than China's, so in absolute terms—at nominal exchange rates—we are spending more than ten times what China is on defense. Some peer competitor! China is simply not in our military league.

But budgets do not constitute capabilities, and capabilities—not how much they cost—are what count strategically and on the battlefield. In this regard, given its size and the speed of its military modernization, China obviously invites special vigilance. It is important for both the United States and China's neighbors to understand what capabilities China is investing in, other than a better-educated and more professional group of officers and enlisted personnel. Does the direction of Chinese military spending suggest a pending shift in the roles and missions assigned to the PLA over the next decade or so?

In point of fact, the ways in which the Chinese military is modernizing seem fully consistent with its traditional roles and missions. China remains engaged in a systematic effort to acquire the capabilities necessary to deter Taiwan from seceding or American or Japanese forces from returning to that island. This has involved building the capacity to inflict convincing damage on Taiwan or on any foreign force that might intervene to shield Taiwan from the military consequences of an attempt to gain independence. No one has been able to identify a weapons system or doctrine being developed by China that cannot be clearly related to this mission or to the security of China's other land and sea borders.

China's defense modernization efforts are therefore impressive, but fall well short of mobilization for war. China does not accept the logic of mutually assured destruction; its nuclear arsenal is being upgraded but remains deliberately modest. China is not procuring the strategic lift, bomber forces, carrier strike groups, amphibious warfare, or command, control, communications, intelligence, surveillance, and reconnaissance capabilities that give the United States' armed forces their unrivaled capacity to conduct offensive operations in faraway places.

There are, of course, those in the United States who wish the Chinese would get on with building aircraft carriers, a fleet of nuclear submarines, and other means of global power projection. Without such a threat from China it is increasingly difficult to justify perpetuating the huge force structure and defense industrial base we developed to do battle with the USSR. So there is a lot of selective listening going on among American securocrats and pundits, who filter out Chinese explanations of what China is doing and replace these with their own speculation and conjecture about what the Chinese ought to be doing to be able to contend with us for global hegemony. But there is no need to manufacture elaborately speculative explanations for modernization programs whose projected outcomes are entirely consistent with the far more limited purposes the Chinese proclaim. Occam's razor applies: all things being equal, the simplest explanation is almost always the best.

Of course, if there is no evidence that Beijing is tempted to recapitulate the Soviet Union's suicidal effort to seek military parity with the United States, it does not follow that China's rapid military modernization should be of no concern. Quite aside from its impact in the Taiwan Strait, the growth in Chinese military strength is altering the military balances between China and regional powers like Japan, Russia, India, Indonesia, and Australia. With the exception of Japan, which seems perplexed and uncertain about what security role it should take up in this century, the region is accommodating these shifts reasonably smoothly. But they are especially challenging to the United States and fully justify a high degree of American attention. China is, after all, a giant. The only Pacific nation—perhaps the only nation in the world—with the scale to match what China may be in the process of becoming in economic and cultural terms and what it could become, should it want to do so, in military terms, is America.

For most of the past sixty years, the United States has relied on its military power to frustrate China's efforts to bring the Chinese civil war to a conclusion by using force to reincorporate Taiwan into the rest of China. For China, the most important defense task has long been the maintenance of territorial integrity by putting sufficient military pressure on Taiwan to cause it to think seriously about political accommodation and to rule out any thought of permanent separation from the rest of China. China's current military modernization is directed in large measure at achieving military superiority over Taiwan that is sufficiently convincing to deter the island from making decisions that would compel the use of force against it. As the United States has thrown its weight more openly behind Taiwan in an effort to balance growing Chinese capabilities, China has also become increasingly focused on how to counter American intervention. While neither China nor the United States wants war, each has become heavily engaged in contingency planning for a war with the other.

The Taiwan issue pits Chinese nationalism and the legitimacy of the Chinese government against Taiwanese identity politics and the American sense of national honor. It remains the only conceivable cause of a future Sino-American armed conflict. A shared sense of this risk has given Beijing and Washington a common interest in deterring Taipei from making rash decisions that could provoke a conflict, but neither can actually prevent Taipei from making such decisions.

A war over the question of Taiwan's relationship or non-relationship to the China mainland would not be a trivial event. It could easily escalate to the level of nuclear exchanges or protracted global conflict between China and the United States. Whatever the outcome for Taiwan's status, its democracy and prosperity would be destroyed.

Fortunately, long-term trends in the Taiwan Strait are enhancing the prospects for a peaceful resolution of the unsettled relationship between its two sides. The danger of war is thus declining. But our European friends present here today need to understand how very serious the Taiwan issue is for both the United States and China. American allies and friends of China alike must act cautiously when their actions might affect it.

Beyond the possibly apocalyptic consequences of missteps over Taiwan, China's advance could be derailed by several possible scenarios only indirectly related to the problems I mentioned at the outset. I don't expect any of these to happen, but they bear consideration. Among the negative possibilities to guard against, let me single out the following four scenarios (in no particular order):

First, global depression or a failed attempt at currency and capital market reform in China.

The undervaluation of the Chinese currency has made China unduly dependent on exports for the continued economic growth necessary to sustain political stability. But while China piles up reserves, the world has been playing American roulette with an overvalued U.S. currency and dollar debt instruments. That's a game where the last one standing gets to hold a bagful of devalued greenbacks. The risk of a sudden dollar collapse, though seldom mentioned in polite company, is on the mind of all the players. The consequences for the global economy would be severe. For the Chinese government and its reform policies, they could be fatal.

So China does not have to make a mistake to be taken down. It, the United States, and the world have yet to chart a path to the realignment in currency values and reform of the international monetary system needed to ensure continued economic health. With the United States Senate conducting a remarkably illiterate debate on Chinese currency reform and China still excluded from some of the key global institutions that deal with these issues, how confident can we be that we will to do so?

A related problem arises from the self-destructive gambling instincts of Chinese small investors and the shakiness of China's newly established equity markets. The immaturity of China's capital markets and financial system as a whole skews the economy in unhealthy directions; it is a drag on Chinese efforts to develop an innovative society. It also poses a risk to the country's stability. A nineteenth-century-style market crash in China, followed by widespread unemployment and unrest, is not impossible to imagine. A halt in economic advance, regardless of its cause, could severely erode domestic Chinese support for continued economic opening and reform. That, in turn, could have very adverse effects on the prospects for the global economy and injure the livelihoods of many who have no idea where China is or why they should care about it.

A second scenario could involve China failing to secure enough energy and raw materials to continue economic growth.

The world is having a hard time adjusting to China's sudden emergence as the largest consumer of many of its natural resources—first in iron, steel, aluminum, copper, and so forth, and second in overall energy consumption. The flip side of this problem is that China is finding it difficult to line up the supplies it needs to feed its booming economy. The steady appreciation of the Chinese currency will help temper the effect of rising costs. But the disruption of shipping by natural or man-made disasters or severe constraints on energy and raw materials imports could bring the Chinese economy to its knees, with many of the same political consequences as a global economic collapse or a stock market crash.

Inevitably, moreover, as a latecomer to investment in global mining and fossil-fuel exploration and production, China must look to sources from which established—mainly Western—mining and energy companies are absent. This is already drawing China into countries the West has sought to isolate with sanctions and blockades. The resulting reduction in Western leverage over such countries increases friction over China's concomitantly rising influence.

A third set of difficulties could arise from a failed Chinese attempt at democratization.

The Chinese have watched closely as sudden attempts to introduce democracy in places without a tradition of the rule of law or much of a middle class—like the former Yugoslavia, Iraq, or Russia and the Caucasus—have destabilized these societies, triggered ethnic separatism, religious strife, and civil war, or led to kleptocracy or one-man rule. So China is very unlikely to be incautious in reforming its own political system, as its rising middle class demands and as its leaders recognize it must.

But it is worth noting the risks that mismanaging this political transition could pose to the surprising political, economic, and cultural diversity of greater China or to responsible Chinese behavior on international issues. A citizenry prematurely empowered to do so might well ask:

- why Hong Kong and Macau should not pay taxes to Beijing as other Chinese cities must;

- why minorities should continue to be exempted from the one-child-per-family policy that most agree is necessary to limit population growth;
- why China should compromise with weaker neighbors as it attempts to fix its maritime borders;
- why China should not use its growing military ascendancy in the Taiwan Strait to settle the issue once and for all; or
- why government policies should not more fully reflect popular anger against foreign governments when they—for example—bomb Chinese embassies abroad, operate spy planes in aggressive patrols along China's coasts, sell weapons to Taiwan, or come up with particularly florid ways to deny history.

Laudable as it may be, no one has claimed that democratization increases *sang-froid*. And we now have a lot of evidence that it can be very destabilizing.

Lastly, there is the somewhat related danger of severe nationalist overreaction to perceived insults from the United States or Japan.

Without being at all aware of how we sound, we Americans—including our political leaders— insult our Chinese counterparts daily through statements denigrating their legitimacy, expressing contempt for their political system, condemning them as evil "Communists," barring them from international gatherings because they do not represent a democracy, attributing malevolent intent to them, branding them as current or prospective enemies who should not be allowed to import technology from us, and so forth. From the Chinese perspective, dealing with the United States is now a constant exercise in forbearance, in the interest of avoiding quarrels and contests that could mire the country in zero-sum games with a rhetorically strident and militarily aggressive opponent. And, with all due respect to our Japanese allies, on occasion they seem even more tone-deaf and less empathetic than we.

Our gratuitous put-downs of the Chinese make domestically appealing sound bites, but they accumulate ill will amongst a pragmatic but proud people. Despite the best intentions of leaders on both sides, an incident could cause the dam to break, releasing a torrent of angry condemnation and sweeping away Chinese willingness to cooperate with us. All we or the Japanese have to do to make China an enemy is to treat it like one. In some ways, we are both perilously close to doing that.

Frankly, I remain optimistic about both China and the prospects for Sino-American relations. I do not expect any of these scenarios to unfold. China is rich in both human and natural resources. Chinese are neither xenophobic nor hostile to the current world order. China has got its domestic policy environment mostly right and it is working with all deliberate speed to improve it further. Its people are blessed with an entrepreneurial culture, show no fear of change, and are willing to learn from their mistakes.

China's leaders have so far been up to the immense challenge of managing transition on a scale that is unprecedented in human history. Collectively, they are very likely the most economically literate leadership on the planet. Politically, they have demonstrated an impressive degree of self-control, steady nerves, and a patient instinct for avoiding premature initiatives. There is every reason to expect they will continue to do so.

So, titillating as it is to imagine the worst for China—as I was asked to do today—I do not predict it. Contemplating the worst serves instead to underscore the very great stake the world has in avoiding it by encouraging China's continuing success. And, if it is self-defeating to assume the worst, it is more harmful still to act as if the worst is inevitable. Pessimism all too easily becomes self-fulfilling paranoia.

How China will invest its resources and the ends to which it will exercise its influence have yet to be determined. We have everything to gain by encouraging China to act in ways that harness its growing wealth and power to the common benefit. We cannot hope to do this by approaching the Chinese with suspicion and hostility or by savoring the prospect of their possible failure. China's continued success will benefit the world. A China that is in difficulty will not.

Chapter 8

U.S.-China Relations and the Emerging World Order

While American sinologists remain focused on China as an East Asian country, it is also, of course, a Central and South Asian nation. As China's international reach expands, the United States is having to learn to engage with China in a widening range of variable politico-economic geometries as well as strategic domains. In the three sections of this chapter that follow, I look at the present and likely future evolution of some of these interactions, concluding with a set of observations about U.S.-Indian strategic interaction in this context.

In the first section, "China's Challenge to American Hegemony," I examine the question of whether China is likely to displace America as the dominant global power or join it in global hegemony, as some other great powers have feared. In the second section, "The United States, China, and the New Global Geometry," I ponder the implications of China's rise amidst the steady decay of the American-dominated post–World War II international order. I conclude with an effort to relate the rise of India to that of China in assessing the prospects for regional and global order: "India and America in the Strategic Times to Come."

> **Find More in the Online Archive**
> For a look at some of the effects of Bush administration policies on China's relations with other regions, like Europe, and the ways in which those relations are evolving, see "Sino-American Relations in Trans-Atlantic Perspective"at http://bit.ly/interesting-times.

China's Challenge to American Hegemony[1]
January 2010

Napoleon is said to have predicted that, when China woke from its slumbers, it would "astonish the world." The Little Corporal was a loquacious fellow who got much wrong, but he seems to have gotten this right. In a mere three decades, China has risen from impotence and backwardness to a leading position in global affairs. This year it will become the second biggest producer of goods and services, something projected just five years ago to happen only in 2020. China is clearly on the way to regaining its historic position as the world's largest economy, displacing the United States. (Given continued rapid growth in the Chinese economy, slow growth elsewhere, and progressive revaluation of the Renminbi yuan, this could happen much sooner than many expect.) The prospect of transcendent Chinese wealth and power, coupled with America's devaluation of its own political and economic prestige, has led to mounting speculation about China's emergence as a global hegemon to rival and, perhaps in time, surpass the United States.

Not so long ago, in the Cold War, the world order was defined by the relationship between the Soviet Union and America as the overlords of rival blocs of nations. Recalling this, some pundits foresee the reemergence of a bipolar world in which the United States and China exercise joint leadership in a so-called "G-2." With the collapse of the USSR, there have been no rivals to American leadership when Washington has chosen to lead. The United States—which spends more on its military than the rest of the world combined—has enjoyed absolute military superiority in every region of the globe. Some imagine China as a "peer competitor" for global dominance.

Since 1974, when Deng Xiaoping addressed the United Nations General Assembly in New York, China has been at pains to deny any possibility that it might seek such dominance. As the Chinese defense "white paper" put it last year: "China will never seek hegemony or engage in military expansion now or in the future, no matter how developed it becomes." In saying this, China is inadvertently echoing the American isolationists of the nineteenth and early twentieth centuries. The United States did not then seek to dominate or control the international state system, nor did it pursue military solutions to problems far from its shores. In time and in reaction to events, however, America came to do both.

Why has China, alone among nations, felt obliged to assert that it does not aspire to regional or global hegemony? Is this simply propaganda, intended to distinguish Beijing from Brezhnev's Moscow or from the militarism of contemporary Washington? Is it a contrite acknowledgment and repudiation of imperial China's past hegemonic status in East Asia? Or is it sincere counsel to future generations of Chinese not to bully their neighbors or the world once they have the power to do so? If so, is there something unique about China that causes its leaders to believe they must make a special effort to resist deep-seated hegemonic impulses?

This has become a timely question. After a couple of bad centuries, China is back. China brims with confidence that it can regain its former dominance, which it considers the natural order of affairs, and that it will do so in this century. Analogies to other rising powers with shallower histories—France, the United States, Germany, Japan, and the USSR—are not helpful in predicting the consequences of China's rise. China has no messianic ideology to export; no doctrine of "manifest destiny" to advance; no belief in social Darwinism or imperative of territorial expansion to act upon; no cult of the warrior to animate militarism or glorify war; no exclusion from contemporary global governance to overcome; no satellite states to garrison; no overseas colonies or ideological dependencies to protect; no history of power projection or military intervention beyond its immediate frontiers; no entangling alliances or bases abroad.

China has a very persuasive explanation of its national interests. It says it needs domestic tranquility and peace on its borders in order to pursue its continued modernization and economic development. It seems very comfortable with a multipolar world order, where peace and economic growth prevail. But anyone with experience of negotiating with the Chinese can attest that they are capable of both haughtiness and petulance. Some of this sort of conduct seems to have been on display at Copenhagen last month. How a still-more-powerful China conducts itself in the future will be decided in part by Chinese realities as shaped by Chinese history. But Chinese behavior will also reflect how the rest of the world, including most notably the incumbent hegemon—the United States—reacts and interacts with China as China rises. And future Chinese conduct cannot be separated from the character of China's domestic politics. An autocracy that feels free to ignore the rule of law at home is unlikely to defer to international law and procedure abroad.

Whatever the meaning of China's assurances that it will not pursue hegemony or engage in military expansionism in the future, we cannot be certain that it will not. There are grounds for optimism, especially with respect to China's use of military power. China's history includes examples of aggressive actions along its borders—especially in Korea and Vietnam. But overall China has been notable for its cautious, defensive, and inward-looking national security posture. The Great Wall stands as a symbol of this, as does the scuttling of the Ming fleet in 1437. Despite a formidable history of innovation in military technology and warfare on a scale commensurate with its huge population and vast size, the Chinese strategic tradition stresses that weapons are inauspicious instruments to be used only when the use of force is unavoidable.

The People's Republic of China has used force when measures short of war have proven inadequate to secure its borders or strategic interests (as in Korea, India, and Vietnam), but, by marked contrast with India in Goa or Indonesia in East Timor, it gave diplomacy the decades needed to resolve the Hong Kong and Macau issues without bloodshed. Beijing has shown a similar preference for negotiations rather than the use of force to settle the Taiwan issue. Cross-Strait tensions are lessening. It should be encouraging that China has insisted on United Nations authorization for its military activities abroad, which are directed at peacekeeping and against piracy.

Still, China is modernizing its military at a peculiar moment of history. The United States inherited worldwide military superiority from the collapse of its Soviet rival. Without much discussion, it has embraced the neoconservative agenda of sustaining this superiority at all costs. But rising Chinese defense capabilities erode American supremacy. China's new anti-carrier weapons endanger U.S. force projection capabilities in the Western Pacific; its anti-satellite programs imperil U.S. global surveillance and communication capabilities; its growing operations in cyberspace menace U.S. government operations and the economy of the American homeland alike. These are serious challenges not just to American hegemony but to core U.S. interests. They have begun to draw a response.

The result is a deeply troubled Sino-American military relationship despite the diminishing prospects for war in the Taiwan Strait. China will persevere in its efforts to build a credible counter to American coercion. The United States will not soon abandon its obsession with retaining absolute military superiority everywhere. A less hegemonic objective would allow the U.S. to accommodate a more powerful China while retaining the ability to prevail in any conflict with it. As things are, increasingly overt military confrontation between China and the United States is likely.

These inherent tensions—along with those arising from the huge bilateral trade imbalance in favor of China—are why the idea of a U.S.-China duopoly like the so-called G-2 is infeasible even if it were desirable, which it is not. Still, the world economy is about to see the displacement of the United States from its twentieth-century preeminence. China will join the U.S., the EU, and Japan at the top. India, Brazil, Russia, and others in the G-20 will follow. What is in prospect is not the hegemony of one or two countries but its opposite—a multipolar balance of economic power.

China, like Japan, is, of course, a country with a population vastly larger than it can prosperously support on its own resource base, large as that is.

And China is late in the search for access to raw materials for its burgeoning industries. (So is India.) China has a vital interest in the perpetuation of a global economic order open to trade and investment. China is now enmeshed in multilateral organizations in which it must daily demonstrate its dedication to the sovereign equality of nations, great and small. All this enforces the respect for comity that is the essence of a "responsible stakeholder." It informed People's Bank of China governor Zhou Xiaochuan's cautious suggestion last spring that it would be better to manage the dollar down to a sustainable international role than to have it collapse.

But America is out of practice at dealing with independent power centers. For the past two decades the United States has been the undisputed global hegemon. For forty years before that, it was the indispensable arbiter of the bloc of nations known as the "free world." American politicians are unaccustomed to formulating policy through multilateral consultations with other nations. Beijing isn't very good at this either, but seems more open to it than Washington. The United States will, as always, do what must be done, after it has exhausted all of the alternatives. But this will take time and cost the United States further prestige and influence. Meanwhile, China's global role will grow, especially if Beijing sustains the modesty and competence for which its diplomats have become known, rather than the arrogance that some of its domestic officials increasingly exemplify.

The Chinese Communist Party has delivered prosperity to ordinary Chinese, which is why it enjoys their support. Eighty-six percent of Chinese think their country is on the right track. Chinese see proof of the superiority of their political economy in the apparent effectiveness of its response to the financial crash and its aftermath. Their government's policies have so far succeeded in sustaining high rates of economic growth through programs that enhance long-term economic and intellectual competitiveness. The contrast with the muddled self-indulgence of Washington's response to the crisis, in particular, is striking. Americans have so far shrunk from the hard decisions necessary to restore fiscal integrity to their government or to reverse serious decay in their nation's human and physical infrastructure. The recession has joined foreign wars and continuing deterioration in relations with the Islamic world as a factor accelerating American decline.

China seems certain to emerge from the crisis with a much larger and more competitive economy. The generation born under the single-child policy is coming of age. It is far more inclined to consumption than its frugal predecessors. A faster transition to growth driven by domestic consumption than many have thought possible seems in prospect. China's imports are now rising much more rapidly than its exports. Its balance-of-payments surplus, huge as it still is, fell by half in 2009. Continuing economic growth, deepened ties with Asian neighbors, the progressive internationalization of a yuan that is rising in value—all promise domestic stability and greater international stature for China in coming years.

The current self-congratulatory mood in China is therefore entirely understandable. Yet it masks the underlying weakness of the Chinese political system. Government in contemporary China derives its legitimacy almost entirely from its ability to deliver continued rapid economic growth. It stands for no credible values, neither trusts nor is trusted by those it rules, suffers from a high level of corruption, and has no clear vision for self-improvement. If America's politics are widely viewed as so venal as to be dysfunctional, the Chinese system is seen as cynically manipulative and of questionable legitimacy. Without political reform, China will remain vulnerable to unrest should the economy falter. If there is no rule of law in China, Beijing's word will be doubted abroad. Despite its economic successes and growing defense capabilities, China's international influence will remain limited as long as it fails to evolve an attractive political system. It is not impossible that it may do so, but there is no evidence at present to suggest that it will.

A Chinese perception that the United States is attempting to leverage its military superiority to keep China down could goad Beijing into efforts to dislodge America from its position of global dominance. Given the continuing disparities in national power, the ensuing struggle would be a long one. The trigger would probably be some incident derived from U.S. military operations off Chinese shores or from the Taiwan issue, to which Sino-American relations remain hostage. This is unlikely, but, unfortunately, it is not impossible to imagine.

As I speak, for example, China is actively considering how to put effective pressure on the United States to halt arms sales to Taiwan. China wants Washington to live up to Ronald Reagan's commitment to restrain and reduce such sales in return for credible pursuit by Beijing of a peaceful settlement of its differences with Taipei. Sanctions on selected American companies—modeled on those the U.S. Congress has imposed on Chinese companies selling objectionable items to others—are apparently among the options before China's leaders. In the current economic climate, any such move by China could trigger a nasty confrontation and unleash an orgy of American protectionist retaliation that would likely set off a trade war. I do not consider such a development likely. If nothing else, however, the possible consequences of miscalculation by Beijing or Washington illustrate the global stake in continuing prudent management of the Sino-American relationship by both sides.

It is important to see China as it is, not as we wish or fear it to be. In 1943, President Franklin Roosevelt declared that China "has become one of the great democracies of the world." That was nonsense, of course. But so, I believe, are perceptions of China as an emerging anti-democratic hegemon. The more likely prospect is that China will take its place alongside the United States and others at the head of a multilateralized system of global governance. In such an oligarchic world order, China will have great prestige but no monopoly on power comparable to that which the United States has recently enjoyed.

America has already lost its global political hegemony. But, for all the reasons I have mentioned, China is neither inclined toward nor capable of succeeding to this role. The Anglo-American financial model is much tarnished by recent events. But no alternative to it has yet emerged. It seems certain that whatever does replace it will be crafted by many hands, only some of which will be Chinese. American consumption is no longer the sole driver of the global economy. The China market has come to play an important part in sustaining world growth. But China is not the only economy that is rising. In some areas of global trade and investment, China will be a dominant factor; in others, it will not be. In the military arena, even if fiscal limitations force retrenchment, the United States will, for many years to come, remain the only power with global reach.

Americans will find it difficult to adjust to a world in which we are no longer all-powerful in all spheres. But we are a flexible and resilient people who can and will accommodate change. Neither we nor the Chinese will cease to pursue our national interests as we see them. In many instances, these views will more or less coincide. On such matters, if others agree, there will be global progress. Where we disagree, we will come under pressure from others to search for common ground. Neither of us will be so powerful that we can ignore such pressure.

In short, the world in the future will be more "democratic" and, likely, more muddled than in the past because many countries, not just the United States or China, will share power in it. There will be ample opportunity for countries with trusted relationships with Washington and Beijing to influence how they participate in global affairs. There will be no hegemon, and there will be no G-2.

The United States, China, and the New Global Geometry[2]
November 2010

It is only natural that when Chinese and Americans meet these days, we should discuss the changing balance between us. There is indeed a shift in relative economic and military power. It is less profound than many imagine. More important, in our mutual fascination with our bilateral interaction, Americans and Chinese often fail to notice a set of transformations with much more far-reaching implications for both of us. The international geometry within which we conduct our respective foreign policies is morphing in ways that demand major adjustments in the strategies of all the world's powers, including both China and the United States. Inherited strategies are unlikely to fit the new circumstances without substantial, ongoing adjustment. Entirely new policies may be more appropriate and efficacious. This was the case after World War II as well. The United States then rose to the challenge of geopolitical change. The absence of a comparable American response this time is striking.

The United States has in many respects disqualified itself or retreated from its past status as the ultimate arbiter of the world's politico-economic order. No other country (certainly not China) yet shows any sign of stepping into this role. By default, regional powers are filling the political vacuum left by the recession of U.S. global hegemony at the regional as well as the global level. In doing so, they are recrafting regional orders to suit their interests rather than those of the United States, the European Union, China, or other external powers. They are also beginning to buttress one another's efforts to manage affairs of concern in their respective regions. A case in point is Brazil's recent backing for Turkey's diplomatic intervention in the Iranian nuclear issue.

The final collapse of the World Trade Organization's sputtering "Doha Round" in 2008 accelerated a parallel trend toward the liberalization of trade and investment through regional rather than global trade agreements. You can see this trend clearly in Asia. As of this year, Asian economies have signed fifty-five free trade agreements. They are negotiating eighty-two additional bilateral agreements, four-fifths of them with countries outside the region. The same thing is happening elsewhere, as the development of Mercosur and the establishment of the Union of South American Nations (UNASUR) in South America attest. The current level of interregional cooperation on economic matters is also vigorous.

All this is a reminder that China is, after all, not alone in rising to greater wealth, power, and regional influence. Brazil, Russia, Turkey, Iran, Saudi Arabia, India, and South Africa are now preeminent participants in shaping new regional orders that slight the stated interests and policies of powers outside their immediate environs. Brazil and others in South America openly challenge U.S. dominance in the Western Hemisphere even as they build more robust relationships with China, Europe, and the Islamic world. Russia is once again a more relevant reference point for the policies of those around it than the United States or other NATO member countries. Turkey has rediscovered its diplomatic centrality in West Asia as well as its Islamic identity. Iran has been empowered by American and Israeli blunders in Iraq, Lebanon, Syria, and Palestine. Saudi Arabia's leadership continuity and wealth have made it the new diplomatic center of the Arab world. India long ago consolidated a far more assertively dominant position in its part of the world than China seeks, and it too is on the rise. South Africa aspires to lead the rest of Africa while Africans increasingly look to Asia rather than Europe or America for development partners.

Nor is the United States the only power to suffer something of a crisis of self-confidence. Japan is stuck in the economic doldrums. It is undecided about how to cope with China's eclipse of it in Asia and with America's ebbing global prestige. Europe remains self-absorbed, less than the sum of its parts, undecided about its relationships with Russia and Turkey, and out of sorts with both the United States and China. Britain is cutting its military power and diluting its reliance on America while building new links to Brazil, India, and even France. The Franco-German partnership that provided the core for European unity has weakened. And the European Union's fiscal and monetary consensus is under severe strain.

The result of these changes is that the major institutions of global governance birthed by American leadership after World War II are no longer congruent with current or foreseeable future configurations of global and regional political, economic, military, and cultural power. European representation in these bodies is both overweighted and unreflective of Europe's post–Cold War reorganization and evolution. The great powers of Asia—China, India, Japan, Indonesia—are underweighted, unrepresented, or both. The growing roles in global affairs of Brazil, the Arab and Islamic worlds, and South Africa also remain unacknowledged. American dominance in international organizations, even as the United States exempts itself from many of their rules, is now widely seen as both an anachronism and an overweening abuse of power.

That the United Nations Security Council, the International Monetary Fund, the World Bank, and other international organizations find themselves misaligned with emerging realities saps their legitimacy. It renders them increasingly incapable of managing the political and economic domains they were established to oversee. The crisis in global governance is equally evident in the realm of trade and investment.

The World Trade Organization (WTO) still provides a quasi-judicial brake on protectionism but no longer serves as an effective vehicle for the realization of expanded economic growth through liberalized rules for trade and investment. The G-7, having proved unable to deal with the global financial crisis of 2007, has been succeeded by the G-20. This brings together leaders who can speak for about 85 percent of global economic power. In theory, this could enable the G-20 to concert necessary reforms in global financial affairs. In practice, however, the new grouping has yet to show that it can or will discharge this function.

The failure of any other country or group of countries to attempt to lead the world to solutions to its problems, as the United States once did, underscores the bankruptcy of existing mechanisms for global decision-making. The result is a worldwide version of the replacement of regulation by the laissez-faire approaches to systems management that facilitated the 2007–08 crash of Wall Street and the global financial sector. This is not a situation with which the United States, China, or any other country should be comfortable.

Neglect is visibly ripening some issues into comprehensive disasters. To cite a few examples: There is no strategy or agreed mechanism for mitigating or managing climate change. No doctrine or system has been developed to curtail the human toll of anarchy in failed and failing states in Africa, Southwest Asia, or elsewhere. Environmental degradation—including mounting pollution of the world's oceans and the collapse of fish populations as well as their underlying food chains—faces no countermeasures agreed upon by the international community. Consensus on key elements of the rule of law is breaking down and yielding to scofflaw practices based on the concept that "might makes right."

As Asia returns to wealth and power, the Islamic world reasserts itself, and other regions throw off the legacy of European colonialism, it is unclear how many of the key ideas and elements of the existing rule-bound international order will survive. The irony of this should be evident to any Chinese audience. What is in jeopardy, after all, is the peaceful world order that China embraced to enable it to climb to renewed wealth and power. In the absence of rules, fortune favors the fierce. It is not out of the realm of possibility that the world may be in the process of reverting to levels of strife that have not been seen since the *Pax Americana* was instituted sixty-five years ago. That should please no one. It would be the very opposite of the harmonious world China says it sees as in its interest.

At the same time, the United States may not be able much longer to provide the free public goods upon which China and other countries have been able to rely to sustain a peaceful international environment in which to develop. I refer to benefits like the American protection of global freedom of navigation, secure access to energy supplies, a global economic system based on the dollar as a universal medium of exchange, an open trading and investment regime, constraints on the proliferation of weapons of mass destruction, and other elements of the mostly benign world order created after World War II. The financial ailments of the United

States menace all this. They risk budgetary collapse at home and economic convulsions abroad.

The U.S. federal government's revenues from all sources will total $2.2 trillion this year. Transfer payments to individuals for unemployment, pensions, health care, and other entitlements of a decent and civilized society will total $2.4 trillion. America must borrow $200 billion before it even begins to pay for basic government operations, including its wars and other military operations. To sustain these, the United States will borrow another $1.3 trillion this year, much of it from abroad. In sum, every dollar the U.S. government spends on operations other than welfare payments is borrowed. Though many Americans remain in denial, it is obvious that this cannot go on indefinitely.

It is quite clear that the United States will not be able to afford a continuing role as the sole provider of free but essential police and other services to the world. U.S. strategy and policies are destined to change as America falls back to a less ambitious role. The only question is whether the change will be gradual or abrupt. Either way change occurs, the United States is not the only nation that must adjust to it.

In many ways, we seem to be on the verge of a world in which there will be no global paramount power. In such a world, the responsibility for global governance will devolve willy-nilly to regional sub-orders. Problems of common concern will be addressed—if at all—by shifting confederacies of regions and their leading powers and by ad hoc conferences rather than through standing bodies at the global level. This is not, of course, the only possible alternative to the crumbling *status quo*. But as the transition to some sort of new world order proceeds—however it is configured—many questions arise. Among them: Who will enforce the peace in increasingly divergent regions? Will the United States seek partners to share its strategic burdens or walk away from them? Will China and other countries take an active role in sustaining a harmonious international order? The challenges of sustaining peace and development should not be underestimated.

For the first time in many years, these challenges do not center on Europe. Thrice in the last century (in World War I, World War II, and the Cold War), confrontations on that continent set off struggles for global supremacy between the world's great powers. The creation and steady enlargement of the European Union make any reenactment of this history implausible. But Europe is alone in having crafted so cooperative and durable a regional zone of peace and prosperity. It is unique in posing no threat to other centers of global power. Unfortunately, it also remains badly incapacitated as a unified international actor.

In the Western Hemisphere, the American system—symbolized by the Monroe Doctrine, the Rio Treaty, and the Organization of American

States—is breaking down. No one can yet say what will replace this system, but many expect that whatever succeeds it will be at least partly made in Brazil. The United States will not welcome this change, but will cope with it and may even benefit from it.

In West Asia, a new regional order is being shaped by interaction between Ankara, Tehran, and Riyadh. The Islamic world as a whole, however, is in ideological turmoil, driven to frenzy by foreign intrusions and perceived humiliation. An extremist Muslim minority now seeks to change the political and social landscape of Islam by driving any non-Muslim presence from its soil. Powerless to accomplish this by conventional means, this minority has turned to terrorism, first against Israel and now against America, its European allies, and Russia as well as moderate Muslim regimes. India's turbulent hold on predominantly Muslim Kashmir has made it, too, a major target of such terrorism. The spreading chaos has already touched China. It is far from clear how it can be contained.

African nations are experiencing crises in domestic governance amidst the collapse of efforts to coordinate international cooperation with them. More than a few states have failed or are faltering, including some that previously seemed destined for wealth and power. Genocidal anarchy prevails in others. One, Somalia, has become a base for piracy directed at shipping in a major sea lane. Only a handful are clear successes. Neither the African Union, the continent's few great powers, global institutions, the former colonial powers, Africa's new partners in the development of its natural resources, nor anyone else has responded effectively to these challenges.

Russia may no longer qualify as "a riddle wrapped in a mystery inside an enigma," as Winston Churchill once described the Soviet Union. He might today call the Russian government a protection racket atop a great energy power that retains nuclear forces sized to support outmoded ambitions. However one describes it, Russia remains a puzzling work in progress. It has yet to find stability as a polity or in its relationships with its neighbors, including Europe, Ukraine and the Caucasus, Turkey, Iran, India, Japan, or China, let alone the United States.

The Shanghai Cooperation Organization provides a cooperative security mechanism for tempering any resurgence of Russian imperialism in Central Asia. But nothing precludes Russia from returning to its rivalry with America or its alliance with others—like India and Japan—to counter China, should it come to see either course as necessary or desirable. Post–Cold War alignments on the Eurasian landmass and its periphery have yet to be sorted out. It is unclear whether they will evolve to China's advantage or disadvantage or what their implications might be for the United States.

The American alliances with Japan and south Korea have till now assured a Japanese ideology of armed pacifism and fostered meek Japanese policies internationally and in Asia. They have also assured stability on the Korean Peninsula by freezing its politico-military division in place. All this may now be in flux.

Stability on the Korean Peninsula is a matter of rising concern. The south is secure, prideful, prosperous, and stable. But there are new uncertainties about the heavily militarized and impoverished north. North Koreans starve as their government boosts its investment in nuclear weapons, goose-steps its way through an inscrutable leadership succession, and bellows at all the world except China, whose advice it politely ignores.

Meanwhile, the emergence of a north Korean missile and nuclear threat to Japan has pushed the Japanese into strengthening their self-defense capabilities and tightening their alliance with the United States. Recent flare-ups over unresolved territorial issues with China have accelerated these trends. They have also led Japan to consider making additional military investments and enlisting other potential partners—like India and Vietnam—to strengthen its hand against China.

Apprehensions among Southeast Asian states about how an increasingly powerful China might ultimately handle territorial and other disputes have long been at the heart of their discreetly expressed concerns about China as a possible future threat to their security and independence. Continuing delay in resolving these polarizing disputes aggravates them. It ensures ongoing efforts by some in the region to draw in other countries to balance China. As in the case of Northeast Asia, seldom has so compelling a strategic trend been driven by such intrinsically trivial islets, reefs, and rocks.

As a new world order emerges, India finds itself in the enviable position of being courted by every significant party. India sees itself as the natural rival to China for influence in Asia and welcomes some partnerships as part of an effort to balance China. Arab states see enhanced relations with India as offsetting over-reliance on the United States. Israel perceives India as a fellow antagonist in its escalating struggle with Islam. Iran believes that closer ties with India can offset American efforts to isolate it. Russia pursues relations with India to defend its former preeminence there, including its arms market. Europe seeks expanded trade and investment in a rapidly growing economy long dominated by British mercantilism or enfeebled by Fabian socialism with Soviet characteristics.

The United States seeks partnership with India for many of these reasons. It sees India as an ideologically compatible and rising Asian great power with which to complement engagement with China. China pursues better relations with India in part to preclude its enmity. Both China and the United States have separate relationships with Pakistan that belie India's aspirations for regional hegemony but seek to avoid entanglement in the fractious issue of Kashmir. India is in a position to make strategic choices that will influence the prospects for peace and security in Asia for decades to come.

The last time that the international environment saw massive shifts in wealth and power similar to those we see today was sixty to seventy years ago, during World War II and its aftermath. As the Cold War began, the world met the challenge of change with the creation of major new systems of global governance and rules of behavior. These were exemplified by the United Nations, the General Agreement on Tariffs and Trade, and the Bretton Woods accord. The United States played the key role in all of these developments as well as in the adoption of the grand strategy known as "containment" that walled off the Soviet Union until it collapsed of its own infirmities.

In the post–Cold War era, however, the United States has yet to outline any principles, articulate any vision, or formulate any strategy for reforming international institutions and practices, making fiscal and monetary adjustments, or maintaining a peaceful international environment. So far, America has cast itself as the military defender of vested interests in a crumbling *status quo*. It has not sought to craft a new strategic order or a more effective international system. For many reasons, some of the most important of which I have mentioned, I do not believe the current—mainly military—American response to change can either succeed or be sustained.

In this context, it matters greatly whether the United States and China recognize the imperative to work together to rebuild mechanisms for global decision-making and to reforge a rule-bound global order. Both countries have a major stake in effective global governance, constraints on unilateral action, the coordination of policies to promote worldwide prosperity, and a stable and predictable international economic order. We will be greatly affected by the decisions that other key international actors make. Our actions and our interaction will influence how Europe, India, Japan, Russia, and many other countries and communities orient themselves not just with respect to us but with respect to each other. To one degree or another, whether we cooperate or contend with each other will help to shape the transitions underway in places as far apart as Afghanistan (where our interests clearly converge), Cuba (where the era of the Castro brothers is drawing to a close), or Korea (where sudden change could come at any time).

It is in our mutual interest and that of the world that the United States and China cooperate, but this will not be easy for either of us. For Americans, it will require setting aside our vain effort to perpetuate the global military hegemony that the collapse of the Soviet Union conferred on us. This effort makes the global distribution of power into a zero-sum game, turning the rise of other powers, even in remote regions, into a perceived threat to American dominance that must be countered by additions to U.S. military power. The pursuit of such dominance sends a message of suspicion and hostility to newly wealthy and powerful countries like China. It inclines them to focus on how to frustrate and deter America rather than how to work with it. Dominance of this kind is also unaffordable. So the pursuit of it will sooner or later be abandoned. That will help.

For China, cooperating with the United States will require a level of activism, imagination, and diplomatic leadership that contrasts with the Chinese foreign-policy tradition of passivity, reticence, and risk aversion. It would help greatly if China could reduce its neighbors' fears of its future power by settling its maritime boundary disputes as skillfully as it has settled its land frontiers in inner Asia. The United States is not a party to these maritime disputes, but its relationships with allies and friends in the region mean that, in practice, it cannot avoid being implicated in them.

Finally, for both Americans and Chinese, building a more cooperative relationship will require a measure of humility, rhetorical self-restraint, and caution that have not recently been much in evidence in either country's foreign policies. This would facilitate mutually considerate strategic dialogue between us. Without such dialogue, we will be unable to respond effectively to the challenges of rapidly evolving global and regional environments. We owe it to ourselves and to our posterity to try harder to work together to advance the many strategic interests we have in common.

India and America in the Strategic Times to Come[3]
January 2011

As the second decade of the twenty-first century begins, no great regional power is as sought after as India. Over the past few months, the prime ministers and presidents of China, France, Russia, and the United States have all come here to Delhi to make the case for enhanced relationships with India. Earlier, Britain's new leader also came a-courting. Why all the sudden attention to this previously underappreciated corner of the globe?

It is not just the stunning beauty of India's women, though that is a compelling enticement revealed to all the world by Bollywood. Nor is it the dynamic growth of the Indian economy, though India is clearly on its way to becoming once again a big factor in the global marketplace. It is not the vibrancy of India's democracy, though India's politicians—like those back home in America—regularly astonish citizens with their legislative stratagems, scalawaggery, shell games, and shenanigans. All these things are part of India's contemporary image. But what most attracts foreign leaders to India is its strategic empowerment by the changing constellation of global power.

I want to speak briefly with you today about shifting patterns in the world and regional political and economic orders and how they may affect India, its neighbors, the United States, and the world. I will begin with a bow to strategic geography and history.

Isolated behind adjoining deserts, mountains, and seas, the Indian subcontinent was long the target, not the instigator, of strategic change. The fabled riches of South Asia were in the main the creation of its own intellectual, human, and natural capital, supplemented by gains from trade with West Asia, North Africa, Europe, Southeast Asia, and China. Indians inhabit a distinct geopolitical zone, separated in normal times from all these others. This region is easy to defend, but it has proven vulnerable to occasional transforming invasions from Central and West Asia, and, at last, the sea.

Until their British rulers joined them to a global empire, Indians seldom ventured abroad except as traders or missionaries. The Islam of Southeast Asia, like its Hinduism and Buddhism, is a legacy of this politically isolationist tradition of outreach primarily through commerce and the force of spiritual example. The wide attractive power of Indian culture (and the broad reach of the Chola Dynasty) notwithstanding, historically, India has been—in the main—content to keep its armies and navies at home. Its political and economic ties to its east have long been especially tenuous.

The arrival of European colonialism drew India out of its strategic shell and involved it in the quarrels of Europe. British India actively defended its lines of communication with the "mother country" against disruption by pirates or rival powers. The Raj sought to buffer its marches against Russian expansionism. To this end, it sent mostly Indian armies to conquer and garrison the shores of the Arabian Sea and the Persian Gulf as well as Iraq. It mounted repeated military expeditions to Afghanistan and Tibet to keep the great powers behind them at bay. Until the Japanese Empire turned on it, British India saw no threat to its security from the east. Its dominion over India's oceans was unchallenged.

It is said that history does not repeat itself, but often rhymes. One may, I think, be forgiven for perceiving some resonance in India's strategic thinking today with that of its British past. And one cannot help but observe that many of the conflicts that trouble India and Pakistan have their roots in lines that British bureaucrats in Delhi drew on maps of terrain they had never seen, in dispensations of communal power they made or failed to make, and in dispositions of territory they proposed but never made effective. But let us leave the Johnson, McMahon, and Durand lines, the pain of the partition, and the continuing insurgency in Kashmir aside in order to focus on the realities they helped create and the relevance of these realities to India's foreign relations today.

The contours of India's strategic environment are in rapid evolution. More important still, the balances of wealth and power on the great Eurasian landmass and in the world as a whole are visibly shifting. To the northwest, secular India's Muslim sister state of Pakistan remains locked in sibling rivalry with it over the unsettled status of Kashmir, Pakistan's fears of Hindu hegemony, and Islamabad's apprehension of yet another Indian vivisection of its territory. The emergence of a nuclear standoff between Pakistan and India has pushed this rivalry into asymmetric modes. These avoid the nuclear threshold but entail terrorism, low-intensity conflict, and a contest for strategic denial or presence in Afghanistan.

Meanwhile, Pakistan functions not as a friendly buffer state, as India might wish, but as an obstacle to Indian access to Central Asia. India is ever more dependent on energy imports from the Red Sea and the Persian Gulf. Its need for energy and access to inner Asia, as well as its impulse to flank Pakistan, have led it to seek close ties with Iran. Piracy has returned to the Gulf of Aden, and there is fear that the Strait of Hormuz might be closed by a war begun by Israel or the United States.

These considerations have revived India's awareness of its vital interests in freedom of navigation and the security of lines of communication in the Arabian Sea and Indian Ocean. They have also underscored India's stake in the peace and stability of the region to which the American naval strategist Admiral Alfred Thayer Mahan, thinking of India in relation to Europe, first applied the name "Middle East." It is not hard to imagine India having to step forward in the future to play a role in offshore balancing in the Persian Gulf region, especially in the wake of any significant reduction in the American military presence there.

With the notable exception of India's attachment to Iran, India's interests largely resemble those of the United States. America too has been troubled by terrorism from Pakistan and its turbulent border regions. The United States is engaged in low-intensity conflict in Afghanistan, where it has sought to bolster the Indian-aligned government of Hamid Karzai. Americans too seek a Central Asia open to the world and free of great-power rivalry. The United States shares India's interest in reliable access to energy supplies in Arabia and adjacent areas and her concern to assure the security of navigation to and from there. So, by the way, do China and other nations. Any attempt from any quarter to interfere with the energy trade for whatever reason would quickly evoke a widening coalition against its perpetrator.

The obvious overlaps as well as the contradictions in American and Indian interests in West Asia nicely illustrate both the potential and the limitations of Indo-American relations. Where our interests are parallel, it will be to our respective advantage to coordinate parallel policies. Where our interests differ, we may find ourselves in contention or even cooperating with others against each other. In this regard, Indo-American relations will not be at all exceptional. We appear to be entering an era in which the norm will be entente—limited cooperation on limited issues for limited periods of time—rather than fixed alliances. The coordinated pursuit of shared interests will be a great challenge to our respective democracies, each of which has an unrealistic habit of expecting uncritical commitments—even public adoration—from foreign partners.

To India's east, the rise to wealth and power of Japan, south Korea, and now the various parts of Greater China is well along in moving the world's economic center of gravity from the Atlantic to Eastern Asia. The combination of globalization and supply-chain-based business relationships is rapidly integrating Northeast Asian economies with those of Southeast Asia. Although India is still not fully part of this process, it is being pulled eastward into complex relationships with nations beyond the Andaman Sea. In many respects, these relationships have no historical precedent.

China is now India's largest trading partner. Projections by Goldman Sachs and others suggest that in 2050, a mere forty years from now, the Indian GDP may have grown to well over $35 trillion in current dollars, matching that of the United States then—but, at $70 trillion, China's economy could be almost twice as large as either India's or America's. The Indian government's decision to offer training in Chinese to the coming generation reflects awareness of this prospect and its effects on the country's future interests and orientation.

Of course, any projection—even one from a very clever banker—is simply an extrapolation into the future of our imperfect understanding of the present. We can be sure that the world of 2050 will not be as we now imagine it. Still, a look back at the world of forty years ago underscores that astonishing changes cannot be ruled out over the next forty years.

In 1970, the world was dominated by the contest between the U.S. and an apparently ascendant USSR. The dominant political concern everywhere was the war in Vietnam. China was poor and isolated by its own ideology as well as by an embargo originally imposed by the United Nations. Europe was divided and seen as the possible epicenter of the next world war. Bangladesh was still East Pakistan. The global economy was still on the indirect gold standard crafted at Bretton Woods. Japan had yet to become a great economic power. There was no Internet and no such thing as outsourcing. India's economists, like those elsewhere, were earnestly studying the supposedly inevitable transition from capitalism to socialism rather than, as turned out to be much more relevant, the transition from socialism to various forms of capitalism. And so forth. No one then foresaw the world of today.

Clearly, we cannot predict with precision what is to come. But for much of history India and China were, respectively, one-fifth and one-third or more of the global economy. This lends credence to the thesis that they are in the process of regaining such weight in world affairs. And it strongly suggests that Sino-Indian interaction will be a major factor shaping not just the future of Asia but of the globe. Is that something to be welcomed or feared? It is certainly something of concern to all the world's peoples, not just Indians and Chinese. Hence the new global attention to India's views.

In both India and the United States, there are now scholars who earn their keep and think tanks that make their way by urging us to be afraid—very afraid—of China's return to wealth and power. There is a ready market for titillating alarmism and there are always people ready to exploit it, especially when it serves the interests of military-industrial complexes. In the resulting debate, speculation is transformed into supposed fact and conjecture becomes imminent certainty. Thus India is said to be about to be strangled by a Chinese string of pearls—though this concept originates with a Washington consultancy, not with the Chinese General Staff, and does not compute. The Indian Navy is told its primary mission is to fend off a Chinese Indian Ocean fleet that does not yet exist and may never exist. India justly condemns long-standing but outmoded and absurdly impractical Chinese claims to what is now a fully integrated part of India—Arunachal Pradesh—even as it continues to press equally outmoded and impractical claims to what is now a fully integrated part of Chinese Tibet—Aksai Chin. Chinese pushback against reinvigorated Indian patrolling along the line of control in the Himalayas and Karakorams is said to be evidence of Chinese assertiveness, not just truculence or a negative feedback loop. And as the pundits issue dire predictions, the Indian and Chinese economies become ever more interdependent.

Paranoia can be self-fulfilling, and there is plenty of it to go around. The Sino-Indian border war of 1962 reminds us how aggressive patrols intended either to challenge or bolster lines of actual control can provoke both unintended conflict and strategic realignment. That war poisoned Indo-Chinese relations and catalyzed China's support of Pakistan as a hedge against Indian hegemony in South Asia. It is distressing that, as Sino-Indian talks about fixing a frontier drone on, many of the same warning signs that preceded conflict five decades ago are reappearing.

Whatever its outcome, renewed conflict in the Himalayas would be a strategic disaster. It would not gain either side's acceptance of the *de facto* border of nearly six decades, nor would it achieve a permanent alteration of that frontier. It could instead create an intra-Asian Cold War. It would likely deepen the Chinese partnership with Pakistan, stimulate Chinese efforts to undermine Indian dominance of the South Asian region, and lead to precisely the sort of Chinese naval challenges that Indian Sinophobes keep predicting.

There is nothing inevitable about such a scenario. Demarcating the Sino-Indian frontier more or less on the basis of the *status quo*, rather than by reference to the capricious cartography of colonial bureaucrats, would be politically difficult but strategically wise. It would remove a major flashpoint. Even then, however, some measure of competition between India and China is surely to be expected. Both Northeast and Southeast Asians seem likely to seek more robust relationships with India, as well as with the United States and others, to help offset the pull of a vastly larger and more powerful China. India will almost certainly be drawn into more active political, economic, cultural and other relationships—including military relationships—with countries on China's periphery.

India will derive its own benefits from such ties, as will China from comparable links to some of India's neighbors. But neither balancing nor competition need mean antagonism, still less enmity. This is all the more so given the wide range of interests that India, China, and other East Asian nations have in common with each other and with the United States. Prominent among these, as previously mentioned, are the need to preclude disruptive conflict in the Middle East, reliable access to energy there, and safe passage to and from the Persian Gulf and Red Sea. These tasks demand multinational diplomatic and naval cooperation rather than rivalry in the Indian Ocean and elsewhere.

Similarly, as densely populated, rapidly growing countries, India and China share an interest in the efficient access to commodities and the expanded markets that only a globally open trading and investment regime can provide. It's hard to imagine a country with a greater stake in Africa's stability and progress than India, unless it is now China. The two countries have parallel concerns about transnational issues like climate change, pandemic disease, and the functioning of many aspects of international law. Their economies are broadly complementary in ways that invite cross-investment, with India disproportionately strong in services and China in industrial production. Then, too, as an economic great power, India—like China, Europe, Japan, and the United States—will be called upon to contribute, in its own interest, to sustaining global financial health and economic prosperity. This will entail cooperation with wider coalitions of countries.

The world in which India is coming into its own is one that no longer has a paramount political or economic power. The United States has built and deployed armed forces structured to enforce its will throughout the globe. In the years since the Soviet collapse, preserving global military supremacy against all comers has become the barely questioned goal of American national security policy. But the fiscal hole at the heart of America's body politic raises serious questions about the sustainability of so expansive a mission. In the years to come, the United States is more likely to be in search of new partners to assist its diplomacy than new military interventions to undertake. The same is true of other established powers as well as newly rising or resurgent regional actors from Brazil to South Africa or Indonesia to Turkey.

In this context, the prospect of America's relinquishment of its self-appointed role as the world's policeman simply accentuates already troubling questions about how to assure the protection of the global commons. The central institutions for managing world affairs no longer perform with adequacy the tasks for which they were established. The Security Council does not enforce the UN Charter or international law. The Geneva Conventions no longer protect combatants against torture or other abuses. The World Trade Organization provides a forum to which to refer trade disputes but no longer leads a credible process for liberalizing trade and investment flows. The International Monetary Fund does not even pretend to regulate the global monetary system or its financial imbalances. The newly formed G-20 has yet to prove its capacity to promote the prosperity of the global economy. No mechanism has been devised to put together an effective international response to global warming and climate change. The world is in the midst of a crisis of global governance.

It seems more likely that this gap in the world's problem-solving capacity will be filled by cooperation within and between regions through ad hoc arrangements rather than by the restoration or creation of global institutions. We see this pattern in last year's Turkish-Brazilian diplomatic cooperation vis-à-vis Iran. It is also evident in processes like the six-party talks on Korean denuclearization, the Quartet's intermittent activities on peace between Israel and its captive Arab populations, recent Latin American efforts to bolster the international community's recognition of a Palestinian state that might coexist with Israel, the EU lead on nuclear talks with Iran, and many other less well-known situations. Ironically, just as an international consensus that India should be accorded a permanent seat on the UN Security Council is consolidating, the relevance of this status to world affairs is visibly lessening. India deserves the prestige of such a seat. But it is not an alternative to the coalition-building that is the essence of sound diplomacy and the central feature of the emerging international system.

Given the growing weight of India in world affairs, it will increasingly be called upon to form and lead coalitions to address both regional and global problems. In many but not all such efforts, the United States can and—I am confident—*will* play a significant supporting role. But, this pattern of entente rather than alliance challenges long-standing strategic predispositions in both countries. The United States needs to understand that cooperation with India on various matters will not be translated into and cannot be equated with alliance. India needs to recognize that cooperation with America in pursuit of common interests, far from compromising its nonalignment, is in fact an affirmation of its independent sovereignty. And, if America must learn to accept the leadership of others, including India, on an expanding range of matters, India must accustom itself to sometimes taking the lead with regard to issues beyond its immediate environs.

I first lived and worked in India forty-five years ago. It is impossible not to be encouraged by what India has accomplished in the interim and by the spirit with which it now faces the future. There is a sense of dynamism here, as in other reemerging great powers, that inspires optimism that the new international order now taking shape will be able in time effectively to address issues that are currently neglected or deferred. Most Americans take pleasure in India's return to wealth and power. The world at large is ready—I believe—for India to play a leading role in regional and world affairs. But only Indians can determine whether India itself is ready for such responsibilities. I, for one, hope that it is.

Chapter 9

China's Global and Regional Impact

China is emerging as an immovable diplomatic and military object, if not an irresistible diplomatic and military force. China's rapidly increasing interactions with regional and global powers are giving it increasing weight in the foreign policy, economic, and national security calculus of countries in every region of the world. It is now impossible to imagine solutions to most global issues without the cooperation or at least the acquiescence of China. This, and the rise of other great regional powers like India and Brazil, is altering the global geometry and bringing into being a new world order—one the United States no longer dominates.

China's gravitational pull, of course, now extends well beyond the Eurasian landmass to embrace Africa and the Americas as well as Australia. I have spoken about China's role in all of these regions as it has grown. In the five sections of this chapter, I look only at the impact of China's rise on the global political economy on Asia as a whole and on the various regions of Asia. These observations are contained in pieces titled, respectively, "China in the Times to Come," "China and the Global Resource Balance," "The Idea of Asia Becomes Real," "East Asia's Engagement with the Arab Countries of the Persian Gulf," and "India, Pakistan, and China."

China in the Times to Come[1]
March 2007

We are here to inaugurate a new center for research, analysis, and education about China, a country far to our west that never stops challenging the minds of those who study it or the character of those who rule it. No country has had a history of comparable continuity. None so well illustrates how seldom the future repeats the past but how easily it can rhyme with what has gone before.

China had a couple of bad centuries, but it is back, and it is on the way to the center of global affairs. As China restores itself to wealth and power, its leaders display a resolute confidence in the future. But they are also mindful that no one has ever before tried to govern a republic of one and one-third billion people in a territorial expanse the size of a continent, still less to transform so many ambitious individuals and obstreperous regions into a harmonious but innovative whole. What are the implications of China's success or failure at this task?

Our country came into being as the age of Atlantic dominance and the industrial revolution began to eclipse China and India. Americans therefore have no experience with the more normal condition of human history, in which Asia was for millennia the global center of gravity. One way or another, in the twenty-first century, China and its neighbors will determine what the resumption of Asian leadership in more and more fields of human endeavor means for an emerging postindustrial world, including for us Americans. Despite the challenges of doing so, we have ample reason to try to understand China and other Asian countries as they are, not as our politicians and pundits prefer to depict them.

At the birth of the United States of America, what some then called the "Celestial Kingdom" loomed large in our imagination. At that time, China was well over a third—nearly two-fifths—of the world's economy. We were accordingly obsessed with breaking past our former British rulers into a direct relationship with the Chinese economy. We knew little of China itself, but we had inhaled the European idealization of it as the most ethically advanced and orderly, as well as the most populous, realm on the planet. As they designed our system of government, the brilliant political engineers who were our founding fathers drew on Leibniz's and Voltaire's musings on the secrets of the "good society" China exemplified to its Jesuit admirers. And they took note of Montesquieu's condemnation of China's reliance on civility and the rule of manners rather than the rule of law to assure public tranquility.

Of course, none of them really knew what they were talking about. We are fortunate that our founding fathers' ambitions to build a better system of government than those in Europe, though based in part on Eurocentric misinterpretations of Chinese politics and society, were so very well realized. It turns out that ignorance can sometimes stimulate creative speculation as well as error. Mistaken European notions about China ended up contributing to theories that inspired our Constitution, a living document that continually challenges us to respect the extraordinary wisdom it incarnates.

China has now once again captured the American imagination. And, as always, it is a place where ignorance remains no impediment to confident prediction. So it is not surprising that politically expedient assertions about China have become as American as fortune cookies, and as sententiously meretricious as the prophecies and advice they encase.

Almost every ideological faction and interest group in our country now asserts its own vision of the People's Republic. Some do so out of fascination; others out of dread. Many seek to use China to prove their point in our political process or to raise money for the cause to which they are committed. Sometimes, for example, in the matters of Taiwan, Tibet, or the democracy movement in Hong Kong, Americans are enlisted by lobbyists acting on behalf of separatist or dissident movements in Greater China. Those who wish America to go abroad in search of monsters to destroy can always find one worthy of our attention there. China has become a screen on which Americans can project both our reveries and our nightmares.

Some points of discord can't be helped. Benedict XVI is understandably no fonder of Hu Jintao and the patriotic Catholic movement in China than Clement VII was of Henry VIII and the breakaway bishops of the Anglican Church. The fact that the majority of Chinese are agnostics has always been an affront to American Protestant evangelists. Chinese, for their part, have bad memories of gunboats escorting foreign missionaries up their great rivers and of tens of millions of deaths from rebellions instigated by cult religions like the Taiping version of Christianity. Some Americans will always stand with His Holiness the Dalai Lama against Chinese sovereignty in Tibet, but Chinese proponents of Tibetan independence are rarer than British advocates of discarding Wales. China's family planning practices are anathema to the abortion-obsessed religious right in our country, but Chinese consider that if we had their ratio of arable land to population, as many as three billion people would live in the United States and Americans might well see population control as a public policy imperative, too. And so forth.

These, and other tensions deriving from things that China rightly or wrongly regards as its own business rather than ours, rest on honest differences between Americans and Chinese that will not be resolved unless we or they change. Neither side is likely to do that anytime soon. So if we are to cooperate to mutual advantage in less contentious arenas, we must manage the bilateral tensions that differing moral judgments about more controversial ones make inevitable. To do this, we must not only understand why each side feels as it does, but what it is and isn't actually doing and what the real—as opposed to the imagined consequences of what it is doing—are likely to be. Such insights are even more clearly essential when it comes to elements of our bilateral and global interactions that affect our vital interests in economic prosperity, national well-being, or security. Here the stakes are considerably higher for both societies.

For better or ill, China is an independent actor in these areas, not an appendage of American policy or politics. And it is an extraordinarily diverse country, including as it does not just Han Chinese and numerous minority cultures but also Hong Kong, the freest market economy on the planet, and Macau, once an Asian version of Boston's "combat zone," now an ever-glitzier "Oriental Las Vegas" and the playground of princelings from all over. With two million Taiwanese—10 percent of whom now live on the Chinese mainland—Taiwan is also *de facto* part of "Greater China," despite its still-unsettled political relationship with the other parts of the emerging Chinese commonwealth.

To deal effectively with China, Americans need to understand it in terms of its own complexities and authentic aspirations. This is unlikely to be achieved by officials engaged in writing narrowly focused and highly tendentious reports mandated by Congress to justify the single-issue agendas of our military-industrial complex or, for that matter, our humanitarian-industrial complex. Nor can it be accomplished by analysts stir-frying intelligence to suit the political appetites of those for whom they work. Government-friendly but politically independent study centers like the one we are inaugurating tonight have a vitally important role to play in keeping our country from developing the world's first genuinely autistic national security establishment, if only in relation to China.

Predictions about China based on *a priori* reasoning, ideologically induced delusions, hearsay, conjecture, or mirror-imaging have been frequent and numerous. They have racked up a remarkable record of unreliability. To cite a few relevant examples: contrary to repeated forecasts, the many imperfections of China's legal system have neither prevented it from developing a vigorous market economy nor inhibited foreign investment—of which China continues to attract more than any other country, including our own. China's failure to democratize and its continuing censorship of its media, including the Internet, have not stifled its economic progress or capacity to innovate, which are increasingly impressive. China's perverse practices with respect to human rights have not cost China's Communist Party or its government their legitimacy. On the contrary, polling data suggests that Chinese have a very much higher regard for their political leaders and government than Americans currently do for ours.

Furthermore, despite our apparent nostalgia for the aggressive expansionism of our now inconveniently vanished Soviet rivals, there is no evidence that Beijing is at all tempted to recapitulate Moscow's suicidal effort to seek military parity with the United States. As a developing nation with fourteen countries on its borders, including such formidable former adversaries as Russia, Japan, Korea, Vietnam, and India, plus an unfinished civil war with other Chinese on Taiwan and the US Navy and Air Force just off its shores, China has plenty of reasons to focus on building a credible capacity to defend its own territory and few, if any, to develop a capability to project force around the globe. And if it were somehow to forget these reasons and to seek to compete with us militarily for global dominion, we would have plenty of warning.

None of this means that we should cease to care about the things we care about or refrain from seeking ways to stand with those within China who share our perspective about what is good for their country. Nor does it suggest that we should be unconcerned about how China may exercise its increasing wealth and power or abandon worst-case analysis of this. But it does emphasize that we cannot afford to confuse prescription with description or to focus on the China of our dreams or nightmares rather than the one that exists. The actual China is one that has plenty of problems that are remote from our recent experience.

The fact is that, while China is no longer a weak country and is no longer the least bit isolated, it is still a poor country and parts of it remain desperately primitive. Chinese leaders' modesty in the face of foreign amazement at their country's economic progress is not feigned. It reflects a realistic appreciation, borne of personal experience with conditions in places like Gansu and Tibet, of the enormous challenges and the several decades their country must traverse before it can achieve its national goal of becoming a moderately well-off society. In this context, China's oft-stated obsession with assuring a peaceful international environment in which it can concentrate on domestic social and economic development makes perfect sense. It is therefore credible. As the United States once did, China focuses on domestic development and seeks friends and commerce abroad, not enemies or entangling alliances. But, poor and backward as much of it may be, China's rapid growth and its sheer size—more than a fifth of the human race, living in an area about the size of the United States—call it to an ever-more-important role in the management of the world's affairs.

A few examples: Chinese capital markets remain only semi-developed and far short of their potential, but we've just seen that when Shanghai has heartburn, the world's stockbrokers get the hiccups. Quite amazingly, one can now rouse an American audience from slumber by talking about the dollar-yuan exchange rate or China's plan to set up an official "investment company" and cut back on purchases of US treasury bonds! Four years ago, China's initial fumbling as it tried to control severe acute respiratory syndrome (SARS) gave the world a real scare. (We must all hope it will do better with the flu pandemic that its poultry farms may now be brewing up.) Polls show that, despite its singularly unappealing political system, China has become, by a considerable margin, the most admired country all around the world. No one still dismisses the PLA as a "junkyard army." China's recent anti-satellite test, growing participation in UN peacekeeping missions, and near tripling of defense spending since 2000 mark its emergence as a considerable military power. A little soft power here, a little hard power there, and Chinese leaders could get a bit bumptious, as many suggest ours have. Will they?

They could. But, so far, the Chinese are showing that they accept that they should—as we have prescribed—be "responsible stakeholders" in the established order of regional and global affairs. Assertions that China has yet to make a choice in this regard are, quite frankly, more an embarrassing commentary on the dated outlook and political myopia of the American officials who make them than evidence of insight or serious thought on their part. For the time being, Chinese seem willing in most respects to accept continued American management of the world's affairs. But we cannot expect them to agree that the United States is entitled to act as the "controlling stakeholder" of those affairs. As the world turns and confronts new challenges, China will increasingly demand full participation in crafting responses to them. That is appropriate and in our interest, for, increasingly, such challenges will be unaddressable without China.

This is already the case with respect to the world monetary system, in which the Renminbi yuan is poised to emerge as a major trading and reserve currency within the coming decade. We are making a big mistake by not including China in the G-8 or, better yet, replacing the G-8 with a body that more accurately reflects global financial and economic power and China's growing share in both. China is already central to the global trade in energy, minerals, and other raw materials, in which rapidly rising Chinese demand increasingly drives prices. As an example, well before the end of this decade, China will be importing more than 600 million tons of iron ore and making more than 500 million tons of steel each year—over five times what we do. And this growth shows no sign of ending. Having cumulatively produced only 2.5 billion tons of steel to our 7.5 billion, China will have to produce another 30 billion or more tons to match our per-capita level of capital accumulation. Don't bet it won't! What standing do we have to ask it not to?

Even American "dead-enders" now accept that global warming and spreading environmental degradation, as well as the constant danger of epidemic disease, present increasingly serious public policy challenges to all of humanity. As all the horror stories in our press and as tens of thousands of protests by affected people in China attest, the stress Chinese now put on their environment is much greater than we have ever placed on ours. What China does at home and what the world is able to do about a widening range of global problems have become inextricably connected. In all the global commons—the seas, the air, space—there can be neither progress nor security without China's full participation as well as our own. If we were to ask for that participation, which we have not, would it be forthcoming? Could China rise to that challenge?

I am optimistic. China's leaders are trying hard, in connection with the Seventeenth Chinese Communist Party Congress to be held this fall, to develop a restatement of ideological principles that emphasizes the imperatives of societal and international harmony and the sinicization of Western-originated theories of innovation in science and technology. They want their country's ideology to include comprehensive guidelines to promote the investigative and inductive reasoning processes characteristic of the earliest and best social science, to draw pragmatic conclusions from the past thirty years of socioeconomic development in China, to follow Confucius and Mencius by laying out principles for ethical behavior at home and abroad, and to recreate on Chinese soil the spirit of innovation in science and technology that inspired the industrial revolution in the Atlantic region. We should all wish the Chinese leadership well in this ambitious endeavor. The world will be a better place if they succeed in elaborating an ideology that commits them to their own and others' peace and development.

If China can both do this and continue its progress toward a reasonably well-off society, it is not unreasonable to consider the possibilities that, by 2025:

- the Chinese yuan may have long since joined the dollar and euro as one of the principal currencies in world trade and reserves and helped bring into being a new and more flexible global financial system in a world more secure in its prosperity;
- those here tonight who are into wealth management—and still alive—may be as heavily invested in the Hong Kong and Shanghai stock exchanges as in New York or London, and private Chinese investment may play a significant, sometimes dominant, role in global markets, including our own;
- thanks to continued economic growth and the appreciation of its currency, China may have the largest economy on the planet while we continue, by a considerable margin, to have its most formidable military;

- the nature of Taiwan's relationship to the rest of China may have been peacefully resolved, taking with it the only conceivable *casus belli* between the United States and China;
- China may have evolved a system in which rule by law, if not perhaps the rule of law, has brought about a high level of domestic predictability and tranquility;
- the habits of consultation based on mutual respect and the policy transparency that characterize democracy at its best may have become integral to Chinese politics, even as the Chinese Communist Party continues in power (whether under that or another, more accurately descriptive name);
- China and the United States may both be in the process of establishing a sustainable presence on Earth's moon;
- contributions to the advancement of science and technology by Chinese may once again be at least proportional to China's share of the world's population;
- China may have begun, with us, to lead the way not in the destruction of the global environment but in its rehabilitation;
- the mounting attractiveness of China's political and economic success may have challenged us to rediscover and reassert the values and practices that have long made others see America as the last, best hope of humankind; and
- China may have joined a united Europe, India, Japan, Brazil, Russia, the United States, and other major powers in a concert of nations that can actually accomplish some of what President Roosevelt hoped the United Nations could do—bringing about a harmonious and largely peaceful world order, increasingly free of both want and fear and respectful of individual and collective rights as well as of the cultural diversity of humankind.

There are, of course, many far darker scenarios than these. You have heard them all. All that is required to realize them is to behave as if they are inevitable, and to interact with China as though they were. But there is surely nothing more inevitable about pessimistic outcomes than about the brighter possibilities I have outlined, which are, I think, close to what most Chinese would very much prefer. Such outcomes are not beyond our common grasp, if we work to achieve them.

Whether one is by nature optimistic or pessimistic, what is at stake in China's return to its historic eminence in human affairs surely illustrates that FDR was right long ago to attempt—over the resistance of our European allies—to incorporate China into the governing councils of the world. That effort failed soon after its inception. If we fail now to recognize the potential for cooperation with China, as well as other nations with rapidly strengthening capabilities, and if we lack the vision to enlist the Chinese as partners in the pursuit of a better future, we will make mutually disadvantageous outcomes much more likely. Preparation to confront the worst, if unaccompanied by a vision of the better, is not "hedging"; it is a belligerent strategy of despair based on self-fulfilling paranoia.

To take the right path forward, we need to know both where we are and where we want to go. We must find the potential for a better future in present realities. It is there to be found by those who look. To identify common interests with the Chinese or to cope with conflicts of interest where these exist, we need to understand Chinese perceptions and concerns, not just our own. Helping Americans to do that is one of the main purposes of CNA's newly established China Studies Center.

China and the Global Resource Balance[2]
July 2007

Next year, 2008, will mark the thirtieth anniversary of Deng Xiaoping's liberation of the Chinese people. In 1978, he replaced bureaucratic central planning with the invisible hand of the market economy. This must be counted as one of the most momentous events in modern history. In terms of current prices, it has brought about a fifty-eight-fold increase in China's gross domestic product (GDP). GDP per capita in China is now forty times what it was in 1978. The country has been transformed by this—and so has the world. China is rapidly acquiring a first-class infrastructure that provides a credible basis for further progress toward affluence.

Deng's revolution in economic affairs is now creating a lot of consumption as well as investment and industrial production. It seems much more likely that current trends will continue than that they will not, but there is nothing inevitable about this. Still, even if growth turns out to be much slower than most people now expect, the net effect will be to stretch out the impact of China's reemergence into wealth and power, not to halt it, and to reduce but not eliminate the implications of a growing Chinese economy for global commodities supplies, prices, investment opportunities, and the environment. Most of what I will have to say about China and its global impact refers to current realities, not projections into the future.

Energy is very much part of this picture, but there has been a lot said about it elsewhere. I want to focus instead on other natural resource import requirements. Chinese industry is set to grow by almost 17 percent this year and that generates a lot of demand for raw materials. Of course, much of what's happening with respect to these raw materials applies equally to oil and gas and to the ships and pipelines by which it is being siphoned up by the Chinese market.

Rapid growth in industrial demand is, however, far from the only cause of the rapid rise in China's imports of commodities. In the first quarter of 2007, the per-person disposable income of urban Chinese rose by almost 17 percent year-on-year in real terms, while average cash incomes in the countryside increased by more than 12 percent. That's a lot of demand for basic consumer goods, furniture, home electronics, foodstuffs, recreation, personal products, you name it.

There is also the phenomenon of China's emergence as the final assembly point in global supply chains and as a formidable processor of raw materials into products for export, like furniture. (The fifty thousand furniture companies in China now have half the global market and, with logging banned in China, are competing with each other to buy up the rest of the world's wood.)

Industrial production and consumption by newly affluent people in China are the twin forces now tightening supplies and driving prices in global commodity markets upward—not just minerals, metals, wood, and petrochemicals, but feed grains, meat, dairy products, and a host of other things. Retailers report that in newly rich cities, like Beijing, the average apartment owner now spends the equivalent of $30,000 on infill and decor. In China's major metropolitan areas, 78 percent of the registered population own their own homes, up from zero two decades ago. (The comparable figure for home ownership in the United States is about 69 percent.)

Without many outsiders noticing, China has acquired a vast property-owning middle class of around 300 million people—about as many as the total population of the United States. At nominal exchange rates—not converted for purchasing power parity, there are already about 50 million Chinese with incomes over $25,000 per year. (In China, that amount will buy five or six times what it will here, so these people are, by any standard, upper middle class.) By 2025, McKinsey projects that this Chinese upper middle class will have grown to about 520 million, even without appreciation of the Chinese currency in relation to the dollar—which seems virtually certain to occur. You don't have to believe that projection of current trends—though I think it's plausible—to grasp how China has become the fastest-growing part of the global market served by North American business—and everyone else.

China's growth is throwing up huge requirements for domestic infrastructure—highways, railways, housing, offices, factories, power plants, pipelines, ports, airports, and so forth. The Chinese are currently spending more than 9 percent of their GDP on modernizing their own infrastructure, not counting what they're spending on building infrastructure abroad in order to ship raw materials home. What China is building is big and it is efficient. It has a lot to do with the astonishing gains in productivity that the Chinese economy continues to register. (In the United States, we are spending less than 1 percent on developing or sustaining our infrastructure—and it shows.) Before I get to its long-term implications, let me cite a few examples of the speed with which development is unfolding in China.

China's first expressway opened seventeen years ago. There are now about thirty thousand miles of expressways, many of them privately financed, built, and operated. (They say the only robbers allowed on these highways are in the toll booths.) By 2020, China expects to have fifty-three thousand miles of superhighways, a high-speed road network 15 percent larger than the interstate highway system in the United States. China will build and pave about half a million miles of ordinary highways over the next five years alone, including, of course, the controversial road it is now building for tourists determined to drive up Mount Everest rather than hike it. All these roads will get heavy use.

Twenty-five years ago, there were a handful of private cars in China. The country still has only about seven cars for every thousand people—a level of market penetration for the automobile that we achieved in North America in 1915. But the car is fast becoming as Chinese as the *sampan*. By 2009, it is forecast, income levels will have risen enough to allow most middle-income Chinese families to buy cars. Auto sales are projected at 10 million by 2010 and 20 million by 2020. China will then, by a considerable margin, be the world's largest car market.

This has all sorts of implications beyond additional demand for petroleum products like asphalt, diesel, and gasoline, not to mention the output of exhaust fumes, used tires, and the like. China now accounts for only a tiny percentage of the world's cars and trucks—but no one who's been there recently will be surprised to learn that it has more than one-fifth of the world's traffic accidents. You can bet that some entrepreneur is already thinking about the huge opportunities in both health care and funeral services as more Chinese compatriots take to the roads! McDonald's has just partnered with Sinopec to add drive-in hamburger joints at filling stations throughout the country. Can the drive-in movie, backseat sexual acrobatics, and ambulance-chasing tort lawyers be far behind?

The economic boom has also generated soaring demand for rail transport. China has only 6 percent of the world's railway mileage. But last year Chinese railways handled 25 percent of the world's passengers and freight, carrying 662.2 billion passenger-kilometers—2.7 times the figure for rail-dense Japan—and 2.87 billion tons of cargo, a billion tons more than the

U.S., and 4.8 times as much as heavily rail-dependent India. China projects expansion of at least 35 percent in its rail network by 2020. It has just introduced the first intercity bullet trains, with more to come.

China's economy is increasingly powered by its domestic market rather than foreign trade, but it is becoming heavily dependent on imports for continued growth. Over the coming five years, Chinese ports will add 42 percent to their current handling capacity, which is already the largest in the world. China has built seven of the world's twenty largest container ports, with major technological innovation and expansion under way to handle volumes of trade that could hardly have been imagined only a few years ago. The country is also the world's fastest-growing aviation market. Air passenger traffic has been going up by about 15 percent and air cargo by 19 percent each year. Over the coming five years, China will build fifty new airports and double its inventory of commercial aircraft.

All this development is occurring apace with urbanization at a rate and on a scale unprecedented in human history. Over the past quarter century, China's urban population has doubled. Over the next twenty-five years, it is expected to double again as 500 million or more people move to China's cities. There are now more than one hundred Chinese cities with populations over one million. Each year, urban areas must find room for 20 million new arrivals from the countryside. Not surprisingly, China accounts for over half of world construction by area. It is building about 8 billion square feet (800 million square meters) of new housing annually.

One result of this is huge new requirements for minerals and metals. China makes 44 percent of the world's cement. More to the point, thanks to rapidly rising Chinese demand, the global mining industry has never been as hyperactive or as profitable as it is now. Mining revenue rose to $249 billion in 2006 from $181.5 billion in 2005. The industry's net profits skyrocketed 64 percent. New mining companies are swarming forth like mosquitoes in the rainy season. There is no end to the boom in sight.

This year, China will make about 500 million tons of steel, over two-fifths of the global total. This is six times as much as the United States produces. It is more than the entire world made ten years ago, and 23.5 percent more than China itself produced last year. To make this steel, China will import about 400 million tons of iron ore, supplementing the rapidly rising output of mines on its own territory. Chinese buyers dominate worldwide scrap markets. Already the largest producer of stainless steel, China managed to increase production last year by another 45 percent, setting off a boom in nickel and ferrochrome. To the delight of countries like Australia, Brazil, and India, as well as shipbuilders everywhere, Chinese iron-ore imports are expected to rise to at least 600 million tons by 2010.

Similar trends are evident in other minerals and metals. Chinese demand is driving major expansion in mining in Australia, Bolivia, Brazil, Canada, Chile, Guyana, India, Indonesia, Laos, Peru, the Philippines, Russia, South Africa, and Tanzania, to name just a few of the countries where large China-connected projects are currently in progress. But China is not just an importer. It is the dominant factor in the production of many minerals and metals. It produces 96 percent of the world's rare earths, 87 percent of its tungsten, 86 percent of its antimony, 75 percent of its magnesium, half of its fluorspar, one-third of its tin and lead, one-fourth of its aluminum and zinc, and one-fifth of its molybdenum. Chinese domestic consumption of all these commodities is rising apace with industrial production, so exports of rare-earth elements, tin, and tungsten are declining even as domestic consumption of these and other commodities continues its dizzy rise.

How long can such growth in Chinese production and consumption be sustained? The answer appears to be that it can go on for a very long time, providing that new sources of raw materials are discovered, that the huge investments necessary to develop and transport them are made, and that new strategies to increase recycling, remanufacturing, and reuse are elaborated.

Take steel as an indicator. Steel is a capital good that, once produced, is constantly recycled. To date, China has produced a cumulative total of about 4 billion tons of steel, four-fifths the total produced by Japan and half that of the United States. The Chinese are well aware that to reach U.S. levels of per-capita capital accumulation, they will have to make another 32 or 33 billion tons of steel. At current production rates, high as these already are, that will take another sixty-five or so years. For China to match Japan will take over a century. It is much more likely that Chinese production will speed up its rise than that it will slow down or decline.

That, plus the impact of other emerging economic great powers like India, will keep mineral supplies tight and prices high. It will make recycling more profitable and encourage the use of substitute materials. It will also keep profits in the global mining industry robust and stimulate major new investment in the economies of Africa, Latin America, Australia, Southeast and Central Asia, and Russia. China is already very aggressively seeking new natural resource supplies in all these regions.

In Africa, Chinese companies are now, by a wide margin, the largest foreign investors. They have strong financial backing from their government, which thinks the business of business is *business*, not the moral transformation of those with whom Chinese companies do it. This is, of course, intensely annoying to Western non-governmental organizations (NGOs), which had become accustomed to having Africa to themselves as a sort of humanitarian theme park in which capitalists and their business interests seldom intruded.

In connection with this, environmentalists are very concerned, and rightly so, by the implications for African rainforests of China's apparently insatiable demand for tropical hardwoods. The most farsighted NGOs are looking for ways to work with the Chinese government and to help it guide its companies toward environmentally responsible behavior. There is reason to hope this may work. China was sufficiently concerned about the environment to double its own forest cover over the past fifty years, to 18 percent. It has recently put forward a "sustainable forests" initiative to govern its purchases of wood from abroad.

More to the point, there is no feasible alternative to working with China. The emergence of the Chinese economy as a driving factor in the global commodities trade has ended the West's ability to determine international policy with respect to global extractive industries, even as it has put an end to the efficacy of coercive sanctions not endorsed by the United Nations on behalf of the entire international community. The arrival of India as another huge consumer of imported resources will give the *coup de grâce* to the age of American and European tutelage of the Third World. Two hundred and fifty years ago, the West began to dominate the globe. As the twenty-first century proceeds, that dominance is fading away. To cite the example of energy: not so long ago, the twenty largest energy firms, ranked by market cap, were in the United States or Europe. Today, 35 percent originate in China, Brazil, Russia, and India. A similar pattern is rapidly emerging in the mining sector.

Chinese companies are not prepared to take on a "*mission civilisatrice*"—the task of implanting their or other foreign norms on African soil so as to transform it. They promise to make Africa and other places in which they invest or do business richer. Whether or not these places also become better is—in their view—for the people who live there, not outsiders, to work out. For their part, Africans want to do business on their own terms, not to depend on handouts dispensed on terms set by others claiming to be wiser and more moral than they. Now that Africans finally have a choice of international partners, they—not foreigners, and certainly not Chinese—will decide how natural resources are exploited in Africa and by whom. Blaming China or India or someone else for this global paradigm shift is not just futile. It is counterproductive.

Quite aside from their politics, the new financial aspects of Sino-African relations are impressive. The loans China offered Africa in 2006 were three times the total development aid from the rich countries that make up the Organization for Economic Co-operation and Development (OECD). Since 2000, China has canceled more than $10 billion in debt for thirty-one African countries and given $5.5 billion in development aid, with a promise of a further $2.6 billion in 2007 and 2008. In 2005, China committed $8 billion in lending to Nigeria, Angola, and Mozambique alone. In that same year the World Bank spent $2.3 billion in all of Africa. In 2007, lending by China's Import-Export Bank to Africa is expected to be about $17.5 billion. And so it goes.

In Latin America, some of the same trends are evident. Trade with China has grown from a couple of hundred million dollars in 1978 to more than $70 billion last year. It is expected to rise to at least $100 billion by 2010. Argentina and Brazil have emerged as major suppliers of soybeans and other agricultural commodities to the Chinese market. Unlike Africa, however—where Chinese direct investment is opening mines and building the roads, railroads, and ports necessary to export their output—in Latin America most of the investment in new production for export to China is locally chartered and financed or conducted by joint ventures with Chinese companies.

This pattern of interaction is one reason that direct investment from China in Latin America has appeared to be much lower than Chinese and Latin American officials had forecast. Frankly, Latin Americans—like North Americans—continue to misunderstand both the nature of the current Chinese economy and its relationship to the Chinese government. They imagine that China's economy consists of a few large state-owned corporations that officials can direct to invest where the Chinese state would like them, for strategic reasons, to invest. By and large, however, Chinese industry is much, much more highly fractured than in the West. It consists of hundreds or even thousands of companies that compete with each other for trade and investment opportunities and resources. Business has to be done with these companies, not with Chinese ministries and their personnel.

Chinese companies do not believe that they are in the charity business; nor are they inclined to serve as disbursement agencies for altruistic Chinese government donations, which are—in any event—as hard to quantify as the Sasquatch population of British Columbia and the state of Washington. The Chinese government can, as it has in Africa, publicize opportunities and create financial incentives that favor the development of investment by Chinese companies, but it cannot substitute its business judgment for theirs and, by and large, does not attempt to do so. A lot of credit arrangements proffered by Beijing for business development in Latin America remain underutilized.

Let me conclude with a cowardly act of preemptive capitulation. I completely agree that the phenomena I have described pose serious challenges on multiple fronts. Global commodity prices are more likely to climb than to decline, as they did for the past two hundred years. There will be a premium on reusing some materials; substitutes will have to be found for still others we have taken for granted. There will be large environmental problems as Chinese and Indian demand for forest products and agricultural commodities rises and mining activities get under way in virgin areas. Western countries are indeed losing the privileged position of monopoly control they had over global extractive industries throughout the twentieth century. There is a major shift in the global balance of economic power going on; it is already evident in American and European friction with China and other non-Western countries over policies toward places like Iran, Myanmar, Sudan, Venezuela, and Zimbabwe. Non-Western countries, not surprisingly, feel no obligation to impose Western values or policy objectives they do not share on their trading partners. Our frustration with their unwillingness to do what we say—even if it isn't what we ourselves have been up to for the past 120 years—will lead to still greater friction.

With these admissions out of the way, I'd like to spend a final few minutes looking at the opportunities presented by the changes I have been describing. How can outsiders profit from the rising appetite for natural resources of the Chinese dragon—or the Indian lion that is coming up behind it?

There are many ways that come to mind, but they break down into a few categories:

- Investors can invest in companies that have the potential and intention to supply China with the energy, industrial minerals, metals, forestry, and agricultural products it needs. This suggests a hard look at natural resource companies operating in currently underdeveloped areas of Africa, Australia, Brazil, Canada, India, Indonesia, Papua New Guinea, Russia, southern Africa, and the southern cone of South America—Argentina, Bolivia, and Chile—and at the many new companies being organized to do this for the Chinese and Indian markets.

- Financiers can help Chinese investors leverage their capital with that of others to create companies and acquire properties at home or abroad. China has a very strong domestic mining industry but it has yet to develop the capability to structure its mining investments to maximum financial advantage. That's where Western financial expertise can come in. There is a lot more capital in China—and, for that matter, among overseas Chinese and in the Arab world—than there are people who know how to make it work most profitably for them.

- Private equity investors can help new companies or pull together currently unrelated Chinese natural resource–related operations with a view to taking the resulting new companies public in Hong Kong, now the site of the largest number of IPOs in the world, or elsewhere—and eventually in equity markets in China itself. In the last six months, with not many people noticing, the price-earnings ratios of companies in the extractive industries have doubled on the Hong Kong exchange. Someone needs to help new companies establish themselves and existing companies to consolidate. Why not do these things in the most profitable way possible?

- Fund managers can invest in the creation of new infrastructure in China: for example roads, logistics management facilities like port, airport, and warehouse operations and real estate. Investors in funds can invest in some of the four hundred or so venture capital and private equity funds that have been established in China.
- Individuals and groups of investors can buy shares in Chinese companies that extract oil, gas, minerals, or metals. Not a few such companies are strong performers with rich dividends. Many are listed in equity markets outside China. New companies are being formed constantly. They can be good investments in their own right but have the added advantage that, with their underlying assets denominated in Chinese yuan, their book value will rise along with the yuan exchange rate. Some will need help making IPOs.
- Entrepreneurs can invest in companies that are focused on improving energy and materials efficiency or the profitable recycling, remanufacturing, and reuse of industrial materials. As supplies tighten and prices rise, companies in this business will prosper proportionately.

A lot of these approaches are very well suited to private equity. Some may not be. But I trust I have made my point. Not so very long ago, Deng Xiaoping declared that "to get rich is glorious." His countrymen have taken him seriously. That's causing some problems. But China's demand for natural resources seems to me to represent some real opportunities for those in private equity who agree with the Chinese people that Deng knew what he was talking about and are prepared, like them, to take a risk or two to achieve the kind of glory he foresaw.

Asia Takes Shape[3]

February 2011

The Greeks are to blame for many things. Not least of these is the somewhat preposterous idea of "Asia." For thousands of years after strategists in Greece came up with this Eurocentric notion, the many non-European peoples who inhabited the Eurasian landmass were blissfully unaware that they were supposed to share an identity as "Asians." After all, except during the near-unification of Asia under the Mongols, they had little to do with each other. Arabs and Chinese, like Indians, Japanese, Malays, Persians, Russians, Turks, and others, had different histories, cultures, languages, religious heritages, and political traditions. Their economies were only tenuously connected by the gossamer strands of the Silk Road and its maritime counterpart.

But all this is now changing. "Asia" is leaving the realm of Greek myth and becoming a reality. Asians are drawing together as they rise in wealth and power. Their companies and their influence now extend throughout their own continent and beyond. In the twentieth century, the world had to adapt to American domination of its global political economy. Americans must now adapt to a political economy increasingly centered on Asia.

In much of Asia, as late as the last decades of the past century, postcolonial hangovers deranged politics with love-hate relationships that distorted attitudes toward the West. This is easy to understand. After all, Western colonialism had humbled the armies, crushed the self-esteem, and suppressed the values and political traditions of societies from Turkey to China.

In West Asia, Turks, Arabs, and Persians bit by bit yielded their autonomy, territory, and national dignity to predatory Europeans. In India, the British overthrew Muslim rule, imposed a single sovereignty, and embroiled the once-isolated subcontinent in the quarrels of Europe. States in South Asia that had for long contributed about one-fifth of the global economy were subordinated to British mercantilism and subjected to British rule.

The East Indies and Indochina also fell to European imperialism. In East Asia, only Thailand and Japan embraced key elements of Westernization with sufficient alacrity to keep the West more or less at bay. Japan did this with such drive and discipline that it soon imposed its own colonial rule in Korea and parts of China. In the Russo-Japanese War and World War II, Japan went on to demonstrate that, when allied to modern technology, its martial traditions would let it punch far above its nominal military and economic weight.

Russia gobbled up Central Asia. It gnawed away at China from the north as Western powers nibbled at it from the south and east. Foreigners carved China into spheres of influence, annexed parts of its territory, and placed bits and pieces of it under their extraterritorial jurisdiction. Europeans and Americans had to do this, we said, to be able to exercise our right to peddle narcotics and proselytize an alien religious ideology to the Chinese people over the outlandish objections of their rulers.

The colonial order in Asia collapsed in the wake of World War II. As the rest of Asia rejected a reassertion of foreign control, America occupied Japan and placed it under our tutelage and protection. China defiantly "stood up," expelling foreigners and their influence from its soil. Southeast Asia revolted against its various colonial masters and their American allies. India hived off Pakistan as both took their freedom from the British. Iran reemerged as an aspirant to regional power. Turkey took its place as the stalwart eastern bulwark of Europe's defenses against an expanded Soviet empire. A new era began.

Only in West Asia—where Africa, Asia, and Europe intersect, where Judaism and Christianity began, where Islam is centered, and where the world's energy resources are concentrated—did major elements of the pre–World War II order persist. In the last days of colonialism, European Jews conquered and colonized four-fifths of the Holy Land, displacing many of its inhabitants. Both Palestinian Arabs and others in the region reacted with shock and horror at this unexpected culmination of both European anti-Semitism and the age of imperialism. Neither the shock nor the horror has yet been cured by Israeli or Western diplomacy.

During the Cold War, the states of the Middle East sank into uneasy dependence on the contending superpowers, which handled conflicts among them as proxy wars. Israel aside, leaders in the region became noted for their fatalistic deference to powerful foreign patrons and their feckless accommodation of European, Soviet, and American insults to the sovereignty, independence, and cultural identities of the peoples over whom they ruled. The first rip in the fabric of this neocolonial order came in the Islamic revolution of 1979 in Iran. That ended Iran's role as "America's gendarme" in the Middle East and forced the United States to switch to military reliance on Saudi Arabia and Egypt. Nearly simultaneously, Egypt's American-brokered peace with Israel made the preservation of the autocratic *status quo* in the region an overriding priority of U.S. policy.

Even a cursory reading of the Camp David accords is a poignant reminder that they were explicitly premised on Israel's undertaking to end its occupation of the West Bank and Gaza and to facilitate self-determination for Palestinians. Failure to do either ensured that the peace between Israel and Egypt was a cold one that could not warm. The Palestinians gained no relief from humiliation and injustice. Instead they saw both intensify. Peace with Israel lost any chance to gain legitimacy in Egypt or elsewhere. In large measure due to this, Israel and the United States have become thoroughly detested in Egypt, by other Arabs, and in the Islamic world as a whole.

America's willingness to underwrite the Mubarak dictatorship and the Hashemite monarchy in Jordan with cash, weapons, and moral support bought the Camp David framework at least the appearance of durability. But the ability of the United States to substitute conflict avoidance for a real effort to make peace has probably expired along with the Mubarak regime. Since Israel continues adamantly to prefer the expansion of its borders to peace with either the Palestinians or its neighbors, and since there has not been a serious "peace process' for more than a decade, it is now unclear how America will continue to stabilize and contain the Israel-Palestine conflict. It is in fact unclear how much influence, if any, we Americans will now exercise in the region as a whole.

The recent uprisings of Arab citizens against their rulers have cast aside the fatalistic sense of impotence and obsequious deference to foreign power with which Arabs long hobbled themselves. They see the United States as having cynically supported despotism over democracy to keep Israel safe from Arab reactions to its behavior. Neither Israeli nor American interests have been the immediate target of these revolutions. But the decisions of Egyptians and other Arabs to seize control of their own future will affect both Israelis and Americans. Thirty years after the Iranian upheaval, the postcolonial order in the Middle East is at last collapsing.

The spreading disorder in West Asia comes after American policies in the opening decade of this century thoroughly discredited the United States, devalued its military power, and cemented Iran's influence in Iraq, Lebanon, Gaza, and Syria. Regionwide political change is occurring as America withdraws from Iraq, leaving behind a ruined country riven by secular passions and with no sure strategic orientation. Meanwhile, the United States' armed forces are generating more terrorists than they are killing in Afghanistan and Pakistan. This is the context in which western Asia's ties to other parts of the continent are thickening. Some might consider it ominous.

The Arabs, Turks, and others in West Asia were trying to reduce their dependence on the United States even before current events illustrated how much contempt they feel for our perceived hypocrisy and how little weight the American word now has among them. They are, of course, well aware that they cannot avoid a measure of reliance on America. The United States is still the only military world power; it is able to invade, if not impose its will on, every corner of the globe. Americans account for over one-fifth of global consumption and are the world's greatest debtors. The United States may no longer be the global source of new ideas for managing world and regional affairs it once was, but it has the ability to block reform initiatives from others. So, like other Asians, Middle Easterners are locked in a Catholic marriage with America. Much as some of them—the Iranians, for example—might wish to send the United States packing, no divorce is possible. But they, of course, are mostly Muslim and untroubled by polygamy. So they are busily contracting new relationships to offset their still-substantial ties to America.

China and India, in particular, are happy to oblige. They are not only the fastest-growing large economies in the world, but the fastest-growing markets for Persian Gulf oil and gas. Over the decade to come, China and India are expected to account for over half the growth in global energy demand. The spectacular rise of Asia's industrious East and South has fueled a boom in its energy-rich West. Chinese construction companies, having proven their capabilities in vast infrastructure projects at home, are building big things from Mecca to Tehran. If the current emblems of the United States in the region are bombers, boots on the ground, and lethally armed drones, China increasingly evokes images of tower and gantry cranes, engineers, and containers full of consumer goods.

The Chinese are succeeding in establishing an influential presence in the region for the same reasons Americans once did. They pay cash, deliver value for money, and make no demands on business partners or hosts to conform to their values, endorse their political preferences, or help them advance an imperial agenda. In these respects, America has met a rival, and it is *us, as we used to be.* But if China is admired for its apparent modesty and competence, no one in the region, still less elsewhere in Asia, sees it as an exemplar of relevant political ideals, as many, if not most, once saw America.

This underscores a key feature of Asia's integration. It is driven by economic and financial factors, not politics or ideology. Trade between the Persian Gulf region, China, and India has been growing at 30 to 40 percent each year for the past decade. (Over that same period, China grew from 10 percent of the size of the U.S. economy to 40 percent. By 2050, only forty years from now, China's economy may be twice the size of America's. And India's economy will match our own in size. We are talking serious economic growth in Asia, with serious geostrategic consequences.

Oil, engineers, and consumer goods are not the only factors drawing West Asia toward the East. Arab investors are flush with cash. They once had a very strong preference for putting their money to work in the United States. American Islamophobia and the reawakening of ancient Islamic ties to China as well as Central and Southeast Asia are well along in curing them of this preference. Meanwhile, both public and private Arab investment in China's petrochemical industries, services, banks, telecommunications, and real estate have surged. The same trend is setting in with India, though it is hampered by corruption scandals and the apparent inability of Indian politicians, like ours, to resist the opportunity to grandstand on specific transactions.

Asia's newfound integration is not limited to trade and investment. Islamic banking, with its now very appealing avoidance of leverage and derivatives, is as much a feature of finance in Malaysia as in the Persian Gulf. It is being taken up in China and elsewhere. Tourism, religious pilgrimages, student exchanges, and language learning are all on a rapid upswing. A few years ago, some were stunned to see China's president Hu Jintao shown around the world's largest oil company, Saudi Aramco, by a series of Chinese-speaking Saudi graduates of China's best engineering schools. In China, dozens of universities and institutes now teach Arabic. Hundreds of Chinese are enrolled in Arab universities. In a few trading centers in China, like the city of Yiwu in Zhejiang Province, Arabic now rivals English as the second language of Chinese merchants. Chinese Central Television has a twenty-four-hour Arabic-language service.

The appearance of Chinese officials who speak fluent Arabic on satellite news services like Al Jazeera has long since ceased to be a novelty. The success of Chinese oil companies in acquiring exploration and production rights in Iraq owes much to the Arabic proficiency of Chinese officials and businessmen. Similarly, fluency in Russian—the *lingua franca* of Central Asia—has been key to China's ability to secure widening access to energy supplies there. Overall, the foreign student population in China has been growing by 20 percent per year. The largest numbers of such students come from other East Asian societies, like south Korea, but there are now also thousands of Indians studying in China. In an effort to boost competitiveness, India is adding the study of Chinese to the national primary-school curriculum.

This development reflects the astonishing advance of Sino-Indian ties—despite India's view of itself as China's strategic rival in Asia. Sino-Indian trade grew from $200 million in 1989 to about $60 billion last year. China surpassed the United States to become India's largest trading partner in 2007. The target for Sino-Indian trade in 2015 is $100 billion. Prospects for Sino-Indian economic cooperation are particularly promising. The two countries' economies are broadly complementary in ways that invite cross-investment, with India disproportionately strong in services and China in industrial production. Investment had lagged until late last year. But Premier Wen Jiabao's year-end visit to South Asia was the occasion for new Chinese investment commitments to India and Pakistan of almost $16 billion each.

Both China and India depend on growing levels of raw materials imports from Africa and Latin America and energy shipments from Africa and the Middle East. Despite their obvious common interests in securing sea lines of communication, there is, however, real reason to doubt whether they will be able to cooperate militarily. The Sino-Indian frontier is about as long as the U.S. border with Mexico, but a lot less peaceful. It is now the only land boundary that China has been unable to settle through peaceful negotiations. China and India fought a brief war along it in 1962, and there are still frequent clashes between their military patrols. Indian apprehensions about growing Chinese military power now play as large a part in driving its defense modernization as do its hostile relationship with Pakistan and the related conflict in Kashmir.

India's concerns about China have pushed it to strengthen military ties with the United States. They have also led it to open security dialogue with similarly apprehensive countries to its east, like Vietnam and Japan. Since the Meiji Restoration of 1868, Japan has been accustomed to being "number one" in Asia. But last year, China's economy displaced Japan's as the world's second largest. The rise of China has pushed Japan off balance psychologically and left it strategically perplexed—unsure about how to cope with its changing place in the Asian pecking order. Some in Tokyo see a defense relationship with India as a useful hedge against China, as the American political and economic global leadership on which Japan has long relied continues to erode.

Last September's collision (in 2010) between a Chinese fishing boat with a drunken captain and Japanese coast guard vessels off the disputed Senkaku (or Diaoyu) Islands alarmed many in Japan. It pushed Tokyo closer, at least for a time, to Washington. It catalyzed the redeployment of Japanese self-defense forces away from Russia and toward the perceived threat of China. It also stimulated Japan to explore prospects for military cooperation with south Korea, something that deeply rooted antipathies on both sides had long made politically impossible. Still, many factors—including rising dependence on growth in the Chinese economy for its future prosperity—continue to draw Japan ever closer to China. A full 20 percent of Japan's trade is now with China, which surpassed the United States as Japan's top economic partner some years ago. At more than 25 percent, south Korea's dependence on the China market is even greater.

All of Eastern Asia (including Japanese and Korean companies as well as those in China and Southeast Asia) is now inseparably connected through supply-chain relationships. India is beginning to be drawn into these as well as other relationships with Eastern Asia. Its choice of Indonesia's president as its chief guest at this year's Republic Day celebrations in New Delhi is a big straw in this wind.

The importance of Southeast Asia as a crucible for Asian economic integration is hard to overstate. Chinese communities there played a key role in the creation of cadre capitalism in China, which incorporates many elements of overseas Chinese commercial and financial culture. The pan-Chinese consensus is that "the business of China and its people is business"—to paraphrase Calvin Coolidge's trenchant description of early-twentieth-century America. This has facilitated the setting aside of territorial claims and other potential conflicts so that everyone can get on with making money, not war.

As he hoped it would, Deng Xiaoping's notion that "to get rich is glorious" has birthed a Greater China. It is healing the rift between Chinese on either side of the Taiwan Strait. Greater China includes the systemically distinctive political economies of the China mainland, Hong Kong, Macau, and Taiwan. Its ideology, to the extent it has one, is best expressed in the orderly meritocracy and pragmatic use of industrial policy seen in Singapore. The economies of Greater China, the members of the Association of Southeast Asian Nations (ASEAN), and—to a lesser extent—traditionally protectionist Japan and south Korea, are now well along in forming a huge free-trade area with which India and other South Asian countries are interested in associating themselves.

Asia's remaining great power—Russia—stands somewhat apart from these processes of integration, but not entirely. It remains a primary source of weapons systems and technology for both India and China. It is becoming a significant energy supplier to China as well as Europe. The beaches of Hainan Island, Vietnam, and India are now the winter playgrounds of the Russian middle class. Lots of Russians are studying and working in China and other countries throughout Asia.

Moscow joined with Beijing and Central Asian nations to form the Shanghai Cooperation Organization (SCO). The SCO seeks to deny the region to great-power rivalries, Islamic extremism, and Chinese ethnic separatists. But Russia seems more focused on relationships with Europe than with Asia. Chinese linkages to Central Asia's energy supplies and transportation corridors are eroding Russia's traditional dominance there. Its sparsely populated but natural resource–rich far-eastern regions are being drawn into the Chinese, Japanese, and Korean economic orbits. Siberian agriculture is increasingly reliant on Chinese migrant labor. Russia's future relationship with the rest of Asia remains a bit of a wild card—as ill-defined and undetermined as the Russian identity, political system, or role in Europe and the Middle East.

The implications of Asia's emergence as a much more integrated set of economies and societies are only beginning to become apparent, but they promise to be vast. Asianization is likely to join globalization as a defining phenomenon of this century. We are already seeing this in the emergence of Asian supply-chain economics as both the heart and circulatory system of global trade. Most financial analysts expect that Asian currencies like the Chinese yuan will in time dilute the now-dominant role of the dollar as the denominator of trade and international monetary reserves. The human and natural resource diversity of an ever-more-integrated Asia provides a firm basis for continued economic expansion amidst rapidly rising productivity.

In 2050—less than forty years from now—our best bankers and economists say that China should have a GDP of over $70 trillion in current dollars. (By way of comparison, U.S. GDP is now about $14 trillion; by 2050 it might be as large as $35 trillion.) That same year, India's GDP should, we are told, be the same or even bigger than that of the United States. Other Asian economies, like that of Indonesia, should have grown proportionately. The figures may be disputable but there is little reason to doubt that, by mid-century, the world's economic center of gravity will be in Asia, somewhere between Beijing and New Delhi. Arabs and Indonesians, Turks and Japanese, Indians and Americans, Europeans, Africans, Latin Americans, and others will be there alongside Chinese. A rising China and India now lift all Asians. Asia has begun to lift the world.

Three centuries ago, Europe, followed by America, displaced Asia from its long-standing preeminence in scientific and technological innovation. (Think of the invention of the zero, the compass, the rocket, paper money, movable type, chemistry, the beauty parlor, and the bank check, for example. These are, respectively, Indian, Chinese, Korean, Arab, and Islamic contributions to human civilization.) But the ranks of the Asian educated are swelling, and institutions that can translate ideas into products—like research universities and venture capitalism—have already taken root on the continent. As this century proceeds, no one should be surprised to see Asia resume its seat at the head of the class.

The prestige and influence of Asian culture can also be expected to grow. We seldom reflect on the extent to which Asian ways have already infiltrated our daily lives. A prior generation of Americans would have found our delight in sushi and sashimi unimaginable. ("Seaweed-wrapped rice and raw fish for dinner? You can't be serious!") Indian-style body piercings, studs, and hanging ornaments, once seen as barbarously exotic, now adorn or—depending on your viewpoint—disfigure many Americans, young and old. The hookah has come to our cities in the form of shisha parlors. Sudoku is all the rage. People pay attention to *feng shui* and our kids study the martial arts. What next from Asia? There will surely be something that now seems improbable. Before long, we will make it too ours, take it for granted, and forget its Asian origins.

Before I close, I want to put forward a few observations on every American's favorite subject—the search for plausible enemies to replace the late Soviet Union. That Russian-dominated empire very irresponsibly dropped out of the race to dominate the world, leaving us to do so—but giving us a bad case of enemy-deprivation syndrome. We need an existential threat to rationalize spending more on our military than the rest of the world combined and to justify exempting defense spending from the budget cuts necessitated by impending national bankruptcy. Russia just isn't up to this anymore. So we have come up with two alternative candidates to do us in—one centered in Asia's West and one in its East: Islam and China. But neither really rises to the role we have assigned it.

Muslims desire to resume a place of dignity in the world's affairs. They have been conducting an escalating and occasionally violent argument among themselves about how to order their societies. Some strongly oppose the influence of our culture on theirs and want to exclude it. Others, as the examples of Tunisia and Egypt show, embrace elements of the ideals in which modern Western political systems are grounded, without wishing to adopt either our model or our mores. All resent our backing of Israel against their co-religionists and all but a few are horrified by our armed invasions of Muslim lands and their results. Most want us gone so they can sort out their differences among themselves. Few have any aspiration to convert us to their faith. None has the capacity to conquer us. Islam doesn't pass the existential-threat test. It is a menace to our military domination of the countries that profess it, not a challenge to the independence, values, or security of a secular America.

As for China, we seem most of all to fear that it might become like us—a country animated by armed evangelism, equipped with a military designed for power projection, and imbued with an impulse to impose its values on the world. In Chinese, the two ideograms that make up the word "China" do mean "central country." In this century, China is very likely once again to live up to the sense of this name in many spheres of human endeavor. But China is in the middle of things in other respects as well. It is hemmed in by militarily powerful neighbors—Russia, India, Japan, Korea, Vietnam, and, of course, the United States, which has a formidable naval presence right up against its twelve-mile territorial sea boundaries and powerful land and air forces in Afghanistan and other places along its western marches. China must manage many challenges to its national security, only a few of which directly concern the United States and none of which are remote from its frontiers.

In short, China faces too many immediate military, social, and economic development problems to be able to follow the United States in attempting to dominate the world—even if it were tempted to do so. The security environment in twenty-first-century Asia will be characterized by shifting coalitions and balances with and against China. In this respect, Asia will resemble nineteenth-century Europe. It too will offer an opportunity for offshore balancing, should the United States wish to draw on the experience of Great Britain then. The British buttressed actors on the continent when and where they needed reinforcement to dissuade the ambitions of neighbors, but seldom intervened directly. Not bad for government work!

As a final illustration of the complexity of emerging Asian military realities, I want briefly to consider their nuclear dimension. Not counting the United States (which has nuclear-capable forces on three sides of it), Asia is already home to six of the world's nine nuclear-armed powers. In time, many suspect, Iran could make this seven out of ten. Even without Iran, the nuclear geometry in Asia is already pretty complex. China, Russia, and the United States aim at each other. North Korea targets Japan and south Korea and would target the United States if it could. India targets Pakistan and China. Pakistan targets India. So does China. Nobody with nuclear weapons yet targets Israel but Israel aims its arsenal at everyone around it. Neither India, nor Israel, nor Pakistan is a party to the Non-Proliferation Treaty (NPT); north Korea has thumbed its nose at it. This is one reason that the continuing U.S. focus on preventing proliferation now seems so quaint. The tigers are out of their cages. Asia is where theories of nuclear deterrence face their final exam. In this context, the grotesquely overbuilt nuclear arsenals that Russia and the United States inherited from our Cold War experiment with mutually assured destruction are irrelevant and a huge waste of money.

The same could be said about some but not all of the now-well-established American hysteria about nuclear attacks by non-state actors. Every nation that has a bomb made a big investment to build it and has a compelling security problem its bomb is intended to address. No one is going to give such a precious thing away. Concerns about the deliberate transfer of weapons to terrorists seem greatly exaggerated, if not delusional.

But there is a possibility that a breakdown of order within a state with nuclear weapons might offer disgruntled elements or murderous extremists in it the chance to pilfer a bomb or two. In this context, at present, Pakistani militants or Israeli settlers come to mind. Over the course of the decades to come, there are likely to be other situations like these to worry about unless the sources of the conflicts that animate fanaticism can be addressed. Vigilance is therefore justified. So is a renewed focus on resolving civilizational conflicts, ending oppression, and building peace, justice, and prosperity in Asia as elsewhere.

To sum up: the challenge to the United States is to harness Asia's progress to our own, not to dominate the continent or retard its advance. Asian prosperity is essential to American wealth and well-being. Asian intellectual excellence and economic productivity should spur us to raise our own performance standards, not seek to lower theirs. Asian innovations must be met by a renewed American commitment to science and technology, not closed minds and protectionism. Intra-Asian dynamics invite agile

American diplomacy that can reduce our defense burden while containing conflict, not militaristic lurches into armed intervention there.

We will not succeed if we fail to recognize that, after a couple of bad millennia for the Greek concept of "Asia," it's back. A large organism that fits the description is actually emerging. We cannot hope to handle this beast—let's think of it as an elephant—if we have a policy for its hindquarters but not for its trunk, head, legs, or belly. Each part of the Asian anatomy presents its own problems and calls for its own policy tools—but, in some respects, the greatest challenge we face may be to see the continent as a whole and to conceive our strategy and act accordingly. Neither the current organization of our academies and government nor our past experience will be at all helpful in this regard. But it must be done. Understanding the increasing interconnectedness of Asia is a prerequisite both for restored American leadership there and for effective global governance in the decades to come. Both are sorely needed.

East Asia's Engagement with the Arab Countries of the Persian Gulf[4]
October 2011

No one should be surprised that the countries of West and East Asia are rapidly drawing closer. On both sides, the interests driving economic cooperation and political rapprochement are compelling. For the countries of the Gulf in particular, whether on the Arab or Persian side of it, the allure of East Asia is not new. Today, as in the past, it is fueled by ties of religion as well as by the desire to profit from economic exchange.

In 650 CE, the Caliph Uthman ibn Affan sent one of the companions of the Prophet Mohammed (PBUH) as an emissary to the newly established Tang Dynasty. That date marks the beginning of Islam in China. Ever since, Muslims have played a prominent role in Chinese society. The great Ming admiral Zheng He [郑和], who visited Arabia in the early fifteenth century, is a case in point. His grandfather and great-grandfather were both hajjis. Admiral Zheng was the great-great-great-grandson of Sayyid Ajjal Shams al-Din Omar al-Bukhari [赛典赤·赡思丁], a Persian who served as governor of Yunnan Province during the early Yuan Dynasty.

Much evidence suggests that the number of Chinese who consider themselves Muslim is now well over 100 million, though the official count remains less than a quarter of that. As the example of Admiral Zheng attests, Chinese Muslims have long been active in sustaining contacts between their homeland and Arabs, Persians, Turks, and other Muslim peoples.

This cross-cultural liaison was, of course, interrupted by the reorientation of international relations imposed by Western colonialism. The postcolonial era in the Middle East and the return of China to wealth and power are fostering its resumption. Some 13,500 Chinese performed the hajj in 2010. There are now direct flights to Mecca from Beijing, Urumqi, Lanzhou, Yinchuan, and Kunming.

Meanwhile, the Gulf's ties with Indonesia, the world's most populous Muslim state, and its Malay sister states, Malaysia and Brunei, have also been invigorated. The main drivers of the Gulf's ties with the East have always been commerce, navigation, and religious pilgrimage, not politics or security affairs. The Arabian peninsula is where Africa, Asia, and Europe intersect. From the Roman era to the age of European colonialism, much of its wealth derived from the role of local merchants as intermediaries in the Mediterranean region's importation of silk and spices from Asia. The emergence of Dubai as a major crossroads for trade between Asia, Africa, and Europe is a modern expression of this strategic location.

The region was once thought fortunate to have a near-monopoly on commodities such as frankincense and myrrh. Now it harbors over half the world's proven oil reserves and a third of its natural gas. But even without such resources, the Gulf Arab states' natural role as trading hubs and communication corridors would make them of strategic interest to Europe, Asia, and Africa. The rapid growth of aviation, logistics management, and port services as contributors to the GDP of the six states of the Gulf Cooperation Council (GCC) is testimony to this geographic importance.

However, for Asia, as for the rest of the world, the Gulf is regarded first and foremost as the center of the world's energy production and, increasingly, its petrochemical products, including fertilizer. Arabs and Persians produce oil and gas and Asians are major consumers of both. The complementarities are inescapable. Neither can the international orientation of the Arab states of the Gulf, as well as Iran, fail to be affected by the fact that the fastest-growing and largest markets for their energy and chemical products are in East and South Asia, especially in China. The emergence of China as the global center of economic gravity is uniting the disparate parts of Asia as never before. West Asia is distant, so the gravitational pull of China on the Gulf is somewhat attenuated, but it is nonetheless very apparent and becoming more so.

China alone currently accounts for about 20 percent of the world's population, 10 percent of its economic production, and 40 percent of its energy demand growth. Within a decade, its economy is expected to overtake those of the United States and then the European Union in size.

China has already become the world's greatest consumer of energy and its second-greatest importer of oil, after the United States. (China will probably not surpass America as an oil importer until the late 2020s). Nearly three-fifths of current Chinese oil imports are from the Gulf. Meanwhile, Japan, India, south Korea, and Taiwan are, respectively, the world's third, fifth, sixth, and tenth largest importers of oil.

In addition to its importance as an energy market, Asia now takes 40 percent of the GCC's non-energy exports. Such exports are growing fast. As an example, Saudi Arabia recently became the leading petrochemical supplier to China's textile industry. The East is not just the future of the Gulf's export-oriented economies; it is also, to a great extent, their present orientation.

Oil, gas, petrochemicals, air routes, shipping, and the region's reestablished role as an intermediary trading center have led to explosive growth in the wealth of the GCC economies. This growth has been accompanied by massive investment in human and physical infrastructure as well as defense equipment and services.

In the early stages of their modernization, the Gulf Arab states, as well as Iran, looked primarily to Americans and Europeans for engineering services, construction management, equipment, and durable goods. European and American engineers and technicians remain active in the Arab states of the Gulf but have been succeeded in many roles sequentially by Japanese, Korean, and now, increasingly, Chinese firms and workforces.

Political confrontations and sanctions have meanwhile eliminated the American presence in Iran and greatly reduced the European presence. Asian companies have filled the vacuum. Japanese and Korean manufacturers started to seize market share from their American and European competitors three decades ago. They continue to play a leading role in heavy engineering projects in the Gulf, including oil refinery and desalination plant construction as well as in the construction of the great office and residential towers that symbolize the region's leap to modernity.

Japan is now, by a wide margin, the largest source of foreign investment in Saudi Arabia. South Koreans won the huge bids for new nuclear power plants in the United Arab Emirates. Over the past decade, China has come to dominate the GCC's consumer-goods markets. Chinese construction companies are now omnipresent. Increasing numbers of Chinese laborers are joining the six million Indian expatriate workers now present in the Gulf, in addition to the nearly three million Filipino and Bangladeshi workers and more than two million Pakistani expatriate workers.

The number of Chinese workers in the Gulf is, however, not likely to approach those of Filipinos or South Asians. The GCC countries are finally coming to grips with the imperative of favoring indigenous over imported labor. The years to come should see a reduction rather than an increase in the GCC's reliance on guest workers. The number of Asian businessmen and women resident in the region should, however, continue to grow. Dubai is already home to thousands of Chinese companies, which have made the emirate both the showroom and the distribution center for their sales in West Asian and African markets.

Some enclaves within the GCC countries exempt foreigners from the gender inequality, forced abstention from alcohol, and religious and social isolation that cause them to demand premium pay and hardship allowances. To the extent that these practices continue or even expand, such enclaves will remain highly competitive locations in which Asian as well as Western businesses can comfortably prosper.

Quite aside from their entrepôt role, the GCC counties, like Iran and Iraq, have become significant markets for automobiles and other manufactured goods from East Asia. The GCC signed its first collective free trade agreement (FTA) in 2008 with Singapore. It has started talks on additional FTAs with China, Japan, south Korea, India, and Pakistan, plus Australia and New Zealand. Three decades ago, four-fifths of GCC trade was with Europe and North America. Now about one-half of the region's trade is with Asia—one-quarter with Japan and Korea and another one-third with the member states of ASEAN, China, and India.

After the 1973 Arab oil embargo and price rise, the GCC became a significant source of capital for the world, including North America and Europe. In the wake of the September 11, 2001, terrorist attacks on New York and Washington, America became a considerably less welcoming and secure destination for investment by wealthy Muslim investors and institutions. More recently, though for different reasons, Europe has also come to be seen as a much riskier place to invest. As a result, Gulf Arab money has flowed in increasing volumes to Asia. Arab money has been welcomed throughout Asia, indeed sought after, as south Korea's increasing issuance of *sukuk* (sharia-compliant bonds) testifies.

There has also been a great deal of unsung financial cooperation between East Asia and the Arab Gulf in the development of new institutions and financial practices. Malaysia pioneered a number of the innovative approaches to Islamic banking that have become an ever-more-prominent part of global financial practices as well as those of the Gulf. Kuala Lumpur remains home to the largest market for *sukuk* in the world. (It is about to issue the first Chinese Renminbi yuan *sukuk*.) Since the outbreak of the Great Recession in the West, interest in unleveraged forms of finance has naturally greatly increased. Islamic banking practices are therefore spreading well beyond the realm of Islam. Meanwhile, China has viewed sovereign wealth funds in the Gulf as models for its own. Chinese sovereign wealth funds have emulated and benefitted greatly from the informal advice of the Gulf region's very professionally managed funds.

The effects of expanding financial and commercial ties between the Gulf and East Asia are far from one-sided. Cultural cross-fertilization is less advanced. The Prophet Mohammed (PBUH) is said to have advised Muslims to "seek knowledge even unto China." In recent years, however, not many from the Gulf have made this intellectual journey. Asians have invested a great deal more time and effort in mastering Arabic and understanding the history and culture of the GCC than Gulf Arabs have been willing to devote to learning Chinese, Japanese, Korean, or Malay, though some have done so. (One thinks of the several dozen Saudi Aramco engineers who learned Chinese to earn degrees from Chinese universities.)

In the absence of well-trained interpreters and translators, the sometimes-poor English language skills of East Asians can and do lead to mutual frustration and misunderstanding. Still, non-Muslim Asians seem relatively free of the off-putting Islamophobia and resistance to local customs that have affected many Westerners since 9/11. Business is being done between the two ends of Asia at an accelerating rate. So far this business does not include much trade in weaponry or defense services, though there have been a few arms sales to GCC countries by both south Korea and China. (Japan still bars weapons exports, though this may be about to change. Other Asian countries are mainly importers rather than exporters of military technology).

East Asians may in time become serious competitors in the region's arms markets, which have long been dominated by European and American suppliers. But neither South nor East Asians are prepared to take a role in the security of the Gulf comparable to that of Europeans and Americans in the nineteenth and twentieth centuries. The sole exception to this has been Pakistan, which has long been a supplier or military expertise and personnel in the Gulf and which seeks the strategic depth that close ties with fellow Muslim nations can provide against India. In time, out of self-interest as well as rivalry with Pakistan, India may also become involved in providing troops and security guarantees in the Gulf. There is a precedent for this in the heavy involvement of British India (including what are now Bangladesh, India, and Pakistan) in the Gulf during the colonial era. But there is no apparent willingness on the part of Chinese, Indonesians, Japanese, or Koreans to consider participating in the defense of the Gulf or of the freedom of navigation to and through it.

In general (Malaysia has sometimes been a notable exception), East Asians seek to avoid taking controversial stands on political issues or entangling themselves in the various disputes that disturb the peace in West Asia. These include the conflicts between Israelis, Palestinians, and other Arabs; Israelis and Iranians; Israelis and Turks; Arabs and Iranians; or sectarian struggles between Sunnis and Shiites. From the perspective of the Gulf Arabs, this noncommittal stance makes Asians limited partners at best. They are easier to deal with than ideologically insistent and geopolitically demanding Americans and Europeans. But, by the same token, they are not interested in making military commitments. They are easy to recruit as arms suppliers but not as allies or security guarantors.

No East Asian nation currently has the force projection capabilities necessary to intervene in the region, even if it were so inclined. East Asians have no imperial history in the region. They do not appear to have imperial aspirations. There is a great deal of speculation—mostly a product of India's obsessive rivalry with China—that China might develop such capabilities in the future, but there is no evidence that it actually intends to do so. China has made no commitments to this end.

Despite the rise in northeast Asian energy and commercial interest in the GCC, for the foreseeable future these countries are very unlikely to act as rivals of the West or to present alternatives to the member countries of NATO as potential guarantors of either Gulf security or regional military balances. To the frustration of the GCC countries, which would like to dilute their dependence on the United States and other Western powers, military relationships between East Asia and the Gulf are likely to remain transactional rather than broadly collaborative. The absence of contributions other than arms sales by Asian nations to the Gulf security architecture will necessarily limit their influence, despite many shared interests.

There is broad scope for cooperation between the nations of East, West, and South Asia in the resculpting of the decaying international order. They share an interest in the managed and orderly replacement of the remnants of the American "unipolar moment" that followed the Cold War with new arrangements more reflective of their interests. The current crisis of global governance affects these interests and demands the redesign and rebuilding of a wide range of international institutions, organizations, and practices.

The challenges before the world encompass politics, economics, and the relationship of the human species to our natural environment. They include developing better strategies for dealing with failing states, sectarian strife, terrorism, piracy, and peacemaking as well as peacekeeping. They embrace requirements for reform of the international monetary and financial system, the further liberalization of trade and investment flows, and the orderly management of the production and consumption of energy and other natural resources. They entail the need to develop effective means of mitigating or remediating human-induced changes in the world's climate, environment, and ecology. None of these issues can be successfully addressed without the participation of the wealthy Muslim countries of the

Gulf or the rising powers of East and South Asia. Engagement between all concerned seems destined to intensify.

While progress toward the forging of closer diplomatic, commercial, financial, and cultural ties has been both rapid and robust, the new relationships are still in their early days. Their further development faces significant challenges. Despite nostalgia borne of the revival of ancient intercourse, there remain radical differences in the political and business cultures, religious traditions, social conditions, and socioeconomic structures of the GCC and most Asian countries, especially the industrialized states of Northeast Asia. The two sides have just begun to rub up against each other. Friction is inevitable as they learn to work with each other to the common advantage.

Such frictions are readily apparent to anyone in a position to observe commercial and financial transactions. The lives of Gulf Arabs remain regulated by the religious calendar and individual obligations to extended families, princely entourages, and other patronage networks. Life in East Asia today combines fondly remembered, but skeptically regarded, native traditions with the commercial calendar invented by the West, organizational allegiances, and reciprocal obligations. Small republics of cousins and genealogy play the role in the Gulf that the Party and ideology do in China. Relationships in the Gulf are organized in large measure hierarchically. In East Asia, they are more horizontal. The Gulf and East Asia share a devotion to the duties of hosts to guests, but the Arab emphasis on family honor contrasts with the East Asian emphasis on individual "face." All this leads to confusion about relationships and the obligations they entail as well as in approaches to dispute resolution.

Then, too, days, months, and years pass in the two regions on different and often incompatible timetables. In some ways, Arab business culture today resembles that of China in the nineteenth and early twentieth centuries. Chinese were then notoriously unpunctual, casual about preparations for both negotiating and implementing agreements, and indifferent to the letter of contract provisions other than those favoring themselves. Today's Chinese, Japanese, and Koreans, by contrast, are obsessively punctual, meticulousness about planning, and personally in touch with (if not pleased by) the legal complexities of international transactions. Asian rulers and business tycoons then employed specialists—in China, they were called "compradors"—to manage their interactions with foreign businesses and to keep them at bay. For much the same purposes, the wealthy and powerful in the Gulf rely today on expatriate experts to deal with foreign trading and investment partners.

The fact that Westerners and Gulf Arabs have been able to deal successfully with parallel barriers to business transactions and financial cooperation strongly suggests that, with time and mutual effort, these inhibitions and obstacles to cooperation can and will be overcome. (Of course, there is a contractual cost to perceived risk based on the frustrations that arise from mutual misperception and misunderstanding. In time, Chinese, like their more experienced Japanese and Korean competitors, will learn how much to allow for it in their bids on projects in the GCC.) Issues of commercial culture aside, however, in many ways the obstacles to cooperation seem less formidable than those with the West.

The great Mongol leader Genghis Khan and his descendants subjected all of Asia—including, ultimately, large parts of the Arab and Muslim world—to conquest and pillage. The Mongols drafted East Asians as technical advisers, siege engineers, and logistical auxiliaries. Other than this, East Asians have no history of colonial or imperial adventurism in the Middle East and North Africa. They did not take part in the implantation of the Jewish state of Israel in the region. They have remained aloof from the Israel-Palestine conflict and related disputes. They have neither a history nor any realistic prospect of military intervention in the Gulf. (If their distance from GCC militaries limits their potential influence, as noted, it also limits their political risk.) Asians have no client states in the Gulf to whose interests they must tend. They are identified neither with the Crusades nor with other, less violent forms of expeditionary evangelism. They display no inclination to interfere in the internal affairs of the region's states in order to reform their politics, societies, or mores. They espouse no principles they deem to be universal and therefore sinful for others not to adopt.

Now the post-postcolonial era has begun in the Middle East and North Africa, the US-dominated global order that followed the Cold War is in recession, and Asia is re-emerging as the center of global wealth and power. East Asians are innocent of most of the political baggage that burdens the major Western powers. The GCC needs their cooperation, and they need the GCC's, to address the international agenda that these changes are ineluctably establishing. In these circumstances, the prospects for cooperation between East Asia and the GCC seem unprecedentedly promising.

India, Pakistan, and China[5]
December 2010

I have been asked to speak about the strategic interaction between India, Pakistan, and China—the three great powers of South Asia. The legacies of the British Empire and the early years of the Cold War trump geographic features like the Himalayas and Karakorams in determining the region's strategic geometry. The past continues to describe the framework within which its major actors form and follow their respective national security policies. So far, sea power's role in their interaction is more speculative than actual. In this case, byplay in the land and in the air will most likely determine what happens in the surrounding Indian Ocean.

The British, for the first time in history, united the entire subcontinent under a single sovereignty. In doing so, they displaced its Muslim overlords from power. When the British left India, rather than accept a subordinate political status under majority Hindu rule, Muslim-majority regions sought self-determination in the state of Pakistan. In many respects, Indo-Pakistani interaction resembles an uncompleted civil war as much or more than an international conflict. In this context, the continuing strife in Kashmir has never ceased to be the defining center of South Asian communal conflict. Meanwhile, the Delhi-centered hegemony of the British Raj lives on, with all in the region except Pakistan and Chinese Tibet subordinate to tutelage from Delhi.

As India's rulers, the British sought to establish Tibet and Afghanistan as buffer states within the orbit of their Raj. To this end, they sent repeated Anglo-Indian military expeditions into both. They drew lines on maps of unfamiliar terrain to demarcate spheres of influence for India. Within these spheres, they sought to exercise direct or indirect control in order to deny strategic advantages to great-power rivals in areas adjacent to India.

At their independence, India and Pakistan both claimed these unilaterally imposed British lines as their legal frontiers, though India subsequently redrew the McMahon line to push it farther into historically Tibetan territory. For their part, China and Afghanistan have never accepted the legitimacy of these frontiers. Still, with the exception of the never-implemented, British-backed claim of Kashmir to part of the Tibetan plateau (Aksai Chin), both have honored these lines in practice. To a remarkable extent, the lines the British drew—or in the case of Kashmir, did not draw—and the outcomes of policies the viceroys adopted are at the root of many of South Asia's ongoing tensions.

China's 1950s-era offer to settle its border with India on the basis of *uti possidetis juris*—establishment of borders on the basis of actual control rather than notional lines on colonial maps—was rejected by India. The Sino-Indian war of 1962 reestablished the line of actual control earlier fixed by China, but also gave rise to a related territorial dispute between India and Nepal. Intermittent discussions of a border settlement have since failed to resolve either Sino-Indian or Indian-Nepalese differences. In the wake of the hostilities between India and China, in 1963

Pakistan reached an interim settlement of its border with China on the basis of *uti possidetis juris*, pending resolution of the status of Kashmir. Today, India's northern borders are once again in a state of escalating politico-military tension.

In the 1950s, India colluded with American covert action programs aimed at strategically distracting China through the destabilization of Tibet. When these programs helped produce a failed revolt and the flight of the Dalai Lama from Tibet in 1959, India became the site of a Tibetan government in exile. In 1961, Prime Minister Jawaharlal Nehru adopted a "forward policy" of military challenge to enforce territorial claims to areas north of the Chinese line of control in the Himalayas. Having become convinced that independent India was, like British India, intent on challenging its control of Tibet—this time with both American and Soviet encouragement—China pushed Indian forces away from the border in 1962.

Many of the elements of this tragic scenario are now back in play. In the absence of any Indo-American covert action program, Chinese paranoia readily supplies one by misconstruing international support for the Dalai Lama and sympathy for violent Tibetan rioters. India continues to augment its forces along the Sino-Indian frontier and to step up its patrols. It appears to China to be once again challenging the line of actual control. China has accelerated the construction of railroads and roads that will facilitate rapid deployment of its forces to the border region if they are needed there. This infrastructure will, not incidentally, make Tibetan natural resources available for the first time to the Chinese national economy.

Meanwhile, resumed talks on a border settlement have catalyzed restatements by both sides of claims that draw angry rejection from the other. Many in India seem to be clamoring for some sort of redress for the country's military humiliation by China nearly five decades ago. It is unclear how seriously this should be taken. Still, despite the rapid growth of interdependence between the Indian and Chinese economies, the escalating tensions in the Himalayas constitute a dangerous situation that bears close watching. They also have the potential to complicate strategic cooperation between the United States and India.

So does the worsening situation in Kashmir. The emergence of a nuclear standoff between India and Pakistan made India's overwhelming conventional military superiority over Pakistan much less relevant than it had been. This shifted the military contention between the two countries into the realm of unconventional and asymmetric warfare. Pakistan is not unhappy that the escalating insurgency in Kashmir ties down hundreds of thousands of Indian troops and security forces. At the same time, the situation in Kashmir fuels a campaign of terrorism against India by various groups there, in India proper, and in Pakistan. India, for its part, has become much more active in Afghanistan, Pakistan's strategic backyard, where the Hamid Karzai government has its roots in the Indian-backed Northern Alliance.

If India's interaction with the Tibetan region of China is in many respects analogous to that of the country's British past, Pakistan too has fallen heir to the policies of British India. Islamabad has sought strategic denial of Afghanistan to its enemies, both Russia (in the form of the 1980s Soviet Union) and contemporary India. As Americans are learning to our distress, policies in South Asia—especially those directed at the region around the Durand Line—that ignore Indo-Pakistani strategic rivalry do not work.

Since its inception in 1947, Muslim Pakistan has been desperately concerned to secure its independence from its Hindu brethren in the far larger, more powerful republic of India, which "vivisected" it in 1971. This has led Pakistan into an erratic alliance with the United States, with which it has worked against common enemies—as a member of the Baghdad Pact, as a launch point for U-2 overflights of the USSR, in jihad against the Soviet occupation of Afghanistan, and, more recently, against the terrorists with global reach in its Afghan borderlands. When Sino-Indian rivalry burst into the open in 1962, this catalyzed a relationship of long-term Pakistani strategic dependence on China.

On several occasions, Pakistan has been able to serve as the common partner of both the United States and China. The U.S. opening to China in 1971 was, of course, brokered through Pakistan, and China was a full partner in Pakistan's American-backed effort to dislodge the USSR from Afghanistan. Pakistan's ability to conduct parallel programs of cooperation intermittently with both the United States and China has, however, never enabled it to craft joint Sino-American actions or to develop a reliable long-term partnership with Washington as well as Beijing.

For its part, China's interaction with India and Pakistan has been remarkably consistent over the decades. China's interests in the region are dominated by its desire to avoid challenges to its sovereignty and territorial integrity in that part of its territory—Tibet—that makes China part of South Asia. This is a fundamentally defensive posture, consistent with China's efforts to preserve a peaceful international environment on its periphery. Tranquil borders are essential to Chinese national efforts to achieve renewal, development, and prosperity.

Given these interests, all things being equal, China can be counted upon to be fully supportive of the South Asian *status quo*. China has *de facto* control of the borders it claims for Tibet with India, including Kashmir as well as with Pakistan. It seeks to confirm rather than alter these borders. In the absence of external backing for India against it, despite acute apprehensions in Delhi, China has not in fact sought to challenge Indian hegemony where it is effective, as in Bangladesh, Bhutan, the Maldives, or Sri Lanka. Nor, of course, has it been prepared to aid or abet Indian domination of buffer states like Nepal or strategic adversaries like Pakistan.

But when India is allied with a great power hostile to China, as it was in the British era or during India's Cold War flirtation with the U.S. and *de facto* alignment with the USSR, China responds with efforts to counter India. China's willingness to step up support for Pakistan in the 1960s is a case in point. China was not deterred by the fact that Pakistan's American allies were still determined to isolate and overthrow the government in Beijing. The potential for a vigorous Chinese effort to undermine Indian hegemony in South Asia needs to be borne in mind. The anti-China entente in Asia that some propose—to unite India, Japan, and Vietnam with the United States in balancing China—could come with a high price tag. Is it in India's or America's interest to risk stimulating Chinese policies directed at altering the South Asian *status quo*? By any standard, that *status quo* is now highly favorable to India.

In this connection, it is noteworthy that India clearly regards China as its principal rival for influence in Asia, but China has not viewed India in the same light. China still sees India in South Asian regional, not pan-Asian, terms. For China, India is both the dominant power in South Asia and a potential source of interference in the Tibet Autonomous Region, not a rival in the broader arenas of the Eurasian landmass or its adjacent seas. The imbalance in the weight India and China assign each other in their national security strategies galls many Indians, who see it as China slighting their country. But it is arguably a much more secure position for India than the alternative.

Most projections suggest that in 2050, China will have a GDP that is about twice as large as the United States or India, which will have achieved parity with the United States in economic size. An India that has succeeded on that scale need not fear Pakistan. A China that has grown to that extent will not fear rivalry with Americans and Indians, but should continue to see the advantages of cooperation with both. Such an outcome would be facilitated by an early end to tussling over the line of control in the Himalayas and the establishment of an order in Kashmir that is accepted as legitimate by its inhabitants. Neither task is easy. But accomplishing both, not inviting tests of strength or inventing new forms of adversarial relationships, should be the focus of Chinese, Indian, Pakistani, and American policy.

Chapter 10

Military Interactions

The early post–Cold War period saw the beginning of a trend toward the rapid modernization of Asia's armed forces. As countries in the region approach developed-country status, it is entirely natural for them to aspire to build armed forces comparable to those of Europe and other regions that industrialized before them. Asian countries have taken to heart the concept of sovereignty introduced to them by occupying Western powers. It is therefore also natural that they should wish to assert and secure their sovereignty by defining defensible postcolonial borders. Throughout the region, militaries that once focused on maintaining domestic order now define their missions increasingly in terms of external defense, a task that requires a higher level of military capability.

The People's Republic of China represents a special case among Asian-Pacific countries. China's economic reforms and military restructuring are taking place amidst a nearly universal expectation that it will in time become a world power in both economic and military terms—i.e., that China will be a country whose economic and military influence spans the globe. (Whether Beijing achieves comparable stature in political terms depends on whether it follows its economic reforms with political reforms that make China less unattractive to its neighbors and the world.) The requirement to prepare, on a contingency basis, for the military conquest of Taiwan has given the modernization of the People's Liberation Army (PLA) the focus it previously lacked. This requirement, more than anything else, now drives China's force restructuring, training, research and development, and equipment and technology acquisitions.

China's defense modernization—and regional apprehensions about China's rise—have been the driving force in most Asian nations' restructuring and modernization of their forces. By 2012, the world's five largest arms importers were Asian states. From 2007 through 2011, India was the world's largest recipient of arms, accounting for 10 percent of the global arms trade. It was followed by south Korea (6 percent), Pakistan (5 percent), China (5 percent), and Singapore (4 percent). In the same year, Asian spending on defense overtook that of Europe. A major factor in this was China. Chinese military budgets have been doubling every five years.

The least developed and most problematic element of Sino-American relations is their military dimension. Americans imposed sanctions after the Tiananmen incident of 1989 and continue to introduce ideologically motivated legislation to bar many forms of military exchanges with the PLA. These factors combine to ensure that Americans continue to know far less and have less interaction with the PLA than we did with the Soviet Red Army at the height of the Cold War. The two militaries' absence of mutual familiarity leads to serious missteps on both sides during times of tension or incidents. There are many examples of this, including the bilateral military confrontations in the Taiwan Strait in 1996, the bombing of the Chinese embassy in Belgrade in 1999, and the midair collision between a U.S. reconnaissance aircraft and a Chinese interceptor near Hainan Island in 2001. This bodes ill for escalation control during a crisis in the Taiwan Strait, the Korean Peninsula, or the South China Sea.

During the Cold War, the U.S. military and the PLA enjoyed a steadily closer relationship. That ended abruptly in 1989, when the collapse of the Soviet empire ended the strategic rationale for cooperation. The bloody suppression of the student uprising in Tiananmen, as well as progress toward democracy in Taiwan, recharged American policy with ideological opposition to Chinese Communism, draining Sino-American relations of their previous warmth. There was no dialogue between the two militaries from June 1989 to early November 1993 when, as assistant secretary of defense, I traveled to Beijing to reopen military dialogue with the PLA.

The purpose of renewed military relations was to mitigate, if not preclude, the kind of mutual hostility that has since become a dominant feature of Sino-American interaction. Despite interest on both sides, the agenda I pursued nearly twenty years ago of developing, through exchanges and exercises, the ability to cooperate in search-and-rescue operations, disaster relief, anti-piracy and anti-terrorist operations, and support for United Nations peacekeeping operations remains unrealized. Mutual suspicion, legal barriers, and the absence of any proposals by either side for military cooperation in pursuit of common objectives—as well as Chinese reactions to Sino-American military confrontations and U.S. arms sales to Taiwan—continue to obstruct efforts to improve mutual understanding.

In the first of the two pieces below, "American Economic and Security Interests in China," I examine American interests in the military relationship as they appeared in the aftermath of the 1996 Taiwan Strait crisis. The factors *it identifies remain operative in the bilateral relationship.[1] Chinese defense spending has doubled every five years since Beijing realized in 1999 that it had to develop the military capability to hold the United States at bay while devastating Taiwan, should it conclude that Taipei's actions justified this.[2])*

Current military interactions between the United States and China are covered in the second section: "Beijing, Washington, and the Shifting Balance of Prestige." For a discussion of the so-called U.S. "pivot" to Asia, see the first section of Chapter 4 (The United States and China Forty Years On), and the final section of Chapter 11 (Indo-Pacific Dynamics in Trans-Pacific Perspective).

American Economic and Security Interests in China[3]
January 1997

Most Americans now accept that China is destined, early in the coming century, to resume its millennial pre-1850 status as the world's largest economy.[4] Later, they expect, it will become a world-class military power. There is, however, no agreement about the impact of China's rise to wealth and power on American interests. Many worry that growing Chinese military prowess could overturn the Asian-Pacific balance of power, challenging American leadership and gradually imposing a Chinese sphere of influence in the region. Others see a modernized and internationally engaged Chinese military as having the potential to contribute to regional stability and the maintenance of global order. Many are apprehensive that China's economic expansion may disrupt the international trading and investment system formed under American leadership over the past fifty years. Still others argue that, if Beijing can be assimilated to the norms of the global economy, China's rapid economic development can help lift American living standards.

The United States emerged on the world stage over the course of the century between the Mexican War of 1846–48 and the Second World War of 1939–45. This period coincided with the century of China's eclipse (from the Opium War of 1839–42 to the civil war of 1946–49). Fifty years of transition (roughly coterminous with U.S. preoccupation with the Cold War) have set China on the path to reattaining the "comprehensive strength" it has long sought. The United States is having difficulty adjusting to a non-bipolar world in which China is an assertively independent actor. For its part, China has yet to learn how to behave with the responsible assurance of a strong and confident country rather than the thin-skinned suspicion of a weak and traumatized one.

Implications for American Security Interests

Whether the shifts in the balance of power that China's rise entails harm or help U.S. security, they promise to challenge long-vested American interests over the coming decades. Among the American security interests in doubt are:

- the capacity of the United States to regulate global transfers of sensitive technology, and to inhibit the transfer of weapons systems ("weapons of mass destruction") that could threaten the military-technological superiority of the United States or U.S. allies and friends in regions like the Middle East and Persian Gulf;
- the unilateral U.S. guarantee that China cannot impose reunification on its lost province of Taiwan by force;
- the freedom of the United States to intervene militarily in East Asia without fear of retaliation against the American homeland;
- the position of the United States as the dominant external actor and security partner in the Korean Peninsula and Southeast Asia and as the primary influence on South Asian politico-military balance;
- the post–World War II status of Japan an American auxiliary rather than an independent military actor in the Western Pacific;
- the century-old U.S. interest in preventing the domination of either end of the Eurasian landmass, i.e., the eastern Atlantic and Western Europe or the western Pacific and East Asia, by another great power; and
- the post–Cold War status of the United States, in security terms, as the sole world power, i.e., as the only nation whose military reach spans the globe.

Whether these challenges to American security interests eventuate depends in the first instance, of course, on the extent to which China's economic resources are directed at building up its military strength. So far the evidence in this regard is hardly alarming. Despite China's rapid economic growth, its defense budget remains modest in relation to the military challenges before the Chinese PLA. This reflects the low priority China has assigned to military, as opposed to other, aspects of modernization.

In almost every direction, a defensively deployed PLA faces forces that are significantly more modern and capable than its best units. (China's defense planners must consider threats to territories China considers its own from Russia, India, Vietnam and other ASEAN members, Taiwan, Korea, and Japan, not to mention the United States.) The PLA has, nonetheless, been on short rations, forced to pursue modernization through downsizing and the retirement of obsolete equipment. For most of the past fifteen years of rapid economic growth in China, the country's defense budget has been flat or declining (after discounting inflation). Meanwhile, the share of GDP available as revenue to the Chinese central government has been declining. This raises doubts about China's capacity to fund a major military modernization program, should its priorities shift in this direction. Both the level of Chinese military effort and the resources available to fund it may now again be rising, but it will be a long time before Chinese forces can match those of its neighbors in quality, still less those of the United States.[5]

Security challenges are, however, not decided by the relative size of economies. Nor is the outcome of war decided by levels of technology alone. When Japan reacted to American sanctions (intended to signal Washington's objections to Tokyo's hegemony in East Asia) by attacking Pearl Harbor, Japanese GDP was about a tenth that of the United States. Japan nevertheless proved a difficult enemy for the United States to overcome. Overwhelming American economic and technological superiority did not gain a U.S. victory in Korea, and failed to prevent defeat in Vietnam. Clearly, other factors can outweigh economics and technology in war.

Among these factors is the balance of fervor between contending parties. When one side in a conflict believes its supreme interest in national survival or its vital interests (such as territorial integrity) to be at stake, while the other has less compelling strategic interests in the outcome of a dispute, its willingness to make disproportionate sacrifices can overcome technical factors like a disparity in economic strength or technology. Will, as well as strategic acumen, counts heavily even in the nuclear age.

In estimating the Chinese challenge, therefore, one must start by considering Chinese national purposes and the degree of fervor attached to them. There is no reason to doubt China's sincerity in seeking a "peaceful international environment" in which to continue its economic reconstruction. To that end, China has settled its territorial disputes with Russia and is forging a broad partnership with it. It has developed mutually beneficial economic cooperation and security dialogue with Japan and Western European nations. China would like a similarly stable relationship with the United States. Many of its regional objectives are congruent with those of the United States. Beijing has sought to avoid chaos or war on the Korean Peninsula, to preserve Pakistan as a counter to Indian hegemony in South Asia, and to promote amicable relations with Southeast Asian nations. China's military objectives remain modest and—in its view—limited to the defense of Chinese sovereignty and territorial integrity.

The mission assigned to the PLA is:

- defending the borders and territories currently controlled by China against further efforts by foreign nations to alter or detach them;
- backing Chinese diplomatic efforts to avoid permanent separation and ultimately recover territories wrested from China by great-power intervention, such as the European seizures of Hong Kong and Macao, the Japanese annexation of Taiwan and the Senkaku (Diaoyu) archipelago, and U.S. Cold War efforts to foster a rival Chinese regime on Taiwan;
- establishing secure and recognized maritime boundaries for the Chinese state where long-standing Chinese claims are now subject to challenge, as in the case of post-independence claims by the Philippines, Malaysia, Brunei, and Vietnam to islets and reefs in the South China Sea and by the Koreas and Indonesia to continental-shelf and other seabed resources;
- retaking Taiwan by force, should Chinese diplomacy fail (unlike Hong Kong and Macao, where it has succeeded);
- protecting other borders, should these be subjected to military challenge (e.g., by Russia, India, Vietnam, or other member states of ASEAN);
- guaranteeing the Chinese state against external intervention, coercion, or dictation by other great powers; and
- backing ultimate Chinese emergence as a world power with "comprehensive strength."

Notably absent from this list are many of the aspirations and objectives that made the rise of other great powers, such as the United States, Germany, Japan, or the Soviet Union, so disruptive of international peace and security. China asserts no doctrine of "manifest destiny" or hemispheric exclusion. It has no ideology of *Lebensraum* to motivate territorial expansion. Its revanchism does not extend to areas inhabited and claimed by non-Chinese. China does not seek to bring additional minority (non-Han) peoples within its borders. Beijing has no universal set of values and beliefs it can explain to its own people, still less an ideology it seeks to impose on others. China appears to believe that access to distant resources is best guaranteed by an open international trading system rather than by power projection.[6] It has no colonies or satellites and no apparent impulse to establish them. China stations no troops beyond its own borders, as it defines them. It vehemently denies its desire to establish an East Asian order similar to that of the pre-Western colonial era, when Beijing's power overawed China's neighbors.

However limited Chinese objectives may be, however, some of them directly affect the interests of the United States and its allies, especially Japan. China's determination to retain its distinctive political system contradicts the American impulse to enlarge the zone of adherence to the liberal values of American constitutional democracy. Ultimately, China's aspirations conflict with the understandable American desire to remain unchallenged as the single global power.

The principal issue between the United States and China arises, however, from China's ambition to undo its dismemberment by past foreign intervention—specifically, to reincorporate Taiwan, if only symbolically, under a single Chinese sovereignty. This imperative is at the very heart of modern Chinese nationalism. Despite Beijing's patient preference for a political solution of the problem of Taiwan's relationship to the rest of China,[7] there can be no doubt about its willingness to use force against Taiwan, if it must. Beijing has made it clear that it will intervene militarily if the island's politics, aided and abetted by American or other forces (e.g., Japanese sympathy for Taiwanese separatism), seem to be taking Taiwan toward independence or otherwise foreclosing the possibility of Taiwan's ultimate reassociation with "China" under a single sovereignty.

That is, unfortunately, precisely where Beijing believes Taipei is now headed. The need to deter Taiwanese separatism and possible American military backing for it has given Chinese military modernization the sense of urgency and focus it had previously lacked. Beijing has long had the capability to intimidate Taiwan through military measures short of war, as it showed from July 1995 through March 1996. The PLA's post–March 1996 obsession with building the capability to conquer Taiwan—and with being able to sink American aircraft carriers, if it must, to do so—will not produce a credible invasion capability for a decade or so. Eventually, however, it will.

The good news is that China's focus on Taiwan diverts resources that might otherwise have been devoted to build power projection capabilities and gives Beijing incentives to compose conflicts with its neighbors on less important border issues. (Recent Chinese diplomacy toward Central Asia, India, and Southeast Asia reflects this.) The bad news is that China is preparing for the possible requirement to use force on the one issue that might set off armed conflict between it and the United States and that these preparations involve building a formidable amphibious warfare capability. Aware of the heavy costs military action against Taiwan would entail, Beijing will remain reluctant to use force against the island unless provoked by developments there. The Taiwanese drive for an international status separate from "China," however, virtually guarantees that such provocations will be forthcoming.

Beijing's and Taipei's policies now [as of 1997] seem diametrically opposed and premised on confrontation rather than accommodation. Beijing:

- strives to sustain the principle of "one China" as the basis of policy toward Taiwan in the United States, Japan, Southeast Asia, and elsewhere, and to persuade foreigners to refrain from intervention in the quarrel between Chinese on either side of the Taiwan Strait;
- has put Taipei on probation, indicating that it reserves the right to punish Taiwan for any further efforts Taipei may make to separate itself from "China" or otherwise alter the *status quo* in the Taiwan Strait;
- actively promotes economic and cultural interdependence across the Strait to ease the path to future reunification;
- seeks to defer political dialogue with Taipei until Hong Kong and Macao have been absorbed, Lee Teng-hui has left office, and Taipei has agreed that the basis of discussion will be the idea of "one China, two systems"; and
- is seeking to build a credible military capability to invade and conquer Taiwan should efforts to achieve reunification through cross-Strait negotiations ultimately fail.

Taipei:

- seeks to establish an official principle of "one China, two equal political entities" and to enter the United Nations as a state separate from the People's Republic of China under the name "Republic of China." Taiwan's main opposition party, meanwhile, lobbies internationally for support for Taiwan independence and UN membership under the name "Republic of Taiwan";
- while keeping a wary eye on Beijing, strives to accumulate the attributes of independent statehood internationally wherever and however it can;
- now officially opposes economic and cultural interdependence with the Chinese mainland despite the opposition of the Taiwanese business community, which is continuing to develop such interdependence through trade and investment across the Strait;
- demands political dialogue with Beijing as an "equal political entity" to establish its status as a state separate from the People's Republic of China; and
- is seeking to buy additional advanced weaponry from the United States to strengthen deterrence and to consolidate a U.S. commitment to come to its aid if war breaks out in the Taiwan Strait.

Taipei's determination to alter its status in the direction of *de jure* inde-pendence, and Beijing's determination to maintain the "one China" *status quo de jure*, pending negotiations on the terms of reunification, make it certain that the Taiwan issue will continue to flare up from time to time.

This means that, as the twenty-first century begins, the United States may face an increasingly stark choice: whether to prepare for eventual war with China over Taiwan's international status or to promote a political solution to cross-Strait relations that finesses the danger of war and conse-quent Sino-American conflict. Gearing up for possible war with a steadily strengthening China would require major increases in U.S. defense spend-ing. A Sino-American conflict over Taiwan would not necessarily be local or regional; it could escalate into general, trans-Pacific war.[8] Even in the absence of armed conflict in the Taiwan Strait, however, emotional Sino-American confrontation over the Taiwan issue has the potential to poison the relationship between Washington and Beijing and to set off a pattern of hostile noncooperation and contention between them, first in the Asia-Pacific region and then, as China's power grows, globally.

Promoting a political accommodation in the Taiwan Strait to avoid this unpleasant prospect would, however, place heavy demands on presidential leadership. The president would have to create a large measure of domestic U.S. consensus on an issue that has, historically, divided Americans. The Chinese civil war and its Taiwan legacy have, historically, been an especially contentious issue between Congress and the executive branch. Promoting peace would require the United States to go beyond the deterrence of war in the Taiwan Strait. It would very likely demand that the president take an ideologically unpalatable stand against the Taiwanese aspirations for self-determination that constitute the Chinese *casus belli* in the Strait and embrace the cause of Chinese reunification, even as he continued to warn Beijing against the use of force to achieve it.

Assuming that American diplomacy can nonetheless somehow restore a *modus vivendi* and credible prospects for a peaceful settlement between Chinese on either side of the Taiwan Strait, the United States, like China's neighbors, will still face the problem of how to deal with the massive shifts in regional power balances that China's rise implies. The specific matters at issue between China and its neighbors are as small as the uninhabited islands and reefs whose sovereignty they contest. Only minor territorial adjustments would be required to settle these disputes. How such adjust-ments take place, however, has very large implications for the future pat-tern of politics in the region and for the American role in it.

China has sought to reassure its neighbors by deferring, rather than pressing, negotiations to establish its maritime borders. Koreans, Japanese, and Southeast Asians may be forgiven, however, for viewing Chinese procrastination with apprehension. China, they calculate, may wish to wait until the balance of power in the region has shifted decisively in its favor. China might then seek to dictate solutions to its neighbors, rather than to compromise with them. This risk would exist even with a continuing, active, and assertive American military presence in the region. Without such a presence, however, no combination of Asian-Pacific states could hope ultimately to balance Chinese power. China's neighbors would have no alternative but to appease it. These realities are at the heart of the regional concerns about Chinese hegemony, which have not been allayed by Beijing's denunciations of "the erroneous theory of a Chinese threat."

Whether the United States can maintain the military presence and play the balancing role in the region that its allies and friends see as desirable depends, in the first instance, on whether the American people are willing to shoulder that burden. It also depends, however, on the character of Sino-American politico-military relations. If these relations are constructive and cordial, Asian-Pacific states will see much benefit and little cost in continued cooperation with the U.S. military. If, however, the Taiwan issue or other factors cause Sino-American relations to settle into tension and hostility, Asian-Pacific states will see continued military identification with the United States as risking embroilment in conflict with China. Few, if any, will wish to assume that risk. This, more than any other reason, is why military "containment" (confrontation and isolation) of China is not a viable option for the United States.

Implications for American Economic Interests

If military containment of China is not a realistic option for the United States, neither is economic containment.[9] For better or ill, China will clearly play an increasingly large part in both the regional and global economies. The question is not whether this can be prevented, but what its consequences will be. The issues for the United States are: first, how to assure that China's economic growth does not adversely affect U.S. interests or how to mitigate such adverse effects; and, second, how to assure that Americans enjoy open and nondiscriminatory ("most favored nation") access to growing Chinese markets.[10]

Among the American economic interests that China's growth might challenge are the following:

- maintenance of the integrity and effective operation of the global trading and investment system built under the past fifty years of American economic leadership, on whose increasingly open markets and orderly management of economic conflict American prosperity has come progressively to depend;

- the peerless leadership role and bargaining power of the United States within the global economic system, as China's economy grows to be larger than the American economy, and, ultimately, larger than the U.S. and Japanese economies combined;
- stability in sectors (especially labor-intensive sectors) of the American economy (and the jobs associated with them) where China enjoys comparative advantage (e.g., in labor costs or indifference to environmental and other socially dictated production costs);
- U.S. export growth, should political tensions result in U.S. sanctions or Chinese discrimination against American sales to a Chinese economy that will constitute an increasing percentage of the overall global market;
- long-standing U.S. dominance of certain third-country foreign markets, if China feels free to follow predatory marketing practices;
- protection of intellectual property rights central to the continued competitiveness of the U.S. economy;
- the continued structural reliance of the American economy on cheap energy from low-priced oil imports, as Chinese demand bids up international energy prices;
- the ability of the United States to finance its budgetary and current account deficits with foreign capital, as China competes for an increasing percentage of global capital flows; and
- avoidance of threats to the global and American quality of life stemming from irresponsible Chinese neglect of the environmental consequences of rapid industrialization.

Some of these challenges are unavoidable consequences of the emergence of a major new player on the global trade and investment scene. Painful adjustments in the structure of American industry and agriculture are always taking place in response to changes in patterns of international trade and finance, not just changes produced by the rise of China. Such adjustments, however, have special political consequences when they can be attributed to developments or patterns of behavior in a particular foreign country. Perceived unfair Chinese competition with domestic U.S. industry, the loss of jobs as imports from China rise in particular sectors of the U.S. market, and the highly visible U.S. bilateral trade deficit with China all serve to generate pressure for a tough American stand on short-term trade and investment issues with China. This, in turn, can create an atmosphere of bilateral confrontation. The only way to mitigate this effect of trade and investment disputes between the two countries is to assure that other elements of the relationship are sufficiently positive to offset it.

Other possible economic challenges from China, however, will be greatly affected by the character of U.S.-China relations and U.S. policies toward China's role in the global economy. It makes a big difference whether Chinese and Americans see themselves as engaged in a zero-sum game or as interacting to advance the common prosperity. The key, in this regard, is whether the United States acts to include or exclude China from the international rule-making bodies it helped to create and continues to lead.

It is impossible to imagine that the current global trading and investment system could function effectively were the United States—as the world's largest economy—not fully part of it and prepared to play by its rules. That system will also be unable to function effectively if China is not fully part of it and playing by its rules, once China's economic weight has grown to match or surpass that of the United States. That is why Americans and other non-Chinese have such a large stake in bringing China into the world's economic institutions and regulatory regimes[11] on terms that buttress rather than distort their operation. The fact that China's bargaining power is growing apace with its economy makes it desirable to negotiate China's inclusion sooner rather than later. This is all the more so because China's idiosyncratic pattern of economic growth is creating a widening range of vested interests by Chinese organizations and individuals against the painful internal adjustments Beijing would have to make to conform to global norms. As China's self-confidence grows, moreover, its willingness to trade substantive concessions for international acceptance is diminishing.

The Connection between Security and Economic Interaction

If the security relationship between China and the United States becomes consistently adversarial, it is hard to imagine that the economic relationship between the two countries can develop smoothly. Sino-American contention over security matters raises issues of national pride and creates political tensions that make it difficult, if not impossible, for the two sides to engage in the kind of framework-setting necessary to promote freer trade and investment between them. Such tensions engender political interference with commercial transactions from both sides.[12] They reduce the willingness of politicians in either country to risk appearing to make concessions to the other on economic as well as political matters.

Conversely, however, a cooperative economic relationship is no guarantee of a nonadversarial security relationship or political cooperation. History is full of examples of countries with strong and growing economic ties that nevertheless went to war with each other. Nor does bilateral economic confrontation over trade and investment issues necessarily translate into military tension. That has not been the U.S. experience with allies like Japan or the member states of the European Union (EU).

A bilateral relationship can be damaged by economic tensions, to be sure, but only tensions in the security arena have the potential to destroy it. More than anything else, the difficulty the United States and China have been having in conducting their relations to mutual satisfaction stems from the failure of either side to invest much effort in building political understanding with the other. Since the Chinese suppression of the June 4, 1989, student uprising at Tiananmen, interaction with China has been viewed as politically incorrect by most Americans. For much of the seven-year period since then, the United States has gone out of its way to demonstrate its contempt for the Chinese political system and its distaste and distrust of the Chinese leadership.[13] China responded with a reflexively counterproductive mixture of passivity, protest, suspicion, and reprisal. In 1993, the administration adopted a declared policy of comprehensive engagement with China, but failed to carry it out. This has not been a constructive or productive time in Sino-American relations.

Toward "Comprehensive Engagement?"

The United States has now apparently decided actually to carry out its declared policy of engagement with China. In a May 1997 speech in New York, and in more detail in a November speech in Shanghai, Secretary of State Christopher signaled an American resolve to replace derogatory diatribe with respectful dialogue between the two countries. He called for regular summit meetings and institutionalization of other high-level exchanges. These speeches, and National Security Council Advisor Lake's July visit to Beijing (the first by such an American official since December 1989), began to articulate an organizing principle for Sino-American relations. (Such a framework has long been needed to replace the collapsed Washington-Beijing-Moscow strategic triangle.) The administration will now work with China to integrate it fully into the international state system as a responsible member of the councils of the great powers. It has, meanwhile, adopted a more cautious approach to the issue of Taiwan. The questions now are whether the administration's new policy will survive the change in its foreign policy team; whether the Chinese, after nearly seven years of frustration and pique with Washington, will be ready to meet the United States halfway; and whether positive Sino-American engagement can survive the inevitable setbacks and attacks it can expect to face from political forces in both countries and in Taiwan.[14]

If so, there is a chance that the improved political atmosphere between the two countries would allow the United States to:

- maneuver Taipei and Beijing away from the course of confrontation on which they are now embarked and toward a refashioned *modus vivendi* in which they can resume exploration of a mutually acceptable long-term relationship;
- strike an acceptable Sino-American deal on China's entry into the WTO that phases in China's adherence to the global norms governing international trade and investment and opens China's economy to greatly expanded American exports;
- end the cycle of U.S. sanctions and Chinese counteractions that has acted to depress bilateral trade, especially U.S. exports to China;
- work with China to broker a reduction of tensions on the Korean Peninsula and between India and Pakistan;
- stimulate China and ASEAN nations to begin active negotiations to compose their differences over islands and resources in the South China Sea;
- bring China into the MTCR and other international bodies that set standards for the international transfer of sensitive technologies, thereby binding China to current and future norms on these matters; and
- help China to remove blockages to successful modernization (such as the absence of an adequate legal system) and to address problems its rapid economic development is causing for it, its neighbors, and the global community (such as environmental damage to its own territory and uncontrolled contributions to global warming).

Both the security and economic interests of the United States, as well as U.S. relations with Asian-Pacific allies, would be well served by a well-coordinated U.S. policy that aimed at these objectives.

Beijing, Washington, and the Shifting Balance of Prestige[15]
May 2011

The organizers of this conference on China's claims and capabilities in its "near seas" recruited me to address it because I am a sort of living fossil. As a certified antique, exhumed from the diplomatic strata of the past, they thought I could not avoid having an historical perspective on things. While you were pondering naval matters today, they were sure that I would be contemplating my navel and reminiscing about ancient events. I don't want to disappoint them, so bear with me as I speak of things as they were forty years ago today—on Monday, the tenth of May, 1971.

I had then just returned from training in Mandarin and Taiwanese. In the inscrutable wisdom of government personnel systems, this was thought somehow to qualify me to become, among other things, the officer-in-charge of the United States' virtually nonexistent economic interaction with the China mainland. (In all of 1971, bilateral trade came to less than $5 million. We do more trade with China in a single hour now.) Instead of focusing on that not-very-demanding aspect of my job, on that Monday, forty years ago, I was busy at other things. Like a few other colleagues in the State Department's Office of Asian Communist Affairs, I was writing papers in support of Henry Kissinger's secret visit to "Pei-p'ing," as political correctness then demanded we call it. The United States had spent more than two decades trying to destabilize and overthrow the People's Republic, championing the lost cause of its defeated rival in the Chinese civil war, and excluding it from participation in international councils.

This was hardly an auspicious basis on which to enlist China in what was then our quarter-century-old grand strategy of containment of the Soviet Union. The shift from antagonism to attempted cooperation reflected realistic judgments about our international circumstances and the trajectory we were then on as a country. President Nixon recognized that our interests would be best served by abandoning failed policies and preconceptions. He boldly sought to seize previously unimagined strategic advantages for our country. To the surprise of many, he brought this off.

To reach an accommodation with China, the United States had to choose between our long-standing politico-military commitment to Taipei and the imperatives of our national interests as affected by the Cold War. Then, as now, the Taiwan issue constrained our relations with Beijing. It threatened an eventual bloody rendezvous between Chinese nationalism and American military power. Then, as now, war would have been disastrous for both sides. Washington and Beijing crafted our rapprochement by deferring to later resolution the *casus belli* between us—the question of Taiwan's relationship with the rest of China. Both this issue and the American role in it remain unresolved. Neither Chinese nationalism nor the Taiwan issue has gone away.

China has been patient for four decades, but it is now actively pondering how best to remove the United States from what is—from its point of view—our very unhelpful residual military role in cross-Strait relations so that Beijing's negotiators can settle the Taiwan issue with their counterparts in Taipei. That, I take it, is a principal focus of the national review of policy toward the United States that China is reportedly poised to launch. Americans cannot safely assume that China's recent objections to U.S.

arms sales to Taiwan or other military actions on our part are *pro forma* or "just more of the same." It's at least as likely that we will soon once again confront the necessity to choose between the self-imposed shackles of long-standing policy and the imperatives of our long-term strategic interests.

The underlying issue today is at root the same as forty years ago—the contradiction between U.S. policies designed to frustrate China's achievement of its core objective of national unity and our need to reduce enmity and increase cooperation with China. But the context in which we must wrestle with this contradiction today is radically different. The balance of prestige, if not yet the balance of power, between the United States and China has shifted.

In international affairs, prestige is the shadow cast by the power of states to shape systems, attitudes, trends, and events. It is generated by the perceived decisiveness of a nation's political system, its economic strength, and the vision and wisdom of its leadership as well as its military prowess. Prestige is a major determinant of the ability of a nation to preserve the privileges of the past or frame the freedoms of the future. Current trends in this regard do not favor the United States over China.

It is not just that China and others are regaining the regional preeminence they enjoyed before the now-defunct era of Western colonialism. It is also that America's fractious politics are now dispiriting rather than inspiring to foreigners and citizens alike. The financial system and economic model of the United States have been discredited in the world's eyes. Few look to us for leadership on either global or regional issues, whatever their nature. Only our military power is fully respected. But, as we have shown the world in Afghanistan, Iraq, and now Libya, there are limits to what military power alone can accomplish. China is widely seen as having its act together. The United States is universally viewed as in big trouble on a dismaying range of issues and not doing much, if anything, about any of them, other than more of the same.

Our fiscal situation is a central element of this perception. Total federal revenue, from all sources (income, corporate, excise, social security, and Medicare taxes) is now $2.2 trillion annually. Total federal transfer payments to individuals for unemployment, pensions, medical care, and the like come to $2.4 trillion. The U.S. government is out of cash; it has to borrow $200 billion even before it begins to fund its operations. The $1.3 trillion it costs to run the government is, in effect, all borrowed, much of it from foreigners. About $700 billion is for the defense budget. Another $300 billion or more is military-related but in other budgets. Total U.S. military spending comes to well over $1 trillion. Most of our politicians remain in denial, but growing numbers of them have begun to realize that

America can't afford to continue anything like this level of outlays for our armed forces.

To our creditors, America now looks like a huge, insolvent insurance company with a mostly military workforce living on credit rollovers. Washington can't even pass a budget, let alone devise a credible plan to pay down our debt. Increasingly, America's creditors see the United States as a bad bet, not a safe haven for their money. This is not good. And it is not smart, in such circumstances, to enter a race with the People's Liberation Army, as we did with Soviet armed forces, to see who can spend whom into the ground.

Unlike the Soviet Union, China has a highly successful economy that is widely seen as a model combination of industrial policy with market economics. Not everybody likes China, but it has a reputation for coherent strategic vision. China does not operate an empire of captive satellite nations, have a history of global power projection, seek to export an ideology, or propose to expand beyond its traditional frontiers. It has not configured its forces for an attack on our homeland, even if it has made provision for retaliation against us in the event we strike its homeland. China has begun, however, to object to American naval operations in its near seas that it considers hostile to it. By its attempts to deny our right to carry out such operations, China jeopardizes our exercise of at least a portion of the global hegemony to which we have recently become accustomed. And the Chinese seem bent on developing defenses we cannot easily overwhelm. These are threats to our omnipotence even if they are not threats to our homeland.

China is also beginning to show a capacity to innovate militarily in ways that challenge American ingenuity. The good news is that China thus stimulates expensive new U.S. research and development projects as well as procurement and a conference or two. It is becoming a justification for "military Keynesianism." But, as the numbers show, even without China as a major driver, military spending is already an unaffordable burden on the U.S. economy. In marked contrast, China's defense budget is neither a significant strain on its economy nor likely to become one. With a GDP that seems destined to dwarf that of the United States in the foreseeable future, China does not anticipate resource constraints as it seeks to counter and outmatch the threat to it from America.

The United States is now fiscally hollow. Yet we are entering a long-term military rivalry with China on terms that are easily bearable by China but fiscally ruinous for us. This rivalry is all the more disadvantageous because China is competing in notably cost-effective ways, and we are not.

Aggressive reconnaissance in cyberspace is a less expensive and fatiguing way than naval and air patrols by which to probe military capabilities and map targets in other nations. Ballistic and submarine-launched cruise missiles can kill capital ships like aircraft carriers at a fraction of what it costs to build them. It's much cheaper to shatter or blind satellites than to launch, maintain, or protect them. Defensive measures are less demanding of human and material resources than power projection against them.

This should give us pause. In some disturbing ways, Sino-American competition is beginning to parallel the contest between us and the Soviet Union in the Cold War. This time, however, the United States is in the fiscally precarious position of the USSR, while China plays the economically robust role we once did. The political and economic weaknesses of the USSR made it unable to compete with us on any terms other than military. The huge expense of a military contest with an economically fitter enemy ultimately bankrupted the Soviet state and brought it down. Moscow's conviction that the best defense is an overwhelmingly strong offense locked it into a military competition that, in retrospect, was as unnecessary as it was ultimately fatal.

Based on parallel logic, we have come to spend as much as the rest of the world combined on capabilities for military coercion. Our current force structure and global military posture are *not* dedicated to the defense of our homeland but to sustaining a credible capacity to overwhelm other nations' ability to defend their homelands and adjacent areas, including their near seas. Americans do not worry that foreigners will impose their will on us. Our armed forces exist to impose our will on those who challenge or resist it. In this context, China's improving defenses are only part of what drives our military strategy. Still, they loom ever larger in its sights.

As their strong preference for asymmetric counters to the instruments of American power projection illustrates, the Chinese are not just seeking security, but affordable security. Perhaps, given the state of our finances, we should do so too. But it's hard to see how an objective of affordable security for the United States could be compatible with maintaining the assured ability to overpower China's constantly improving defenses.

The subject you are discussing—China's strategy for its near seas—is very relevant. The Chinese have begun to make it clear that they will not be prepared to tolerate the long-term menace of provocative foreign naval operations near their homeland's coasts indefinitely. So it is in its near seas that China's determination to carve out an exception to America's global dominion is finding its clearest expression. This determination does not make China a threat to the United States, but it reinforces the point that China is a threat to U.S. military supremacy in Asia and possibly beyond it.

In this context, as in others, it would seem wise to minimize activities that increase rather than diminish China's perceived need to prepare itself for future combat with the United States. To the extent that the U.S. and

PLA navies come to confront each other in China's near seas, the stimulus for China to focus on ridding these seas of foreign threats simply increases. There is, after all, an ineluctable asymmetry at play. The United States can cease to patrol China's near seas if it chooses, but China cannot cease to abut them.

The U.S. Navy insists on the right to conduct all sorts of operations in exclusive economic zones—EEZs—as an essential legal underpinning of our national interest in maintaining a dominant naval presence around the world. China sees its maritime perimeter through its experience of national humiliation by repeated assaults from the sea. What is a legal principle for Americans is a defense imperative for China. Such differences are unlikely to be resolved anytime soon. Nor can we assume that bringing them to a head would necessarily resolve them in our favor.

The United States is not a party to the UN Convention on the Law of the Sea (UNCLOS) and so not in a position to avail ourselves of its dispute resolution mechanisms. International law evolves to reflect changes in military preoccupations, technologies, and balances. Hence, the worldwide move—which the U.S. Navy stoutly resisted—from a three- to a twelve-mile territorial limit. Hence the subsequent creation, also initially opposed by the United States, of a two-hundred-mile EEZ. It's hard to argue that American views enjoy greater international deference today than they did thirty or forty years ago.

There are many countries concerned, like China, to secure themselves from potential attack from the sea. In the post–Cold War era, there are not many nations interested in preserving conditions conducive to global power projection or worldwide naval operations. If push came to shove, a majority of UNCLOS member states might support China's views over ours. If the Chinese were to mount their own aggressive reconnaissance operations off Guam, Pearl Harbor, San Diego, and Puget Sound, even our own politicians might object to their right to do this. In a world of more than one large and competent navy, the application of the golden rule to naval operations is an ever-present, if perhaps novel and unwelcome, possibility.

In sum, having a legal right to do something does not make it wise to rub others' noses in it. Lurking offshore to satisfy a prurient interest in the military preparedness of other nations to defend themselves can clearly be useful. Possibly, in some circumstances, it could be essential. But the best way to preserve the right to do it may be to refrain from doing it too obviously, too frequently, or too intrusively.

Antagonistic encounters in China's near seas are a significant factor in worsening Sino-American military relations but they do not have the impact of U.S. moves to shore up Taiwan's resistance to reunion with the mainland. The Taiwan issue is the only one with the potential to ignite a war between China and the United States. To the PLA, U.S. programs with Taiwan signal fundamental American hostility to the return of China to the status of a great power under the People's Republic. America's continuing arms sales, training, and military counsel to Taiwan's armed forces represent potent challenges to China's pride, nationalism, and rising power as well as to its military planners. These U.S. programs appear to reflect judgments by the American elite that the Communist dictatorship on the mainland is fundamentally illegitimate and should be prevented from extending its sway to other parts of China even by peaceful means. U.S. interactions with Taiwan and Tibet belie the lip service American officials pay to the notion of "one China." The message China's civilian and military elite get from these interactions is that the United States wants "one China in name but not in fact—not now, and perhaps never, if America has anything to say about it." The Chinese don't think we should have anything to say about it.

The kind of long-term relationship of friendship and cooperation China and America want with each other is incompatible with our emotionally fraught differences over the Taiwan issue. These differences propel mutual hostility and the sort of ruinous military rivalry between the two countries that has already begun. We are coming to a point at which we can no longer finesse our differences over Taiwan. We must either resolve them or live with the increasingly adverse consequences of our failure to do so.

For Chinese, the Taiwan issue presents an increasingly stark choice between national pride commensurate with rising prestige and continuing deference to America's waning power. With Taiwan and the mainland integrating in practice, China sees the policies of the United States as the last effective barrier to the arrival of a ripe moment for the achievement of national unity under a single, internationally respected sovereignty. Dignity and unity have been and remain the core ambitions of the Chinese revolution. China may, for now, continue to emphasize the avoidance of conflict with the United States. But the political dynamics of national honor will sooner or later force Beijing to adopt less risk-averse policies than it now espouses.

For Americans, the Taiwan issue presents an unwelcome choice between potential long-term military antagonism with China and the perpetuation, despite rapid cross-Strait economic and social integration, of Taiwan's *de facto* political separation from the mainland. So far, the United States has in practice given priority to Taiwan in what is now best described as an effort to retard the speeding tilt of the cross-Strait military balance against Taiwan. Given the huge stakes for the United States in our strategic interaction with China, this choice might well strike someone looking afresh at the situation as oddly misguided.

American priorities look all the more inverted when one considers that Beijing has offered to negotiate what amounts to purely symbolic reunification with Taiwan, forgoing any political or military presence of its own on the island. This offer cannot be dismissed as incredible. China's willingness to tolerate amazingly different politico-economic orders on what is nominally its territory has been amply demonstrated in both Hong Kong and Macau. Its proposal to Taipei offers far greater autonomy than either of these city-states enjoy. Is it worth a war with China to prevent such an outcome? If not, why are we behaving as if it is?

Both our global military posture and our approach to China seem unlikely to work out well for us. Perhaps it's once again time to throw off the intellectual shackles imposed by long-standing policy and address the imperatives of long-term strategic interests. Just something to think about as you plot a course for the U.S. Navy in China's near seas.

Chapter 11

Managing Sino-American Relations

America's policy toward China has been driven by different objectives in different periods. The initial opening of 1971–72 reflected little beyond a desire to put strategic pressure on the USSR and north Vietnam, with which the United States was then at war. The normalization of U.S.-China relations on January 1, 1979, began a five-year drive to bring every dimension of these relations to the level they might have achieved had the two countries not been without such ties for the previous three decades. The Soviet invasion of Afghanistan on December 24, 1979, challenged the strategic interests of both the United States and China. It kicked bilateral relations into high gear, ushering in a decade of overt and active strategic cooperation, including assistance to China's military modernization as well as the massive purchase of Chinese weapons for the Afghan resistance.

The era of strategic cooperation against the USSR came to an end in 1989. On June 4 of that year, Deng Xiaoping's belated suppression through violence of defiant, months-long student protests in Tiananmen Square and elsewhere drained the warmth from Sino-American relations. In response to this, the United States ended its military relationship with China and imposed sanctions on various other forms of cooperation with it. The November 9, 1989, collapse of the Soviet empire—symbolized by the fall of the Berlin Wall—then deprived the relationship of its principal strategic rationale. High-level visits and dialogue between the two countries outside multilateral contexts essentially ended.

In 1992, the United States set aside the constraints on arms sales to Taiwan to which Ronald Reagan and Deng Xiaoping had agreed on August 17, 1982. That year's U.S. election campaign featured attacks on "the butchers of Beijing" by the Democratic Party candidate, Bill Clinton, who was elected president on November 3. The first term of the Clinton administration began with policies toward China that were focused almost exclusively on efforts to shame the Chinese into embracing Western concepts of human rights. Although a slow process of renormalization of relations gradually unfolded,[1] the U.S. relationship with China remained essentially adrift throughout Clinton's first term in office (1993–96). It took a clash of opposing shows of force in the Taiwan area to remind Americans of what was at stake in the careful management of a relationship with China that was not limited to human rights issues.

Since then, Sino-American relations have developed lopsidedly. The economies of the two countries are now very interdependent and, as in many such relationships, are characterized by frequent bickering. Political cooperation on international issues, while limited, is sometimes effective. But military relationships between the United States and China are underdeveloped and tinged with mutual animosity.

Sino-American relations will determine, to a great extent, what the course of the twenty-first century is, not only for the U.S. and China but for the world. This book concludes with a few thoughts on how to manage these relations to preserve the domestic tranquility, enhance the security, and bolster the prosperity of both societies.

The review of China policy in this chapter's first section, "Back to Basics," which became an article in Foreign Policy magazine, was an effort to imagine a basis on which the president to be elected later that year (1996) might restabilize and reinvigorate Sino-American relations. Much of it anticipated the evolution of China policies during President Clinton's second term (1997–2000). Its analysis of the Taiwan issue proved prescient but its recommendations did not, for the most part, become policy. In many respects, despite the lapse of a decade and a half, the questions I raised and the policy framework I proposed for managing U.S. relations with China retain their relevance.

In the second section, "The Promise of Sino-American Relations," I review the ideological and other barriers to realizing the full potential for U.S.-China cooperation and propose an agenda for such cooperation. In the third, "A China Policy for the Twenty-First Century," I imagine a grand strategy for dealing with China's return to wealth and power.

And in the final section, "Indo-Pacific Dynamics in Trans-Pacific Perspective," I analyze the reactions of China's East and South Asian neighbors to its growing influence, the response of the United States to their concerns, and the prospects for a more harmonious and cooperative order in the region.

Find More in the Online Archive

Written before the current global depression, "China: Three Challenges and One Surprise" argues that, in our obsession with bilateral and military factors, the United States has failed to perceive more fundamental challenges that the rise of China poses to U.S. global financial and economic supremacy, scientific and technological leadership, and political hegemony: http://bit.ly/interesting-times.

In addition, many years after I studied ancient and modern European languages, Tamil, Chinese (Mandarin and Taiwanese), Thai, or Arabic, I was honored by a request to help present an award for excellence in language learning to the students at the United States Military Academy at West Point. The result was an essay called "On Learning Chinese and Other Foreign Languages," available at http://bit.ly/interesting-times.

Back to Basics[2]
April 1996

No one would now dispute the judgment of Chinese premier Li Peng that "Sino-American relations are highly volatile." The uncertainties affecting Washington's ties with Beijing have raised a large question mark over prospects for continued peace and stability in the Asia-Pacific region. There is rising apprehension among business and academic circles in both countries that escalating political and military tensions between the two governments over a widening range of issues could soon blight their flourishing economic and cultural interaction. In both Beijing and Washington, discussions of Sino-American relations now ponder the adverse consequences of estrangement and strategic hostility rather than the advantages of friendship and entente. Some in both China and the United States now foresee a twenty-first century dominated by contention between Beijing and Washington. Few are optimistic about Sino-American relations. Almost no one seems to envision the possibility of broad cooperation between the United States and China in the coming decades.

The contrast with the late Cold War period, from 1971 to 1989, when five successive American and Chinese administrations worked to advance a positive vision of Sino-American relations, could not be starker. Over those years, relations between Washington and Beijing improved fairly steadily, though with some setbacks. They did so under three guiding principles.

Sino-American Rapprochement

First, in the words of the Shanghai Communiqué of 1972, both sides recognized that "there are essential differences between China and the United States in their social systems and foreign policies." By mutual agreement, Washington and Beijing avoided ideological arguments. Instead, they conducted an active dialogue to seek common ground for joint, parallel, coordinated, or at least deconflicted policies. By adopting this approach, both sides sought to create an auspicious context for isolating and narrowing their differences step by step. This worked. China changed a great deal more than the United States as a result.

Second, the two sides worked together to integrate China into global and regional institutions. Washington sought thereby both to expand the effectiveness of these institutions and to transform China from a threat to the existing world order into a stabilizing element of it. This also worked. When China was admitted to the club, it accepted and learned to play by the club rules. For example, China's accession to the World Bank facilitated its adoption of a market economy. Its membership in the United Nations led in time to its accession to the Nuclear Non-Proliferation Treaty, its support of UN actions to liberate Kuwait from Iraqi aggression, and its participation in the successful UN peacekeeping effort in Cambodia.

Third, the two sides sought to promote conditions conducive to peaceful resolution of the problems arising from China's division into very different societies on the Chinese mainland, in Hong Kong and Macao, and on Taiwan. This also worked. By contrast with India, which took Goa by force, China negotiated the peaceful retrocession of both Hong Kong and Macao. Tensions in the Taiwan Strait abated, allowing Taiwan to end martial law and blossom into a prosperous democracy. Peaceful dialogue and interaction replaced confrontation between Taipei and Beijing.

Sino-American Estrangement

The two U.S. and two Chinese administrations that have been in power since 1989 have abandoned these principles in favor of a different approach. The results speak for themselves.

Rather than continuing the search for common ground, Washington and Beijing focused on their differences, especially essentially irreconcilable ideological differences over issues like human rights and Tibetan separatism. They deferred discussion of possible common interests and the harmonization of their policies to a later date that never seems to come. The result was bickering and posturing by both sides, punctuated by occasional acts or threats of retaliation by each side against perceived slights. Each side has come to distrust the other.

Meanwhile, neither Chinese nor American leaders made any real effort to develop a post–Cold War rationale for cooperative relations. The policy vacuum left by the collapse of the Soviet Union and the consequent disappearance of the Washington-Beijing-Moscow strategic triangle therefore remained unfilled. The result was strategic drift in Sino-American relations, U.S. policies driven by Congress and special interests rather than by the administration, and Chinese policies based on the conviction that the United States seeks to dismember China, overthrow its government, and frustrate its economic modernization.

At the insistence of Asian nations, China was admitted to regional institutions like the Asia-Pacific Economic Cooperation (APEC) and the ASEAN Regional Forum (ARF). The United States, however, ceased to make any effort to integrate China into global institutions. New organizations like the Missile Technology Control Regime (MTCR), the World Trade Organization (WTO), and the "New Forum" (successor to COCOM) exclude China. The end of the effort to include China in international regulatory regimes slowed the process of bringing Chinese behavior into conformity with global norms favored by the United States. This let China pick and choose the rules by which it would play. Even more damaging, it left matters of worldwide and regional concern to be dealt with as issues in U.S.-China bilateral relations rather than as multilateral concerns. American attempts to act as the world's conscience in forcing global norms on China more often than not left the United States isolated from or unsupported by its allies.

Taiwan's newly democratic politics led it to challenge the diplomatic *status quo*—and hence to upset the previous *modus vivendi* in the Taiwan Strait. Taipei enlisted the support of the U.S. Congress in its drive to overturn long-standing agreements between Washington and Beijing. Under congressional pressure, the U.S. executive branch altered its policies on arms sales and cabinet-level dialogue with Taipei as well as visits by Taiwan's leaders, while brushing aside Beijing's protests with increasingly unpersuasive denials that there had been any policy change.

Washington, meanwhile, shrank from dialogue with either Beijing or Taipei about how to preserve and enhance the prospects for peaceful cross-Strait relations. (Talking with Beijing was seen as politically incorrect. Talking with Taipei was viewed as diplomatically awkward.) Beijing lost confidence in the U.S. administration's willingness to adhere to Sino-American agreements on the management of the Taiwan problem, while Taipei fell into the habit of using Congress to end-run or roll the administration. Lee Teng-hui's visit to Cornell in June 1995—a private visit undertaken for official purposes and for domestic political advantage in Taiwan—was a case in point. This event, more than any other, served to convince Beijing that Washington might collude with separatist forces in Taipei to detach the island once and for all from China. Chinese on both the mainland and Taiwan read the visit as a signal that Taipei could count on American backing for policies provocative to Beijing, regardless of the views of the U.S. executive branch.

The absence of an American vision of how to manage relations with China as China rises to wealth and power equivalent to that of the United States has been matched by the absence of a vision in China of how it should conduct itself as a great economic and military power. Both countries have stressed the need to talk with each other, but neither seems to know what to talk about. In practice, the United States has talked to China only when it has had a congressionally mandated peeve to register or a sanction to threaten. China has talked to the United States only when it has had a protest to register or a retort to deliver. There has been no broader dialogue to set a positive agenda for Sino-American relations.

Why Talk?

The sudden return of tensions in the Taiwan Strait after more than a decade of peace finally stimulated Secretary of State Warren Christopher (in a speech in May 1996) to propose more frequent and intensive high-level talks with Beijing, including regularly scheduled summit meetings—but 1996 is an election year in the United States. Such talks must, in practice, wait until 1997. This gives Washington time to ponder the question: Talks about what? What does the United States want from China? How does the United States propose to get it?

The answer is that the United States needs to talk to China about American interests that cannot be advanced and issues that cannot be managed or resolved without contributions from China as well as the United States. There is a rapidly growing list of such interests and issues.

1. China is the world's most populous country and the world's fastest-growing economy. Most economists predict that China will overtake the United States as the world's largest economy sometime in the next twenty-five to thirty years. No effort to regulate global trade and investment to assure the common prosperity can succeed if China is not part of it.

2. China is now the only great power to have had significant parts of its territory detached by the actions of other great powers—European powers in the cases of Macao and Hong Kong; Japan and the United States in the case of Taiwan. China is determined not to allow these imperialist and Cold War divisions of its territory to become permanent. The United States has an indirect but substantial stake in the

success of the agreed-upon transitions in Hong Kong and Macao. The United States has an even larger stake in assuring that changes in the relationship between Taipei and Beijing take place peacefully, by agreement between the two, rather than through unilateral action from either side.

3. China lacks secure and recognized borders. It feels a need to establish such borders—by negotiation, if possible; by force, if necessary. The list of minor territorial adjustments to be worked out between China and its neighbors is long—seabed boundaries with both Korean states; the Senkaku (Diaoyu) Archipelago with Japan; and in the "no man's land" of the South China Sea, territorial disputes with the Philippines, Vietnam, Malaysia, and Brunei as well as a seabed dispute with Indonesia and an unsettled border with India. The United States has a big stake in peaceful adjustment of these disputes. Each requires only relatively small compromises for resolution. In the aggregate, however, how such adjustments are arranged will determine whether the Western Pacific is peaceful or tense and whether U.S.-China relations are cooperative or confrontational.

4. China's industrial and technological capacity is rapidly advancing along with China's involvement in international trade. No effort to regulate the global transfer of sensitive technology or weaponry can hope to succeed if China is not part of it.

5. China is the fastest-growing contributor to greenhouse gas emissions on the planet. It is now second only to the United States as a contributor to global warming, and will soon overtake the United States. No effort to address global environmental problems can succeed if the United States and China are not full partners in it.

6. China is the largest country in Asia. Its territory is now being used by international drug traffickers and organized crime. Its people are being smuggled to the United States and other countries under conditions that rival those of the African slave trade of two centuries ago. Neither drugs nor crime nor illegal migration can be combated successfully without effective cooperation between the United States and China.

A Positive Agenda for U.S.-China Dialogue

The failure of the approach to U.S.-China relations adopted since 1989 suggests that both countries would be wise to conduct their talks under the principles that worked from 1971 to 1989. The factors listed above suggest a ten-part agenda for positive American engagement with China to advance U.S. interests. The questions leaders in Washington and Beijing need to discuss include:

1. What are the responsibilities of the United States and China—as two of the world's greatest powers, both permanent members of the United Nations Security Council—for the maintenance of a stable and decent world order? This is not an abstract question. The Sino-American contretemps over the extension of UN intervention in Haiti earlier this year illustrates the perils of Sino-American discord in the Security Council. The successful UN operations in the Gulf and Cambodia illustrate the benefits of a harmonious Sino-American working relationship.

2. What are the responsibilities of the United States and China, as two of the world's largest economies, for the management of trade and investment policies to maximize global, regional, and bilateral prosperity? How can Sino-American cooperation promote these ends? In this connection, it is clearly an anomaly that Russia's declining, semi-marketized economy is represented in the G-7 while China's rapidly growing market economy is not. Should China not be invited to join the G-7? Similarly, the global trading system envisaged by the WTO cannot hope to function effectively for long if China's economy remains outside it. How can the United States achieve the most rapid feasible phase-in of WTO policies and practices by China? Given the relatively primitive state of Beijing's legal and administrative capabilities, does China require assistance to enable it to speed up such a phase-in and make it fully effective? If so, how can the United States and other major members of the WTO most efficiently provide such assistance to China?

3. How can the United States and China work together to ameliorate the effects on the global environment of China's rapid industrialization and urbanization?

4. How can the United States and China best assure strategic stability in Asia? Specifically, how can Japan be reassured that its national security will not be threatened as Chinese power grows? Neither China nor the United States nor the Japanese people themselves wish Japan to feel forced to rearm or to pursue independent military policies in Asia. How can the United States and China best help Japan to avoid feeling it faces such choices? How do the two countries manage the inevitable reemergence of Russia as an active strategic player in the region early next century so as to buttress rather than threaten Asian strategic stability? How can the United

States facilitate peaceful settlement of the long list of relatively minor Chinese territorial disputes with its Asian neighbors?

5. Can the United States and China, as the two greatest military powers in Asia, translate their common interests in the prevention of war and the relaxation of tensions in Korea, South Asia, and the Persian Gulf into parallel or coordinated policies that promote these objectives?

6. If the two countries can do this, how can they work together to prevent the proliferation of weapons of mass destruction and their delivery systems to these regions—all of which are far closer to China than the United States? It has clearly not been effective to insist bilaterally that China harmonize its policies and export control practices with those of the United States and other members of the Missile Technology Control Regime, the Australia Group, the Nuclear Suppliers Group, and the New Forum. If China is not a member of the club, it does not feel bound by the club rules. China needs to be brought into these groupings as a member in its own right, rather than left outside them to act in disregard or defiance of their decisions.

7. How can the United States and China work most effectively together to suppress the international trade in narcotics? To frustrate international crime? To curb illegal migration? To prevent hijacking, piracy, and terrorism?

8. Can China build the central government institutions and national administrative and judicial structures it needs to be able to do what we want it to do? Where China has reached agreement with the United States it must be held to its word. But when China lacks the administrative skills and capabilities to assure the immediate, full, effective implementation of what it has agreed to—as in the case of intellectual-property rights—it does little good and much harm simply to charge the Chinese with lack of sincerity. Rather than threatening to cut off billions of dollars in American sales to China and cost tens of thousands of American workers their jobs every time China stumbles at implementing accords with the United States, Washington should be prepared to spend a few hundred thousand dollars to work with China to fix problems both sides agree need fixing. If the U.S. government can't find the money to do this, could it not help coordinate a private-sector effort to fund foundations or other nongovernmental organizations to do the job?

9. Is there not room for American cooperation as well as contention with China on human rights? Beijing increasingly recognizes the need for the rule of law. China wants to build a modern legal and

judicial system. Such a system is essential not only to protect the rights of individual Chinese but also to provide the dispute resolution mechanisms and predictable business climate essential to trade and investment decisions in a market economy. The United States helped the Chinese authorities in Taipei to strengthen legal institutions and the rule of law even as Washington continued to call violations of human rights to Taipei's attention. This approach worked in Taiwan. It worked in Korea. Why abandon it in China in favor of an approach to human rights based only on public castigation and condemnation?

Washington needs to put its money where its mouth is on human rights in China. If China's nineteenth-century living standards produce Dickensian horrors in Chinese orphanages, the United States should not hesitate to call these horrors to the attention of the Chinese government. But, at the same time, Americans should work with the National People's Congress and relevant Chinese ministries to help them correct such abuses. Americans should work with Chinese universities and the Chinese judiciary to strengthen legal education for judges and to improve judicial administration. It took time for Koreans and for Chinese in Taiwan to build the rule of law and respect for human rights. It will take time for Chinese on the mainland to do the same. But it will take less time with U.S. help than without it.

10. How can the United States manage the question of Taiwan and promote the American interest in a *modus vivendi* and peaceful settlement between Beijing and Taipei? Taiwan's politics may have changed, but its geographic position has not. Taiwan cannot enjoy security without either a working relationship with Chinese across the Strait or strong backing from a powerful enemy of China. Does the United States wish to play the role of such an enemy of China?

The Taiwan Problem Reemerges

When the United States switched recognition from Taipei to Beijing and ended its defense treaty with Taiwan in 1979, exchanges of artillery fire between the People's Liberation Army (PLA) and Taiwan's armed forces ceased. Tensions in the Taiwan Strait greatly diminished. Reassured by restrained but substantial U.S. sales of defensive weapons, Taiwan's growing sense of security allowed it to end martial law. Until last year, under conditions buttressed by American diplomacy, both Taipei and Beijing assumed that there were only two possible futures for Taiwan— the *status quo*, as amended by peaceful interaction across the Taiwan

Strait, or some sort of agreement on reunification. In these circumstances, there was a *modus vivendi*. Taiwan was not an urgent issue for Beijing. Nor were relations with the Chinese across the Strait an urgent issue for Taipei. The island prospered and emerged as a wealthy, democratic society. Chinese on the mainland did not object to this. Indeed, they benefited from it.

Dialogue gradually superseded military confrontation in the Taiwan Strait. Peaceful interaction between Chinese on Taiwan and the mainland increased at a dizzying pace. A million and a half Taiwanese visited the mainland each year. The mainland became Taiwan's largest export market. Taiwan's entrepreneurs invested perhaps $25 billion there. There was no part of the mainland, however remote, that Taiwanese were not involved in modernizing. Taiwan's experience in the modernization of Chinese society was being successfully exported to the Chinese mainland. The influx of ideas from across the Strait, including the staging of local elections throughout the mainland under procedures modeled on the initial stages of democratization in Taiwan, steadily increased the prospects for the ultimate emergence on the mainland of a more decent civil society. These developments were good for Taiwan, good for China, good for Asia, and good for the United States. They represented a major achievement for U.S. foreign policy.

U.S. policies were based on the recognition that American interests would be far better served by the gradual coming together of the two sides of the Strait than by their separation. These policies promoted rather than opposed rapprochement across the Strait. They favored the creation of conditions conducive to negotiation between Taipei and Beijing and resisted unilateralism from either side.

The rebirth of tensions in the Taiwan Strait is the result of the breakdown of this policy framework. It arose as a result of Taiwan's understandable dissatisfaction with the *status quo*, which denies Taiwan the international recognition to which it feels entitled as a modernized, democratic society and a major trading economy. In the absence of a firm hand in Washington, Taipei's unilateral actions to alter the *status quo* led to Beijing's unilateral actions to enforce it. As Taipei sought to introduce the idea of "two Chinas" or "one China, one Taiwan" as alternatives to either the *status quo* or reunification, the *modus vivendi* that had benefited both sides (as well as the U.S. interest in peace and stability in the Western Pacific) collapsed.

American diplomats brokered the emergence of that *modus vivendi*. If it cannot be restored, the United States will face a stark choice between joining Taiwan in military confrontation with the People's Republic of China or accepting the eventual conquest of Taiwan by the People's Liberation

Army. In either case, Taiwan's prosperity and democracy will be among the principal victims.

From Beijing's point of view, Taipei's "pragmatic diplomacy" over the past three years seemed intended to acquire the attributes of independent statehood one by one, on the diplomatic installment plan. This diplomacy sought to raise Taiwan's international profile as a political entity separate from "China." Taipei worked hard to establish diplomatic relations and set up embassies in capitals where Beijing was also represented. (This approach has registered success mainly in impecunious African capitals.) Taipei also offered the United Nations $1 billion for a separate seat in the General Assembly. Beijing, not surprisingly, interpreted these initiatives as an effort to establish Taipei as the capital of a separate state—something Beijing has always said it would not tolerate.

Beijing Confronts Taipei

When political means failed to produce such a change of course by Taipei, Beijing turned to military means. Despite the sound and fury in the Taiwan Strait, however, Chinese objectives remained limited. Beijing did not seek to make Taiwan do anything in particular. It aimed instead at persuading Taiwan to stop doing things that appeared to challenge the *status quo* or to prejudice prospects for ultimate reunification across the Strait. But the strategic costs to China of its military shows of force were quite disproportionate to Beijing's modest objectives. The PLA's actions in the Taiwan Strait provoked U.S. naval deployments to counter them. American and Japanese concern about long-term Chinese intentions toward Taiwan and other territorial issues grew. The rise of anti-China sentiment in the United States and Japan was matched by an upsurge of anti-Americanism in China.

Ironically, Beijing does not seek reunification with Taiwan anytime soon. Chinese leaders have said they will address this issue with Taipei only after the reintegration of Hong Kong and Macao has been accomplished. That means sometime well after 1999—under a new generation of leaders in both Beijing and Taipei. Even if Beijing decides that it has no alternative to invading and conquering Taiwan, it will take it at least a decade to complete the military build-up necessary to guarantee success.

Nor does Beijing seek to roll back Taiwan's democratization, though it has been convenient for politicians in Taiwan to make that claim. Even under its proposals for reunification, Beijing does not seek to alter Taiwan's political or economic system. The issue for China is not how Taiwan selects its leaders or how these leaders make decisions. The issue is the decisions Taiwan's leaders make.

Prospects for Peaceful Reunification

Chinese military pressure greatly increased the percentage of Taiwan's electorate that preferred prolonging the *status quo* to making decisions about either reunification or independence. In response, Lee Teng-hui began to stress that, once reelected as Taiwan's president, he would seek a renewed *modus vivendi* with Chinese across the Strait. It appeared for a time that Lee might be prepared to refrain from further actions that could provoke Beijing, standing down from "pragmatic diplomacy" while stepping up emphasis on cross-Strait relations. It was said that Lee planned to use his inaugural address to announce a major relaxation of Taipei's restrictions on direct trade, transport, and telecommunications links to the mainland. China's leaders clearly signaled that if Lee ceased "separatist" actions, they would stand down the PLA. Cross-Strait talks, based on the principle of "one China," might then resume.

As Taiwan's presidential election approached, however, the PLA stepped up its military maneuvers, conducting missile firings that threatened to shut down trade through Taiwan's major ports. This was a challenge to the long-standing American policy of preventing conflict in the Western Pacific. The United States deployed two aircraft carrier battle groups to the area. The purpose was to underscore the abiding American interest in a peaceful settlement between Chinese on both sides of the Taiwan Strait. The ironic result of this Sino-American naval confrontation was, however, to set back prospects for the restraint and dialogue between Taipei and Beijing that are essential to such a settlement.

U.S. intervention to counter China's use of military measures short of war relieved Taipei of pressure to heed Beijing's concerns or to accommodate them. It reemboldened those in Taiwan who count on being able to enlist the United States (or at least the U.S. Congress) in backing their drive for separation from China under either a "two Chinas" or "one China, one Taiwan" formula. In the end, Lee Teng-hui's inaugural address devoted surprisingly little time to cross-Strait relations and announced no policy changes. Lee vowed to "continue to promote pragmatic diplomacy" and stated that problems in the cross-Strait relationship had arisen "because the Chinese Communists have refused to admit . . . that the Republic of China exists." He offered to make a "journey of peace" to the China mainland to discuss "how to terminate the state of hostility" between the two sides, linking this vaguely to the "historic task of unification." In a forecast of Beijing's probable reaction, the Taipei stock market fell by over four percent.

Even before these events, President Jiang Zemin and other civilian leaders in Beijing had found it hard to argue that prospects for peaceful reunification with Taiwan remained credible. China began its military maneuvers because it judged that political trends on the island were such that only pressure through military threats could deter separatism and, ultimately, bring Taipei to discuss some sort of reunification with the rest of China. If Beijing believes that only military pressure can rein in Taipei's drive for international recognition as a state separate from China but perceives that any effort to exert such pressure will be offset and neutralized by the United States, what hope can it have for peaceful reunification? Many in Beijing have now concluded that Taiwan's continued status as part of China can be guaranteed only by conquest of the island, even if this risks conflict with the United States. Unless this calculus can be altered, the prospects for continued peace in the Taiwan Strait, as well as peace between the United States and China, must be judged as poor. Lee Teng-hui's proposed meetings on the mainland now represent the only obvious opportunity to resurrect faith in the possibility of a negotiated relationship between Taiwan and the rest of China.

Even if Lee opens a direct dialogue with Beijing, the PLA now seems likely to get the budget increases necessary to acquire the capability to blockade or invade Taiwan against possible U.S. intervention sometime in the first decades of the next century. (The recent consolidation of Sino-Russian relations promises to make a widening range of Russian equipment and technology available to the PLA.) Given the enormous price that war with Taiwan would exact, Beijing will continue to seek a peaceful settlement even as it carries out its military build-up in the Taiwan Strait. That is why questions of protocol and other difficulties in the way of Lee's travel across the Strait are likely to be resolved. If the contest between Taipei and Beijing is remilitarized, however, the consequences for Taiwan, in particular, will be profound. Taiwan's superior political and economic system give it major advantages in nonmilitary competition with the Chinese mainland. The island cannot hope to win an open-ended arms race with Beijing even if the United States backs it in such a military contest.

As it focuses on developing military options vis-à-vis Taiwan, Beijing will be at pains to reassure its Asian neighbors that they have no cause to fear Chinese "hegemonism" or expansionism. China's ratification of the UN Convention on the Law of the Sea (UNCLOS) in May 1996 and other gestures it is making to the member states of ASEAN seem to foreshadow a serious effort by China to settle territorial issues in the South China Sea. Such a settlement would reinforce the desire of ASEAN members to keep a healthy distance between themselves and any conflict in the Taiwan Strait. For similar reasons, China may also become more open to resolution of its disputes with Japan over the Senkaku (Diaoyu) Archipelago and with Korea over the seabed boundary in the Yellow Sea.

U.S. Policy on the Taiwan Issue

Recent events have convinced many on both sides of the Strait that, despite American lip service to the principle of "one China," the United States sees some sort of advantage in supporting Taiwan's permanent separation from the rest of China. If credibility cannot be restored to a process of reunification through cross-Strait negotiation, this thesis may ultimately be tested in war. Restoring prospects for a peaceful settlement between Chinese on either side of the Taiwan Strait has therefore become the most urgent task before U.S. China policy.

Rather than helping remilitarize the Taiwan issue, U.S. policy should promote alternatives to arms races and conflict. Americans should seek to avoid ever having to answer the question of what we would do if our policy failed and armed conflict returned to the Taiwan Strait. U.S. actions earlier this year made it clear to Beijing that Americans care what happens to the admirably modernized, democratic Chinese society that has emerged in Taiwan. Beijing now understands that Americans may be prepared to go to war to resist the subjugation of Taiwan by force. Taipei has all the backing it needs to bargain with Beijing. Unless the United States is prepared to settle into a long-term relationship of hostile confrontation and possible war with China, however, Washington cannot afford to leave Taiwanese with the impression that they have a blank check they can fill out with American blood. Despite the difficulties of doing so, the United States must now insist that Taipei and Beijing begin to define a relationship between themselves that both can accept.

Accomplishing this will require an intensified dialogue with both Taipei and Beijing by the administration that will take office on January 20, 1997. The Taiwan Relations Act provides appropriately discreet channels for such a dialogue between Washington and Taipei. The growing American consensus to step up high-level contact with China's leaders provides the political opening for such a dialogue with Beijing. In these dialogues and in its public articulation of its policy, the United States must stress to both Chinese parties that it favors rapprochement, encourages negotiation, and seeks to promote an end to military tension and arms races between the two sides of the Taiwan Strait. The United States must make it clear that it will act with restraint and refrain from actions that it judges might undercut these objectives.

No administration can hope to conduct a policy successfully if it is under constant attack from Congress and subject to reversal by lobbyists representing foreign governments and interests. The Bush administration made negotiating a pact with Congress about Central America its first order of foreign policy business. Having achieved peace in Washington, Secretary of State Baker turned vigorously to the achievement of peace in

Central America. The next administration will need to do the same with regard to China.

Conclusion

The United States and China need to recognize the extent to which problems of great importance to both countries cannot be addressed without dialogue and cooperation between them. Washington and Beijing have much to gain by refocusing on common purposes while launching a patient effort to narrow differences in their views and policies. This approach worked when there were fewer common interests and many more points of difference between the two countries than there are now. There is little reason to doubt that, with sufficient effort on both sides, it can work again.

No such cooperation will be possible, however, if the situation in the Taiwan Strait is allowed to drift into long-term confrontation. The United States and China share a vital interest in avoiding such conflict. It would poison Sino-American relations, risk Japanese rearmament against China, engender disastrous alterations in the Asian strategic balance, severely damage both Taiwan's democracy, and set back prospects for successful economic and political modernization on the Chinese mainland. The failure to refashion a *modus vivendi* in the Taiwan Strait could lead to a Sino-American military confrontation that would rival the costs of the Cold War and replicate its perils to both the United States and China.

The Promise of Sino-American Relations[3]
February 2008

On a chill, gray Monday morning, exactly thirty-six years ago today, I stood on the steps of the old Hongqiao Airport terminal. I had arrived in Shanghai twenty minutes in advance of President Nixon. I had studied Chinese in Taiwan, but this was, of course, my first encounter with the Chinese mainland. My eye was drawn to a billboard that defiantly proclaimed, much as those at the airport in Taipei did at the time (with seven of the same eight ideograms), "We have friends all over the world." As Air Force One pulled up and cut its engines to refuel and take on a Chinese navigator before flying onward to Beijing, I heard a bird sing. Judging from the presence of birds but the absence of aircraft at Hongqiao, I deduced, all those foreign friends of China couldn't be conducting their comradely visits by air.

As our president and his wife disembarked for an off-camera cup of tea, I struck up a conversation with a Chinese foreign ministry official, the first I had ever met. I was, it turned out, also the first American official with whom he had ever spoken. That day, February 21, 1972, culminated in President Nixon's meeting with Chairman Mao and dinner with much of the Chinese Communist Party Central Committee in Beijing. It was a day of mutual discovery for many Chinese and Americans—not just for me and others who took part in some or all of its events, but for all whose stereotypes were blown away by the images on television.

In the past thirty-six years, China has changed so much and become so much part of the world, and Sino-American relations have become so tangled in multiple intimacies, that the international solitude China then enjoyed can no longer be imagined. There is no birdsong now at the Hongqiao or Pudong airports. Instead, there are hundreds of jet aircraft arriving and departing for every corner of China and the globe. Last year, China overtook the United States as the world's third-largest destination for foreign visitors. And the human ties between almost every sector of our two formerly estranged societies are now rich, ubiquitous, intricate, and warm.

Yet China and the United States began our contemporary relationship not with affection but with cold, strategic calculation. The American intention was to alter the world's strategic geometry, not to change China by opening it to outside influence. Ours was a marriage between hostile parties arranged by geopolitics. It took place despite bitter disagreement on many matters and highly negative images of each other.

Today, when people think of the Shanghai Communiqué, they remember the way in which it finessed differences over the question of Taiwan's relationship to the rest of China and pointed to the need for Chinese on the two sides of the Strait to craft their own peaceful resolution. That language was, of course, a major achievement for both sides. But, in diplomatic history, the most innovative element of the Shanghai Communiqué was not the creative ambiguity of its language about Taiwan. It was the unprecedented candor with which the text recorded sharp differences between the United States and China on many regional and global issues.

And, in terms of the broad national security and foreign policies of our two countries, the essential paragraph was not that about Taiwan. It was our mutual acknowledgment that, while "there are essential differences between China and the United States in their social systems and foreign policies," we could and should set aside these differences in the interest of sustaining a mutually advantageous international security order and pursuing common purposes in accordance with international law and comity. I do not paraphrase by much.

Such realism and mutual respect, tempered by deference to the rules of international conduct, was a wise basis on which to open a relationship between two great nations with the capacity greatly to help or hurt each other. It also delivered the strategic results both sides intended. The essence of this approach was 求大同存小异—preventing differences on relatively minor matters from obstructing the search for agreement on others of greater importance. Tonight I wish to focus on the implications of common interests, not areas of discord.

It would, however, be inappropriate not to acknowledge the continuing challenges posed by the two long-standing barriers to the realization of the full potential of Sino-America relations. These barriers to greater cooperation are well known. They are: first, the possibility that decisions or events in Taiwan outside the control of Beijing and Washington could ignite a conflict in the Taiwan Strait and trigger a widening war between us that neither desires; and, second, the effects of ideological stereotypes in the domestic politics of both countries. But there is no need for me to dwell on these problems. Too much ink has already been spilled over improbable contingencies and the sometimes-willful mischaracterization by each side of the other's intentions. Today there is growing reason to be optimistic about even these impediments to improved relations.

After all, to speak first of Taiwan, despite occasional moments of reckless political gamesmanship, the general trend has been toward cross-Strait integration. The net effect of Chen Shui-bian's drive to reverse this trend has been to push Washington and Beijing into parallel action to preserve the prospects for peaceful resolution of cross-Strait differences. To this end, each has reaffirmed the one-China principle and opposed moves from Taipei to abandon it. A growing majority on Taiwan is coming to grips with the reality that Taiwan's future depends on friendship and collaboration with the Chinese mainland and that the world will neither welcome nor endorse efforts to determine their island's status unilaterally. On this side of the Strait, too, the clear working assumption is now that progress in cross-Strait relations is best achieved by mutual agreement and that this requires deference to public opinion in Taiwan as well as on the mainland. And while the limited use of force for deterrent purposes has not been ruled out, there is widespread recognition that attempting to impose reunification coercively or by conquest would be both fruitless and counterproductive.

The Shanghai Communiqué's premise that the question of Taiwan can and should be resolved peacefully by the Chinese parties to it has therefore never been more apposite. The conceptual differences between the two sides of the Strait once again appear to be narrowing. Both sides have begun anew to think creatively about how to assure peace and stability in the Taiwan Strait so that, with wisdom and patience, people on both sides of it can craft a mutually agreeable accommodation. All these factors have made the Taiwan issue less contentious between Washington and Beijing than it has been for some time. We may now be in a brief period of heightened risk, but there is growing reason for optimism.

The other major obstacle to the development of our relations, ideology, has waxed and waned over the years. At various times, anticapitalist dogma, anticommunism, the radical ideology of the Gang of Four, zeal for democracy and human rights, and other passionately held beliefs on one side or the other have stood in the way of forward progress. And yet our relations have moved forward. With time and experience, we seem to be rediscovering the pragmatic spirit of the Nixon opening of thirty-six years ago. There are many disputes between the two countries but, with few exceptions, they have to do with the specific policies of one side or the other, not insurmountable differences of principle.

Of course, our relationship is not built on shared values. This leads polemicists, both here and in the United States, to posit ideologically driven contention between us. And a few indignant ideologues are moved to diatribe. But these apostles of strife are the exception and have, so far, been utterly wrong in their predictions. What is, in fact, most surprising to someone like me, who can remember the very sharp ideological arguments of the past, is how many similarities there now are between American and Chinese views of the world and its problems.

One reason for the decline of ideology as an impediment to better relations is the great increase in contact between Americans and Chinese. On both sides of the Pacific a new generation of scholars and businesspeople has sprung up. They owe much to their elders but face no barrier to living, studying, and working in the countries they are trying to understand, travel frequently in them, have easy access to their officials, and are at home in them. Ignorant *a priori* reasoning about each other has not vanished from either country, but it is in retreat. That is important, for both nations have changed greatly since we reencountered each other decades ago. China, in particular, has changed and continues to change with unprecedented speed. One cannot visit the same China twice. What even knowledgeable Americans think they know about China must therefore constantly be checked against the latest realities on the ground.

The course of Sino-American relations since their normalization also gives grounds for optimism. In the perspective of decades, despite some twists and turns, it is a remarkable record of success.

Immediately after normalization in 1979, the United States had two broad objectives for our bilateral relations. We wanted to bring

U.S.-China relations to the level of mutual engagement and confidence they would have attained if we had not spent three decades in a state of mutual isolation. And we wanted to draw China into the world order from which we had systematically excluded it during that period of non-intercourse. As it happened, these objectives coincided almost perfectly with those of China's greatest twentieth-century leader, Deng Xiaoping. Vice Premier Deng sought to enlist America in his bold effort to change China. He succeeded. He believed that China could benefit from becoming what World Bank president Robert Zoelleck has called a "responsible stakeholder" in the existing world order, rather than railing against that order or trying to overthrow it. Results prove Mr. Deng to have been very much right about this too.

By the last years of the 1980s, our bilateral relations had essentially matured. With the notable exception of military cooperation and exchanges, they were able to survive and eventually recover from the setbacks of 1989. That year, the events of June 4 in Tiananmen squeezed the warmth from our ties. The collapse of the Soviet empire robbed them of their strategic rationale. And the democratization of Taiwan began to give identity politics a loud voice there.

Nonetheless, by the mid-nineties, we were able to resume addressing the second objective, the admission of China to the status of full participant in global governance. The twentieth century concluded with Sino-American agreement on Chinese entry into the World Trade Organization. China's successful adaptation of its economy to the global norms of the WTO has contributed importantly to its remarkable economic progress since then. As this century began, China's actual accession to the WTO marked a major milestone in its integration into the governing councils of the world, a process that now lacks little to complete it. Since then, China's skill in addressing security issues on the Korean Peninsula and elsewhere has won global respect for its diplomacy and leadership.

Along with China's emergence as a great economic and diplomatic power has come a diversification of its international relations beyond the predominant reliance on the United States that marked the early stages of reform and opening. For China, America is no longer the measure of all things, nor is it central to all issues. This is a natural result of the maturation of Mr. Deng's reform process. In part, however, it also reflects the gradual emergence of a new world order. Today, while military capability to operate throughout the globe remains an American monopoly, other elements of power—political, economic, cultural and informational—are increasingly widely dispersed. The European Union, not the United States, is now China's largest trading partner and Chinese increasingly look to it, not the United States, for both education and political inspiration. Korean, Japanese, and other cultural influences now vie with American-inspired trends among Chinese youth. And China is forging its own vigorous pattern of cooperation with Africa, India, Latin America, the Middle East, and Russia, without reference to the United States. But amidst all this diversification of Chinese connections to the world beyond it, relations between Chinese and Americans too continue to ramify and grow in scale and depth.

The fractal complexity of contemporary China's foreign relationships now makes it impossible to describe Sino-American relations in simple terms. They cannot be reduced to a straightforward hierarchy of a few national interests or interactions. Along with this complexity has come a fog of detail no single mind can embrace. It is very difficult to see beyond what is immediately in front of us; both sides have become accustomed to muddling along with no clear idea of where we want to go. There is nothing exceptional about this approach to managing bilateral relations. Proceeding ad hoc has enabled us to avoid conflict. Not all relationships require agreement on a strategic concept. But the absence of such a concept guarantees that we miss opportunities to seize opportunities and that our interaction continues to fall well short of its potential to benefit each of us. Perhaps it is time to blow away the fog, look again at what's in this relationship for each side, and to develop a common agenda on which to move forward together.

The inauguration of a new president in the United States in 2009 will offer an opportunity for such a mutual review. There is a growing range of issues that cannot be addressed and opportunities that cannot be seized without joint or parallel action by China and the United States. On these issues, neither country can hope to lead a successful international response without the support of the other. Such issues now embrace every element of national interest and every facet of national power. Each country can benefit from seizing the opportunity to address them in concert with the other. Both risk suffering if we lack the will to do so.

The most obvious of such issues, of course, is the linked challenges of environmental degradation and climate change. Environmental degradation is an issue that greatly worries Chinese; global warming is of rising concern to Americans. These are trends that negatively affect all humanity and the future of life on this planet. The situation calls out for leadership from both China and the United States. But neither country has been prepared to take the lead and each has described itself as unable to move unless the other moves first. This has disappointed the world. The immobility on both sides persists despite the fact that there are obvious complementarities and opportunities for trade-offs implicit in our respective conditions. This is a bilateral impasse that wise leaders in both countries can and must resolve. If our two countries move together, the world will follow.

As two of the main engines driving global growth, the prosperity of our respective economies is of interest not just to Americans and Chinese but to everyone else in the world. The squabbles we have been having about exchange rates are part of an emerging global pattern of monetary difficulties. With about one-fourth of the global economy and a much higher proportion of its debt, the United States' currency can no longer bear the burden of providing three-fifths of the world's reserves. Nor, if the United States succeeds in halting its economic hemorrhaging by restoring balance between imports and exports, will it continue to export enough of its currency to provide other countries with dollars to hold in reserve. Europe can take up some but not all of this slack; neither China nor Japan is in a position to help do so.

There is an increasingly obvious need for a new international monetary order in which all nations share burdens and benefits to global advantage. A reform proposal from China and the United States would, I am confident, be welcomed by Europe, Japan, Saudi Arabia, and the other monetary great powers. The semi-annual strategic economic dialogue between cabinet-level officials in both governments, begun a year and a half ago in Beijing, provides a forum and mechanism within which we could begin to craft such a proposal.

There are other economic issues, like the revitalization of the Doha round of talks on trade liberalization, where leadership from both our countries is also essential and potentially advantageous to both. But the need for Sino-American initiative is not limited to the economic sphere.

The United States and China have serious differences about how intrusive the international community's response to domestic disorder and unrest in sovereign nations should be. Rather than engaging in mutual recrimination, we need to discuss these differences honestly and, to the extent we can, narrow them. But the fact that we differ on some matters should not prevent us from making common cause on others. Nor should it preclude our assisting in the formation of ad hoc multilateral groupings to accomplish mutually advantageous purposes. As currently constituted, the United Nations and other institutions we inherited from the last century cannot always serve this purpose.

Some of the problems and opportunities before us are regional in nature. For example, sudden transitions on the Korean Peninsula cannot be ruled out. They have the potential to destabilize northeast Asia to the detriment of American as well as Chinese, Japanese, and Russian interests, not to mention the safety and well-being of Koreans themselves. Similarly, I believe, we have acquired a common interest with others in helping Central Asians enjoy peace and development without being drawn into great-power rivalry in that region. And we have repeatedly shown that we share a concern about the nuclear standoff in South Asia. These and other regional issues have implications for China and the United States as well as those directly implicated in them. We may hope for the best but must prepare for the worst. It is none too soon to begin to create the regional security consultative and contingency planning arrangements we need to help manage possible crises at the regional level.

There is also, of course, a global dimension to some of the problems I have just cited. For instance, neither China nor the United States wants to see the further spread of nuclear weapons, whether on the periphery of China or farther afield. Yet the Nuclear Non-Proliferation Treaty no longer provides a basis for dealing with declared and undeclared nuclear weapons states, nuclear arsenals are no longer being downsized, and the inhibitions on proliferation are steadily weakening as more and more nations seek sovereign control of every aspect of the nuclear fuel cycle. Our two nations have been cooperating with others in the effort to secure a nuclear-free Korean Peninsula, but this begs the question of the larger global context. If we do not expand our cooperation to create a new and more credible nonproliferation regime with universal applicability, further proliferation is a certainty.

As the twenty-first century nears its second decade, China and the United States have the capacity to help the world collectively to address many pressing issues, if our leaders can muster the imagination and will to do so. We both want to preserve a peaceful international environment. But we must ask ourselves: is it enough to sustain peace by coping with problems as they arise, or should we seek a more harmonious world order that can actively use that peace to create a better life for ourselves and our descendants? I hope that our leaders will answer that question by rising to the challenge of guiding change to the advantage of both our peoples and those of other nations, great and small.

From the outset, the promise of Sino-American relations has transcended the bilateral benefits they could bring to both of us. Our interactions move the world. When linked to a broader vision, they have the capacity to move it for the better. We owe it to our posterity to work together to that end.

A China Policy for the Twenty-First Century[4]
April 2008

If today were January 20, 2009—which not a few here must wish it were—the forty-fourth president of the United States would be in his or her first day on the job. Our new president will inherit a dismaying list of foreign policy messes that clamor for an urgent fix, but, barring the unexpected, relations with China probably won't be on that list. During the Bush administration, the United States' best relationships have been with the nations of the Asia-Pacific region, among them—much to the surprise of many—China. If nothing goes badly wrong between now and the inauguration, Mr. Bush's successor will be able to savor memories of the cathartic China-bashing of the campaign but to succumb to the temptation to put the actual development of a strategy for handling China onto the back burner.

After all, the new president will have to deal with recession; inflation; mounting foreign debt amidst a credit crisis; public and private pension systems that are slouching toward insolvency; a massive budget deficit with a built-in fiscal time bomb of unsustainable tax cuts that are due to expire; a health insurance system that is driving individual Americans to distraction and businesses over the edge; an educational system that saps rather than fuels the competitiveness of the U.S. economy; a workforce unnerved by broken immigration policies and the fact that industrial jobs are now less than 10 percent of our labor market and falling; an energy policy that celebrates self-indulgence and continually deepens import dependence; increasingly shabby infrastructure, complete with collapsing bridges, terminally gridlocked traffic, and man-eating potholes; and an almost universal disbelief in the capacity of Washington politicians to do anything about any of these things.

And then there's foreign policy.

Unless something fundamental changes, when the next president takes office, Osama bin Laden will still be at large and al-Qaeda will be planning something to one-up 9/11; most of our land combat capacity will still be committed to reinforcing strategic failure in Iraq; no one will have yet come up with a plausible endgame for our intervention in Afghanistan; Pakistan will still be a catastrophe waiting to happen; the threat of terrorist reprisal for our intrusions into the realm of Islam will continue to escalate; an outmoded international monetary and reserve system will still menace our prosperity; withering alliances will ensure that we are without international cover or backup for our foreign policies and overseas operations; Israel will remain a pariah state in its own region, besieging others in anticipation of their besieging it, losing friends and alienating people throughout the world; Iran will be farther along in its efforts to develop a complete nuclear fuel cycle as the basis for an independent nuclear deterrent; Russia will continue its regression toward its czarist past; Turkey's estrangement from the United States will be a work in progress nearing completion; trans-Atlantic relations will remain rancorously adrift and Western values will still lack the long-term, unified backing they need to prevail over competing ideas; Venezuela and other Latin American nations will be working on new and ingenious ways to undermine American leadership of hemispheric affairs; Africans will stay on the road to alignment with a resurgent China and a reinvigorated India; ASEAN will persist in preferring Chinese attentiveness and flattery to American scolding and neglect; Japan will remain strategically perplexed; no one will be doing much to stop the Earth from warming; the United States will still be isolated, resented, or ignored in the United Nations and other multilateral fora; and very few foreign nations will accept American leadership.

Thus, we arrive at the question at hand. How should we deal with China, in all its dimensions—global, regional, bilateral, multilateral, and domestic? Given everything else on his or her plate, the new president could well decide that the condition of U.S.-China relations is good enough for government work, and defer the task of developing a comprehensive strategy for dealing with it. But that would be a mistake. China and our relations with it will determine a good deal of what happens in this century and how we fare in it.

It would be nice if China were on our side—or at least not against us—on the formidable range of foreign and domestic challenges we have accumulated since the end of the Cold War. It would be reassuring to be confident that we are not headed into a new cold war, this one with China—a nation that manifestly lacks the ideological rigidity, military overextension, and economic dysfunction that enabled us to box in the Soviet Union until it collapsed of its own infirmities. We were able to encapsulate our strategy for dealing with the Soviet challenge to our values and interests in a single word: "containment." Both China and the international context in which it is rising are vastly more complex. No bumper sticker suffices to describe a relationship that is simultaneously cooperative and competitive, distant and close, wary and warm.

In economic terms, China is already a world power. It is beginning to extend its diplomatic influence well beyond its immediate region, to recover its ancient cultural eminence, and to resume its historic contributions to the advance of science and technology. It is a significant regional military power with an increasingly formidable capacity to defend its borders and the approaches to them. China is a growing contributor to peacekeeping operations under the United Nations flag. It may, in time, extend its military reach more widely, though at this moment there is no clear evidence that this is its intention. The global expectation that China is destined to assume a world leadership role, however, gives it political influence that its unappealing political system would otherwise deny it.

There is no American consensus about how we should deal with growing Chinese power. Nor is there a unified U.S. government strategy for doing so. Members of Congress, as usual, are too busy seeking favors or passing condemnatory resolutions on behalf of special interests and single-issue activists to think about how their actions could affect the broader national interest in a cooperative relationship with China. A small group of members seeks to equate hostility toward China with patriotism. These members have sought to raise public alarm about China through special commissions and annual reports and passing legislation to bar contacts and dialogue with the People's Liberation Army. The lowest common denominator of these disparate views is very low indeed—a tapestry woven of a little bit of pandering and a whole lot of slandering—the opposite of strategy.

Amidst the cacophony, the executive branch has often seemed to consist of disconnected departments and agencies, each doing its own thing—or not doing it—with Beijing. In a speech in 2005, former Deputy Secretary of State Zoelleck made a noteworthy attempt to synthesize a strategy from all this bureaucratic Brownian motion, quirky indiscipline, and ideological knuckle-dragging. He coined the phrase "responsible stakeholder" to describe the kind of China we would like to work with, but the incoherence didn't really go away. The phrase lingers on, but not the ideas behind it. More recently, Treasury Secretary Paulson has tried to pull together a comprehensive approach to economic aspects of our interaction with China.

It is a long time since there has been an effort at the presidential level to articulate a comprehensive statement of objectives vis-à-vis China, and there is no overall plan. Nor has there been any effort by the executive branch to educate the public on the challenges we face and do not face in our relations with China and the Asia-Pacific region. Perhaps this reflects the fact that China has become the subject of such a wide range of celebrity and interest-group politics that our leaders fear that saying what they want to do with China might get in the way of actually doing it.

Whatever the reason for it, the absence of a unifying concept has left us and everybody else to figure out for ourselves what the United States is actually trying to do with or to China. The Chinese, it must be said, are particularly bad at this kind of analysis. The majority of Chinese appear to believe, for example, that public reaction here to the recent race riots by Tibetans and to unrest among other Chinese minorities proves the existence of a plan by the United States and its Western allies to divide, dismember, weaken, and humiliate China. President Bush's admirably stiff upper lip in the face of these events and unwillingness to politicize the Olympics will, I hope, help convince them that they are wrong. But I wouldn't count on it. The level of patriotic indignation in China against posturing by American and European politicians over Tibet is already so high that a long-term clampdown in Tibet seems inevitable, while public support in China for continued cooperation with the West can no longer be taken for granted.

Even if we make it through the Olympics without more riots and recriminations, there will still be a good deal to be said for taking the guess-work out of China strategy and its supporting policies. Doing so could help establish a better-coordinated and more disciplined approach in executive branch departments and agencies while dispelling counterproductive mis-impressions abroad and rebutting conspiracy theories in China itself.

It is not enough simply to have relations with China. Those relations should be grounded in reality and calculated, directed, and managed to advance our interests—or at least to save them from harm. The next president needs to find an early occasion to restate our objectives with respect to China and the reasoning behind them. I hope he or she will do so both realistically and with a selfish regard for American interests.

Before I talk about some of the elements of such a statement of objectives, given the military focus of this audience, I'd like to put forward a few sobering observations about the post–Cold War era and the limits of American coercive power in relation to the rise of China. There is, after all, no point in responding to China's return to wealth and power with daydreams about options that do not in fact exist.

Even if we wanted to do so (and it is not immediately obvious why we should), we could not hold China down. In the globalized economy of today, no effort—even by a country as great as our own—to organize the isolation of China could succeed. Opposing China's rise will not stop it. It will simply earn us the enmity of China's once-again-proud people. The observation of the founding father of modern conservatism, Edmund Burke, applies. "The heart of diplomacy," he said, "is to grant graciously what you no longer have the power to withhold." Only by co-opting what one cannot stop can one hope to direct its trajectory and thereby shape the future to one's advantage.

Some of the same Americans who promised marvelous strategic results from the invasion of Iraq continue to argue for the containment of China. The fact is that an attempt to implement such a policy would isolate the United States from our allies and friends to an even greater extent than our policies in the Middle East have. It would raise almost as much distrust of our intentions in Delhi, Hanoi, Islamabad, and Tokyo as in Beijing. From Japan and Korea, through Southeast Asia to India and Pakistan, and onward through Central Asia and Russia, every nation on China's periphery is well along in warily accommodating it. None of China's neighbors sees an effort to isolate it, weaken it, or divide it as feasible, and none is prepared to incur the high costs of attempting to do so.

Though all nations desire continued participation by the United States in the Asian-Pacific balance of power, none wants the United States to act as the sole balancer of Chinese power. None favors American confrontation with China or the division of Asia into spheres of influence like those of the Cold War. All wish to see a regional and global balance that incorporates rather than excludes China, India, and other emerging great powers, as well as Japan, which cannot forever hide behind Uncle Sam. This is as true outside the Asia-Pacific region as within it. Although the European Union bans weapons sales to China, it does so on human rights grounds, not geopolitical grounds, and in deference to American concerns, not out of strategic conviction.

The strategically inclusive approach to China favored by our allies is not contradicted by the Taiwan problem, the only issue that anyone has been able to identify that could ignite a war between China and the United States. There is broad regional and international appreciation of the United States' role in blocking unilateral moves to alter the *status quo* by either Beijing or Taipei. Still, no U.S. ally has committed itself to participating in a defense of Taiwan's continued separation from the rest of China. Our most stalwart allies in the Pacific, the Australians and south Koreans, who have fought alongside us in every other conflict over the past half-century, have made it clear that they would sit out such a fight. Despite its oft-expressed apprehensions about China's return to Asian primacy, even Japan is undecided about whether and to what extent it would facilitate military operations from U.S. bases on its territory in a war to define Taiwan's relationship to China.

In the only war with China that anyone can imagine, then, for all practical purposes, we would be on our own. Given how much more capable our navy and air force are than those of the People's Liberation Army, and despite the disagreeable experiences of the Korean War, I have little doubt that we would prevail in any battle with the PLA. What no one can tell me is how we would limit the conflict or win the war. Unlike Korea and the proxy war we fought in Indochina, a U.S.-China war over Taiwan would not be fought in a third country. It would take place on territory that all Chinese agree is theirs, and in the Chinese homeland. Strikes on the Chinese homeland would elicit counterstrikes by the PLA on ours, by fair means or foul. After we took out Chinese forces in the Taiwan area and beyond it, much of Taiwan would be a smoking ruin; China and its nationalism would still be there to rebuild the capabilities to have another go at it. We would have made a permanent enemy of China. This is not an appealing scenario and it's hard to see much in it for us or anyone else.

These are some of the reasons that the aim of U.S. policy with respect to Taiwan has wisely been to ensure that no war over it ever occurs. This policy now seems once again to be bearing fruit, as Taipei and Beijing prepare for negotiations on a wide range of initiatives to further the already-extensive integration of their economies and societies and to establish a long-term framework for peace and stability in the Taiwan Strait. Americans need to make it clear that there is a corollary to our opposition to coercion and unilateral efforts to change the *status quo*, and that is our willingness to embrace and act to support changes upon which the two sides of the Strait mutually agree. We should do nothing to disrupt their crafting of such changes. We must ensure that as Taiwan negotiates, it does not do so from a position of weakness—but we should encourage it to negotiate. Asia—and the world—would be a better place and U.S. interests would be well served if the Taiwan issue were peacefully resolved.

The Taiwan problem has been a persistent constraint on the development of U.S.-China relations and an intermittent source of bilateral crises that destabilize the region and alarm our allies and friends. Ironically, the principal beneficiaries of Sino-American tensions over Taiwan have been the Russians and other countries with territorial disputes with China. They have been able to exploit Beijing's obsession with the great rent in China's territorial integrity that Taiwan represents. One result has been border demarcation agreements and military confidence-building measures along their borders with China that are considerably more generous than they might otherwise have been. Another has been the emergence of China as Russia's biggest arms market, alongside India. Of course, Taiwan has also become a major destination for U.S. arms sales, a market we monopolize because no other arms-exporting country is prepared to sell there. It is a fact that our military-industrial complex has acquired a vested interest in demonizing China while talking up Taiwan's defense needs.

To the dismay of some, Taiwan has recently become much more selective about what it buys from us. This reflects its recognition that an island of 23 million people cannot hope to sustain a long-term military balance with a society of 1.3 billion and growing. This would be true even if China were not driven by other factors unrelated to Taiwan to reequip and modernize its military. But it is. Even as the PLA builds preparedness for Taiwan contingencies, it must mount a credible defense along fourteen land borders and against other powerful nations that, like Japan, have a history of invading China. Ironically, any U.S. military planner charged with planning China's defense would demand a vastly greater level of defense spending than the PLA has been able to wangle.

Both Beijing and Taipei want to end their military confrontation. Both now seek to negotiate a formula that would permit the long-term peaceful coexistence of Taiwan's political economy with the quite different systems now flourishing on the mainland, in Hong Kong, and in Macau. Working out such a formula, consistent with the principle of "one China," is the stated objective of the administration that will take office in Taipei on May 20. Doing so will not constitute "reunification." Discussion of arrangements for that could be deferred, perhaps indefinitely. In the meantime, both sides are committed to exploring—I quote—"a formal ending to the cross-Strait state of hostilities" and "the establishment of a military mutual trust mechanism, to avoid cross-Strait military conflict." The United States should express willingness to help secure any new *status quo* that may be agreed between Taipei and Beijing and to act accordingly.

If Taipei and Beijing can achieve what they now hope they can, Taiwan's democracy will, for the first time, be unthreatened and a major burden on our relationships in the area—not just with China but with other countries—will be lifted. Concern on the part of the Republic of Korea about our embroiling Koreans in a war with China over Taiwan has been the principal obstacle to the transformation of our alliance into a partnership for power projection. A somewhat similar concern has kept our alliance with Japan from achieving its full potential. Obviously, new possibilities for a strategic relationship with China, leveraging its capabilities to serve our purposes, would also arise.

The downside is, of course, that the credibility of China as a putative "peer competitor" of the United States would be greatly diminished. Our defense industries would be thrust back into another season of "enemy deprivation syndrome"—the queasy feeling they get when their enemy goes away and they have to find a new one to justify defense acquisition programs. I am sure they would prove to be up to that challenge! A moment of disorientation in the military-industrial complex would, in any event, be a small price to pay for greater security in the Western Pacific and the end of any serious prospect of armed conflict with China.

With this prospect in mind, let me return to the broader issue of U.S. objectives vis-à-vis China. I think these should be to ensure, to the extent possible,

- that Americans benefit rather than suffer from China's emergence as an economic great power;

- that China becomes a committed guardian and follower of good practices of global governance within a rule-bound international order favorable to American as well as Chinese interests;
- that China pulls with us rather than against us as we tackle global, regional, and transnational problems;
- that the Taiwan issue is resolved peacefully on terms acceptable to both sides of the Taiwan Strait; and
- that disputes, including China's few remaining territorial issues with its neighbors, are also resolved by peaceful means.

Serious pursuit of these objectives would demand of us a degree of far-sightedness and diplomatic creativity like those we evidenced six decades ago, when the now-vanished world for which we built our present international institutions and practices was still new. It would require us to recognize that the alliances and multilateral structures we set up to deal with the threats of fascism and Soviet Communism need reform, supplementation, or replacement to be able to deal with the very different challenges and opportunities of the post–Cold War era. These challenges cannot be met with coalitions or through gatherings that do not include those with the capacity to wreck the solutions we craft, as well as those essential to crafting them. We need new diplomatic and security architectures to manage new global and regional problems. Creating them will require us to combine vision with pragmatism and to set aside our rigid insistence that nations demonstrate democratic credentials before we will work with them.

China is very relevant in this regard. There is a growing range of problems that cannot be addressed and opportunities that cannot be seized without China's cooperation or acquiescence. Such issues now embrace every element of our national interest and every facet of national power. They may sound abstract, but they can help ordinary Americans—or hit us where it hurts. Fortunately, the prospect for Chinese cooperation on many of them is good, especially if Taipei and Beijing succeed in taking the Taiwan issue progressively off the Sino-American agenda. Whether that happens or not, let me mention just a few things the next president could usefully take up with the Chinese to serve the objectives I've outlined.

One of these is the trade imbalance and the dollar-yuan exchange rate. These problems are linked politically. They now also connect to a broader issue of global concern. With about one-fourth of the global economy and a much higher proportion of its debt, our currency can no longer bear the burden of providing three-fifths of the world's reserves. Americans need to return to funding our economic advance with our own savings rather than through foreign borrowing. China and other high dollar-surplus countries need to know that their long free ride on the dollar is coming to an end. They will have to pick up their fair share of sustaining the health of the global economy and the international monetary and reserve system on which it depends. We need urgently to sit down with the Chinese and others to begin to work out a new system that would include full convertibility for the yuan but preserve as much as possible of the value of China's, Japan's, and other countries' hard-earned dollar reserves. The aim should be to begin to craft a joint proposal for international monetary reform that we could put before the world's great financial powers.

Consider also the questions of international good governance and the rule of law. One of the lessons Americans may well take away from Iraq is that we should get out of the business of trying to propagate democracy in foreign lands and instead focus on making it work here, counting on the good example we set to inspire others to emulate us. But we have a big stake in the extent to which China internalizes the idea of the rule of law. This is not just because China is becoming an increasingly important element in the forces shaping world order, but because no nation that is a scofflaw at home can be trusted to follow the rules abroad. (The reverse of this, that scofflaw behavior abroad fosters unconstitutional corner-cutting at home, is also true, as our own government has recently reminded us.) We need to set a good example at home to have credibility abroad. But we must do more than that.

We need to work with the Chinese to improve the performance of their courts, enhance their legal education, upgrade their forensic standards, and modernize their law enforcement practices. This, not public condemnation and verbal abuse, is how we helped south Korea and Taiwan become democratic societies characterized by a high degree of respect for human rights. Twenty years after the student uprising in Tiananmen, it is time to do away with the sanctions—self-imposed restrictions—that prevent us from working with the Chinese government to help the vastly larger society of the mainland attain comparable standards of civilized behavior.

Yet another challenge that tests our willingness to explore partnership with China is environmental degradation and climate change. Nothing the United States can do will have much effect on the deteriorating global environment without parallel or complementary action from China. It has been all too easy to use this fact as an excuse for doing nothing. The next president should use it as a reason to challenge China to join us in tackling the problem.

If the Bush administration succeeds, as it yet may, in removing the nuclear issue as an obstacle to a permanent peace on the Korean Peninsula and normal relations with north Korea, its successor will have something to build on in terms of creating a northeast Asian security system that can help with crisis management and dispute resolution in that region. China would be an essential partner in any such arrangement, as it has been in the six-party talks. China would also be an indispensable participant in any broader concert of Asia-Pacific powers, including not just our allies in Japan and Korea, but also India, ASEAN, Australia, and others. Such a gathering could advance our objective of assuring that territorial and other disputes are worked out by measures short of war.

Finally, to return very briefly to military matters, it is shocking that we had more contact and were more familiar with the reasoning processes of our Soviet enemies than we are today with the Chinese, who are not and need not become our enemies, and with whom we share many common concerns. At present, if there were an abrupt transition in Korea or Pakistan, or an incident in Central Asia, we would not have the mutual confidence and familiarity necessary to work with the Chinese to address the resulting problems, despite the almost certain desire of both of us to do so. Military dialogue and exchanges need a lot of work on both sides.

The United States faces a daunting array of foreign and domestic problems, many of which we cannot hope to solve on our own. We cannot take China's cooperation with us on these problems for granted, even though in some cases it is indispensable. Equally, however, we have no basis for presupposing China's opposition or indifference on these issues. How the United States conceives of our relations with China and how we approach these relations will determine whether China is helpful or hostile on matters of concern to us. We will do better, I think, with a less stridently critical and militaristic approach than the one we have recently followed.

Diplomacy is not just about preventing problems or deterring others from creating them, though both are part of it. Diplomacy is equally, as the Truman and Nixon administrations showed in the past century, about responding to broad strategic challenges, about redefining the world and regional orders, about creating opportunities to advance the national interest, and about crafting strategic architecture that embraces the capacities needed to pursue these opportunities. In 2009, Sino-American relations are likely to be ripe for redefinition, renewal, and mutually beneficial enlargement.

It will fall to the president who takes office next January 20 to compose a comprehensive strategy to accomplish this and to devise realistic policies to implement that strategy. But, as former Secretary of State Kissinger once wisely remarked, "no foreign policy—no matter how ingenious—has any chance of success if it is born in the minds of a few and carried in the hearts of none." The next president must also lead the American people toward a better-informed consensus on how we can best compete and cooperate with an increasingly influential and powerful China.

The potential for partnership between the United States and China is great; the costs of antagonism are greater. China's leaders have said on many occasions that they want a strategic partnership with America. To test whether that is possible, Americans must decide what we want from such a partnership and be constant in our pursuit of it.

✑

Indo-Pacific Dynamics in Trans-Pacific Perspective[5]
April 2012

Since the end of the Cold War, the Indo-Pacific region has emerged as the world's most dynamic geopolitical zone. Shifting balances of power there are reshaping international perceptions. They are also fueling apprehensions about economic, military, and political trends; hardening territorial disputes; and driving change in the U.S. economic, political, and military roles in Asia. The uncertainties these shifts entail are causing Asian nations to seek reassurance in reaffirmations of civilizational, cultural, and historical identity. They are redefining relationships with the United States. The principal, but far from the only, force at work in these complex interactions is the return of China to wealth and power.

The psychological impact of China's rise has been amplified by its apparent competence at simultaneously coping with immediate problems, removing structural barriers to future prosperity, and strengthening national competitiveness. (This view may be about to be overtaken by events, but never mind that for now.) China's global and regional peers brood about their apparent inability to do nearly as well. China has advanced amidst repeated demonstrations of European entropy, Japanese political palsy and economic torpor, temporizing in India that threatens that country's much-ballyhooed reincarnation as a great power, and disarray and dysfunction in many, if not most systems of global governance. Meanwhile, a dismaying mix of fiscal embarrassment, economic lethargy, and political paralysis continues to erode American self-confidence and clout.

For the past two decades, Asian economies have been growing steadily more interconnected. By a significant margin, almost every Asian country now has China rather than the United States as its largest trading partner, and China's share continues to grow. In the case of Japan, trade with China is now a bit over 20 percent of the total, while the United States accounts for just 12.5 percent. In the case of India, China trade is one-sixth and U.S. trade one-eighth of the total. south Korea's trade with China is equal to the total of its trade with both the United States and Japan. Indonesia's trade is 14 percent with Japan, 12.5 percent with China, and 7 percent with the United States. As a sign of the times, total U.S. trade with greater China—including Hong Kong and Taiwan—is now greater than U.S. trade with Canada!

Asian prosperity—and to a lesser extent that of the world—has therefore come to depend more on continued Chinese success than American, even though the American market powered the initial Asian lift-off. The result is an increasingly integrated economic region that is at once Sinocentric and less dependent on North American and European markets than in the past. The United States has recently embraced the Trans-Pacific Partnership (TPP). This has been portrayed as a move to offset Chinese influence in Asia. But the TPP will not alter, still less reverse, current trends, even if it is realized in the foreseeable future. (For many reasons, this seems unlikely.)

Asian nations remain intimately connected with the United States. For example, there are nearly 160,000 Chinese students here, more than 100,000 from India, nearly 75,000 from south Korea, almost 25,000 from Taiwan, and a bit more than 20,000 from Japan. China, by contrast, hosts only 10,000 Indian students at present. Amazingly, however, for a country that only recently opened its universities to foreigners, there are now more Japanese and almost as many south Korean students in China as in the United States. (More students from Taiwan now study on the Chinese mainland than in the U.S.) Both the trends and the future seem clear.

More to the immediate point, China's neighbors have become actively engaged with it in a remarkable range of fora, dialogues, and consultations on matters of mutual concern or interest. Still, China's emergence as an immovable military object—if not yet an irresistible military force—concerns them. Those nations with active territorial disputes with China—a list that includes India, Japan, Korea, the Philippines, and Vietnam—are particularly apprehensive.

The responses of individual Asian nations to these trends differ, but they follow a common pattern. No Asian country, including China, wants to see a Cold War–style division of the Indo-Pacific region into competing spheres of influence. Rather than countering potential Chinese hegemony by re-embracing that of the United States, Asians seek to craft a rule- and relationship-bound regional order. They hope that this can maximize economic potential and mitigate political risks while enhancing national strategic autonomy. Each Asian country strives to consolidate its own borders and boundaries while reducing the danger of armed conflict with China or others over disputed territories.

Outreach to the United States by U.S. allies and former adversaries in Asia is an important part of this effort on their part to adjust to change. In some ways, however, it is less significant than their efforts to accommodate themselves to China's rising power. Generally, enhancements to their cooperation with the United States are followed by equal and opposite enlargements in their interactions with China. Meanwhile, all Asian nations, other than China, aim to balance regional intercourse with diversified global relationships. None wishes either to provoke China or to become a pawn in Sino-American strategic rivalry.

As China has risen in influence and prestige, U.S. allies as well as other Asian nations have therefore reacted cautiously. Few, other than India, are actively concerned about the prospect of military conflict with China. But all feel intimidated by China's huge size and growing military weight.

All have been attempting to strengthen themselves both economically and militarily, while reaching out for the added reassurance of American and other foreign backing. At the same time, all have been cultivating cordial relations with China. Their objective is to incorporate China peacefully into a stable balance of power in the Indo-Pacific region, not to exclude it. In their view, the American role should be to stabilize the process of accommodating the realities of Chinese power, not to obstruct this process. The sharper their differences with China with regard to territorial disputes, therefore, the more they seek to offset their bickering by drawing closer to China.

Almost all Asian nations have initiated some form of security dialogue and mechanism for crisis management with the PLA. They do this bilaterally, rather than as groups of nations. In addition to beefing up their armed forces, however, some have also been building new relationships that hint at the potential for future intra-regional coalitions. Japan and Vietnam are particularly active in this regard, as illustrated by their recent courtships of India.

The America that must deal with this evolving new order in the Indo-Pacific is not the same country that hunkered down there after World War II. The Cold War both militarized U.S. foreign policy and birthed a fiscally insatiable American military-industrial complex. The political vector of these developments has made militarism a defining element in contemporary American national identity. We have come to see security issues in predominantly military and coercive terms. In Asia, in particular, we equate military presence with influence.

But military power is only one aspect of national security or, for that matter, of influence. Concepts of both power and security in and around Eurasia are less unidimensional than ours. Despite the tremendous diversity of Asia, there is recognition from India to Japan that national security involves much more than the ability to mount an effective military defense of the homeland or to impose the national will on foreigners by force. The use of force is seen as but one of many means by which to change people's minds and alter their behavior—and, in most respects, as the least desirable.

Outside the United States, including in China, national security is widely seen to derive from domestic tranquility, social unity, economic resilience, and strategic vision as well as from military prowess. National security policy has as its objective the preservation of what Chinese, Japanese, and Koreans once called the "national essence" [国粹 (guocui)/ kokusui/kuksu], a concept that is civilizational, cultural, historical, and sometimes racial, but not ideological. In Asia, by contrast with America, national security doctrine does not posit a need to export any value system or impose any particular political culture on others. Preserving national independence, dignity, and pride entails sound statecraft that can recruit allies, frustrate enemies, and deflect domestic and foreign challenges to the geography, cultural traits, and social structures that define a nation. It does not require converting others to one's national value system. Security is measured in the welfare of citizens and their families, their confidence in their futures, and the tranquility of their lives as well as in the projected outcome of potential armed clashes with foreigners.

In this context, ironically, while others see rising Chinese strength, China's leaders fear the prospect of *internal* instability born of policy missteps, foreign humiliations, or natural disasters. Where our military has been schooled to the thought that "there is no substitute for victory," the Chinese military tradition sees such a substitute in the achievement of desired political results through right-sized efforts on the battlefield. China's rulers are, for the most part, risk-averse, conservative, and patient. But they are very much aware of the great power their country is acquiring.

Americans, by contrast, increasingly dread a future of lessened prestige and diminished international sway. This predisposes us both to strut our stuff and to take risks. Our political culture leads us to emphasize military and coercive means to solve problems or meet challenges. But U.S. allies and partners in Asia view combat and threats to engage in it as an undesirable last resort. They consider persuasion more likely to yield lasting diplomatic success than intimidation. They distrust Chinese assurances that China "will never seek hegemony," but they are also wary about entrusting their national security to possibly trigger-happy Americans.

American policy has now officially recognized that the Indo-Pacific region is the world's new economic center of gravity and that the balance of power within it is evolving. Notwithstanding the clumsiness of our proclamation of a military "pivot" to hold China in place, our response to this evolution has been more than military. To ensure continuing influence on the region's economic policies, we have—as I mentioned—joined the expansion process of the Chilean-Singaporean–initiated Trans-Pacific Partnership.

To raise our political profile, President Obama is now committed to regular participation in annual East Asia Summits. With Indo-Pacific economies the consumers of as much as 60 percent of Iran's oil and gas exports, the American effort to dictate terms to Iran on nuclear matters through sanctions and military threats has necessarily focused heavily on Asia. This has tested the ability of American leadership to bring our Asian trading partners in line with our policy.

These initiatives demonstrate U.S. attention to the region. Paradoxically, however, they also illustrate the handicaps that hobble efforts to shore up American influence in Asia. Those taking part in the TPP expansion process have greatly welcomed the prospect of American participation in the vast free trade zone they are attempting to create. But many object to the U.S. insistence on imposing various American special-interest agendas on other members. They consider this to exemplify American overreach and overestimation of U.S. leverage in changing times. (The U.S. demands a radical rewrite of the global norms for intellectual-property rights as well as the adoption of American-style financial deregulation, labor standards, environmental regulations, waivers of sovereign immunity in the litigation of investment disputes, and other idiosyncratic elements of the currently troubled U.S. economic system.)

Others note that the American proposals seem calculated to engineer the exclusion of China from TPP. They understand the gamesmanship but question the logic of this, given the importance of China to regional and global prosperity and the fact that China is fast becoming the world's largest economy. And all are aware of the United States' history of extracting concessions from other countries in return for undertakings that the U.S. Congress then balks at implementing. Frankly, most observers rank the prospects for the far-more-accommodating Chinese-backed East Asian Free Trade Area as considerably better than those for TPP.

Asian leaders universally welcome the renewed American attention to them, but many do not appreciate the introduction of elements of the U.S. global agenda into their discussions. This is particularly true of U.S. policies in the greater Middle East, which not a few view as anti-Islamic or unilateralist. In Indonesia, Malaysia, and Brunei—to one extent or another—Islam is an important component of national identity. And no nation likes to have policies based on interests it doesn't share imposed on it.

The United States' treatment of the dollar as a sovereign instrument by which to compel others to conform to unilaterally formulated American policies has elicited a significant passive-aggressive reaction. In addition to its role as the U.S. currency, the dollar is the principal unit of account for global trade settlement. By blocking its use by banks in transactions with Iran, including money transfers for oil and gas purchases, the United States has been able to override the energy strategies and economic interests of our Asian allies and trading partners without making any sacrifices ourselves. We have considerably narrowed Asians' access to energy supplies in the process. Meanwhile, of course, the possibility that Iran might react to an Israeli or American attack on it by closing off energy exports from the Persian Gulf has boosted oil prices. That has had a depressing effect on the global economy, including Asia.

One unfortunate side effect of the U.S. campaign to subdue Ahmadinejad and the ayatollahs has been to stimulate China, India, and other Asian nations to begin to create workarounds to avoid using the dollar in settling international trade accounts. This quiet revolt against "dollar despotism" promises to accelerate the global erosion of U.S. financial power. More importantly, in terms of relations with the Indo-Pacific region, the bullying style of leadership we have exhibited compares poorly with the more deferential approach taken by China. Asian power and influence on the global stage are growing. The ability of the United States to enlist Asian support for policies in which Asian interests are not directly engaged has not been enhanced by recent experience.

Quite apart from than these politico-economic interactions, the military "pivot"—now officially designated the "rebalancing"—has been presented as the centerpiece of the U.S. refocus on Asia. At more or less the same time it was announced, the United States proclaimed a new operational concept—called "air-sea battle"—that envisages strikes deep inside Chinese territory in response to conflicts on China's periphery. There is no evidence that the authors of this concept considered how a nuclear-armed China might respond to such an attack. The scenario that "air-sea battle" is directed at deterring is a resumption of the Chinese civil war in the Taiwan Strait. This is universally assessed as increasingly implausible. So the United States seems to be escalating its capacity to conduct offensive operations against a declining threat from a China that is increasingly able to defend itself. We appear to be acting to counter China's rise, not to blunt or alter China's policies.

Not surprisingly, China's leaders see this as evidence that America has veered toward overt enmity. They appear to have reacted calmly by boosting long-term funding for military R&D rather than current defense spending. Conversely, American "rebalancing" has not reduced the defense spending of those in the region concerned about Chinese military power. Instead, it has emboldened some to escalate their claims to islets, reefs, and rocks in the South China Sea—now referred to in Manila as the

"West Philippine Sea"—and the East China Sea, where barren islands now bear newly minted Japanese names.

Those in the region whom the U.S. "rebalancing" was meant to reassure—as well as China's experts on the United States—have, in fact, been somewhat skeptical about both the "pivot" and "air-sea battle." They suspect that both may turn out to be fiscally infeasible. The United States has already announced cuts in projected defense spending. "Sequestration"[6] or its equivalent will force further, larger cuts, but even those won't be enough to cure U.S. insolvency. Still more cuts in military outlays will be necessary to make ends meet.

Then, too, "rebalancing" presupposes that the United States can now pay less military attention to the Middle East. This seems a queer thesis to advance when war with Iran is a serious possibility and Israel faces the prospect of a collapse of the U.S.-brokered Camp David framework that has guaranteed its security for more than three decades. In some respects, "rebalancing" looks like yet another worrisome instance of an American propensity to confuse the sum of particular bureaucratic, armed service, and special interests with the U.S. national and global interest.

Finally, it is not at all clear that recent U.S. initiatives are consistent or compatible with the strategies of those they are supposed to support. No one in the Asia-Pacific region shares the U.S. defense commitment to Taiwan or considers the threat to Taiwan from the Chinese mainland to be growing. But that's the scenario driving U.S. policy. No one in the region wants the United States to threaten China or to stimulate it to see a need to expand its defense perimeter to include other Asian nations from which U.S. forces might attack it. Yet it is entirely possible that the net effect of U.S. policy will now be to do both.

No one in Asia seeks to deny China an appropriate role in regional security architecture. But, through Chinese eyes, the aim of U.S. policy seems to be to perpetuate U.S. dominance while confining China to the sidelines of a newly reinforced American sphere of influence. No one in the Indo-Pacific region wishes to see it divided between rival hegemonies, still less between foreign and Asian hegemonies. Yet that outcome is implicit in the current trajectory of U.S.-China relations.

These questions are much larger than those raised by the specific issues of the South or East China Seas or even Taiwan. They are also too important to be left unaddressed by the participants in the security and other dilemmas that frame them. Their outcomes will determine much more than the future American role in Asia. The Indo-Pacific region is now the fulcrum of global geopolitics. How these questions are answered will decide what sort of world we live in and how it is managed.

So Americans and Asians need a serious dialogue about how to craft a more harmonious and cooperative order in the Indo-Pacific region. The United States, echoed by others, has long demanded greater transparency from China with regard to its policies and actions, especially in the military sphere. China and other Asians now have cause to demand a greater measure of transparency from the United States.

Sometimes opacity is a mask for clear but concealed intentions. More often, however, it is the face of confusion, inconsistency, and incoherence in national objectives. It is time for Americans, Chinese, and other Asians to clarify our intentions, aspirations, and strategies—not just to each other, but to ourselves.

Notes

NOTES: Introduction

1. A version of this introductory essay appeared (in Italian) in the December 2012 issue of the Italian geopolitical quarterly *Limes*.
2. See, for example, "Forecasting Change in China: Where China Seemed to Be Going in 1980," at http://bit.ly/interesting-times.
3. How China transformed itself is discussed at length in supplementary materials that can be accessed at http://bit.ly/interesting-times.

NOTES: Chapter 1—What Mr. Nixon Wrought

1. Unbeknownst to Mr. Nixon, I had produced the first draft of his proposed remarks. I had included no poetry. That was added later by the White House.
2. My 1995 interview with the Foreign Affairs Oral History Collection of the Association for Diplomatic Studies and Training gives details. It is available at http://1.usa.gov/OzECK7.
3. Speaking as secretary of state, John Quincy Adams famously declared in 1821 that "America does not go abroad in search of monsters to destroy. She is the well-wisher to freedom and independence of all. She is the champion and vindicator only of her own."
4. Remarks to the Center for the National Interest on the Fortieth Anniversary of President Nixon's Opening to China, delivered in Washington, D.C., February 16, 2012, available at http://bit.ly/Y9AZ6x.
5. February 21, 2012.
6. Issued in Shanghai on February 28, 1972, at the conclusion of President Nixon's meetings with Mao Zedong, Zhou Enlai, and other Chinese Communist leaders.
7. In China, ghosts and other spirits are said to travel only along straight lines and to be unable to turn corners. One popular explanation for the privacy ("spirit") walls

that lie behind the "moon gates" through which one goes into household courtyards is that they make it impossible to enter without turning a corner.

8. The "Guam Doctrine," sometimes called the "Nixon Doctrine," was a set of principles for U.S. foreign policy first put forward by President Nixon at a press conference in Guam on July 25, 1969. As he later summarized it in a formal address to the nation on November 3, 1969, the Guam Doctrine consisted of three main points:

   First, the United States will keep all of its treaty commitments.

   Second, we shall provide a shield if a nuclear power threatens the freedom of a nation allied with us or of a nation whose survival we consider vital to our security.

   Third, in cases involving other types of aggression, we shall furnish military and economic assistance when requested in accordance with our treaty commitments. But we shall look to the nation directly threatened to assume the primary responsibility of providing the manpower for its defense.

9. President Nixon visited Beijing, Hangzhou, and Shanghai as a guest of Chinese Communist Party chairman Mao Zedong (whose state and government the United States did not then recognize) from February 21 to 28, 1972.

10. The legacy of this peculiar feature of the Cold War is continuing U.S. difficulty in distinguishing interests from values. Americans routinely see affronts to American values as challenges to U.S. interests and vice versa. American political leaders often misunderstand or misportray foreign objections to U.S. policies as assaults on U.S. beliefs. The confusion that this conflation of interests and values engenders accounts in no small measure for the erratic and often self-destructive course of U.S foreign policy in the post–Cold War era.

11. With Western Europe, Japan, and Brazil allied to the United States, among the world's actual and potential great powers only China (after the Sino-Soviet split of 1960–62), India, and Indonesia could seriously claim to be "nonaligned" during the Cold War. Though estranged from the United States, China was openly at odds with the Soviet Union. India had made the USSR its principal politico-economic partner while striking a wary stance toward America. Indonesia attempted to keep its distance from both superpowers, which obliged it by slighting Indonesia's geopolitical importance and potential.

12. The Shanghai Communiqué of February 28, 1972, is a diplomatic document that is remarkable for its candor. It opens with a lengthy recital of the very sharp differences between American and Chinese views of the global and regional orders and the opposing stands of the two governments on issues like the Second Indochina War, the unfinished war between south and north Korea, the propriety of Japanese rearmament, and the tense relations between India and Pakistan. After committing both sides to peaceful coexistence and a measure of strategic cooperation, it records an interim agreement to disagree about the Taiwan issue.

13. The Carter administration, which made the promotion of "human rights" a central element in U.S. foreign policy, normalized relations with Beijing without seeking concessions on Chinese domestic political practices. Ronald Reagan gave public voice to American democratic ideology but did not in fact push democratization or a human rights agenda with China.

14. "We are America; we are the indispensable nation. We stand tall and we see further than other countries into the future," said Secretary of State Madeleine Albright, February 19, 1998.

15. Despite its oft-declared antipathy to "industrial policies," the United States has an economy that is just as guided by government as others that extol the virtues of such policies. The socioeconomic outcomes favored by government in the U.S. are embodied not in bulletins of government economic departments but in tax codes, to which individuals and businesses refer closely when making economic decisions. But federal and state tax policies in the United States—the American version of industrial policy—are the product of a hundred years of responsiveness to special interests by many thousands of politicians. They represent so many contradictory choices that they are more often than not an impediment rather than a stimulus to the creative destruction that is the most admirable attribute of capitalism.

16. Examples include terms that are either counterfactual or have misleading connotations like "planned economy," "non-market economy," "centrally planned economy," "mercantilism," etc. Other terms, like "state enterprise," suggest something quite different to Western readers than the enterprises that operate within China's remarkable diversity of ownership systems, levels of government involved in entrepreneurship, and so forth.

17. 食色性也.

18 With the notable exception of the German *Mittelstand*, Western economies are now mostly dominated by oligopolies and large corporate enterprises that are the product of decades of economic consolidation.

19. The CCP has inducted virtually everyone in China with aspirations to participate in politics into its ranks. Its membership is slightly less than 6 percent of the overall Chinese population, somewhat above the proportion of those who are politically active in most other political systems. (In the United States, for example, less than 5 percent of the population can be considered politically active, while no more than 1–2 percent habitually gives time or money to politics.)

20. In 1973, the first Speaker of the United States House of Representatives to visit Shanghai asked the (acting) mayor if he could meet a Chinese lawyer. His request was met with silence. (It was then the Cultural Revolution, during which CCP members were expected to espouse leftist utopianism with Chinese characteristics.) The Speaker reiterated his request. The mayor, faithfully representing traditional canons of Chinese morality as the CCP then interpreted them, replied that "after the liberation of Shanghai, we did a survey of occupations and social classes and it was determined that there were four that would not be required in the new China: pimps, prostitutes, pushers, and lawyers." Sad to say, all are now back in droves. So much for moralizing utopianism.

21. Such corruption can pad costs in China as much or more than reliance in the West on lawyers and litigation to ensure clarity of contractual obligations or to resolve conflicting interpretations. When markets for goods and services are relatively "perfect" and thus characterized by intense price competition, as many currently are in China, competition effectively constrains corruption. But as markets become more

"imperfect," oligopolies emerge to dominate them, or they are reserved for central or regional monopolies, the costs of corruption under cadre capitalism can be very high indeed.

22. The CCP's tolerance of small-scale disturbances focused on economic grievances enables it to correct particularly egregious abuses; to separate the question of its legitimacy from the misbehavior of local officials; to gauge popular discontent with specific policies and practices; and to try out adjustments to both, while purging its ranks of especially venal and politically insensitive cadres. The CCP does not seem much worried about specific protests; it has learned how to manage them. Resolving the controversies that generate disturbances is part of the process of precluding the emergence of patterns of protest that might go beyond particulars and coalesce into a broad challenge to CCP rule.

23. See, for example, Richard Edelman, "Trust 2008," Edelman.com, January 22, 2008, available at http://bit.ly/hI1Qxw.

24. The United States, by contrast, with only 4.6 percent of the world's population, disposes of 29.5 percent of its arable land and about 23 percent of its water. If the U.S. had population-to-arable-land and water-supply ratios similar to China's, it would have about 4 billion inhabitants and very different attitudes toward a wide variety of public policy issues than it does at present.

25. Some estimates of the number of Chinese deaths from the Japanese rampage through China (1931–1945) are as high as 35 million. Even larger numbers of Chinese may have perished in the domestic disturbances that attended the European subordination of China to Western influence in the nineteenth century and in the turmoil that resulted from Chairman Mao Zedong's failed attempts to accelerate China's economic growth and transform its political culture from 1958 through 1976.

26. Let the better hypothesis win!

27. As rapidly as Chinese defense spending has been rising, it has been doing so at a rate below growth in central government budget outlays. In 2011, China's defense budget had fallen to less than 1.5 percent of GDP or slightly less than 7 percent of the central government budget. Military-related expenditures outside the defense budget could add as much as another 40 percent or more to total defense spending, bringing it to something over 2 percent of GDP. (This is not unusual. In the United States, the defense budget amounts to 4.8 percent of GDP, but military-related expenditures outside it raise total defense spending to as much as 6.6 percent of GDP.)

28. From 1979 to 1989, China's defense budget fell at an average annual rate of about 6 percent. Over the ten years since 2001, it nearly tripled. (Over the same period, U.S. defense spending, starting from a much higher base, almost doubled.)

29. The Mongols (Yuan Dynasty) ruled from 1271 to 1368. The Manchus (Qing Dynasty) ruled from 1644 to 1912.

30. Japan annexed Taiwan from 1895 to 1945. U.S. intervention following the outbreak of the Korean War in June 1950 froze the two sides of the Chinese civil war in place, separating Taiwan from the rest of China. To this day, Taiwan remains both politically separate from the rest of China and under U.S. military protection.

31. China has repeatedly stressed that it will not pursue or practice hegemony.

32. These include a war in 1950–54 to prevent the defeat of the pro-Chinese north Korean regime and the presence of U.S. forces on the Sino-Korean border; border skirmishes with India in 1962; a 1964–73 proxy war to support north Vietnam in its battle for a unified Vietnam against U.S. opposition; border skirmishes with Soviet forces at several points along the Sino-Soviet frontier beginning in 1969, the affirmation of a claim to the Paracel Islands against south Vietnam in 1974; a 1979–1982 war to persuade a newly united Vietnam that consolidation of its control of Indochina in association with China's Soviet enemies could not succeed; and minor skirmishes with Vietnam over South China Sea claims in recent years.

33. Notably, China negotiated the return of Hong Kong and Macau to its sovereignty, in 1997 and 1999 respectively, rather than settling these issues by force, as it could readily have done. The Sino-Indian border remains the subject of active if desultory negotiations between China and India. The only arguable exception is China's opportunistic seizure of the south Vietnamese-held portion of the Paracel Islands (西沙群島) in January 1974, but there is some dispute about which side provoked the battle that resulted in the expulsion of south Vietnamese forces from the single island in the group that they had garrisoned.

34. The best account of China's policies on border disputes is to be found in M. Taylor Fravel, *Strong Borders, Secure Nation: Cooperation and Conflict in China's Territorial Disputes* (Princeton, NJ: Princeton University Press, 2008).

35. Dictated by Deng Xiaoping as part of his admonition that China should "avoid the limelight while focusing on self-improvement," a more accurate translation of the phrase, 韬光养晦, which has been tendentiously mistranslated to sound sinister: "hide one's capabilities and bide one's time."

36. Other sections of this book contain extensive discussion of this and other aspects of the Taiwan issue, which remains the core politico-military problem between the United States and China.

37. Once indelicately called "full spectrum dominance," the objective of sustained military supremacy underlies the new U.S. doctrine of "air-sea battle." The inclusion of Iran (which the United States has repeatedly threatened to attack) alongside China as a prime target of this doctrine removes any doubt about its purpose.

38. To counter the power projection capabilities of U.S. aircraft carrier battle groups, China has developed ballistic missiles designed to disrupt their missions. To counter U.S. space-based command, control, and intelligence systems, it has developed anti-satellite capabilities. It matches intelligence collection by U.S. naval and air operations just off its coasts with intrusive cybernetic operations. It may have developed the capability to conduct a cyberattack on U.S. economic infrastructure in response to a U.S. kinetic attack on its military and industrial facilities.

39. On May 7, 1999, a U.S. Air Force B-2 bomber dropped five Joint Direct Attack Munition (JDAM) bombs on China's embassy in Belgrade, killing three Chinese citizens and destroying the embassy's communications center. The United States insisted that this was an accident and apologized for it. Despite this, China remains convinced that the bombing was deliberate.

40. Perhaps the most egregious instance of this was Secretary of Defense Donald Rumsfeld's speech to the Shangri-la Dialogue in Singapore on June 5, 2005. In it, Rumsfeld (ignoring a century and a half of Asian history, the huge increases in the U.S. defense budget then in progress, and his own attention earlier in his remarks to the formidable power projection capabilities of the U.S. Navy) exclaimed: "Since no nation threatens China, one must wonder: Why this growing investment? Why these continuing large and expanding arms purchases? Why these continuing robust deployments?" He then advocated fundamental political change in China, toward "some form of a more open and representative government."

41. Ironically, Americans seem more accepting of a political system that allows the will and interests of the few to prevail over the aspirations and pocketbooks of the many than Chinese may now be.

42. With the implied endorsement of China's likely next premier, the World Bank has produced a blueprint for such transformation of the Chinese economy. (See "China 2030: Building a Modern, Harmonious, and Creative High-Income Society," World Bank/Development Research Center of the State Council, People's Republic of China, February 2012.) No such plan has yet been developed by or for the United States.

43. The Department of Defense (DOD) budget contains about three-fifths of total U.S. military-related spending, with the rest in other budgets like Veterans Affairs, Energy, Homeland Security, etc. Thus, much commentary in the press that equates the DOD budget with defense spending is misleading. The DOD budget is about 4.7 percent of U.S. GDP or about 20 percent of the U.S. federal government budget. Overall military spending is about 6.6 percent of GDP or 26 percent of the federal budget.

44. China's defense budget for 2011 was CNY 583.6 billion (1.4 percent of GDP or 10.7 percent of central government spending). Converted to U.S. dollars at the nominal exchange rate, this was about $91.5 billion. (An increase of 11.2 percent was announced for 2012, bringing the budget to about $106.4 billion or 1.28 percent of GDP.) Clearly, as in the case of the United States and other countries' defense budgets, China's published budget does not include all military-related spending. Foreign estimates of China's actual spending on its military vary widely, but none rest on convincing methodology or can be squared with data on central government revenues.

The most widely cited numbers internationally are those from the U.S. Defense Intelligence Agency (DIA). These appear to be derived by converting the Chinese defense budget into dollars, multiplying by two, and subtracting $3 billion from the result. There is no apparent basis whatsoever for this methodology. It does not rest on reliable insights into Chinese budgeting practices, purchasing-power parity ratios for defense procurement, or anything else. It is best described as "seat-of-the-pants" guesstimating.

The fact is that no one knows the actual level of Chinese defense spending, but it is almost certainly at or below the target of 2 percent of GDP set by NATO for its members. The only things that appear certain are that the Chinese defense budget buys a lot more in Chinese currency than it would in dollars; that it measures the same items from year to year; and that its stated rate of increase should be taken seriously as an indication of overall trends in the importance China assigns to military aspects of its defense.

45. See other sections of this book for detailed discussion of the effects of Lee Teng-hui's self-contrived, quasi-official, congressionally sponsored visit to America in June 1995; the resulting March 1996 naval confrontation in the Taiwan Strait; Lee's July 1999 proclamation of independence in all but name and its politico-military consequences; the March 2000 election of Chen Shui-bian, an open advocate of Taiwan independence; and Kuomintang Chairman Lien Chan's courageous, healing visit to the mainland to meet with his CCP counterpart in April 2005.

46. "Suprastatal" best describes competencies created by agreement of the authorities on both sides of the Taiwan Strait to enable cooperation across it consistent with a vague mutual understanding that there is only "one China." Under such suprastatal arrangements, each side continues to claim its own sovereignty, which the other side avoids either recognizing or challenging, but each side either 1) yields the exercise of a portion of its sovereign authority to an agreed institutional arrangement, or 2) agrees to limit the exercise of its sovereign authority in return for comparable restraint by the other. Such suprastatal arrangements manage or deconflict mutually specified aspects of cross-Strait interaction. They are enforced by concern for "face" and the sustainment of relationships rather than by reference to principles of law. (See discussion of the "Chinese Ideology" above.) Suprastatal arrangements resemble the confederal mechanisms of "supranational" institutions like the European Coal and Steel Community, but differ from them in that they are not "international" agreements, are not negotiated on a government-to-government basis, and do not rest on or imply mutual recognition by the parties delegating powers to the common authority they are creating.

47. China needs to redefine its claims to harmonize its nine-dash line of 1947 with the 1982 United Nations Convention on the Law of the Sea (UNCLOS). All claimants need to seek a common understanding under the UNCLOS of the criteria that enable islands to cast exclusive economic zones of 200 miles rather than simply territorial seas of 12 miles. Maps need to be redrawn to reflect this understanding. China and Vietnam need to set aside historical claims (as China has done in settling many of its land borders) in favor of the principle of *uti possidetis*—by which actual possession of a geographical feature creates a presumptive claim to it. The Philippines needs to curb its newly aggressive territorial ambitions. A negotiating process needs to be set up by which cooperation with other claimants is rewarded and recalcitrance is penalized. The United States needs to keep its military mitts off the cases and controversies the South China Sea generates. Not easy, but not impossible.

48. See the discussion of this issue in Chapters 9 and 10 under the titles "India, Pakistan, and China" and "India and America in the Strategic Times to Come."

49. A desire for a multipolar rather than unipolar world also links India and Russia and, more loosely, the so-called BRICS (Brazil, Russia, India, China, and South Africa) in suspicion of U.S. diplomatic and military policies.

50. Russia first encountered China as a territorial predator in the seventeenth through nineteenth centuries. It became, successively, a participant in foreign military and political interventions in China (1901–1949), an ideological tutor and economic model (1949–1959), an ideological and strategic adversary (1960–1989), and a good neighbor and major trading partner of China (1991 to date).

51. China's northeastern region, Dongbei, comprised of the three provinces of Liaoning, Jilin, and Heilongjiang, was formerly known as Guandong ("East of the Pass") or Manchuria. Sino-Russian border issues in this region were settled in the Sino-Soviet Border Agreement of 1991. The last section of the border was demarcated in 2004 in a Complementary Agreement between the People's Republic of China and the Russian Federation on the Eastern Section of the China-Russia Boundary.

52. As all the world is learning, *Renminbi* (which means "people's money") is the name of the currency (like *Sterling*), which is denominated in *yuan* (like *pounds*).

53. The intimate relationship between levels of government and enterprise in cadre-capitalist China could easily lend such complaints particularly strident political overtones.

54. Consider recent disputes over the "responsibility to protect" and the right of the international community, acting through the United Nations and regional organizations, to take sides in situations of civil strife and civil war like those that have recently roiled societies in West Asia and North Africa (e.g., Libya, Yemen, Bahrain, and Syria).

NOTES: Chapter 2—How Diplomatic Normalization Happened

1. *Beijing* means "capital in the north." In Shanghai dialect, the two ideograms of which *Beijing* is composed are pronounced something like "Peking." This became Beijing's conventional spelling in English prior to the adoption in 1979 of the official Chinese alphabetization of Mandarin as the international standard for rendering Chinese into English. In the summer of 1928, Chiang Kai-shek's forces took most of northern China and renamed Beijing *Beiping*—"peace in the north." The Chiang government's capital was then in Nanjing—pointedly meaning "capital in the south." In the Wade-Giles system then commonly used to transliterate Mandarin, *Beiping* was spelled *Pei-p'ing*. This became the way politically correct English-speaking supporters of Chiang Kai-shek's Republic of China insisted on referring to what became the Chinese Communist capital in 1949.

2. Not until much later did I come to understand the important role India had played as a partner in U.S. covert action programs directed at strategically distracting China by promoting unrest in Tibet. This Indo-American partnership was part of the background to the Sino-Indian border war, reflected in the CIA escort of the Dalai Lama into Indian exile in 1959.

3. As a serving government official, I could not and did not accept payment for this work.

4. Ironically, I had been the author (in 1974–75, during a year at Harvard Law School's East Asian Legal Research Center under Professor Jerome A. Cohen) of the series of detailed legal studies that became the basis for the Taiwan Relations Act (TRA). Some have called me "the intellectual father of the TRA." See Tan Qingshan, *The Making of U.S. China Policy: From Normalization to the Post–Cold War Era* (Boulder and London: Lynne Rienner, 1992).

5. A version of this article, which was written in late 1980 (when the author was Country Director for China and Mongolia Affairs at the United States Department of State), was originally published in *Sino-American Normalization and its Policy Implications*, ed. Gene T. Hsiao & Michael Witunski (New York: Praeger, 1983).

6. Richard M. Nixon, "Asia after Vietnam," *Foreign Affairs*, no. 1 (1967): 111–125. During the 1960 campaign, Nixon had stated: "I can think of nothing more detrimental to freedom or peace than recognition of Communist China."

7. *New York Times*, April 23, 1968.

8. *New York Times*, May 2, 1968.

9. *U.S. Department of State Bulletin*, no. 1511 (1968): 737–740. Hereafter cited as *DSB*.

10. *New York Times*, September 6, 1969.

11. *DSB*, no. 1559 (1969): 397–400.

12. Henry A. Kissinger, *White House Years* (Boston: Little, Brown, 1979), 169–170.

13. *DSB*, no. 1564 (1969): 505.

14. *DSB*, no. 1573 (1969): 126.

15. Kissinger, *White House Years*, 180–181.

16. *DSB*, no. 1578 (1969): 260.

17. U.S. Congress, Senate Committee on Foreign Relations, *Hearings Before the Subcommittee on U.S. Security Agreements and Commitments Abroad*, 91st Congress, 2nd sess., part 4, 1971, 1010.

18. Kissinger, *White House Years*, 188.

19. *DSB*, no. 1594 (1970): 31–32.

20. Richard M. Nixon, *U.S. Foreign Policy for the 1970s: A New Strategy for Peace* (Washington, DC: U.S. Government Printing Office, 1970), 140–142.

21. Kissinger, *White House Years*, 91.

22. *DSB*, no. 1596 (1970): 83.

23. See Jack Anderson's report in *Washington Post*, May 11, 1980.

24. Kissinger, *White House Years*, 687.

25. Ibid., 689.

26. Anderson 1980.

27. Kissinger, *White House Years*, 701.

28. Ibid., 702.

29. Ibid., 703–704.

30. *DSB*, no. 1607 (1970): 496; *DSB*, no. 1659 (1971): 510.

31. *U.S. Federal Register*, Document 71–8520, filed June 18, 1971, vol. 36, no. 119, Rules and Regulations, June 19, 1971, 11811.

32. *U.S. Federal Register*, Document 71–6599, filed May 10, 1971, vol. 36, no. 91, Rules and Regulations, May 11 1971, 8672.

33. Richard M. Nixon, *Public Papers of the Presidents, Richard Nixon, 1971* (Washington, DC: U.S. Government Printing Office, 1972), 276–278.

34. *New York Times*, December 7, 1969.

35. Kissinger, *White House Years*, 709.

36. *DSB*, no. 1666 (1971): 702.

37. Nixon, *Public Papers*, 544.

38. Ibid., 594.

39. *New York Times*, April 29, 1971.

40. *DSB*, no. 1666 (1971): 702. The announcement was made on May 7, 1971.

41. Ibid., 815. This took place on June 10, 1971.

42. Kissinger, *White House Years*, 728.

43. *Public Papers of the Presidents, Richard Nixon, 1971*, 819.

44. Kissinger, *White House Years*, 763–765,

45. Henry A. Kissinger, *A World Restored* (Boston: Houghton Mifflin, 1957), *passim*.

46. Richard C. Holbrooke, *China and the U.S.: Into the 1980s*, in U.S. Department of State, *Current Policy*, no. 187, June 4, 1980. (Disclosure: Though delivered by Assistant Secretary Holbrooke, this speech was drafted in its entirety by the author.)

47. E.g., Zhou Enlai, "Kunming Documents: The Great Victory of Chairman Mao's Revolutionary Line," translated in *Issues and Studies*, June 1974 (Taipei): 102–108. For Zhou's speech, see *Peking Review*, nos. 35–36 (1973): 17.

48. Kissinger, *White House Years*, 749.

49. Ibid., 703, 765, 781–784.

50. *DSB*, no. 1706 (1972): 29.

51. Kissinger, *White House Years*, 1055–1074.

52. Ibid., 1084.

53. Dr. Kissinger's assertion that a review of the Chinese text was not done is incorrect. It was reviewed by the author. See ibid., 1084–1085.

54. *New York Times*, July 21, 1971.

55. See President Nixon's report to the Congress (May 3, 1973), quoted in U.S. Department of State, "U.S. Policy Toward China, July 15, 1971–January 15, 1979," Selected Documents, no. 9 (January 1979), 14–19.

56. Ibid., 8–9.

57. Ibid., 10.

58. Public Law 93-22, 93rd Congress, 1st sess., in U.S. *Statutes at Large*, vol. 87 (Washington, DC: U.S. Government Printing Office, 1973), 24.

59. U.S. Department of State, Selected Documents, no. 9, 19.

60. *DSB*, no. 1815 (1974): 380.

61. For a discussion of the Japanese model, see Gene T. Hsiao, ed., "The Sino-Japanese Rapprochement: A Relationship of Ambivalence," in *Sino-American Détente and Its Policy Implications* (New York: Praeger, 1974), 160–188.

62. See, for example, Deng Xiaoping's remarks in the *Times* (London), June 3, 1975.

63. *New York Times*, June 9, 1977.

64. Jimmy Carter, *Public Papers of the Presidents, Jimmy Carter, 1977*, vol. 1 (Washington, DC: U.S. Government Printing Office, 1977), 95.

65. President Carter made the remark at a press conference, May 12, 1977. See U.S. Department of State, Selected Documents, no. 9, 1.

66. Ibid., 32–33.

67. U.S. Department of State, *Foreign Affairs Memorandum: Diplomatic Relations with the People's Republic of China and Future Relations with Taiwan* (December 1978): 2–3.

68. See Secretary Cyrus Vance's address, January 15, 1979, in U.S. Department of State, Selected Documents, no. 9, 55.

69. In 1979, several U.S. senators challenged the authority of the president to terminate the Mutual Defense Treaty. The District Court held that the power to terminate the treaty was shared between the Congress and the president, but the Court of Appeals for the District of Columbia, *en banc*, reversed this decision, with four judges holding that the president had the authority to terminate the treaty in question on his own. The Supreme Court vacated the District Court's judgment with instructions to dismiss on the ground that the case presented a political question. One justice, dissenting, reached the substantive issue and upheld the power of the president to terminate the treat in this case as incidental to his power to recognize governments. See Goldwater v. Carter, in *U.S. Federal Supplement*, vol. 481 (St. Paul, MN: West Publishing, 1979), 949.

70. Vance, January 15, 1979, address, 55.

71. Ibid., 55.

72. U.S. Department of State, *Foreign Affairs Memorandum*, 3.

73. Ibid., 3.

74. For reference to the other documents, see U.S. Department of State, *Foreign Affairs Memorandum*, 4.

75. Ibid., 4.

76. *New York Times*, December 18, 1978.

77. *DSB*, no. 2024 (1979): 5.

78. When this essay was originally published in *Sino-American Normalization and Its Policy Implications*, editors Gene T. Hsiao and Michael Witunski noted that year-end 1980 trade results exceeded even the State Department's September estimate. The Chinese mainland became the eleventh largest U.S. export market, ranking immediately behind Taiwan (9) and Australia (10). Two-way trade reached an astonishing $4.9 billion, of which $3.8 billion was U.S. exports. In January 1980, U.S. exports to the mainland of $424 million for the first time exceeded exports to Taiwan of $315 million.

79. See U.S. Department of State, Bureau of Public Affairs, *Gist*, September 1980.

80. As of 1980, there were about a hundred federal laws requiring amendment to make China eligible for U.S. assistance in various fields.

81. Fox Butterfield, "Brown, in Peking, Urges Cooperation to Counter Moscow," *New York Times*, January 7, 1980.

82. *U.S. Federal Register*, Document 80-12796, filed April 24, 1980, vol. 45, no. 82, Rules and Regulations, April 25, 1980, 27922.

83. The officials included Assistant Secretary for East Asian and Pacific Affairs Richard C. Holbrooke; Assistant Secretary for International Narcotics Matters Mathea Falco;

Director for Politico-Military Affairs Reginald Bartholomew; Executive Secretary Peter Tarnoff; and senior National Security Council staff member Roger Sullivan.

84. Bernard Gwertzman, "Soviet Is Cautioned," *New York Times*, February 18, 1979.

85. Warren Christopher, Deputy Secretary of State (February 7, 1979), statement to U.S. Congress, House Committee on Foreign Affairs, *Taiwan Legislation*, 96th Cong., 1st sess., February 7 and 8, 1979, 2–6. The author's role in the conception of this approach is discussed in Qingshan, *Making of U.S. China Policy*, 40–42, 44, 54 (n74).

86. See U.S. Congress, Senate Committee on Foreign Relations, *Taiwan Enabling Act*, 96th Cong., 1st sess., February 22, 1979, 7–8.

87. Ibid., 23–39.

88. U.S. Congress, House Committee on Foreign Affairs, *United States-Taiwan Relations Act*, 96th Cong. 1st sess., March 24, 1979.

89. U.S. Congress, House Committee on Foreign Affairs, *Taiwan Relations Act*, 96th Cong., 1st sess., March 24, 1979.

90. Fox Butterfield, "Senators Cautioned on Taiwan by Deng," *New York Times*, April 20, 1979.

91. Meizhou Huaqiao Ribao (New York), January 30, 1981.

92. These figures are unofficial U.S. government estimates. According to official Hong Kong sources, the value of trade between Taiwan and the mainland by way of the British colony in the first ten months of 1980 increased by twelve times to $164.9 million from $12.5 million in the corresponding period of 1979. Of these, mainland goods transshipped to Taiwan through Hong Kong alone accounted for $65.65 million. See *Dagong Bao* (Hong Kong), January 2, 1981.

93. The figures of U.S. bilateral trade with Taiwan were released by the American Institute in Taiwan (AIT), Arlington, Virginia.

NOTES: Chapter 3—The Origins of the Taiwan Issue

1. As Max Weinreich observed, "A language is a dialect with an army and a navy." Taiwanese (Minnan) is the speech of people who possess both but, when it is written at all, it is written in the same ideographs as Mandarin as well as other dialects of Chinese. Written Minnan, like written Cantonese or Wu (Shanghai dialect), is therefore essentially indistinguishable from Mandarin, which remains the standard of official discourse on both sides of the Taiwan Strait. Taiwanese dialect is almost the same as the Minnan spoken in Xiamen, across the Taiwan Strait.

2. Hakka (Kejia) speakers preceded Minnan speakers in the settlement of Taiwan and continue to make up 15 to 20 percent of the island's population. I was only a week into the study of their dialect when I was transferred to Washington to serve as the principal Mandarin interpreter for the Department of State. Lee Teng-hui (1923–) is a native Hakka rather than Minnan speaker.

3. The Freeman Chair is the creation of the Freeman Foundation, which was endowed by Mansfield Freeman, a scholar-businessman who co-founded the American

International Group (AIG) insurance company in Shanghai in 1919. The Freeman Foundation was for many years chaired by his son, Houghton "Buck" Freeman (1921–2010). Although it appears that my branch of the Freemans shares common ancestors in early seventeenth-century Massachusetts with this Freeman family, for all practical purposes we are not related. The confusion on this point has been compounded by the fact that the Freeman Chair at CSIS was until recently held by my son, Charles III, who, like my daughter (my mother's namesake), Carla Park Freeman, is a sinologist.

4. Originally published in *Remembering and Forgetting: The Legacy of War and Peace in East Asia*, ed. Gerrit W. Gong (Washington, DC: Center for Strategic and International Studies, 1996). Reprinted with permission.

5. Who has since openly acknowledged his ancestry by taking his father's surname, Chiang (or in the contemporary spelling, Jiang).

6. 三民主义 or the "Three Principles of the People" was the political platform of the founder of the Republic of China, Dr. Sun Yat-sen, and the KMT's official ideology. The three principles are 民族 (nationalism), 民权 (democratic rights), and 民生 (social welfare).

7. As of 1995, when this piece was written.

8. 1995. Apartheid ended in South Africa in 1994, when universal suffrage was instituted and Nelson Mandela was elected president. South Africa broke relations with Taipei and recognized Beijing in January 1998.

NOTES: Chapter 4—The Reemergence of the Taiwan Problem

1. President Carter had committed the United States to "sales of carefully selected defensive weapons on a restrained basis."

2. Relevant excerpts of key documents governing U.S. policies on the Taiwan issues are available at http://bit.ly/interesting-times.

3. Not, as the media legend has it, in the Taiwan Strait.

4. A version of this article appeared in the *China Business Review* 22, no. 6, November–December 1995. Reprinted with permission.

5. Beginning in July 1995.

6. A version of this article appeared in *Harvard International Review* XVIII, no. 2, Spring 1996, under the title "Reluctant Guardian: The United States and East Asia."

7. Office of International Security Affairs, "United States Security Strategy for the East Asia-Pacific Region," Washington, DC: Department of Defense, February 1995.

8. A version of this article, written in May 1998, appeared as the lead piece in *Foreign Affairs* 77, no. 4, July–August 1998, under the title "Preventing War in the Taiwan Strait: Restraining Taiwan—and Beijing." Reprinted with permission.

NOTES: Chapter 5—War, Peace, and Taiwan

1. This talk was given at Stanford University on April 22, 2004.
2. The actual production level in 2010 turned out to be more than 600 million tons.
3. April 21, 2004.
4. Ditto.
5. Remarks to the Center for Naval Analysis in Alexandria, Virginia, on Wednesday, September 14, 2011.
6. Notes regarding Blair House meetings, June 26, 1950, reproduced in the Truman Library's online archive "The Korean War and Its Origins, 1945–1953," available at http://bit.ly/TVgzry.
7. Harry Truman, speech delivered January 5, 1950, White House press conference, Washington, D.C., available at http://bit.ly/U5yf7l.
8. In 2011, cross-Strait trade was about $160 billion annually. More than 40 percent of Taiwan's exports were to the mainland, either directly or through Hong Kong. Well over a hundred thousand Taiwan-invested business and projects were underway across the Strait, and cumulative investment in the mainland from Taiwan was about $150 billion. (Investment approved by the Chinese central government stood at about $53 billion.)
9. At any given moment in 2011, 10 percent or more of Taiwan's population (i.e., 2 to 2.5 million people) are at work or play on the China mainland. About 175,000 people from Taiwan have taken up permanent residence across the Strait. At the same time, nearly 250,000 people from the mainland are temporarily in Taiwan, while almost 130,000 have permanent resident status there. In 2010, 1.6 million tourists from the mainland visited Taiwan.
10. The Qing (Manchu) effort to retake Taiwan from the Ming pretender-regime that had retreated to it succeeded only on the last of eleven bloody assaults on the island that took place over the course of two decades.
11. Passed by the National People's Congress in March 2005.

NOTES: Chapter 6—Where Is China Going?

1. See Chapter 4 of this book, which covers the various phases of the "Taiwan Problem."
2. The point of several interlocutors in Beijing and Shanghai was not to disparage American power but to argue that the huge American nuclear arsenal was now irrelevant in the Taiwan context because neither the U.S. nor China would risk escalating a conflict there to the nuclear level. I didn't find this at all startling or particularly noteworthy because I did not foresee how it would be distorted. When the leaks occurred, I was traveling in India and unable to respond to press inquiries. Nor did I feel at liberty to do so, as the meeting had been off the record, a condition by which I felt bound at the time.
3. See the extended discussion of the crisis and its aftermath in Chapter 4 of this book.
4. Actually, Taiwanese-Hakka.

5. Discussion paper prepared for the Bilderberg Conference, Toronto, Ontario, Canada, May 29–June 2, 1996.

6. Japan, of course, disputes sovereignty over the four "Northern Islands" with Russia. Spain and the United Kingdom have differences over Gibraltar. These disputes do not, however, involve significant populations or extensive territories. Nor do they have the emotional force of China's claims to Macao, Hong Kong, and Taiwan.

7. Beginning in 2010, this situation changed, as Japan expanded its efforts to assert greater control of the Senkaku/Diaoyu Archipelago and China stepped up resistance to this. By late 2012, a full-scale crisis between the two claimants was underway.

8. The decision of the United States to interpose itself between China and other claimants deprived the latter of this incentive. Confrontation escalated apace with U.S. policy changes that culminated in the 2011 "pivot to Asia."

9. Ironically, the turn toward cross-Strait compromise that began with KMT Chairman Lien Chan's historic 2005 visit to Beijing altered this calculus. As tensions over Taiwan receded, those over territorial disputes in the South and East China Seas escalated.

NOTES: Chapter 7—Deng's Revolution in Retrospect

1. Remarks to the China Forum, Johns Hopkins School of Advanced International Studies, October 11, 2006.

2. David M. Lampton, professor and director of China Studies at the Paul H. Nitze School of Advanced International Studies at Johns Hopkins University in Washington, D.C.

3. Mao expected China to suffer and survive a nuclear attack from the USSR, the United States, or both. His answer was this slogan. It combined civil defense, preparation against disaster, and righteousness to lay the basis for defeating such an attack.

4. Remarks to the foreign policy group Le Cercle, June 23, 2007, Washington, D.C.

5. As of 2007.

NOTES: Chapter 8—U.S.-China Relations and the Emerging World Order

1. Remarks to the Global Strategy Forum, London, England, January 20, 2010.

2. Remarks at the Hopkins-Nanjing Center, Nanjing, Jiangsu, China, November 10, 2010.

3. Remarks to the Delhi Policy Group and the MIT Center for International Studies, New Delhi, India, January 12, 2011.

NOTES: Chapter 9—China's Global and Regional Impact

1. Remarks to the China Study Center, Washington, D.C., March 27, 2007.
2. Remarks to the Summer Roundtable of the Pacific Pension Institute, July 25, 2007, Victoria, British Columbia, Canada.
3. Remarks to the Camden Conference, Camden, Maine, February 17, 2011, under the title "The Challenge of Asia."
4. Paper delivered at a seminar of the Institute of International Strategic Studies at Manama, Bahrain, October 16, 2011.
5 Remarks to the Center for Naval Analyses Conference with India's National Maritime Foundation, Alexandria, Virginia, December 13, 2010.

NOTES: Chapter 10—Military Interactions

1. The most detailed examination of Chinese budgeting practices available in English remains the report of the United States–China Policy Foundation study group I led to China in November 2006. The group's report, "Defense-Related Spending in China: A Preliminary Analysis and Comparison with American Equivalents," is available online at http://bit.ly/SBh5jk.
2. See Chapter 4.
3. This originally appeared as a working paper prepared for the fourth meeting of the Study Group on "American Interests in Asia: Economic and Security Priorities," sponsored by the Economic Strategy Institute, Washington, D.C., January 16, 1997.
4. Economic historians estimate that, throughout the premodern period, China's economy was between 30 and 40 percent of global GDP, and sometimes more. They dispute whether the Roman Empire, at its height, had an economy larger than China's.
5. In the short term, the qualitative gap between the PLA and its potential adversaries is actually widening, given the pace of military modernization in China's East Asian neighbors—especially Taiwan. The Asia-Pacific region now spends more on defense than all of Europe (excluding the states of the former Soviet Union). East Asia vies with the Middle East as the largest market for international arms exports.
6. "Power projection" is taught in Chinese military academies as part of the course on foreign military doctrines. China seeks to join existing international organizations on as favorable terms as possible, rather than to overthrow or displace such institutions.
7. Unlike India, which seized Goa by force, or Indonesia, which did the same with Irian Jaya and East Timor, China was willing to wait for negotiated solutions of both the Hong Kong and Macao issues. Beijing's opening reunification proposal to Taiwan concedes that the island's economic and political systems would remain unchanged by reunification, that Taiwan could keep its armed forces, and that no civilian or military officials from the mainland would be stationed in Taiwan after reunification. Taiwan would thus enjoy an enhanced version of the "one country, two systems"

scheme to be applied in Hong Kong and Macao. Taipei is naturally skeptical about the sincerity and reliability of these PRC positions, which would symbolically subordinate Taiwan to Beijing.

8. The United States thrice threatened the use of nuclear weapons against China in the 1950s. The desire to gain immunity from such strategic blackmail was a principal motivating factor in China's construction of its current, modest *force de frappe*. China has no credible first-strike capability and therefore has a nuclear policy of "no first use." China has, however, pointed out that it can now retaliate against nuclear or non-nuclear attacks on its territory with counterstrikes on the U.S. homeland or U.S. bases overseas.

9. When the United States adopted its policy of containment against the former Soviet Union, American GDP constituted about two-thirds of the global economy. The U.S. economy today is about one-fifth of global GDP. Nor does the United States now enjoy the undisputed technological superiority and monopolies it did fifty years ago. The USSR was dedicated to economic autarky. China, by contrast, is committed to an increasingly open trading economy. Other countries would not follow the United States in curtailing trade and investment relations with China.

10. Ironically, given the much more open American economy, its commitment to national treatment for foreign firms, its relative immunity to political manipulation, and the legal protections it offers against unfair trading practices, the United States has a much larger stake in receiving most-favored-nation status (MFN) from China than China does in receiving it from the United States. The problem of nondiscriminatory access to the China market is not a new one. The concept of MFN was invented and first applied to obviate unfair competition in the nineteenth-century China trade.

11. Among these are the World Trade Organization (WTO), the Group of Seven (G-7), the Wassenaar Arrangement (successor to COCOM), the Missile Technology Control Regime (MTCR), and the nuclear suppliers group (London Club).

12. U.S. sanctions prohibiting exports to China are met by Chinese inhibitions on imports from the United States. U.S. sanctions on imports from China draw counter-restrictions on Chinese imports from the United States. In both cases, U.S. exports take a major hit. China can usually (though not always) make up the imports it loses under U.S. sanctions by turning to non-American suppliers of similar products (though sometimes products of lesser suitability or quality and higher cost). This mutually counterproductive game has made many Chinese wary of reliance on imports or other forms of cooperation with U.S. firms, caused them to view the United States as an unreliable partner, and placed U.S. firms at a competitive disadvantage. It has also deterred American exporters from long-term commitments to develop a market for their products in China.

13. Over this period, no American president visited Beijing, nor did a Chinese president visit Washington. Contacts between leaders of the two countries occurred only at the margins of international gatherings, like APEC and the UN General Assembly. (An effort to arrange a visit by the Chinese president to Washington foundered over the

unwillingness of the United States to offer full protocol honors to him.) No effective working relationship was established between the two foreign ministers, who concentrated on exploring differences rather than points of common ground between the two countries. The United States sought (successfully) to block the staging of the 2000 Olympics in Beijing. Washington made annual efforts (unsuccessfully) to achieve international condemnation of China at the UN Human Rights Commission and treated the UN conference on women as an opportunity to stage an on-site protest of Chinese human rights practices. The U.S. Congress sought (unsuccessfully) to compel the president to recognize Tibet as a state separate from China, an act of war under international law. The absence of contact reinforced mutual ignorance, as each country misunderstood and misperceived (or failed to perceive) changes taking place in the other. Ignorance created suspicion. Suspicion led to apprehensions of mutual hostility.

14. Among the flashpoints ahead are: the ever-present possibility of another flare-up over Taiwan; the annual MFN debate in the U.S. Congress, which may focus on blocking administration efforts to negotiate Chinese entry into the WTO; the July 1, 1997, reversion of Hong Kong to China, which—even in the absence of a televisable public-relations catastrophe—will likely produce an outpouring of anti-China media commentary and intemperate retorts in the Chinese media; and a September 1997 summit meeting, convened by the government of Panama, to which both Bill Clinton and Lee Teng-hui have been invited.

15. Remarks to the China Maritime Studies Institute, U.S. Naval War College, Newport, Rhode Island, May 10, 2011.

NOTES: Chapter 11—Managing Sino-American Relations

1. I visited Beijing as assistant secretary of defense for international security affairs on November 1–2, 1993. The purpose of my visit was to restore dialogue between the armed forces of the two countries. The White House and Department of State saw this as a means of incentivizing the Chinese military to yield to the U.S. human rights agenda. The Department of Defense did not demur but viewed the reopening of dialogue as a means of reversing the already apparent progression from non-intercourse to estrangement to suspicion to hostility before it could become entrenched. In the end, none of these objectives was satisfactorily attained.

2. A version of this chapter, which is based on a speech at Stanford University's Asia/Pacific Research Center in April 1966, appeared in *Foreign Policy*, 104 (Fall 1996), under the title "Sino-American Relations: Back to Basics." It is reprinted here with permission.

3. A version of this talk was given as the annual lecture in honor of A. Doak Barnett and Michel Oksenberg, Shanghai, China, February 21, 2008.

4. Remarks to the National War College Alumni Association, Washington, D.C., April 25, 2008.

5. Remarks to the George Washington University's Elliott School of Foreign Affairs Conference on "Power, Identity, and Security: Regional Cooperation and the U.S. Role", Washington, D.C., April 16, 2012.

6. "Sequestration" or "the sequester" refers to a package of automatic spending cuts under the Budget Control Act, which was passed in August 2011. This law stipulated that, if there had been no congressional agreement on a $1.2 trillion deficit-reduction package by November 23, 2011, across-the-board cuts in federal spending would take effect beginning January 1, 2012. No deal was reached, and the sequester was triggered. Budget cuts, which are projected to total $1.2 trillion, are scheduled to begin in 2013 and end in 2021, evenly divided over the nine-year period. These cuts are also evenly split between defense spending—with spending on wars exempt—and discretionary domestic spending. If Congress fails to agree on a budget that accomplishes comparable budget balancing, the total cuts to be applied in 2013 are expected to be $109 billion.

Acknowledgments

My thanks to my publisher, Helena Cobban, who encouraged me to put together this compilation of essays and observations on the interaction between the U.S. and China and whose website stores, at http://bit.ly/interesting-times, the archive of commentaries on historical events that supplements what is in print here. My thanks also to Sarah Grey of Grey Editing (http://www.greyediting.com), who very professionally cleaned up the text, and who was in every respect a pleasure to work with. What Sarah edited reflected, as everything I now write does, the merciless eye and blue pencil of my wife, Margaret Van Wagenen Carpenter. She cut the number of prolix sentences and unintelligible complexities substantially, although I was able to sneak a few by her.

CPSIA information can be obtained at www.ICGtesting.com
Printed in the USA
BVOW02s0243201213

339536BV00002B/171/P